T0375147

Gnostic Visions

Uncovering the Greatest Secret of the Ancient World

LUKE A. MYERS

iUniverse, Inc.
Bloomington

Gnostic Visions

Uncovering the Greatest Secret of the Ancient World

iUniverse books may be ordered through booksellers or by contacting:

iUniverse
1663 Liberty Drive
Bloomington, IN 47403
www.iuniverse.com
1-800-Authors (1-800-288-4677)

ISBN: 978-1-4620-0548-2 (sc)
ISBN: 978-1-4620-0547-5 (ebook)
ISBN: 978-1-4620-0546-8 (dj)

Printed in the United States of America

iUniverse rev. date: 4/1/2011

CONTENTS

INTRODUCTION

———————————————————

This book is as much about plants as it is about identifying how Gnostic visions were originally created. We know more about our past and the world in which we live than at any other time in human history. But there is still much that remains lost and forgotten from human history, with some of this only waiting to be rediscovered. About twelve years ago, before the writing of this book, I had my first mystical experience. It took place on the top of a mountain in the middle of the Mojave Desert. From that time forward I began a search for greater insight and understanding into the world's religions. Being raised Christian; I soon began to study Gnosticism. I was quickly intrigued by the many astounding experiences presented in Gnostic texts, experiences of travels to higher dimensional realms, contact with divine beings of light and even the experience and contact with the divine itself. Having collected a series of visionary and mystical experiences of my own by this time, I quickly began to realize that there was something truly great taking place in Gnostic texts that the modern world had not yet fully uncovered. This is when I realized that the modern world had no idea how Gnostic experiences were created. Because of the Gnostics close relationship to the genesis of early Christianity, the Gnostics are profoundly important in helping us to understand not only Christianity's earliest beginnings but also the greatest secrets of the ancient world.

After reading Gnostic texts, one is immediately struck by experiences that are imbedded in visionary and esoteric lore. From studying the Gnostic's visionary experiences we know that their visions take on a particular and defined character. Having spent the better part of a decade studying altered states of consciousness and enthogenic plant use around the world, I knew that the Gnostic's visions were real and that there was only a limited number of ways that they could have been created. After exploring Gnostic scholarship on the topic of how Gnostic visions were created, I came up surprisingly empty handed. Only a handful of scholars ever attempted to explore and try to identify how Gnostic visions were created. None of the ideas presented by any of the big names in Gnostic scholarship at the time even once mentioned the possibility that the Gnostics were creating their visions through the use of naturally available visionary compounds. At the time I began to write this book, the general consensus among Gnostic scholars was that the method for how Gnostic visions were created was unknown, but the leading possible candidates were, meditation, ontological reflection of self, hypnotic trance, and guided group meditation. I quickly realized from these suggestions that these Gnostic scholars had no idea how Gnostic visions were being created. Because I had already gained extensive first hand experience with many psychedelic and entheogenic shamanic plants, I knew that there was a big piece of the picture that these scholars had missed.

In 1990, a doctor by the name of Rick Strassman began work on a little known neural transmitter which at the time had been found to have a direct connection to the experiences created by the brain in Near Death States. In that same year, Dr. Strassman gained approval by the American F.D.A to conduct research on this chemical compound and administer it to live human subjects. Over the course of his research, Strassman documented dozens of unusual reports of powerful visionary experiences that not only closely resembled Near Death Experiences but also the strange and unique experiences we find documented among the Gnostics.

Having already known about Dr. Strassman's research into this chemical compound, known today as DMT, I began to conduct my own research on the substance and its potential connection to Gnostic visions. I quickly discovered that this powerful visionary neural transmitter was not a rare compound locked away in the brain, but that it existed with relative abundance throughout nature and the world of plants. I began to learn everything that I could about these DMT containing plants, their uses among humans, the history of their use, and the people that used them. Soon after doing this, I began experimenting with plants myself. While DMT is present naturally in many types of plants, the body has a natural enzyme called monoxides that are actually designed to break DMT down in the gut before it has time to pass into the body and pass the blood brain barrier. In certain parts of the world, particularly in the Amazon Rainforest, people have learned that these stomach enzymes can be denatured by other plants. When these two plants are mixed together and drank they produce a powerful visionary experience, with the DMT as the primary visionary catalyst. In the South American Amazon, this botanical mixture is known as ayahuasca.

Soon after experiencing ayahuasca myself and learning about how it is made and the cultures that use it, I discovered that it had recently been discovered by botanists that there were two plants in the Middle East that contained the same two chemical compounds found in the brew ayahausca. Because this news was not widely known at the time, very little research had been conducted on the possibility that the two plants could have ever been mixed or consumed for their visionary properties at any point in antiquity. So this is when I started to conduct my research. I started gathering evidence that the two plants that could have made up this visonary brew were known about and used in antiquity. What I found totally surprised me. Not only did I find evidence that the two plants that make up this visonary brew were known about and used in antiquity but there was direct evidence that these same two plants were also known about and used among the Gnostics. Studying the experiences of the Gnostics I soon came to discover that when the visonary experiences of the Gnostics are compared to the effects of Ayahuasca, a direct correlation can be seen between them. The following research of this book represents almost a decade of research into the identification of the lost Gnostic sacrament and the method of how Gnostic visions were created. Before I go on to explore Gnostic visions and present evidence for how their visionary experiences were created, I would first like you to gain a basic understanding of how the spiritual world is contacted and experienced by various peoples in the world today. I would also like you see the research that has been conducted on the identification of other ancient visonary religious experiences and understand the importance of visonary compounds in early human history and religion. So, to understand the Gnostics you must first understand the world that they came from and to do that you must first understand humanity's earliest encounters with the divine.

Part I:

Keys to the Spirit World and Classical Visions

Ch I

Keys to the Spirit World and the Birth of Religion

And the Lord spoke to them, now listen to me! Even with the Prophets, I the Lord communicate by visions and dreams.

Numbers 12:6

In the very beginning of the Torah, as well as in the Bible, one of the very first stories you read after the creation of the world is the story about the transformation and subsequent exoduses of Adam and Eve from the Primordial Garden of Eden, the Garden of Paradise. Many people who have read this age old story never seem to see how it directly relates to what we know today as the history of early human evolution. Many Bible teachers today talk about this age-old legend only as literal evidence for their claim to the start of mankind's original eternal sin and subsequent fall from primordial perfection and divine grace, as if God was still holding a grudge against mankind for eating this fruit, and still cursing mankind after all of these many years. If this is to be taken literally, in this way, then I would really not want to be any part of such a harsh and wrathful God. But if we look at the story as something else, maybe it may open up more possibilities. Maybe this age old legend really was passed down from generation to generation long ago and made its way into the history of the Jewish people, holding a glimpse of truth into one of the greatest mysteries of our own most ancient past:

> But God said, "You shall not eat of the fruit of the tree which is in the midst of the garden, neither shall you touch it, lest you die." But the serpent said to the woman, "You will not die, For God knows that when you eat of it, your eyes will be opened, and you

will be like god, knowing good and evil." So when the woman
saw that the tree was good for food, and that it was a delight to
the eyes, and that the tree was to be desired to make one wise, she
took of its fruit and ate; and she also gave some to her husband,
and he ate. Then the eyes of both of them were opened, and they
knew that they were naked; and they sewed fig leaves together and
made themselves aprons.

Genesis, 3:3

Perhaps the story of Adam and Eve is not about a primordial never-ending curse on mankind for eating the mythical fruit of knowledge. Instead it may actually be about the transformation of primordial mankind from a primitive animal state into the first truly human humans. Perhaps this story of Adam and Eve is not about sin or an eternal curse on mankind as some have suggested, but is instead about the primordial transformation of human consciousness. The story of Adam and Eve shows how the human mind that we know today came about as a result of eating a mind-altering fruit or plant by the first two humans. It is also the first place in Western civilization that we find a prevalent and important theological and cultural legend that implies a clear and direct association between the acquisition of knowledge and the use of a mind-altering plant.

In the story of Adam and Eve, the tree of knowledge was a plant that induced an experience that resulted in mankind's primordial animal mind being forever changed and transformed into something much greater: something truly more human, a mind that can know right from wrong and for the first time, be fully self-aware, self-reflective, and free from the binds of pure animal instinct, a mind truly human.

One of the first people to propose the entheogenic theory of human evolution outside the biblical story of Adam and Eve was the late philosophical ethnobotanist Terence McKenna. McKenna proposed that some early hominids, being omnivorous, would have discovered and ate psychedelic plants and fungus in their daily foraging. In doing so, these plants would have made distinct temporary changes to their everyday consciousness. These plants would have sharpened or heightened the hominids perception, allowing them to better "find" and "sense" predators, even finding better food sources, as well as gain a distinct edge in competition for mates. This plant-based increase in awareness could have also added in the development of higher cognitive functions over time, much better than their other non-psychedelic plant-eating neighbors. This could have given certain groups or individuals a distinct advantage over other proto-humans, allowing for a superior but natural evolutionary edge on their competition, making them more mentally advanced and more suitable to survive.

In studying animal behavior, researchers have found that many animals demonstrate the clear desire to seek out intoxication. Some of these include cats to catnip, birds to intoxicating nectars, reindeer and caribou to Fly Agric mushrooms, elephants to fermented fruits, even cows to intoxicating grasses. There are also countless cases in which the psychoactive or narcotic properties of certain plants have been directly discovered by humans through the observation of animal behavior. But for a long time, there was no hard evidence indicating early primates ever utilized psychoactive plants for their effects or in any of their daily foragings. Because of this, there was very little evidence to support this particular theory of early human evolution at the time. Then a discovery was made while studying animal and primate behavior in a tropical forest of Africa that finally shed light on this ancient theory. [1]

In the forest of Gabon and the Congo in Africa, the Mitsogho shamans, or Nganga as they are called by the locals, reported to animal behavior researchers and various European ethnobotanists exploring the region that male Mandrills were known to use the psychoactive plant Iboga to become intoxicated. Mandrills are closely related to baboons and can be found in the tropical rainforests of West Africa, Southern Nigeria, South Cameroon, Gabon, and the Congo. Mandrills are known to live in wide-spread communities, adhering to a rigid hierarchical social structure. At the top of the social ladder are the Alpha males to whom other powerful males submit; these in turn dominate yet weaker males. When a male Mandrill must engage in combat with another, either to establish a claim to a female or to climb a rung of the hierarchical ladder, he does not begin to fight without forethought. It has been found that many Mandrills will first find and dig up an Iboga bush, eating its psychedelic root; next, they will wait for its effects to hit in full force (which may take from 1-2 hours) and only then does he approach and attack the other male he wants to engage in battle. This peculiar animal behavior is the first of its kind demonstrated among primates, something that clearly demonstrates a high level of premeditation and awareness in the mind of the animal. It also demonstrates some of the first documented reports of psychedelic plant use among certain primate groups, and the use of these substances by these animals for these unique and particular social purposes. These findings stand not only as supporting evidence for the entheogenic theory of human evolution, but also demonstrate the possibility that this age-old western legend of Adam and Eve could actually have had its place in fact, and could, in some fashion, have once really taken place. [2]

If the change in consciousness from animal to modern human ever took place, as at one time it clearly must have done, what was the event that facilitated this change? What started this alteration in consciousness and heightened increased awareness of self that modern humans have over all the other animals on this planet? If the consumption of mind altering plants helped to contribute this change in human evolution and awareness, then the story of Adam and Eve would be a legend that is based on a real primordial event. If such an event ever took place, it seems clear that early humans would have had to deal with the deep-seated anxiety at their newly-perceived separation from their environment. Adam and Eve would have had a sudden sense of their own mortality, and clear awareness of their inevitable death. The down of human consciousness could have been interpreted as a fall from grace to early humans because animal consciousness is more instinctual and more imbedded in its own nature, not burdened by self awareness and the self-conscious weight of human morality.

After this change occurred, the first humans would have found themselves in a world without the innocent, no longer free of anxiety, guilt, and remorse. The first humans were the first to feel the heavy weight of morality. They were now responsible for their own actions. Maybe this is why the tree of knowledge became known as "the tree of the knowledge of good and evil." The first humans saw this as a tree that gave knowledge, a never-ending knowledge and understanding between right and wrong, good and evil, a tree that in some way also separated them from their more primordial animal past and gave them their newfound awareness of their now naked animal bodies.

This newfound change in early humans could have been seen as a fall from grace because of the fall from the grace of their past instincts and ignorance and rise into what we know today as being truly human. So what may have once seemed like a fall from grace really opened their eyes and the doors of the great creative reasoning and insight that is so distinct to the human condition. [3]

This early protohuman behavior could have even later developed into the vocation of the first shamans, healers, or priests; the very same individuals that modern anthropologists have identified with as being the earliest spiritual practitioners and healers on the planet. Remarkably, when we go on to study Shamanism, one of the most unique and central aspects known to unify the worldwide shamanic traditions is the fundamental belief that the alteration of consciousness is essential for accessing and contacting spiritual realities. The system of methodologies found in shamanism for contacting spiritual realities is also held to be the oldest of spiritual practices in the world. The belief in a spirit world or in the existence of a spiritual level of reality that is unseen by the normal human eye is held as the most fundamental component of all major world religions. But the ideas, myths, and symbols used to construct the idea of a spirit world as they are seen in any given major world religion, have their origins in these much older and much more ancient roots. As a matter of fact, the foundations for the belief in a spirit world or spiritual dimension of reality can all find their origins in these earlier and much more ancient shamanic roots and practices. [4]

The Symbolic Revolution

The birth of human language, writing, and religion are known to have started with a prehistoric movement that is characterized today as the Symbolic Revolution. The Symbolic Revolution characterizes the first creation of human symbols and the attachment of purpose and meaning to these symbols, both visual and otherwise. The development of symbolism is known to have been one of the greatest advancements in early human development and evolution. In studying the first defining elements of human existence on this planet, we are led to examine the earliest depictions of mankind. In what are known as the first defining elements of human art, religion, and the belief in supernatural realms, (elements that are all found within the earliest cave paintings of humanity) is a unique phenomenon that mysteriously emerges some time around 40,000 years ago. Before about 40,000 years ago, other than a very few and widely scattered isolated examples, there is nothing in the archeological record left by our ancestors that we would instantly recognize as modern human behavior. After this period in time it is clear that creatures exactly like us had arrived and began to spread across the globe. The first and most noted universal phenomena associated with humanity and the early rise of modern human behavior is the notable and first defining evidence for the belief in supernatural realms, supernatural spirit beings, and the first direct evidence for the birth of religion. [5]

The clearest possible illustration of this is found in cave paintings dating from the prehistoric periods found all around the world. In southwest Europe, some of the most ancient and sophisticated representations of prehistoric religious art can be found. The oldest cave art so far discovered in the world suddenly appears between 40,000 and 30,000 years ago, where it then endures until approximately 12,000 years ago. This is the art of the great painted caves such as Chauvet, Lascaux, Pech Merle, and Altamira. The caves are rightly famous for their realistic images of Ice Age mammals. Much less known is the fact that numerous supernatural beings, often half human, half animal, are also depicted, very reminiscent of patterns found in shamanism, items or beings known as shape shifters a practice known to utilize altered states of consciousness in which the shaman enters a state of trance and experiences visions, supernatural beings, and temporary mental transformations. [6]

For many years, these mysterious items were hotly debated within the academic community and the source of their meaning and inspiration were equally mysterious. Then in an ingenious explanation put forward by an international group of anthropologists and archeologists regarding the bizarre appearance of these cave paintings and the beings found within them, was put forward an idea that was finally able to explain their existence. The essence of their argument was that cave art expresses mankind's first and oldest notions of death and other realms of existence, notions that are now largely believed to have taken shape in altered states of consciousness most likely brought on by the consumption of psychoactive plants. Although not to the liking of some scholars, this has been the most widely accepted theory of cave art since the mid-1990s. Because of this remarkable fact, it is almost an embarrassment that none of the experts currently advocating this theory have ever actually consumed any psychoactive plants themselves; nor do they have any first-hand idea of what an altered state of consciousness is like, or any desire to experience one. This in my view has limited the modern academic understanding of this phenomenon and its various manifestations around the world. While it is a great academic insight, I truly believe that to fully understand and comprehend the complexity of this phenomenon and its relationship and importance to early human history, one must extend this inquiry into the realms of direct first hand experience and knowledge.

Before modern human behavior, no one ancestor in human lineage had ever made use of any form of symbolism before and needless to say no other animal species had ever done so before either. The switching on of humanity's symbol making capacity that took place sometime between 100,000 and 40,000 years ago was an event that not only changed everything in human history, but it was also closely intertwined with humanity's first inquiries into spiritual and supernatural realms. So if altered states of consciousness did help facilitate the switching on of early humanity's symbol-making capacity and our first inquiries into the supernatural as is supported by cave art research, then the relationship between early mankind's evolution and the botanical world is much more closely connected then what has been previously thought.[7]

According to Professor David Lewis Williams, the first leading proponent of this theory of cave art, "such ideas are not part of the normal, predictable current of everyday life but instead arise from the universal human neurological capacity to enter altered states of consciousness." [8] Many anthropologists are convinced that as far back as the Upper Paleolithic, our ancestors placed a high value on hallucinogenic and visionary experiences and made use of psychoactive plants to induce them. In addition, it is well known that rhythmic drumming, dancing, fasting, self mutilation, and sleep deprivation, are also known to induce visionary and hallucinatory experiences. [9]

Supported by David Whitley, one of the leading North American rock-art specialists, Jean Clottes, the world renowned expert on the French prehistoric cave paintings, and Lewis Williams and a growing number of other scholars from many different countries around the world, are beginning to take the view that the first notions of the existence of supernatural realms, beings, and the first religious ideas about them, the first art representing them, and the first mythologies concerning them, were all derived from the visionary experiences of prehistoric shamans.[10] One of the first academic investigators to propose this extraordinary theory of prehistoric cave art was David Lewis Williams. Williams first began to develop his "neuropsychological model" of cave art and the origins of religion in the early 1980s, and has been testing and defending it virtually non stop since 1988, when he and his co-researcher Thomas Downson officially put it before their peers in the scholarly journal *Current Anthropology*.[11]

In examining Williams' research on this topic, it has been pointed out by himself and other cave art researchers that much of the art depicted in the prehistoric caves of southwestern Europe date from around 40,000 to 30,000 years of age and are found to depict animals which would have been familiar to our prehistoric ancestors such as, bison, horses, and woolly mammoths. This originally gave rise to the idea that these prehistoric paintings were a form of magic designed to give humans power over the animals they hunted.[12]

This idea prevailed for much of the twentieth century, but it is hard to see why because it was so blatantly wrong. We can tell what our ancestors ate by the bones discovered in their caves, and these rarely match the creatures depicted on the walls. More importantly, many of the images feature fantastic monsters and supernatural beings that have never existed in everyday physical reality. Therianthropes (from the Greek therion = "wild beast" and anthropos = "man" are depictions of human animal hybrids. These images are inarguably one of the more enigmatic and mysterious features of these prehistoric depictions. [13] One such figure is known as the "Sorcerer" of Trois Freres cave in France, dating back approximately 17,000 years. Deeply engraved into the rock ceiling is an amazing figure with the ears of a wolf, the eyes of an owl, the antlers of a stag, the tail of a horse, the claws of a lion, and the feet and body of a human being. Other bizarre therianthropic images can be found in caves across Europe, and the similarities between them are not only remarkable, but quite often breathtaking.[14]

A horned bison with a man's arms and torso, daubed in red ochre in Fumane cave in northern Italy, matches another bison-man etched in charcoal on a cave ceiling in Chauvet, France, which resembles yet another bison-man at El Castillo in northern Spain. One of the most remarkable features of these unusual cave depictions is the time spans separating their creation.

The Fumane image is 35,000 years old, the Chauvet image was created some 3,000 years later in or around 32,000 years ago, and the El Castillo image was made some 17,000 years after that some time around 15,000 years ago. It is important to also point out that the 17,000 years spanning the creation of these prehistoric cave paintings is a period more than eight times longer than the whole history of the Christian religion. [15] An image must be very powerful to be maintained and repeated over such a great length of time, and just as significant is the fact that similar images can be found all over the world-notably in Africa. In South Africa, for instance, there are paintings of beings that are half man, half praying mantis. In Tanzania, there are strange other worldly images of human bodies with insect heads, including "feelers" and eyes on stalks. Clearly, such images are not depictions of a hunter's prey. They are pictures of "supernatural beings"- i.e. beings that we do not see in everyday life, beings that are encountered in altered states of consciousness, being found in the visionary space. [16]

But the questions remain: how, why, and because of what experiences did our ancestors begin to conceive of the existence of beings like these? In a search for answers, researchers have come to another mysterious set of universal recurring images found in cave and rock art all over the world: enigmatic geometric patterns such as grids, nets, ladders, spirals and zigzag lines. These patterns are central to the research work that was conducted by David Lewis Williams. Williams was intrigued by the results of various neuropsychological experiments in which volunteers under modern laboratory conditions were given psychoactive substances and asked to describe their effects. During these tests, the volunteers reported seeing various kinds of abstract geometric patterns known today as "entopic phenomena." Since scientists believe that neither the average size of our brains nor the basic wiring had changed at all in the last 50,000 years, Williams realized that our prehistoric ancestors would have seen much the same geometric patterns had they entered altered visionary states. He began to speculate that the abstract patterns painted on the cave walls represented what our Paleolithic predecessors saw when they entered deep visionary trance. Williams also pointed out that in addition to the entopic patterns seen in prehistoric art, many modern lab volunteers pointing out identical geometric and spiral patterns. In fact, many volunteers in altered states of consciousness have routinely reported encounters with similar entopic patterns and therianthropic beings throughout the research that has been conducted in this field. This indicates that the modern lab volunteers who were experiencing these altered states of consciousness were reporting many of the same visual phenomena that were left on cave walls found from throughout the prehistoric period. [17]

It was an extraordinary theory at the time, but soon enough Williams would find even more evidence to support it in the testimony of an extinct tribe of Southern African Bushmen known as the San. Until about 1927, it was perfectly legal for white South Africans to hunt and murder the San, whose body parts were kept and boastfully displayed by early white settlers as hunting trophies. So anticipating their annihilation as early as the 1870s, a German linguistic expert named Wilhelm Bleek conducted interviews with the few surviving San tribesmen to record their way of life before it disappeared. The notebooks contained his neatly written transcripts remained hidden in South African archives until David Lewis Williams re-discovered them nearly a century later. [18]

The San were remarkably clear about the beautiful and mysterious rock paintings of their ancestors, which included the praying mantis images I just mentioned. They revealed that the paintings were the work of shamans, whose role it was to travel into the spirit world and negotiate with the inhabitants on behalf of their fellow Bushmen. On their psychic visionary voyages, these shamans were accompanied by spirit guides who appeared to them in animal form and taught them to heal the sick, influence the weather, control the movements of animals and so on. Intriguingly, the San described how the shamans entered the other world by means of an arduous and exhausting form of dance. Williams realized that this would have lead to extreme dehydration and hyperventilation, exactly the conditions that could propel them into visionary trance. When they returned from these visionary out of body journeys, the shamans informed the community about what they had learned and painted some of the strange beings and scenes they had encountered on the rocks and caves surrounding them. This was therefore what led to the existence of their rock art, further demonstrating the validity of Williams' theory. [19]

Williams also realized that the strange geometric patterns the ancient San painted were the same "entoptic phenomena" experienced by Western volunteers many millennia later, patterns that were also identical to patterns found painted on cave walls in Europe many millennia earlier. As for the half-man half-beast therianthropes, the ancient San people said that when their Shamans would enter the other world they would sometimes have to adopt various animal forms and the paintings depicted them at various stages of their shamanic transformations. The fact that similar images can be seen in cave systems across the world supports Lewis-Williams' remarkable theory, that they were all the work of shamans who had entered altered states of consciousness and states of deep visionary trance. Besides ritual dancing, drumming, and eating or drinking psychoactive plants, these visionary states may also have been achieved through physical stress such as body piercing, starvation, or sensory deprivation, possibly even in the caves where the paintings were created. [20]

Prehistoric North Africa

As you have seen, the knowledge and use of visionary experiences goes far beyond recorded human history. Rock paintings and carvings from the prehistoric periods serve as a testimony to the preliterate history of human civilization. Rock art, was the first permanent form of visual communication known to man, and has been found all over the world. This same form of art and visual communication eventually led to the invention of writing and goes back almost to the origins of mankind. In the Tanzania region of Sahara North Africa there have been found rock paintings dating as far back as 40,000 years or more. Archeologists exploring various caves in these regions of the Sahara desert have found other numerous cave paintings dating from 7,000 to 9,000 years of age. Unlike many other cave paintings, these have clear representations of psychedelic plant use. These paintings represent what are now known to be the oldest depictions of shamanic psychedelic mushroom use in the world. These rock paintings depict pictures of people or spirit persons holding large bands of mushrooms in which the explicit use of these mushrooms seems to be taking place for the purpose of ritual or within a sacred setting. Many times these ancient mushroom cave paintings are accompanied by a painting of a large masked man or spirit person whose body is many times also depicted as being covered with these mushrooms. It has also been documented among Scholars that the masked dancers found in the caves of Inaouanrhat and Tassili from the Sahara have apparently influenced the early cultures of the Nile Valley and of West Africa, and one can suspect that the use of masks in both regions particularly in ancient Egypt is one such link. However, there is no stylistic similarity between the mask in Tassili art and those of West Africa or the Nile. But considering the time span that has elapsed between the two traditions it is largely accepted that some stylistic elements may have changed and evolved over time. [21]

Rock art experts have already produced significant evidence supporting that the art of what is now known as the Round Head period from the many depictions of round headed mushroom figures found throughout the Sahara desert region are believed to have been influenced by ecstatic or visionary states induced by the consumption of the many psychoactive mushrooms growing throughout the region. At the time these cave paintings were created, the region was forested, covered with lush vegetation, rivers, and lakes. This time period is known as the Great Humid Holocemic Period and is characterized by the presence of enormous lakes all over the Saharan basin around (10,000 B.C. - 5,500 B.C.). [22] This is also the generally accepted period for the chronology of the Round Heads art. A pollen examination carried out at the Tossili site revealed that during the Round Heads period, this area was covered by vast vegetation and highland flora, as well as the presence of coniferous trees and oaks. It can be presumed that some of the mushrooms represented, specifically the large ones, were indigenous to this wooded area in that they are intimately associated with these species of trees. This vast region of trees, forest, and lush vegetation eventually died out due to the ever increasing drought and climate change that started to grip the region shortly after the end of the last great ice age. According to scholars and archeologists investigating the art in the region, the art was produced by the early hunter gatherers during the end of the Pleistocene and the beginning of the Holecene periods. [23]

Similar works dating back nearly to the same period in history can also be found in various other sites around the world, areas that later became arid or semiarid when the lakes and rivers dried up due to climate change after the last great ice age. From the many works of art these peoples have left us, we have learned that the people who created these amazing works of art were gatherers of wild vegetable foods as well as visionary plants and mushrooms. The scholars who have studied these cave paintings are of the opinion that the works of art of the Round Heads period are the results of particular ecstatic states associated with dance and the use of psychoactive substances. The context, or rather, the "motivations" behind the Round Heads' art, just as with all the other periods of Sahara rock art, are generally of a religious, and perhaps, mystical initiatic nature. The figures who created these astounding works of art are also the same individuals typically found in all prehistoric societies whose main role it is to be a mediator between man and the spirit world. According to Henri Lohte, the discoverer of the Tassili frescoes, it seems evident that these painted cavities were secret sanctuaries of ancient shamanic initiation in which the explicit use of visionary mushrooms was known to have occurred. Scholars have pointed out that the use of visionary substances, where it arises, is historically associated with controlled or supervised rituals. It is perhaps not a chance occurrence that the areas where examples of rock art are found around the world are also areas in which it is most often asserted that the use of psychoactive substances might have taken place. The scenes represented in these ancient cave paintings most likely served as a source of inspiration and are areas where the most famous examples can be found in terms of imagination, mythological significance and early writing. Since most of the works of rock art were related to initiation rites and were part of the religious practices of these ancient people, the idea that these works of art should be associated with the use of naturally occurring visionary substances such as mushrooms, which are well documented for creating such mystical visionary experiences when consumed, should come as no surprise considering the sacred use of such substances by various indigenous people in the world today. [24]

In examining these ancient cave depictions in greater detail, we find images of enormous mythological beings with human or animal form, side by side with a host of small horned and feathered beings in dancing stance found covering the rock shelters on the high plateaus of the Sahara. One of the most important scenes found in the Tin-Tazarift rock art site, at Tassili, is a series of masked figures in line and hieratically dressed or dressed as dancers surrounded by long and lively festoons of geometrical designs of different kinds. Each dancer holds a mushroom-like object in the right hand, with two parallel lines coming out from the mushroom to reach the central part of the head of the dancer, which is in the area of the roots of the two horns. This double line almost seems to signify an indirect association, as if some form of non material fluid or substance is passing from the object held in the right hand and the mind of the individual holding the mushroom. This interpretation coincides with the effects of psychoactive psilocybin mushroom, if we bear in mind the universal mental experience induced by psychoactive mushrooms, which is often of a mystical and spiritual nature, including but not limited to an experience of interconnectedness and higher or elevated awareness. [25]

Another common feature found in these mushroom cave depictions is the presence of mushroom symbols starting from the fore-arms and thighs as well as other that are held in the hand. In the case of the Matalem-Amozar figure, these objects are scattered over the entire area surrounding the body. This mushroom symbol was first interpreted by researchers as an arrowhead, and or a vegetable, probably a flower, or some other undefined enigmatic symbol. But because of the clear abundance of mushroom depictions throughout the cave walls it was clear that researchers could not deny that the form which most closely corresponds to this cult object was in fact that of a large mushroom, most probably of a psychotropic kind, the sacramental and socialized use of which is well represented in gathering and offering scenes throughout these caves and in the depiction of expressive ritual dances depicted on the walls. All of these cave depictions are also accompanied with many characteristic geometrical patterns, elements that are all very characteristic to the Tassili visionary works. Because of this, these two figures could now be interpreted as images of the "spirit of the mushroom," images that are also known to exist in many other cultures that are also known to use visionary mushrooms or other psychotropic vegetables. [26]

In a shelter in Tin - Abouteka, in Tassili, there is a motif that appears at least twice that associates images of mushrooms with fish. Two mushrooms are depicted opposite each other, in a perpendicular position with regard to the fish motif and near the tail. Not far from above here are found other fish which are similar to the aforementioned but without the side-mushrooms. In the same Tin - Abouteka scene, yet another remarkable image could be explained in the light of ethno-mycological enquiry. In the middle we find an anthropomorphous figure traced only by an outline. The image is not complete and the body is bending, it probably also has a bow. Behind this figure, we find two mushrooms which seem to be positioned as though they were coming out from behind the figure. If the mushrooms in question are those which grow in dung, the association between these mushrooms and the rear of the figure may not be purely casual. It is known that many psychotropic mushrooms (above all, Psilocybe and Panaeolus genera) live in dung of certain animals particularly quadrupeds and bovines, such as cattle, horses, and others. [27]

The specific ecological relationship between psychoactive mushrooms and the dung of animals would have also been witnessed by the early hunter gatherers who created these cave depictions. The appearance of these types of animals with mushrooms in these cave paintings would also account for the creation of the mystico-religious relations between the mushroom and the animals which produce its natural habitat. The dung left by herds of quadruped animals were important clues for prehistoric hunters on the lookout for game, and the deepening of such scatological knowledge for hunters probably goes as far back as the Paleolithic period (the long period of human history that saw the hunting of large game). Thus we have a further argument in favor of the events that would have witnessed the mythical associations of these mushrooms with animals and the religious interpretations of this on different occasions, or different seasons of the year. The relationship between these (sacred) animals and the psychoactive mushrooms depicted in these ancient prehistoric caves clearly indicates some of the earliest venerations of these animals as well as their relationship to the use or discovery of psychoactive substances. [28]

In a painting at Jabbaren, one of the most richly endowed Tassili sites, there are at least 5 people portrayed in a row kneeling with their arms held up before them in front of three figures two of which are clearly anthropomorphous. It could be a scene of adoration in which the three figures would represent divinities or mythological figures. The two anthropomorphous figures have large horns while the upper portion of the third figure, behind them, is shaped like a large mushroom. If the scene is indeed a scene of worship of adoration, it is an important testimonial as to Round Heads' mystico-religious beliefs.

These images are important because they not only show signs of early mystical religious veneration but also the role of art among early human population as a means of symbolic expression. The prehistoric art found within these caves represents from a visual stand point, the symbolic representation of these peoples' religious practices, beliefs, and mythology. This clearly indicates a strong connection between the use of these visionary substances and some of the earliest recordings of mankind, records that are clearly of a mystical or visionary religious nature. [29]

In examining these cave depictions further, we find many more-or-less anthropomorphous figures with mushroom shaped heads, items which are also to be found repeatedly in Round Head mushroom Sahara art, some with "hat-heads" of unboned or papillate form, which on two occasions are of a bluish color while others carry a leaf or a small branch. It is important to point out the similarity between the blue color of the mushrooms found in these paintings and the blue color of Psilocybin found in psychoactive Psylocibe mushrooms. While visionary mushrooms are clearly some of the most prominent items found in many of these caves paintings, mushrooms are not the only vegetal substances found in Round Head art. We often find figures in typical costume and in hieratic positions, dancing and holding in their hands small branches or leaves (and in one instance roots) At least two species occur fairly frequently in the images found at *Tassili* and nearby *Acacus*. In fact, the interest which surrounds the use of these psychoactives is always represented within the context of a general interest in mushrooms and the vegetable world, demonstrating that the religious activity and religious initiations of these ancient people was most directly related to the natural vegetable and mycological world. The discovery of these cave paintings also demonstrates that it was from the use of these natural substances, among these ancient peoples, that we can find some of the first representations of individual religious speculation derived from mystical spiritual experiences within an ancient prehistoric community. [30]

Shamanism and Entheogens

The use of psychoactive plants, animals, or fungi for obtaining altered states of consciousness, healing, and creating religious mystical experiences is as old as human kind itself, but the modern academic knowledge of this and these substances importance and use around the world, is actually a relatively new one. Anthropologists have long known that early peoples used plants for many medical and material purposes, but it has only been fairly recently that modern science has started to rediscover the depths of botanical understanding ancient peoples have had for the many uses of the plants around them. Many people today do not know that over 70 percent of the modern pharmacopoeia's plant-based remedies were first discovered by traditional aboriginal societies, and most medications we have today first came from natural plant-based sources.[31] A discussion of human life on this planet would not be complete without a look at the role of plants. A complete record of the many thousands of plant and fungi species used for human functioning would fill volumes, yet historians have often had the tendency "to dismiss plants as less than fundamental in history." [32] In recent years, however, there has been a reawakened scientific interest in the fundamental role plants have played in many cultures throughout the world and throughout human history for medicinal as well as spiritual uses. This growing botanical insight has led to a greater understanding of the role plants have played in human culture, history, and religion.

The use and importance of plants in human culture far transcends their medical or material value. As a matter of fact, the use of plants and fungi for spiritual and religious purposes has been reported by anthropologists throughout the world and on almost every continent. The widespread incorporation of sacred and spiritual plants has led many researchers to believe that the use of plants may be one of the first and oldest technologies of mankind, used for healing and inducing mystical or religious experiences throughout human history. Many researchers have even proposed the possibility that the use of plants in the most ancient history of mankind may even have helped facilitate the very first systems of human spirituality and religion. The fact is that there are many plants throughout the earth that have been known to expand consciousness, increase awareness of self, and initiate one into the nature of spirituality. Thousands of Ph.D. professors all over the world, in fields such as Botany, Ethnobotany, Archaeology, Anthropology, Philosophy, and Psychology, as well as numerous other fields have written thousands of books and papers on the investigation and study of psychedelic plants, the great antiquity of their use, and their modern day incorporation. Many such writings have dealt with the use of such substances by spiritual practitioners in almost every religion formed on the planet, and most people are totally out of the loop in knowing about any of this. [33]

As scholarly and academic knowledge has grown over the years, so has the understanding regarding these plants, the people that use them and the remarkable experiences they are known to create. In 1979, a group of ethnobotanists and scholars created the term "entheogen" to more accurately describe the experiences many shamanic communities were experiencing from using particular psychoactive plants during their visionary religious and healing rituals. The term "entheogen" is translated as "creating the divine within," in the strictest sense of the word, an entheogen is a psychoactive substance, most often some type of plant matter with a psychoactive effect that occasions an enlightening spiritual or mystical experience. Usually this entheogen experience takes place within the parameters of a ritual. The term is usually applied to a natural plant or fungus able to induce such an experience on the user. The use of entheogens in traditional societies has been documented from sites nearly all over the world today, but most predominantly their use has been found among surviving indigenous peoples that are known to still practice their traditional ancient ways, practices which are largely included as various forms of shamanism. [34]

All over the world our ancient ancestors discovered how to maximize human abilities of the mind and spirit for healing and problem solving. The remarkable system and methods they developed is known today as "shamanism," a term that comes from a Siberian tribal word for its practitioners: "shaman" (pronounced SHAH-mahn). Shamans are a type of medicine man or woman especially distinguished by the use of journeys to hidden worlds, known through myths, dreams, and visions. The phenomenon of shamanism as well as the use of mind-altering plants and fungus has been demonstrated to be unfathomably old and amazingly widespread. Evidence for this can be seen in the Australian Aborigines, where shamanism is a fully developed practice among them. The Australian Aborigines are a great example of this due to the clear fact that they were separated from other human populations as much as forty thousand years ago. They were fully isolated on the Australian continent from that time until the arrival of European settlers just a few hundred years ago. [35]

Outside of the modern Western culture, shamanism seems to be something close to a universal human phenomenon. A cross-cultural similarity in shamanic belief systems are found across the world, from Australia to Brazil to Siberia to India and even the highlands of Nepal and the Himalayas. In the vast anthropological literature on shamanic initiations and practices that are many times, experiences that can be understood as the death and mystical resurrection of the candidate by means of a descent to the underworlds of the mind and subsequent ecstatic ascent into heavens of the sky. The candidate, while he or she is undergoing shamanic initiation, receives a massive influx of the sacred. This experience of creating the divine within is a marked characteristic of many shamanic traditions and initiations all over the world today. [36]

One of the traditional ideas and beliefs known to unify the various shamanic traditions around the world is the belief in a spirit world, or a spiritual dimension of reality and the necessary practices, techniques, or tools to directly interact, contact, and experience this other reality or spirit world. Shamanism is also fundamentally known as a healing tradition that has been joined with these various techniques for altering consciousness to heal the sick, interacting with the divine world to gain knowledge or information to heal or aid the community. Shamanism is not a system of religion or faith; it is a system of direct knowledge and experience that has been handed down directly from nature.

This universal theme in shamanism that the spirit world can be directly accessed by altering the normal waking state of consciousness is achieved when a person enters into non-ordinary reality and gains a greater perception and insight into themselves and the world around them. The fact that the alteration of consciousness can lead to the experiences of other dimensions of reality and the acquisition of knowledge is in many ways a very foreign concept to the modern Western mind. The main reason for this is that for the last 1500 years these archaic practices have been actively persecuted, outlawed, and suppressed in the West. In Europe, this eradication campaign first started with the destruction and eradication of the age-old systems of European spirituality and religion during the fall of the Classical age almost 1500 years ago. During this period in history the religious beliefs and traditions of indigenous Europeans were eradicated and assimilated into the dominant religion of Roman Christian Orthodoxy. It was not until the modern age of science and discovery that the knowledge of these practices began to reemerge into the understanding of the modern Western mind.

In more recent years, there has been a growing academic interest in the use of shamanic methodologies in the earliest religions and civilizations of the ancient world. Since many of these consciousness altering techniques, including the use of entheogenic substances, are intrinsic to shamanism and shamanism is known to be the oldest and most widespread human spiritual tradition, researchers have begun to focus on and find evidence for similar methodologies being practiced in many of the world's earliest civilizations. Since shamanic methodologies are based around actual experiences, having knowledge about how these experiences are created and the effects they induce, researchers are able to gain greater insight into these experiences, what they are like, and how similar experiences have been created in the past. In shamanism today, these visionary methodologies are primarily used in healing rituals as well as awakening the human mind to secret unseen inner worlds of consciousness and spirit. But over the years, as Western interest and understanding of shamanism has grown, researchers have come to learn many things about the important place these ancient systems of healing and spiritual practice have had on the spiritual, magical, initiatory, and religious history of many of the world's earliest religions.

Uncovering the Lost Secrets of the Ancient World

The use of altered states of consciousness for obtaining knowledge and contacting spiritual realities has not been confined to indigenous shamanic cultures. As a matter of fact, the very roots of contemporary western civilization demonstrate a wide variety of visionary rituals and experiences that utilized altered states of consciousness as important and integral aspects of their religious practices. The mystical religious experiences of the western world's earliest civilizations were experiences that were taking place long before the rise of many of our own modern day religions. Because most of these ancient religious traditions became persecuted and suppressed into extinction, all evidence of their existence now remains only in the surviving pieces of archeological and literary evidence that have survived from the ancient world attesting to their importance and existence. Because many of these early civilizations were the first to domesticate animals, invent writing, and organize some of the first cities and human populations, many of these early civilizations were also some of the first to organize formal state cults, religious institutions, and mystery traditions. Because shamanism is known as the earliest form of healing and spiritual practice on earth, evidence should be found that many of the earliest civilizations in the world have incorporated many of these earlier shamanic practices into the formation of many of their earliest religious traditions.

In studying the religious practices of the classical world, we quickly come to find that many classical religious institutions held a high regard for the mystical visionary experience, viewing the alteration of consciousness as an important and integral requirement in contacting spiritual realties. Many of these early cults and religious traditions were centered on and around the direct experience of the mystical, many times through the direct religious initiatic experience. In later years of classical antiquity, it became the cults and religious institutions of the ancient world that incorporated these various visionary methods for direct personal experience of the spirit world that became some of the most successful. When the different methodologies for inducing visionary and religious experiences are compared to known religious experiences worldwide, anthropologists have found that many of the groups known to claim contact with other spiritual realities in the world today, are also those that are still known to utilized these age old shamanic practices for entering trance, experiencing visions, and inducing altered states of consciousness. Because most of the world's current population currently practices various forms of religion that have extracted and removed many of these ancient methodologies from their religious practices and no longer incorporate them as necessary components of sacred contact, many people in the world today know very little regarding these ancient methods of spiritual contact or the experience they create, experiences that were once so vitally important to the religious traditions and experiences of our ancestors.

For many years, as research has continued to emerge regarding the use of altered states of consciousness in religious initiatic rituals in many civilizations of the ancient world, our understanding of ancient religious practices has begun to expand and our understanding of the ancient world's greatest mysteries is finally beginning to come to light. In the initial years, many of these early discoveries were heavily persecuted and seen as a largely taboo subject by many academic circles, but with increasing historical and anthropological evidence growing demonstrating that early human populations utilized these methodologies and that from these experiences of altered states of consciousness the very idea and practice of religion may have been born, a reemergence in the investigation and acceptance of such practices has finally started to be accepted throughout the scholarly and academic community. This modern growth of scholarly research and understanding into the experiential nature of many ancient religions is issuing in a new era of academic insight and understanding regarding ancient religious practices as well as the history of the human religious experience.

When we examine the religious practices of the ancient world, we find a surprising array of evidence demonstrating the mystical shamanic roots of these early religious traditions. In studying ancient religion, we find that many religious systems of the ancient world incorporated these earlier shamanic methods for obtaining knowledge, experiencing the spirit world, and initiating individuals into an experience with the divine. When formal state cults popped up many of these ancient practices were woven into the fabric of the early state cults, religious traditions, festivals, and the initiations they created. The mystical and visionary experience was an important and integral aspect of classical pagan religious culture. In more recent years, a growing number of researchers have collected strong and convincing evidence demonstrating that many religious institutions of antiquity were known to have utilized visionary and entheogenic substances in some of their most important initiatic religious practices. While these mystical and visionary experiences were known to modern scholars, they were also surrounded in controversy and mystery, with the true methods of how these visionary experiences were being created remaining completely unknown. It has only been more recently with the growing advancements in the understanding of modern anthropology, ethnobotany, classical studies, and shamanic methodologies, that a more in depth understanding of these ancient cults and their religious practices has finally begun to be understood and the source of their mystical visionary experiences finally come to be identified.

Ch 2
Visions and the Hellenistic Mysteries

We beheld the beautiful Visions and were initiated into the mystery which may be truly called blessed, celebrated by us in a state of innocence. We beheld calm, happy, simple, eternal visions, resplendent in pure light

(Plato, in Phaedrus)

The Delphic Mysteries

The belief that an alteration in consciousness can facilitate a spiritual or mystical experience as well as impart information or knowledge on the experiencer is not a new one; as a matter of fact, it has been demonstrated to be one of the oldest worldwide spiritual belief systems. It is a tradition that is also found to be central within the shamanic tradition, as well as many of the religious practices and traditions of the world's earliest civilizations. In examining the classical Hellenistic world from which much of western civilization was later founded, we find a surprising amount of prominent religious institutions known to have utilized visionary experiences and altered states of consciousness for obtaining knowledge, creating spiritual experiences, and even contacting the divine. One of the best documented Hellenistic Greek religious institutions known to have utilized altered states of consciousness for obtaining prophetic knowledge was the famous Delphic Oracle. The Delphic Oracle was first established in the 8th century B.C. Its last recorded response was given in 393 A.D., when the Christian emperor Theodosius ordered pagan temples to cease operation. During this period the Delphic Oracle was the most prestigious and authoritative oracle in the Greek world. Writers who mention the oracle include Herodotus, Euripides, Sophocles, Plato, Aristotle, and Pindar, among many others. [1]

There are many stories regarding the origins of the Delphic Oracle. One legend, which is first related by the 1st century B.C. by the writer Diodorus Siculus, tells of a goat herder called Kouretas who noticed one day that one of his goats fell into a crack in the earth and was behaving strangely. Upon entering the chasm, he found himself filled with a divine presence and could see outside of the present into the past and the future. Excited by his discovery, he shared it with nearby villagers. Many started visiting the site until one of them was killed by the experience. From that time on, only young girls were allowed to approach the chasm and then only in conditions regulated by a guild of priests and priestesses, and once each year a pure woman was chosen from among this guild of priestesses to take the place as the famous Delphic Oracle. [2]

Delphic Priestess

The Delphic Oracle Priestess was known as the Pythia. The word Pythia is derived from Pytho, which comes to us from Greek mythology. The name comes from the death of the monstrous serpent Python after it was slain by the sun god Apollo. The Pythia were known as women of good character. They were chosen from amongst a guild of priestesses from within the Temple of Apollo. Although some Pythia were married, upon assuming their role as the Pythia, the priestesses ceased all family responsibilities and individual identity after being instituted for training into the priesthood. In the heyday of the Greek oracle, the Pythia may have been a woman chosen from a prominent family, well educated in geography, politics, history, philosophy, and the arts. In later periods, however, uneducated peasant women were chosen for the role. During the height of the oracle's popularity, as many as three women served as Pythia, with two taking turns in giving prophecy and another kept in reserve. [3]

Several other officials were also known to have served the oracle in addition to her priestesses. The other officials associated with the oracle are less understood. These are the *hosioi* ("holy ones") and the *prophetai* (singular *prophētēs*). *Prophētēs* is the origin of the English word "prophet," but a better translation of the Greek word might be "one who speaks on behalf of another person." The *prophetai* are referred to in literary sources, but their function is unclear; it has been suggested that they interpreted the Pythia's prophecies, or even reshaped her utterances into verse, but it has also been argued that the term *prophētēs* is a generic reference to any cult personnel at the sanctuary, including the Pythia. [4]

Oracular Procedure

At any given time after about the year 200 B.C. there were two priests of Apollo who were in charge of the entire sanctuary at Delphi; Plutarch, who served as a priest in the late first century and early second century A.D., gives us the most information about the organization and operation of temple and oracle procedure. Before 200 B.C. there was probably only one priest of Apollo. Priests were chosen from among the leading citizens of Delphi, and were appointed for life. In addition to overseeing the oracle, priests would also conduct sacrifices at other festivals of Apollo, and had charge of the Pythian Games. The Greek Delphic Oracle was known to have given prophecies only between spring and autumn. In the winter months Apollo was said to have deserted his temple, his place being taken by his divine half-brother Dionysus, whose tomb was said to be within the temple. Plutarch informs us that his friend Clea was both a priestess to Apollo and a priestess to the secret rites of Dionysus. Once a month thereafter the oracle would undergo special rites, including fasting, to prepare her for the event, on the seventh day of the month, sacred to Apollo. It was said she would wash in the Castalian Spring. She would then receive inspirations by drinking of the waters of the Kassotis where the water was said to flow right from the inner floor of the temple where she would later come to be seated. [5]

Descending into her chamber, she was mounted on her tripod seat, holding laurel leaves and a cauldron of the Kassotis water into which it is said she gazed. Nearby she was flanked by the two golden eagles of Zeus, and the cleft from which emerged the sacred fumes of prophesy. Consultants carrying laurel branches sacred to Apollo approached the temple along the winding upwards course of the sacred way, bringing a goat for sacrifice in the forecourt of the temple, and a gift of money for the oracle. Petitioners drew lots to determine the order of admission. The goat was first showered with water and observed to ensure that it shivered from the hooves upwards, an auspicious sign that the oracular reading could proceed. Upon sacrifice, the animal's organs, particularly its liver, were examined to ensure the signs were favorable to proceed. [6]

The Oracles of Delphi were known to have survived since ancient times, and over the many hundreds of years spanning the Prophetic utterances of the Oracle in the Greek world over half are said to be historically accurate, and it was this profoundness that gave the Oracle her widely regarded respect and popularity. At times when the Pythia was not operating, consultants obtained information from the future in other ways at the site. It is said that some people would cast lots near the temple, using a simple questioning system of Yes or No devices to get the answers they were seeking. But many Greeks used the counsel of dreams for their Prophetic inspirations in the times the Delphic Oracle was not around. [7]

In an attempt to find a scientific explanation for the Prophetic inspirations of the Oracle, scholars have referred to the ancient writings that have been made on the Oracle. One of these refers to Plutarch's observation that the oracular powers appeared to be linked to vapors from the Castalian Spring that surrounded the Oracle in the inner parts of the temple chamber. Together with the observation that sessions of prophesy would take place in, or be preceded by a visit to an enclosed chamber at the base of the temple. Plutarch had for a long period presided over the Delphic Oracle as a priest at the site. It has often been suggested by many historians that these vapors may have been hallucinogenic gases but it was not until fairly recently that this once controversial theory was actually proven as fact. [8]

Secrets of the Delphic Oracle Revealed

The first excavation of Delphi was conducted by a French team led by Theophile Homolle of the College de France from 1892 to 1894 and reported by Adolphe Paul Oppé in the year 1904, who stated that there were no fissures and no possible means for the production of fumes. Oppé flatly stated that the French excavations had found no evidence for a chasm underneath the temple. [9] Following this definitive statement, such scholars as Frederick Poulson, E.R. Dodds and Joseph Fontenrose all stated that there were no vapours and no chasm underneath the temple. A recent reexamination of the much earlier French excavations, however, has shown that the earlier consensus was gravelly mistaken. In 2001, evidence of the presence of ethylene, a potential hallucinogenic gas was found in the temple's local geology and in a nearby spring by an interdisciplinary team of geologists, archaeologists, a forensic chemist, and a toxicologist. [10] The highest concentrations of ethylene gas were found in the waters of the Kerna spring, just immediately above the temple. Although in small quantities, currently the waters of the Kerma spring are diverted from the site for use by the nearby modern town of Delphi. It is currently unknown the degree to which ethylene or other gases would be produced at the temple should these waters be allowed to run free, as they did in ancient times. [11]

It has also recently been shown that the temple of Delphi lies exactly on the intersection of two major fault lines: the north-south Kerna fault and another east-west Delphic fault paralleling the shore of the Corinthian Gulf. The Rift of the Gulf of Corinth is one of the most geologically active sites on earth. Earth movements there impose immense strains on the earth at accompanying fault lines, heating the rocks and leading to the expulsion of the lighter gasses, such as the hallucinogenic gas ethylene. It has been disputed as to how the adyton was organized, but it appears clear that the Apollo temple was unlike any other in Ancient Greece, in that the supplicant descended a short flight of stairs below the general floor of the temple to enter the sanctuary of the Oracle. It would appear that a natural cleft or chasm at the intersection of fault lines was enlarged to create the main attachment off the center of the temple, and the flowing waters of the underground springs would accumulate the gas, concentrating it in the enclosed space. Plutarch reports that the temple of Apollo was filled with a sweet smell when the spirit of the god was present [12]:

> Not often nor regularly, but occasionally and fortuitously, the room in which the seat of the god's consultants is filled with a fragrance and breeze, as if the adyton were sending forth the essences of the sweetest and most expensive perfumes from a spring. [13]

Of all of the hydrocarbons, ethylene gas is the only one that is known to have such a sweet smell. Inhalation of ethylene in an enclosed space in which the Oracle was in but separated from the consultant by a screen or curtain of some kind, would have exposed the Oracle to sufficiently high concentrations of the narcotic gas, enough to induce a mildly euphoric trance-like state. Frequent earthquakes seem to have been responsible for the observed cracking of the limestone, and the opening up of new channels by which hydrocarbons entered the flowing waters of the Kassotis. This would cause the amounts of ethylene emitted to fluctuate, increasing or decreasing the potency of the drug released, over time. It has been suggested that the decline in the importance of the Oracle after Hadrian was in part due to the fact that there had not been an earthquake in the area for a significant length of time. [14]

Later scientific examination by Isabella Herb found that a dose of 20% ethylene gas administered to a subject was a clear threshold. A dosage much higher than 20% could cause unconsciousness. But with less than 20% a trance state was induced and the subject could sit up, hear questions, and answer them logically, although the tone of their voice might be altered, their speech pattern could be changed, and they may have lost some awareness of their hands and feet, to the point that it was possible to have poked or pricked the subject with a knife or pin and they would not have felt it. [15] When patients were removed from the area where the gas had accumulated, they had no recollection of what had happened, or what they had said. With a dosage of more than 20%, the patient lost control over the movement of their limbs and may even start to thrash wildly, groaning in strange voices, losing balance and repeatedly falling. In such cases, studies show that shortly thereafter the person dies. According to Plutarch, who witnessed many prophecies, all of these symptoms match the experience of the Pythia and the Delphic Oracles in action. Plutarch is also known to have said that the Pythia's life was shortened through the service of Apollo. In the examination it was also found that the sessions were said to be very exhausting. In the classical texts, it was said that at the end of each period the Pythia would be like a runner after a race or a dancer after an ecstatic dance. So it is clear that long term exposure to the gas would have had a profound physical effect on the health of the Pythia, just as the historical informants claimed. [16]

The Delphic Oracle was one of the best documented religious institutions of the classical Greek world. The Delphic Oracle is an excellent example of how altered states of consciousness were understood and utilized in the Classical Hellenistic society, as it has recently been identified that naturally occurring psychedelic ethylene gas, under the temple at Delphi was responsible for the profound prophetic utterances of this ancient Hellenistic oracle. The discovery of psychoactive ethylene gas under the temple of Delphi has profound implications in helping modern scholars understand the religious and theological consciousness of pre-Christian Europeans as well as the religious and spiritual mindsets of people of the ancient Hellenistic world. The fact that the psychoactive potential of ethylene gas was utilized as a tool for facilitating the Delphic oracles prophetic utterances indicates that the Greeks put a strong importance on the alteration of consciousness for obtaining knowledge as well as communicating with spiritual realities.

The Greek Eleusian Mysteries

Mystery religions are known today as various secret cults of the Greco-Roman world that offered individuals religious experience not provided by the public religions. A mystery religion offered its members secret knowledge and wisdom. In a mystery religion, an inner core of belifes, practices, and the religions true nature, were revealed only to those who have been initiated into its secrets. Derived from primitive tribal ceremonies, mystery religions reached their peek of popularity in Greece in the 1st three centuries of the C.E. Their Members met in secret to share meals, take part in dances, ceremonies, and especially initiation rites. The cult of Demeter produced the most famous of the mystery religions, the Eleusinian mysteries. [17]

In fact, the cult of Demeter and its initiation rite, the Eleusinian mysteries, was the most famous of all Greek religious institutions and is also known for creating visionary religious experiences, experiences that took place in a secret initiation ceremony. The rites of Eleusis were usually practiced at least once in one's lifetime by all Hellenistic Greek peoples. Although it was more localized and centralized than most of the other Greek mystery traditions, this early central circumstance did not detract it in any way from its great reputation, or its grand influence in the ancient world. The center for these religious rituals usually took place at Eleusis, on the fertile Rharian plain a few miles from Athens where in prehistoric times the cereal grain goddess Demeter was revered by an agricultural community there. This is where the cult of the Greek goddess Demeter existed for many centuries long before the Christian era, where it has been associated with an antique tradition with roots that ran into prehistoric times. [18]

In order to understand the power of these rituals and what they meant to these ancient people it is necessary to keep in mind the main points of the Eleusinian myth which was developed to explain and justify the cult rites. These are stated with sufficient elaboration in the Homeric Hymn to Demeter, (7th century B.C) as well as in the mythological narrative of Demeter and her daughter Persephone. According to the story, Persephone, daughter of Demeter, Goddess of Vegetation and the giver of goodly crops, was stolen by the lord of the underworld (Hades), known in Roman times as Pluto, and carried off to the underworld to be his bride. This was done with the knowledge and tacit approval of Zeus himself. Demeter frenzied with grief, rushed about the earth for nine days, torch in hand, abstaining from eating and drinking, and searching wildly for her lost daughter. As she rested at the "maiden well of fragrant Eleusis" she was welcomed by Queen Metaneria and the daughters of Celeus, who took her to their father's house for rest and refreshment. Here she finally broke her fast and dwelt for a time. To thank her, Demeter took care of the prince Demophon. Secretly each night Demeter brought the boy near the fire and fed him with the nectar of the ambrosia of the Gods, and she did this to make him immortal. One night the child's mother saw this and she was astonished. [19]

In her strong resentment against Zeus, Demeter brought great famine upon the once fruitful earth so that no crops grew for mankind and no offerings were made to the gods. Finally, an arrangement was made with Hades, whereby Persephone was restored to her sorrowing mother. However, since her daughter had eaten a sweet pomegranate seed in the underworld, she was forced to return there regularly for a portion of each year. Demeter, in her joy at the restoration of her lost daughter, allowed the crops to grow once more and instituted in honor of this great and happy event the Eleusinian mysteries, which it is said she gave to mortals as the assurance of a happy future and afterlife. Such was the myth which stood in the background of thought for all those who participated in the grand Eleusinian rites. [20]

The experiential basis for this story is quite clear. It is a nature myth, a vivid depiction of the action of life in the vegetable world with the changing of the seasons. Each year nature passes through the cycle of apparent death and resurrection. In winter, vegetable life dies while Demeter, the giver of life, grieves for the loss of her daughter. But with the coming of spring, the life of nature revives again, for the sorrowing mother receives her daughter back in her arms with happiness. Through the summer, the great mother abundantly maintains the life of nature until autumn, when again her daughter returns to the underworld and the earth becomes desolate once more. Thus, year after year, nature itself re-enacted the great myth of Eleusis. [21]

While the myth of Demeter may be well known, it was the initiations at Eleusis that gave those who participated in these secret rites and rituals a much closer and more personal experience of the afterlife. Legends of the special initiation of ancient heroes and foreigners like Heracles and the Dioscuri recall the primitive time when membership in the cult was open to citizens of Eleusis only. Then, with the political fusion of Eleusis and Athens into the larger Greek state, the local barriers were broken down and rebuilt along much larger more extended lines. The dominant city-state of Athens adopted the Eleusian cult as her own, brought it under state supervision, and was entrusted with the general management of these great mysteries to the larger Greek world. Inscriptions of the Periclean period attest the well-considered plan of Athens to use the mysteries as a religious support for her political hegemony. This combination of ancient Eleusinian tradition and the official patronage of the Athenian state gave dignity and prestige to the mysteries of Demeter, even in the late first century A.D. [22]

The so-called Homeric Hymn to Demeter is one of the earliest and most valuable of the Eleusinian documents, it invites the whole Greek world to come and participate in the mysteries. Herodotus states that on this day, whoever wished to do so, whether they were Athenians or other Greeks, might come to be initiated. Later, even the Hellenic limitation was removed and persons of any nationality were received, providing they understood the Greek language in which the ritual was conducted. Many significant testimonies have been found that have attested to the popularity and success of the Elusian Mysteries, many given by the philosophers and moralists of the period. Even at the close of the pre-Christian era, Cicero declared it was his personal opinion that Athens had given nothing to the world more excellent or divine than the great Eleusinian mysteries. Even later in early Christian times when the Great Olympian Zeus had lost his ancient supremacy, and the Delphic Oracle and tradition of the great sun god Apollo was reduced greatly in influence, Demeter and the Eleusinian mysteries still enjoyed a high reputation and strong influence throughout the ancient world.

Today, barely a half an hour drive outside of the modern city of Athens can be found the ancient shrine of Eleusis. Now humbled and in ruins, the

Eleusian shrine was once the center of the most famous mystery cult of the classical Hellenistic world. Once a year, thousands of pilgrims from all over Greece used to converge on Eleusis, where the peak of their journey converged on the great Telestron, the dark sacred hall of Initiation where the sacred story of Demeter and Persephone was reenacted in a grand theatrical spectacle. But the initiation was much more than a theatrical reenactment. It was an event where the very spiritual forces of nature were harnessed and came to be utilized. The myth, as in parts of the Eleusian rite, tells the story of Demeter's journey into the underworld to claim back life from the death of her daughter Persephone, a fantastic shamanic like myth that honors the forces of life, death, rebirth, and spiritual regeneration. Like the legendary myth, the people who participated in the initiation rituals at Eleusis were also introduced into the mysterious forces of life, death, and the inner visionary worlds of the spirit.

Unlike many of the traditional rituals of the state religions, which were designed to aid in social cohesion, the mysteries were an individualistic form of spirituality, which offered mystical visions and personal enlightenment. The initiates underwent a secret process of initiation, which profoundly transformed the initiates' state of consciousness. The poet Pindar reveals that an initiate into the mysteries "knows the end of life and its god given beginning." [23] In the classical age, the visionary experience was seen as a very important and sacred experience and it was always related to initiation. Because of this, it was also kept as a very closely guarded secret and never discussed with the uninitiated. The mysteries could only have been given through purification and the experience of initiation. Initiation played a very important role in the ancient western mystical tradition. In these secret mystery traditions, particularly those of the Greeks and Egyptians, these experiences were seen as giving insight and understanding into the worlds of the gods, the spirits, and the dead. Because of this, they also had a very close relationship to the language and experiences of death and the world of spirits. The greatest thinkers, artists and innovators of the antiquities were all initiates of various mystery religions, which all held secret the greatest of their mysteries. The eminent roman statesman Cicero Enthuses stated this about the mystery initiations of the classical Greeks:

> These mysteries have brought us from rustic savagery to a cultivated and refined civilization. The rites of the mysteries are called the "initiations" and the truth we have learned from them the first principals of life. We have gained the understanding not only to live happily but also to die with better hope. [24]

The Rites and Rituals

The name "Eleusinian mysteries" is connected with two Greek words *eleusis,-eos,* meaning- *Arrival tó mystírion,* meaning – *secrecy* or to arrive at secrecy. The people were arriving to this place to perform secret initiation rites called mysteries. The mysteries were kept in absolute secrecy, so it was strictly forbidden to talk about them under penalty of death. Nevertheless, there is some information from many different sources that has been studied and gathered over the years that have been used for the reconstruction and understanding of these ancient events. [25]

When we study the Eleusinian rite, we find that it was divided into four distinct stages: *The Katharsis,* or preliminary purification, *The Sustasis,* or preparatory rites and sacrifices, *The Telete,* i.e., the initiation proper, and *The Epopteia,* or highest grade of initiation. Of these various stages the first two were public, and consequently there is a large amount of information about them. But the last two were very strictly private and therefore known only to those who had been initiated. More than six months before the "great mysteries" in what is today the month of September, the "minor mysteries" were celebrated at Agrae, a suburb of Athens, on the banks of the Eleusis. Clement of Alexandria spoke this about these minor mysteries:

> The minor mysteries which have some foundation of instruction
> and of preliminary preparation for what is to come after [26]

This statement emphasizes the rites conducted at Agrae were seen as an important prerequisite for the greater mysteries to follow. On the day after this initial preliminary instruction, the assembly gathered at the sea where they came to cry, "To the sea, O Mystae!" and the candidates preparing for initiation ran down to the sea to purify themselves in the salt waves of the Mediterranean ocean. This was done as a form of ritual baptism believed by the Greeks to be of greater virtue than that of fresh water. "Sea waves wash away ill sin," said Euripides. The assembly also carried with them a young suckling pig which was first purified by immersion in the waters of the sea. Later the pig was sacrificed and its blood sprinkled on each candidate. The flesh of a pig is very similar to that of a man, so it was believed by the Greeks that by sacrificing a young pig, the pig would consume all the misdeeds and sins of the people asking for forgiveness during this purification and sacrificial ritual. Tertullian, in speaking of this rite, declared:

> At the Eleusinian mysteries men are baptized and they assume
> that the effect of this, their regeneration and the remission of the
> penalties due to their perjuries. [27]

Cleansing by salt water was further enhanced by the sacrifice of the young pig, all for the forgiveness of the initiate's sins. This ritual has long been known by historians to have many striking similarities with the Christian rituals of baptism and the blood of Christ also symbolizing the forgiveness of sins. This also struck ancient Christian writers who themselves applied the new birth comparison to their own experiences in Eleusinian baptism. The rite was believed to be regenerative, and regenerative powers were credited to the ritual, which operated to make the initiate pure from sin and born a new being. It was with this rite particularly, that the Eleusinian devotees associated the idea of personal spiritual transformation and the beginning of true rebirth. [28]

On the thirteenth of September, the "great mysteries" began and lasted a full week. Quote from late pagan writers indicate that the Athenian proclamation included not only ritualistic requirements but elements of moral scrutiny as well. Such an indication can be seen on the carving that has been found over the doorway of the Rhodian temple in which is inscribed the following words:

> Those can rightfully enter who are pure and healthy in hand and
> heart and who have no evil conscience in themselves.[29]

From the many pictures and reliefs of vase paintings that we have related to the Eleusinian mysteries, we find that most of them are concentrated mainly around two themes: Those that are depicting the mythological story about the blessing of agriculture and fertility of the earth, and in the second case, they illustrate the great procession from Athens to Eleusis. After the preliminary purification rites at Athens, the purified candidates are known to have formed in solemn procession on the nineteenth of September and marched to Eleusis where they were to complete the celebration of the festival. Along the way leading from Athens there were many holy places, and this parade for the great mysteries came with performed ritualistic observances en route. The company of followers arrived at Eleusis by torch light late in the evening. The long march was then followed by a midnight revival and celebration out under the stars. From this, the Initiate was prepared for the climactic feature of the celebration which took place in the Telesterion, the great Hall of Initiation. This sacred place was closed to all except the ready and purified initiates, and the events which occurred there were strictly private and shrouded in the densest secrecy. The initiates were under pledge of secrecy not to divulge the revelations given there. Apparently, even public opinion and law enforced this important pledge. [30]

The Ninnion Tablet dated from the first half of the 4th century B.C. now found in the National Archaeological Museum of Athens, shows the procession of initiates with Kore and Iakchos in front of Demeter. We are supposing that people arrived inside the sanctuary. Demeter with a scepter is sitting on the sacred chest, and Kore with torches, is introducing her initiates to the Mysteries. Each of them is keeping branches, which were swung rhythmically along the thirty kilometers of the Sacred Way from Athens to Eleusis. The procession was moving with dancing attendants in a parade. The second row of procession was led by torch-bearer Iakchos in the function of priest at the mysteries who leads the way and held torches for performance of the rites. He is standing near Omphalos while a further unknown figure sitting near the closed sacred chest also known as the *kiste*. Another unknown woman keeps this in her hands with a scepter and a vessel. She is probably a virgin priestess of Demeter carrying the kiste with the sacred symbols during the procession and keeping a vessel with kykeon, the Ritual Drink. On the pediment of this tablet is represented *Pannychis*, the whole-night feast. The festival activities were accompanied by dances, perhaps across the Rharian field. The myth says that this is the place where the first grain ever grew, and later a bull would be sacrificed in the great court of the sanctuary, this was done to honor life and fertility. [31]

To understand what was going on inside the great sacred hall of initiation, scholars must look to any pieces of surviving evidence known to describe the experiences that took place in these ancient rites. Text like the Homeric Hymn to Demeter, Pindar, Sophocles, Euripides, Aristotle, Pausanias and others, give us great insight into these ancient rites and rituals as well as the powerfully mystical visionary effects they were known to have had on the participants. All of these ancient texts give insights into what was actually taking place within the initiation hall. When we look at these ancient writings we quickly find that the authors of these texts were all writing without any doubt to the mystical and spiritual significance of the inner Eleusinian mysteries and its effects on initiates. Many of them believed that the mortals who participated in the initiations were blessed. It is said that after being initiated they knew the beginning and the end of life; they had happiness, while the others, the uninitiated, had only misery and after death had only murky darkness. [32]

As the history goes, the gates at the sanctuary in Eleusis were finally open but only for the initiates: men, women, and foreigners who were admitted, not murderers or barbarians. The initiation rites took place in the Telesterion building (which was made to fit several thousand people) on the 20th and 21st of the month. On each of its sides there were seats from which initiates watched the mysteries. Almost in the center of the hall was built the Anaktoron Palace, a rectangular stone construction for the sacred objects of Demeter. Only the hierophants could enter it to perform the rites and display their sacred things. Two classes of initiates participated in the mysteries - the initiates, who took part for the first time, and the others, who were present for at least a second time. The second group could attain epopteia, the highest stage of initiation, when the hierophant showed the greatest mystery. The next day after the ritual, the initiates honored the dead with libations from special vases. On the 23rd of the month, the celebrations came to an end and everybody returned home. For close to two thousand years, a few of the ancient Greeks passed each year through the portals of Eleusis. There they celebrated the divine gift to mankind of the cultivated grain, and were introduced to the awesome powers of the nether world through initiation into the greatest religious rites of the Hellenistic world. [33]

Indications that the Eleusinian initiation had a close relationship to the experience of death or some other type of mystical spiritual experience can be found throughout the Greek language. Greeks in particular were known to have had a very close relationship between the initiatic experience and the language of death. To the ancient Greeks, initiation and death were intimately intertwined. Evidence of this is implicated in their language: *Telos* means the end, perfection, completion, its plural form; *Telea* was the standard word for the initiation rites, which were also known to offer fullness and completion, but at the same time involved a termination or death. The word is found in many variations, many of which are also found throughout the rights of initiation: *Telein* is "to initiate; and *telesterion* is the hall in which the initiation takes place; the *Telestes* is the initiation priest; the *telete* is the initiation ceremony itself; and finally, the *Teloumenoi* are those who have been initiated. The essence of Greek initiation as with many other mystery traditions of the classical world was a real encounter with the sacred. In the ancient Greek world, initiation lay at the very heart of the cultures earliest recorded spiritual life. [34]

The relationship between the experience of death and the ritual of initiation are related in the words of many classical writers. The Philosopher Thermistius in his treatise "On the soul" gave this secret teaching regarding the mystery initiation of the Greeks. "At the point of death the soul has the same experience as those who are being initiated into the Great Mysteries." Thermistius goes on to inform us that, "to be initiated is to experience the same knowledge as one obtains from death- though, of course, with initiation the seeker returns to this world and does not die." In the following quote related to Themistius that may also have also been written by Plutarch goes on to relate this about his initiation experience in the Mysteries of Eleusis. [35]

At first one wanders and wearily hurries to and fro, and journeys with suspension through the dark as one uninitiated: then come all the terrors before the initiation, shuddering, trembling, sweating, amazement: then one is struck with a marvelous light, one is received into pure regions and meadows, with voices and dances and the majesty of holly sounds and shapes: among these he who has fulfilled initiation wanders free, and released and bearing his crown joins in the divine communion, and consorts with pure and holly men. [36]

Probably the greatest collection of information regarding the inner secret rituals of Eleusis that explains some of what was taking place in the initiation hall at Eleusis has come down to us from later Christian writers who tried to break the sacred secrecy regarding these ancient rituals, much of the information we have today about these inner practices now comes from these other outside sources. In these later writings we find that many of the authors described details from the inner initiation act. One of the most startling discoveries regarding these inner rites is the use and drinking from a sacred ritual drinking cup during the initiation processes and before the onset of the visionary experience. The cup was known as the Kykeon. The Kykeon is what initiates were said to have drank from just before the onset of the visionary experience. This sacred cup was kept with and moved within the precession to the Eleusinian temple, the sacred tools known as the kiste and kalathos (kiste - the sacred chest, kalathos - the basket closed with a lid), which only initiated (mystes) members knew what it concealed. In one quote, found on engraved inscription on the base of the statue of an Elusian initiate, describes the revealing of these sacred items:

O mystae, formerly you saw me coming from the shrine and appearing in the luminous nights. Being in an impressionable state of mind, the mystae must have felt themselves very near to divinity when objects so jealously guarded and of such sanctity were finally exposed to view. [37]

The Sacred Drinking Cup

The more scholars studied the inner ritual experience of the Eleusinian rite the more they started to find strong evidence that the initiation ritual at Eleusis not only included a theatrical drama in the form of an education passion play, but they also contained something else, something that was both very mystical and visionary. The rites in the inner sanctum had a transcendental effect on the mind and emotions of the initiates. While it is known that the initiated were instructed in the doctrine of a state of future rewards and punishments before the initiation took place, the greater Mysteries were obscurely intimate. It is known that inside the initiation hall the initiates were astounded by mystic and splendid visions. According to ancient informants, "the felicity of the soul both here and hereafter was purified from the defilements of a material nature and the soul was constantly elevated to the realities of a grand and intellectual vision." So while it was becoming apparent to researchers that the great inner mysteries of the Eleusinian rites were inducing sacred visionary experiences, the question remained, how were these experiences created?

For years, researchers suspected that the powerful effects of the mysteries were coming from a drug additive inside the ritual drinking cup of the Eleusinian rites. The main problem with this theory at the time was that no one knew exactly what the drink included that could have created a visionary experience. The only thing researchers had to go on was a scattered description of its effects for possible identification. Upon a more in-depth historical cross examination of the inner mysteries, a theory would start to unfold that would finally show that the inner rituals at Eleusis really were able to induce the profound mystical visionary experiences the many philosophers and historical informants were claiming to have experienced in these ancient rites. To identify the potential visionary additive contained in the ritual cup, investigators would have to look for any historical documents known to have survived from the ancient world that indicated what may have been inside the Kykeon that could have been able to create such remarkable visionary experiences. One historical text said that the Kykeon was partially made with barley, water, and mint. But the text never described the use of any visionary ingredients. For many years, researchers thoroughly examined evidence trying to uncover the identity of this lost psychoactive component. As a result of this research, the Eleusian mysteries are now probably one of the most well studied mystery traditions of the classical Hellenistic world. Many great thinkers, poets, and philosophers of the ancient world participated in this great ceremony. Many of the texts we have on this ancient ritual described it as the greatest visually sublime experience of a person's life, an experience that gave both mystical visions and an ecstatic new hope for the afterlife.

For a long time the source of these experiences was not fully understood. It was only relatively recently that researchers started to take into account the central importance that visions played in the inner rites. Once this was done real headway was made in identifying the components that were responsible for their creation. Many scholars pointed out over the years, the many visionary elements of the inner rituals, items that have been found from many written historical text known to describe the ritual and its effects. These pieces of evidence gave researchers a strong indication that the experiences being created in these rituals were being created and induced from a natural visionary additive within the ritual drinking cup, the Kykeon.

Finding an Answer

For many years the visionary component of the Eleusinian rituals remained a mystery. It was only through years of dedicated research and historical examination into these mystery rites that researchers were finally able to explain just how these experiences were actually created. In examining this evidence we find that many Greek relics, statues, and paintings all show the goddess Demeter holding sheaths of grain, the central symbol of the cult. One of the most important elements that were over looked for a long time by early researchers was the sacred color of the goddess, the color purple. If it was clear that the Eleusinian ritual was creating visionary experiences, then maybe there were clues standing right out in front of researchers' eyes, clues passed down from the ancients that could give details regarding the source of their visionary power. Researchers started with the central symbols of the goddess' cult, items such as grain and the color purple. The question they had to answer was: are there any natural substances that were associated with grain, had the color purple in them, and had visionary or mind altering properties? At first, it seemed very unlikely, but the most remarkable thing they came to discover, was that there was in fact a very common Mediterranean substance that fit exactly into this strange set of prerequisites. There is a substance that is both purple and associated with grain, lives or grows abundantly throughout the Mediterranean region, and can induce visionary mystical experiences when consumed; this is the psychoactive grain infecting fungus more commonly known today as Ergot. [38]

Albert Hofmann was one of the first people to fully investigate the historical Ergot-Eleusian relationship as well as one of the first to offer a full scholarly investigation explaining how a psychedelic potion could have been prepared in ancient Greece from the ergot fungus. It took Hofmann two years and much laboratory work to complete his task. Since ergot in contaminated grain was known as a dreaded poison in the Middle Ages, he had to overcome how Eleusian priests could have isolated the psychoactive alkaloids from the more toxic ingredients. What he discovered was that eronovine and lysergic acid amide, the two principal psychoactive compounds in ergot, are both water-soluble, whereas the poisonous alkaloids in ergot, such as ergotamine and ergotoxin are not. Throughout Greece ergot is a parasite of barley, which we know was one of the ingredients of the *Kykeon*, and in Hoffman's opinion it would have been relatively easy for the priest to extract the visionary alkaloids. This is, "the separation of the Hallucinogenic agents by simple water solution from the non-soluble ergotamine and ergio-toxin alkaloids." Hofmann explained that Ergoline alkaloids more or less fall into two categories: non-water soluble peptide alkaloids, which exert more toxic effects, and water soluble Lysergic acid derivatives with psychedelic effects more pronounced and far less toxic. Of the latter that appear in nature the most important are Ergine *(D-lysergic acid amide)* the psychoactive principle of many species of Convolvulaceae, and Ergonovine *(D-lysergic acid-L-2-propanolamide)*. Hofmann reports that he ingested 2.0 mg of Ergonovine Maleate, which is about six times the normal dose used in medicine at the time for ceasing Postpartum Hemorrhaging. He experienced some psychedelic activity that lasted more than five hours. Hofmann stated that the ancient Greeks, or at least some of them, could have made a safe psychedelic beverage with an aqueous infusion of Ergot thereby separating the water soluble alkaloids from more dangerous peptide ones. [39]

Although the priest of Eleusis were dedicated in particular to the cultivation of wheat and barley in the name of Demeter, goddess of grains, fertility, and the Greek mysteries, Hofmann pointed out that an even easier method than washing contaminated barley was available to the ancient priest. Paspalum distichum, a wild grass that grows throughout the Mediterranean, supports Claviceps paspali, another species of ergot which are also known to contain only the psychoactive alkaloids with none that are toxic. Hofmann explained that they could have even been used directly in a powder form enabling the astounding visions of the Eleusinian rituals. Probably one of the greatest pieces of evidence linking the goddess Demeter to this newly suspected psychoactive grain infecting fungus is the fact that Demeter herself the Goddess of Eleusis, was sometimes known by the name of *Erysibe*, which literally means, "ergot." We also read three times in the Hymn to Demeter that her robes as well as those of her priest and priestesses were "dark purple," the same color as the fruiting bodies of the psychoactive ergot. [40]

C.A.P. Ruck, with the assistance of Danny Staples, later rendered a detailed explanation of the Hymn to Demeter and cites the information from related Greek texts that pertain to Demeter's Eleusinian cult. In this and two following writings Ruck (1981; 1983) expounded some historical evidence that ergot was the key ingredient in Demeter's potion, from the fact that Demeter was often called *Ersybe* or ergot and the important correlation of ritual symbolism to the purple color in the Goddesses ritual robes, items which are now believed to have reflected the dark purplish-brown hue of *Claviceps*. According to Hofmann, it seemed that the kykeon contained Ergot of Paspalum and not the barley mixture according to the Homeric Hymn. In Hofmann's opinion barley was not believed to be the psychedelic principle, but a nutrient extract used with the mint. The admixture of mint fits well into the Ergot hypothesis of the kykeon because it is well known that ergot preparations produce light nausea which can be counteracted by mint.

According to the famous Philosopher Aristotle, the mysteries did not teach rules of conduct but rather stimulated the emotions. Aristotle is of the opinion that also Synesitis affirms, "that the initiated learned nothing precisely, but that they received impressions and were put into a certain frame of mind." [41] As I detailed earlier many historical informants considered this ritual the most supreme experience in an initiate's life, both physical and mystical. So profound and sublime was this mystical ritual of the early Greeks that even the greatest of Greek philosophers spoke very highly of them and were all participants. Even the great philosopher Plato is quoted in saying this regarding the Eleusinian experience:

> Those who are initiated into the great mysteries perceive a wondrous light. Purer regions are reached, and fields where there is singing and dancing, sacred words and divine visions, inspire a holy awe. Then the man, perfected and initiated, free and able to move super physically, without constraint, celebrates the mysteries with a crown on his head. He lives among pure men and saints. He sees on earth, the many who have not been initiated and purified, buried in the darkness, and through fear of death, clinging to their ills for want of belief in the happiness of the beyond.
> - Plato (427-347 B.C.)

The initial discovery of Ergots relationship to the Kykeon and the visionary experiences created in the Eleusian rites was first made in an interdisciplinary study based on three different approaches: Ethnomycology, Classical Studies, and Chemistry. The secret rites of the Eleusian mysteries which had remained a mystery for four thousand years, had finally been identified and found to be associated with an intoxication caused by the fungus Claviceps paspali, which grows parasitically on certain grains throughout the Mediterranean region and Greece. But how far back in human history does the use or knowledge of Ergot go? Well Ergot fungus has been infecting and growing parasitically on grain in the Mediterranean longer than humans have been alive on the planet. Ergot spores and fungus have also been found in Neolithic caves throughout Europe. The Greeks themselves said that from the very start of human civilization the Elusian rituals were given to mankind as a blessing, a blessing that came from the grain. This would indicate a very ancient relationship with the fungus as well as the possibility that ergot infected grasses were known about and produced in some of the first agricultural settlements around 9,000 B.C. If this is true, then it is possible that the investigation and use of Ergot for spiritual or visionary purposes could go back millennia. Historically, Ergot is thought to have first been mentioned directly around 600 B.C. by the Assyrians and later by the Roman historian Lucretius (98-55 BC) referred to ergotism as *'Ignis sacer'*, meaning Holy Fire, a name which later became used for plagues of ergotism that started to arise during the later Middle Ages in Europe when knowledge of the fungus fell into decline. [42]

Claviceps Paspali

Claviceps Paspali also known as Ergot can be toxic if taken in high enough doses. Small amounts of the fungus will not hurt, but if one was to consume a large amount of the infected grain, very dangerous side effects could occur. This could include symptoms such as fever, cold sweats, and pain in the joints or extremities, and if the dose is too high, possibly even death. The dangerous and toxic effects of Ergot only seemed to have really first manifested in European history after the fall of the classical world and the destruction of the Eleusinian rituals. The first large plagues of ergotism only really started to occur in the Mediterranean region after this Classical knowledge was lost, the temples destroyed, and priesthood disbanded. Because of this, in the later Middle Ages ergotism grew to its greatest point as a sickness among the common people, people who had lost all knowledge of its toxic potential. Because of this loss of classical wisdom, the knowledge regarding Ergot's intoxicating and visionary potential fell largely into decline. This eventually led to large outbreaks of Holy Fire that would later come to plague the people of Medieval Europe. It was this ancient knowledge that was perpetuated by the Eleusinian priesthood. It was this age old wisdom that told the people not to harvest, bake, or eat these purple infected grains. Once the cults of Demeter vanished, it left uneducated Christian rulers to take control over the lands that were once ruled by pagan peoples who knew of the purple grains potential dangers. When this change took place, as history shows, it would only take a few hundred years for Ergot Plagues to start popping up across Europe.

The word Ergot is derived from an old French word argot, meaning the cock's spur. The violet-purple or black sclerotia formed by Ergot consist of hyphae and may be two to ten times the length of a normal kernel. If bread was prepared without removing the black spurs, epidemics of ergotism would occur. Poor people mainly ate rye especially during famines, when even the spurs were collected because of hunger. The first mention of gangrenous ergotism was in Germany in 857 A.D. and the first epidemic of convulsive ergotism occurred in 945 A.D. in Paris. [43]

These are the two distinct types of ergotism, with the gangrenous type seen mostly in France and the convulsive one in Germany. The name Holy

Fire or St. Anthony's fire, given to Ergot epidemics during the middle Ages, referred to the burning sensation experienced by sufferers in the limbs. In 1582 Adam Lonicer in Germany made the first note of Ergot stimulating uterine contractions and inducing labor. It was the most effective drug for this purpose at the time, resulting in a rapid and sudden termination of labor with a delivery time lasting less than three hours. But Ergot was eventually deemed unsuitable for this purpose as the dosage could not be given accurately due to large variations in the active ingredients. [44]

Infestations of this fungus into the grain supply gave plagues of fever and intoxicating visions. This gave it the name Holy Fire. High doses of infected grain could have been very dangerous and even deadly, giving people high fevers, blisters, and aborting women's pregnancies during high intoxications of the infected grain. St. Anthony, after whom the "Fire" was named, lived as a religious hermit in Egypt. He died at age 105 in 356 A.D. He is named Protecting Saint against Holy Fire, Epilepsy, and Infection. During the Crusades, the knights brought back his remains to France, for burial. Infestations and even plagues of Holy Fire are found throughout later European history. It was not until 1676 that the real cause of ergotism was first discovered and measures of control were set up. But by the 1750s botanists were still uncertain how Ergot grew or why it was toxic. In 1815 the famous botanist A.P. de Candolle proved the fungal infection of the Ergot fungus and in 1818 the Massachusetts doctor Prescott, gave a dissertation on the natural history and medical effects of ergot, which he later published. [45] After Dr. Prescott published his work on the medical properties of the fungus ergot was increasingly being employed in medicine, but it was not officially accepted into the Pharmacopoeia until 1836, and it was not until the 1920s that the active principals of Claviceps Purpurea came to be known. Subsequently a number of other alkaloids were discovered in the fungus. One of which was the psychedelic compound responsible for its powerful visionary effects, the psychoactive compound LSA. [46]

Ergot has a very long and complex relationship with mankind in the Mediterranean region. Evidence of Ergot's long history and awareness in Europe can be seen from the long logistic association that the fungus has throughout the Mediterranean world. There are two dozen words for the Sclerotium in France alone, sixty-two vernacular names in German, Mutterkorn being the most commonly used. There are twenty-one in Dutch, fifteen in Scandinavian, and fourteen in the Italian language. There are also seven in the English language in addition to the borrowed word Ergot. This proliferation of Vernacular terminology clearly indicates the importance and long history of this fungus in many European countries. [47]

Hofmann pointed out that the psychotropic properties of Ergot were quite well-known in antiquity and that such folk knowledge of these properties lingers in Europe even today. Further evidence of this is seen in just some of the many modern names of the fungus throughout Europe names such as Tollkorn ("mad grain") and seigle ivre ("inebriating rye") (Hofmann 1978a), names which clearly give it away as a well-known purple, grain infesting, visionary intoxicant. One of the most interesting and subsequent pieces of evidence demonstrating the visionary properties of the Ergot fungus is its relationship to our own modern history. The Swiss chemist Albert Hofmann long argued in support of the visionary and entheogenic theory of Ergot as the visionary component in the Elusian Mysteries. Hofmann further suggested that the Eleusinian priests may have employed Ergot of the wild grass Paspalum, which produces only the visionary alkaloids and not the more harmful and toxic type of Ergot known to induce fevers or pain in higher dosages. While many historians and researchers felt that the discovery of the Eleusinian mystery's visionary admixture had finally been uncovered, there still remained some skepticism in the historical community. Only a few years after this theory had been fully presented and articulated to the academic world did one of the greatest breakthroughs emerge from the chemical examination and exploration of the ergot fungus. In 1938 Dr. Albert Hofmann made a discovery that would forever change the history of modern western culture, a discovery that was made by investigating and exploring the chemical properties of the Ergot fungus. [48]

Modern Visions

While investigating the chemical and pharmacological properties of Claviceps Paspali, commonly known as Ergot, Dr. Albert Holfman discovered and synthesized for the first time in history the semi-synthetic compound Lysergic Acid Diethylamide, a substance more commonly known today as LSD. His research into the pharmacological properties of Ergot as well as his dedicated research and discoveries regarding the Eleusinian mysteries not only helped change the course of our understanding of the classical world, but directly impacted and changed the course of modern history.

Only 15 years after his remarkable synthesis and discovery of LSD in 1953 did the U.S. Government Agency known as the Central Intelligence Agency or the CIA, authorize the start of a secret government project called MK Ultra. The program was at the time, a top secret U.S. government program centered on assessing the possible military applications of LSD for proposed weaponization and mind control programs, a project that quickly ended due to the substances unpredictable nature and unsuitability for weaponization and use in mind control warfare. [49]

The word psychedelic, meaning "mind-manifesting" was coined in the 1950s during our culture's brief enthusiasm with chemical self-discovery. During these brief years of initial western study, a massive amount of well-documented scientific research accumulated attesting to the positive psychotherapeutic potential of LSD as well as many other psychoactive substances being investigated by science at the time. Many of these substances were studied and found to hold many beneficial and therapeutic properties. As well as the substances well-noted spiritual mental healing properties, such studies also showed LSD to hold strong benefits for the rehabilitation of criminals into society and patients suffering from a wide variety of emotional and mental illnesses. Many scientists presented a wide variety of positive research regarding LSD's positive therapeutic potential for a wide variety of social and psycho-therapeutic applications. Yet despite the wide accumulation of positive academic research pertaining to the therapeutic potential of this and other psychoactive substances in the medical and psychological practices, the widespread and uncontrollable status of them in society coupled with the Government's fear regarding LSD's power, unpredictability, and effects on society resulted in the subsequent total outlaw of all psychedelic compounds in the mid-1960s. With the U.S. Government's outlaw of all psychedelic substances, the mainstream vogue for consciousness expansion quickly ended soon after.

While psychedelics of any form are demonized and repressed in the U.S. and many other western nations today, the visionary compounds found in many plants and fungi are the spiritual sacraments of many tribal cultures around the world. Psychedelic plants have been used constructively and safely in ritual settings around the world for thousands of years. These natural psychedelic plants are considered sacred because they awaken the mind to other levels of awareness and they are seen as gateways to a spiritual and multi-dimensional vision of reality. The chemical responsible for the visionary state of Ergot is known as the compound LSA from which the synthetic compound LSD is derived. For further information on this subject, the social and political history of the compound LSD and its discovery, the reader is referred to the book Acid Dream: the Complete Social History of LSD by Martin A. Lee and Bruce Shlain.

In the year 396 C.E the Sanctuary of Eleusis was finally destroyed by bands of fanatical Christian monks. Before this act of tragic vandalism, the mysteries had been celebrated there for over eleven centuries. At the height of their popularity, people were coming from all over the known world to be initiated. Each year, some 30,000 Athenian citizens embarked on the pilgrimage 30 kilometers bare foot to the sacred site of Eleusis on the coast to celebrate the autumn mysteries of Dionysus. After ritual naked baptisms in the sea and other purification ceremonies, the crowd reached the great doors of the initiation hall. All initiates were sworn to secrecy and held the mysteries so sacred that they kept this oath all of their lives. [50] To this day, much of the Elusian rites still remain a mystery, but we now know that they witnessed a sublime theatrical spectacle and were awed by sounds and dazzling lights. The orchestrated apex of the initiation included the consumption of a drink that gave the initiated a vision of transformation, rebirth, and an experience of spiritual enlightenment. So it seems clear that any great power such as this, which goes untamed, can or will be used for good or bad, both sacred and the profane. So it was in this construction of ritual and mystery that the ancients learned to tame this sacred power and used it for the good, used it to give man a better hope for the future, and a look into his inevitable end. Maybe someday our own culture can regain this delicate balance and once again find a constructive way to elevate our souls and to manifest our minds.

> The Homeric *Hymn to Demeter,* Pindar and Sophocles already praise the bliss of initiates in the Other World, and pity those who die without having ever been initiated.
>
> Plato, *Phaedrus*

CH 3
MYSTERIES OF PAGAN PHILOSOPHY

God is not external to anyone, but is present with all things, though they are ignorant that he is so.

(Platinus 260 A.D)

Before I go on and present the Gnostics and go on to identify how their visionary experiences were created, I would like you to see how the visionary rites of Eleusis affected some of the religious and philosophical teachings of the classical worlds greatest thinkers. In late classical antiquity, the mystical religious experience as it was handed down by the mystery traditions of old, was the primary source of spiritual realization throughout the western world. When we examine the history of these experiences in western civilization, we find that the importance of visionary experience emerged with the most prominent significance during late classical antiquity. This period of history not only saw a growing popularity of mystery traditions that offered initiates secret ancient knowledge and mystical spiritual initiatic experience, but also the growing expansion of mystical and esoteric philosophical speculation. As we saw earlier in the Greek Eleusinian Mysteries, a sacred potion was drank and visions were seen and experienced. Some scholars have refused to examine the evidence that demonstrates the visionary nature of these experiences and have instead decided to interpret these evidences only metaphorically. However other scholars have suggested another possibility's, people such as Wasson, Hofmann and his associates who were some of the first to argue that it was purple Ergot infected grain that was consumed at Eleusis, which made a real psychoactive potion just as the classical writers had claimed. Because of the evidence they presented, it stands to reason that famous participants in these initiatory rites had in fact experienced the visionary effects they claimed and these experiences helped to contribute to the philosophical speculation of their period. In looking for evidence of this we must look at one of the most important and famous of these Eleusinian participants, the great philosopher Plato.

Mysteries of Platonic Thought

Plato is one of the greatest philosophers of all time, and probably the most famous philosopher of the western world. Plato was a participant of the Eleusinian mysteries; he is also known to have had knowledge of these visionary experiences and even to have described them. He has been quoted in saying that his participation in these mystic rites had a notable effect on his philosophical doctrine. If this is true and visions were actually seen and experienced in these rituals as classical authors such as Plato claimed, then this would indicate that the philosophical and mystical ideas found within Plato's writings are not just theoretical constructs but were based on visions that were actually seen and experienced. Plato was widely admired for his philosophical inquiries into the soul as well as the unseen worlds of form, spirit and mind. While it is clear that Plato was known to have had a deeply spiritual and psychological side to his philosophical logic, some of Plato's most popular and important works are those that are related to ethics, society and politics. Plato's political theory was known to have developed in a close connection with his ethics and it is these works that have stood out as a philosophical beacon for western democracy and law. In addition to Plato writing many important works regarding politics, ethics and society, he was also known to have inquired into the philosophical sides of music, art, and the early sciences. But among all of these great intellectual achievements, Plato is credited with founding the first university, the Academy. [1]

Plato was also a very open admirer and initiate into the Greek mysteries of Eleusis. Much of the language that Plato often used regarding the unseen worlds or forms is known to imply in his belief in the existence of a separate world of a transcendental essence. This aspect of Platonic thought is something that fundamentally cannot be denied. But many if not most academics are very resistive to the metaphysical interpretations of many of Plato's teachings. It is strange to see why because many of Plato's philosophical ideals on metaphysics directly relate and have root in the teachings also found and expressed in the mystery traditions of Eleusis. Plato was known to have regarded metaphysics and the spiritual experience as the highest of the three stages of enlightenment in the spiritual progress. This also corresponds to the highest stage of initiation into the mysteries, a term that was known as epopteia, "the supreme vision of the highest reality," an experience tantamount to assimilating oneself insofar as possible into the supreme union with the Godhead, an experience that always took place in the perfecting rites and mysteries of Eleusis. [2]

Plato also stated that, "the true occupation of the philosopher is to allow the soul to be released from the body and run free," this is not only a clear characteristic of the ecstatic and visionary experience, but it is also directly associated with the initiate experiences encountered in the Hellenistic mystery traditions. Because of this, it stands to reason that Plato's philosophical ideas on the soul, the world of spirit, and form, were not merely theoretical constructs as some have assumed, but were in fact based on actual experiences and visions actually lived through and experienced by Plato himself. Plato's philosophical works on the soul and the worlds of form, spirit, and mind are not just mere metaphors as some academics would presume, but rather, there is ample evidence to show that they were based on visions that he had actually seen, and experienced, and clearly come to be incorporated into many of his teachings and philosophical works. While many traditional academic schools still attempt to claim that much of Platonic thought is based around purely theoretical constructs of a reflective and rational mind, with no connection to the visionary experience, and while the visionary roots of Platonic teachings (on such ideas as forms, essence, and mind) may be a controversial subject within many academic circles today, it seems that when considering the surmountable evidence demonstrating the visionary nature of the Eleusinian initiations and Plato's own written statements attesting to their sacred, mystical, and visionary character, it seems very clear to me were Plato found his ideas, and I also believe it was very clear to his contemporaries as well. [3]

Some of the best evidence to demonstrate this fact comes many years after Plato's death, when a new form of philosophy was born from his original thoughts, ideas, and philosophical teachings. This new form of Platonic philosophy is know today as Neo Platonic philosophy, a system of philosophical thought that arose out of Plato's original ideas and teachings. In examining this further, I should point out that the most important and unique aspect of the Neo-Platonic tradition was the importance it put on the visionary and ecstatic experience of creating and contacting the divine. This traditional Platonic quest is found not only in Plato, but also in the later works of the Neo Platonic philosophers as well as the Jewish philosopher and historian Philo of Alexandria. Philo was a great admirer of Plato and just like Plato, Philo of Alexandria was also a well documented visionary himself. Many of Plato's contemporaries were also well known and documented for their visionary experiences, practices, and philosophical speculations; (people such as Valentinus, Albinus, Clement of Alexandria, and especially Plotinus and all the later Neo Platonic philosophers.) All of them shared in common the teachings and understanding of these mystical visionary ascents. Teachings that they stated must first be acted by initial purification, usually also with some form of instruction until the course of the ritual initiation when the mind then becomes absorbed in its single object (the One, the Good, the Beautiful, the Divine) at which point one "suddenly" sees the ultimate source of all these philosophies and intellection giving way to initiation and union with the divine mind and spiritual ecstasy so highly prized by the spiritual seeker. [4]

The visionary and ecstatic experience was very prevalent in the late classical age as well as in the Neo Platonic tradition. The fact that such experiences were held in such high regard to these ancient people clearly attests to their importance in the development of late classical philosophical thought, literature, and intellectual speculation. Because of their tendency to inquire about the nature of the mind, soul, and its relationship to the ecstatic visionary experience, the Neo-Platonic tradition could in many respects be called a philosophy of ecstasy and the spiritual experience. Yet many contemporary schools teaching philosophy today fail to point out these important details regarding the true nature and source of Neo-Platonic wisdom. Instead they only briefly mention them, if they are mentioned at all. They tend to leave out many of the important facts regarding the Neo-platonic tradition's relationship to the visionary ecstatic experience, or state that these visionary ecstatic experiences were not the primary contributing source of its most profound esoteric philosophical wisdom. When these controversial topics are discussed, they are left out as only a side notes in history. It is as if they would rather conceal these unknown controversies in history then to state them as important contributing forces to the development of late classical pagan thought and philosophical inquiry. The fact is, that the late classical systems of pagan thought such as the Neo Platonic tradition and others have been vitally influential in many of the greatest and most important aspects of the western intellectual tradition, so to ignore this entire chapter of its intellectual inquiry is to deny the very sources from which they came, and by doing this we deny the greatest and deepest truths of our own inheritance.

Philo of Alexandria

While Plato may have inspired many great minds of the ancient world, he was not the only great thinker of the ancient world who was known to have had experienced mystical visionary rites and who's thoughts and philosophical writings helped shape and contribute to our world today. Another one of these great men is known as Philo of Alexandria. Philo is known as the chief figure of Jewish Hellenistic Philosophy. Living around the time of Jesus

Christ, Philo was born in 25 B.C. and died some time after 40 A.D. Philo believed that God was personal, as Jewish philosophy teaches, but he is at the same time a pure being, absolutely simple. He does not occupy space or place but rather contains all things within himself. Philo was an educated Jewish intellectual living in the Popular Jewish quarter of Alexandria Egypt around the 1st century A.D. He also had a hearty admiration for the philosophy and the minds of the Greeks. Among gentile authors it was the philosophers of the Greeks whom he most highly esteemed. Parmenides, Empedocles, Zeno, and Cleanthes seemed to him almost divine men and members of a sacred company. While Philo is well known to have had a strong admiration for Greek Philosophers he is also known to have shown the greatest fondness of all, for the great Philosophies of Plato. Philo of Alexandria used words like "Plato the great" and "Plato the most sacred." This leads us to inquire into Philo's own philosophical system, a system partially characterized by the characteristic marks of Platonism. [5]

When we examine Philo's writings, it becomes clear that he was known to borrow freely from many other systems of intellectual thought at the time. The mathematical philosophies of the Pythagorean tradition were also particularly attractive to him. He spoke of this school with veneration and was himself characterized as a Pythagorean, by Clement, of his own city. On the philosophical side, Philo presents a notable example of the eclectic tendencies of the time, and one reason why it is so difficult to reduce his thinking to a definite system of thought, is because of the true syncretistic character of the thoughts in his writings. [6]

In spite of his appreciation of Greek philosophy, Philo yet remained at heart a religionist consciously loyal to the practices of his fathers. It was not one of the thinkers of the Greeks but Moses himself who was the greatest of lawgivers and philosophers. In studying the religious philosophies of Philo and his contemporaries, we quickly find that his teachings were primarily centered on a single phase of religious mysticism. One that we find was centered on the personal religious experience and mystical visionary enlightenment. Like many of the pagan Philosophers, Philo said that his experiences came from his culture's own secret mystical initiation tradition, rituals that had been perpetuated by his own race throughout the ages. It was this direct personal religious experience that Philo, the Egyptian Jew, was so directly interested in experiencing, an experience that involved the immediate relationship of mankind with the very essence and experience of the divine. So Philo understood God as far removed from humanity, but man himself was not so far removed from the divine. [7]

When it came to the central experience of the divine, the mediating agencies were for the most part totally disregarded by Philo. Philo believed that the human soul was only to be left alone with God not within its own self but somehow outside of itself an idea that was also perpetuated by Plato regarding his experience of the divine reality. Philo quotes this on his idea: "If you seek God, O my mind, go forth out of yourself, and seek for him."[8]

Probably one thing that mattered most to Philo was man's real kinship with the divine. Philo strongly believed that this was achieved solely by virtue of mankind's intellect and his mind, but if not by meditation then by what other means? Philo taught that the soul strove for realization, it strove for union with the divine origins of its being; hence there was, in the soul itself an inner urge that impelled it Godward. The ultimate goal of the soul's endeavor was an immediate vision of God itself. This, in Philo's estimation, was the supreme experience of the religious life. [9]

Philo persistently asserted, but usually with some reservation, that the direct vision of the mind, and the immediate apprehension of God, were really possible for humanity. Philo went farther and in terms of real enthusiasm attempted to describe such an immediate experiences of God that he himself was known to have had. Philo viewed God as something truly real, something that humans could also have direct contact and experience with, but God was also something invisible, able only for contact through the mind and soul of a person and accessible only directly through visions of the mind. [10]

Philo also claimed that he possessed knowledge of a secret initiation process in the form of a Jewish Mystery tradition that had been passed down secretly throughout the ages to only a select and chosen few, directly from Moses. Philo not only claimed to be initiated into this Jewish Mystery tradition but he also stated that he was an initiator himself, he claimed to have started his own Jewish mystery school known as; *The Mysterys of Moses.* Philo taught that Moses himself had been or was initiated into the secret mystery tradition by another and that it had been secretly handed down long before him. According to Philo, this initiation process had been handed down and perpetuated overtime to only a select few throughout the millennium. Philo claimed that these Jewish mysteries were far superior to those practiced by other races, such as the Greeks or the Egyptians, both of whom had mystery initiations of their own. Today all knowledge and evidence regarding these Mysteries of Moses, as stated and claimed by Philo, have been lost. The only elements that have survived regarding them are a handful of writings from Philo claiming their existence, and a few cryptic descriptions of some of his own visionary experiences. While the source of Philo's visions seems to elude us today, the specific character of his experiences seem to have shared the most in common with other secret visionary tradition also popular at the time, a tradition that was known to have had a very close connection to Judaism, as well as the visionary traditions surrounding Egypt at the time, the visionary religious traditions of the Hermetic and Gnostic faiths.

Neo Platonic Philosophy

While the written works of Philo of Alexandria may give us great insight into the Jewish mystical tradition circulating in Egypt at the time. Philo's mystical philosophical teachings and strong adoration for Greek philosophy is known to have helped prepare the way for the later development of Neo-Platonism which seemed to have also emerged from Alexandria Egypt a while after his death. With birth of Plotinus in the early 2nd century, Neo Platonism would take on many aspects of these earlier philosophical doctrines such as the transcendence of God, the existence of intermediary beings, and the soul's ascent to God culminating in visionary ecstasy, something that was a very defining attribute of Egyptian mysticism, Gnosticism, and the visionary and philosophical works of Philo and the later Neo Platonic Philosophers. [11]

It wasn't until later in the classical age with the appearance of the Neo Platonic philosophers in Egypt, that we begin to find the greatest influx of visionary and ecstatic experiences beginning to take center stage on the philosophical platform. Neo Platonism is a modern term used to designate the period of Platonic philosophy beginning with the works of Plotinus and ending with the closing of the Platonic Academy by the Emperor Justinian in 529 A.D. This brand of Platonism, which is often described as 'mystical' or religious in nature, developed outside the mainstream of Academic Platonism. The origins of Neoplatonism can be traced back to the era of Hellenistic syncretism, which spawned such movements and schools of thought as Gnosticism and the Hermetic tradition. Neo-Platonism may be considered under three aspects: philosophical and scientific; practical and ethical; and mystical and occult. The philosophical and scientific aspects of Neoplatonism were first recorded by Plotinus. The practical and ethical teachings were stressed by Porphyry, while the mystical and occult side of Neo-Platonism found its most complete expression in the works of Iamblichus. Neo Platonism and the study of the Neo Platonic tradition is important to the research of this book because it allows us to understand the mystical visionary experiences and practices taking place in late classical times, as well as to gain insight into the much more ancient visionary religious traditions and experiences they were known to have studied. [12]

Plotinus

Plotinus is known as the first great Neo-Platonic Philosopher. Plotinus was born in Egypt at about 204 A.D. Plotinus, we are told by his disciple

Porphyry, that he attended the lectures of the various professors at Alexandria until he was 28 when he joined up with a Persian expedition of the Emperor Gordia, in order to make the aquatints of Persian Philosophy. He soon returned to Rome and opened a school. When Plotinus was about sixty years old he received as a pupil the celebrated Porphyry. Porphyry relates that his master experienced ecstatic union with God four times in the six years in which he was his disciple. Neo Platonic thought unarguably was the most saturated with visionary and mystical experiences out of the known collections of classical philosophical systems. In these teachings Plotinus taught that God was absolutely transcendent he is one beyond all beings. He also taught on the soul, the experience of God, as well as on beauty, ethics, and the divine world. But probably some of his greatest works he created were those that related to the ecstatic or entheogenic experience of creating the divine within. In his teachings on this, Plotinus is quoted in saying:

> In this ecstatic union, the soul retains her self consciousness. But all these stages are but preparations for the final stage, that of mystical union with God the one, who transcends beauty, in an ecstasy characterized by the absence of all duality. In thought of God or about God there is no such separation from the Object; but in ecstatic union there is no such separation. There shall a man see, as seeing may be in heaven, both God and Himself: himself mad radiant, filled with intelligible light, or rather grown one with the light in its purity, without any burdened any heaviness, transfigured to Godhead, nay being in the essence of God. This ecstatic union is however, of a brief duration so far as this life is concerned: we looked for its complete and permanent possession in the future state, when we are freed from the hindrances of the body. [13]

Plotinus taught that there is a supreme, totally transcendent "One" Containing no division, multiplicity or distinction. "The One" he said, "can not be any existing thing and can not be merely the sum of all things, but is prior to all that exists. Thus no attributes can be assigned to the One. We can only identify it with the Good and the principals of beauty." Plotinus denies sentience, self awareness, or any other action to "the One," rather if we insist on describing it further we must call the One a sheer dynamis or potentiality without which nothing could exist. "The One," being beyond all attributes including being and non-being, is the source of the world-but not without the act of creation, willful or otherwise, since activity cannot be ascribed to the unchangeable, immutable One. The "less perfect" must, of necessity, "emanate", or issue forth, from the "perfect" or "more perfect." Thus all of creation emanates from "the One" in succeeding stages of lesser and lesser perfection. These stages are not temporally isolated, but occur throughout time as a constant process.

Mind and Soul

The first emanation of the One according to Platinus was "nous" *nous* is known as thought of the divine mind, logos, or order, or reason, identified with the demiurge in Plato's *Timaeus*. It was the first will towards the good. From *nous* proceeds the world soul, which Plotinus subdivided into upper and lower, identifying the lower aspect of the soul with nature. From the world soul proceeds individual human souls, and finally, matter at the lowest level of being and thus the least perfected level of the cosmos. Neo-platonic teachers like the Gnostics and Egyptian mystics believed that the universe was regarded as a series of emanations from the Godhead. Matter itself is merely the lowest of these hyper-dimensional emanations. Although the number and qualities of these emanations differ, most Neo-Platonists insisted that God was both singular and good. Although Neo-Platonists were technically polytheistis, they also clearly embraced a form of monotheism: reality was varied, with varied gods, but they all represented aspects of the one divine reality. When we look back to the doctrine of Speusippus (Plato's successor in the Academy) we find that he states that the One is utterly transcendent and "beyond being," and that the Dyad is the true first principle. Plotinus likewise declared that the One is "alone with itself" and ineffable. The One does not act to produce a cosmos or a spiritual order, but simply generates from within itself, effortlessly, a power (*dunamis*) which is at pure intellect (*nous*) and the object of contemplation (*theôria*). While Plotinus suggests that the One exists by thinking itself as itself, the intellect subsists through thinking itself as *other*, and therefore becomes divided within itself: this act of division within the intellect is the production of being, which is the very principle of expression, creation, and emanation. For this reason, the intellect stands as Plotinus' universal soul this first principal he defined as divine soul and mind all in one. [14]

When Plato spoke of his theories of forms, he asserted that forms and not the material world of change known to us as sensation; possess the highest and fundamental kind of reality. Plato spoke of forms in formulating his solution to the problem of universals. Plotinus likewise believed that out of the inert unity of these Forms, arises the soul, whose task it is to think these forms discursively and creatively, and to thereby produce or create a concrete, living expression of the divine intellect. This activity of the universal soul results in the production of numerous individual souls: living actualizations of the possibilities inherent in all living material forms. Plotinus believed that this divine universal intellect became divided within itself through contemplation, but the human soul becomes divided outside of itself, through the secret actions of mystic ecstasy. This expressive or creative act of the universal soul also referred to as nature is what constituted the creation and formation of the cosmos. When the individual human soul reflects upon its true nature this soul is capable of attaining insight (*gnôsis*) into the essence of intellect; however, when the soul views nature as something objective and external as something to be experienced or undergone, while forgetting its source or root, the soul detaches itself from the creator and forms a mind locking itself within nature. Because of this, evil and suffering ensue, and the human soul looses its connection and awareness of its original divine root. [15]

Plotinus believed that the human soul proceeds from the perfect conception of a universal form (*eidos*). It then emanates into the always flawed expression of this form in what we know today as the materially derived world of matter and human 'personality. This is how the human soul finds itself. Because the soul is this divine spark and the source or essence that is the human soul finds itself in this material manifestation, it risks succumbing to the demands of the material body, and so becomes something less than divine. The Cosmos, according to Plotinus, is not a created order, planned by a deity on whom we can pass the charge of begetting evil; for the Cosmos is the self, the expression of this great divine universal soul/mind. This idea according to Plotinus corresponds, roughly, to Philo's *logos prophorikos*, the *logos endiathetos* which is the Intelligence (nous) of the Cosmos. The Cosmos, in Plutonian terms, is to be understood as the concrete result or 'product' of the universal soul's experience of its own mind (*nous*). Plotinus also explained Nature as the very locus of personality. In the system of Platinus, the intellectual ascent, or salvation through assimilation into the experience and knowledge of god, reached there most complete systematic expression. Philosophy in the Neo Platonic tradition now included not only logic, cosmology, psychology, metaphysics and ethics, but also the theory of religious experience and mysticism. In fact, since the highest type of knowledge is the mystical knowledge of God, and since Plotinus, who most probably based his theory of mysticism on his own personal experiences as well as on past speculation, he evidently regarded the ecstatic mystical experience as the supreme attainment of the true philosopher and thus utilized these experiences as vital aspects of his philosophical work and introspection. [16]

Iamblichus

Iamblichus was among one of the most important Neo Platonic philosophers after Plotinus and while only a fraction of Iamblichus books have survived, most of them having been destroyed during the early Christianization of the Roman Empire. The written philosophical works of Iamblichus were some of the most detailed mystical occult works from the Neo Platonic tradition and have subsequently given us some of the greatest insights into the Neo Platonic experiences and what type of visionary methodologies the Neo Platonic philosophers may have utilized from the many ancient religious traditions circulating at the time. While the works of Plotinus may have centered more around the teachings of Plato and the visonary traditions of the Greeks, the works of Iamblichus go on to demonstrate some of the strongest connections to the mystical occult works of the Egyptian, Chaldaean, and Gnostic mysteries, depicting some of the most visionary esoteric works of late classical pagan thought.

Iamblichus as well as many of the Neo Platonic philosophers spoke very highly of the Egyptians mystical religious priestly knowledge. Iamblichus of Apamea was probably the greatest proponent of Egyptian wisdom as well as the Hermetic and Chaldaean mysteries. Iamblichus even tells us that the Egyptian Hermetic text had originally been written in Egyptian, by Egyptian priests who then rendered them into Greek, but their primary sources originated from within the temples of ancient Egypt. He also stated that the Great Pythagoras and Plato, during their visits to Egypt read through the stelae of Hermes with the help of native priests, indicating Egyptian influences in the philosophical works of some of the Hellenistic world's greatest philosophical minds. [17]

While much of Neo Platonic philosophy was originally born out of Alexandria, Egypt, in later years of its history philosophical schools spread too many other regions of the empire and surrounding Mediterranean. One of the more prominent schools that were known to have existed outside of Egypt in later years was the Neo Platonic school in Syria. The chief figure of the Syrian school of Neo Platonism was Iamblichus. Iamblichus was a pupil of Porphyry and lived in 330 A.D. Iamblichus was born in Chalsis, in Coele Syria, at about the middle of the third century. From the fragments of his life which have been collected by historians, we find that he was a man of great culture and learning, and renowned for his charity and self-denial. His mind was deeply impregnated with Pythagorean doctrines, and in his famous biography of Pythagoras he has set forth the philosophical, ethical, and scientific teachings of the sage in full detail. Iamblichus was also a well studied student of the Egyptian Mysteries and expressed his desire to make available what had been taught only in the mystery schools and under the greatest of secrecy. Iamblichus was also known to have carried much further the Neo Platonic tendency to multiply the members of the hierarchy of beings, which he also combined with the importance of theurgy and the practice of visionary occultism and the Egyptian mysteries. The tendency to multiply the members of the hierarchy of being was present in Neo Platonism from the very beginning but Iamblichus is known to have made the most extensive use of these beings and their philosophical speculation. [18]

Iamblichus introduced the idea of the soul's embodiment in matter, believing matter to be as divine as the rest of the cosmos. This was the most fundamental point of departure between his own ideas and those of his Neo Platonic predecessors, who believed that matter was a deficient concept. Despite the complexities of the make-up of the divine cosmos, Iamblichus, like the Gnostics, still had salvation as his final goal. The embodied soul was to return to divinity by performing certain rites, or theurgy, literally, 'divine-working'. Some translate this as "magic," but the modern connotations of the term do not exactly match what Iamblichus had in mind, which was more along the lines of a religious ritual. Iamblichus believed that the transcendent cannot be grasped with mental contemplation because the transcendent is supra-rational. Theurgy or divine working was thus a series of rituals and operations aimed at recovering the transcendent essence by retracing the divine 'signatures' through the layers of being, this then, according to Iamblichus, was the only way to achieve this experience and knowledge. Iamblichus stated that education was important for comprehending the scheme of things as presented by Aristotle, Plato, and Pythagoras as well as the secret occult wisdom of the Egyptians and ancient Chaldaean Oracles, but it was only through spiritual ecstasy that mankind could truly achieve awareness and union with the one. [19]

Iamblichus was best known for his teachings and practice of theurgy, practices in which Iamblichus is also known to have utilized visionary experiences as integral parts of his divine philosophical work. The magical works of Iamblichus were said to have worked on the lower level, also known as the visual or material level, with physical symbols, and at the higher levels with magic. The theurgy of Iamblichus is said to have been based on the fact that the divine exists within all of material matter, the theurgist by using these materials would then eventually reach the level where the soul's inner divinity would be united with God. This then was the supreme achievement of the Neo-Platonic Philosopher, but it was also the system of secret rituals that Iamblichus used that helped him achieve his secret visionary contact. Iamblichus went on to assert that the source of his visionary spiritual knowledge came from the secrets of the Egyptian and Chaldaean Mysteries.

While the exact sources of these visionary rituals were never fully disclosed in his writings, the surviving texts of Iamblichus describe many of his mystical visionary experiences and their mysteries. Upon examining his writings, one finds many similarities between them and the visionary entheogenic experiences we also find reported in the Chaldaean and Egyptian Gnostic writings of the same time period. [20]

Iamblichus Magic, Nature, and the Keys to the Spirit World

Today religious ecstasy is defined as an altered state of consciousness characterized by greatly reduced external awareness and expanded interior mental and spiritual awareness, which is frequently accompanied by visions and emotional/intuitive insight (and sometimes physical) euphoria. In many if not most cases that these ecstatic experiences are known to have been created and documented, they are found to take place within a handful of consciousness altering techniques that are incorporated as essential practices of various shamanic traditions around the world. In studying the Neo Platonic tradition of ecstasy, it is well documented among scholars that the Neo-Platonic Philosophers incorporated altered states of consciousness to create the ecstatic and visionary experiences so characteristic of their philosophical speculations. Altered states of consciousness were also a defining element of many classical pagan religion's rites, rituals, festivals, and religious initiations. While many Philosophers are known to have been initiated into the secret rituals of various mystery cults of the time, there is evidence that some of these philosophers also perpetuated their own mysteries and had secret doctrines that were based on actual mystical religious experiences just like those seen and experienced in many other pagan mystery traditions of the time. [21]

Throughout history, the land of Egypt was admired for its advanced knowledge of medicine, magic, and science. As you will see later in this book, much of Egyptian magic was related to the occult properties of various natural substances like plants, stones, and herbs. Iamblichus was known to have made the most use of these ancient Egyptian teachings for his own philosophical work. Iamblichus is also known to have founded a school of Theurgic Magic among the Neo-Platonists. At first this school was distinct from those established by Plotinus and Porphyry, both of whom considered the knowledge of practical Theurgy as dangerous to the majority of men. But in the passage of time Porphyry came to adopt Iamblichus' point of view and gave him both encouragement and support. If we would understand the true purpose of Iamblichus' school, we must first learn the real meaning of the word *Magic,* as it was also understood by the ancients. Magic for them was a true sacred science. A practice indissolubly connected with religion. In defining this science, Plato said: "Magic consists of, and is acquired by the worship of the gods." But when Plato spoke of "the gods," he referred simply to the occult powers and potencies of nature. The relationship between nature and the innate occult properties found within nature are as Proclus relates regarding the sacred science of Egyptian magic. [22]

The science of magic includes knowledge of the constitution of nature and of man. Both have their visible, physical side as well as their invisible, indwelling, and energizing aspects, and above these there is the spirit, alone, eternal, and indestructible.

But, as "light and darkness are in the world's eternal ways," the art of magic also falls into two distinct divisions. When the adept uses his knowledge beneficially, with no other thought other than to benefit and heal nature and man, the result is good and thus known as White Magic, or as Iamblichus called it "Theurgy." But when he applies his knowledge of these secret arts to selfish or evil motives, it is known as Black Magic or *Goetia* as Iamblichus called it. Iamblichus, instigated by a pure motive, taught this White Magic. He had two objects in view when he did this: He wanted to uncover the invisible side of nature, to warn men of the perils that lurk in the shadows of this secret "Hall of Learning," and to show how the dangers may be avoided. His second object was to give men who had not been initiated into the Mysteries the means by which they could affect the union of the divine spark in themselves with its parent-flame, the Divine of the All. Porphyry, the teacher of Iamblichus, was also fully aware of the invisible side of nature and warned of the possible bad effects which might occur to those who attempted to practice Theurgy without a thorough preliminary cleansing of the lower material self. [23]

The mystical and visionary occult's aspects of Iamblichus' teachings did not stop with nature and the experience of the divine world. In his instructions, like those in *The Voice of the Silence,* are for those "ignorant of the dangers of the lower unseen worlds known to him as the Iddhi. Iamblichus went on to say that the ancients did not consider the inner worlds (known to him as *Aether*) as a great void but pictured it as a boundless ocean peopled with living forces. This idea of a deep boundless realm of inner spiritual forces in echoed in many shamanic traditions around the world. These are experiences that are as old and as ancient as human kind itself. Finding these ancient methodologies alive and present in the writings of Iamblichus and the late classical pagan philosophers clearly attest to the ancient shamanic roots of classical religion and the mystical spiritual experiences they were known to have created.

In Iamblichus's book *Theurgia or on the Mysteries of Egypt,* Iamblichus goes on to ask some of the following regarding divination and the secret occult practices of his time:

What is it that takes place in divination? For example, when we are asleep, we often come, through dreams, to a perception of things that are about to occur. We are not in ecstasy full of commotion, for the body lies at rest, yet we do not ourselves apprehend these things as clearly as when we are awake. In like manner many also come to a perception of the future through enthusiastic rapture and a divine impulse, when at the same time so thoroughly awake as to have the sense in full activity. Never the less, they by no means follow the matter closely, or at least they do not attend to it as closely as when in their ordinary condition. So, also, certain others of these ecstatics become entheast or inspired when they hear cymbals, drums, or some choral chant; as or example, those who are engaged in the korybantic rites, those who are possessed at the Sabazian festivals, and those who are celebrating the rites of the divine mother. Others, also, are inspired when drinking water, like the priest of the Klarian Apollo at Kolophon; others when sitting over cavities in the earth, like the women who deliver oracles at Delphi; others when affected by the vapor from the water, like the prophetesses at Branchidae; and others when standing in indented marks like those who have been filled with an imperceptible inflowing of the divine plerome. Others who understand themselves in other respects become inspired through the Fancy: taking darkness as accessory, other depending on singing and magical figures and others on employing certain drinks and potions. Some are affected by means of water, others by gazing on a wall, others by the hypethral air, and others by the sun or in some other of the heavenly luminaries. Some have likewise established the technique of searching the future by means of entrails, birds and stars. [24]

In this work, *De Mysteris Aegyptorum*, or *The Mysteries of Egypt*, Iamblichus details many important elements that were used by the ancients in their divine mystical workings. While a great deal of knowledge can be gleamed from the ancient writings of Iamblichus, these texts still only hint into exactly how many of the experiences of the Neo Platonic philosophers were created. While the above statement is only one of a few statements directly detailing the mystic, ecstatic, and shamanic experiences of the ancient world, the surviving written works of Iamblichus give us some of the most clearly defined descriptions of these cult practices and the experiences they created. From examining his writings it becomes obvious that altered states of consciousness were used within many pagan religious rites, rituals, and religious traditions of the time. Anyone familiar with Shamanic methodologies for entering altered states of consciousness and contacting spiritual realities, will find many striking and important statements in the above quote and many other of his surviving writings. It is also interesting and important to point out the use of shamanic drumming and the induction of trance dance states in the korybantic rites of Dionysus, the rituals of the great mother, and at the Sabazian festivals. While the visionary and ecstatic experience was a fundamental and important attribute of Neo Platonic philosophy, it is clear that the Neo Platonic philosophers were not only familiar with a wide range of ecstatic experiences available to them at the time, but that they also had first hand experience with them as well.

When we examine the surviving writings of these ancient philosophers they show us a world that was heavily steeped in the experience of the mystical and highly desirous for absorption into the divine. The experience of the visionary realms and the beings residing within these realms were of the utmost importance to Iamblichus. In his many visionary experiences Iamblichus encounters various visionary supernatural beings, angels, gods and daemons. These beings encountered in the visionary realms, gave direct insight into the worlds of spirit. In his writings on this, Iamblichus is quoted saying some of the following:

In the Epoptic Vision the figures of the gods shine brilliantly; those of the archangels are awe-inspirering and yet gentle; those of the angels are milder; those of the daemons are alarming....The images of the Gods glow with abundance of light, and those of the archangels are surprisingly luminous. Those of the angels are resplendent with light, but daemons present the appearance of smoldering fire. [25]

In another visionary experience Iamblichus goes on to elaborate:

There flashes out from the Gods beauty which seems inconceivable, holding the beholders fixed with wonder, imparting to them an unutterable gladness, displaying its self to view with ineffable symmetry, and carrying off the palm from other forms of comeliness. The glorious views of the archangels have themselves very great beauty, but it is by no means ineffable and admired as that of the Gods. Those of the angels partake in a degree of the beauty which they receive from the archangels. When the archangels appear, there are certain regions of the world set into motion, and a divided luminance goes before them. [26]

The explorations of the inner visionary worlds were not unique to the philosophical works of Iamblichus, but were well known among the Neo-

Platonic Philosophers. Porphyry, the teacher of Iamblichus, talked about spiritual beings that were subject to characterization by the human will, and that they may appear to us as either good or bad. Porphyry describes them in this way [27]:

> Daemons are invisible. But they know how to clothe themselves with forms and configurations subject to numerous variations, which can be explained by their nature having much of the corporeal in itself. When they can escape the vigilance of the good Daemons, there is no mischief they will not dare commit, one time they employ brute force; another time, cunning, but there is another class of entities that which reside in the Astral Light. [28]

Iamblichus, like many Neo-Platonic philosophers, claimed that the source of their mystical and philosophical wisdom came through the ecstatic alteration of consciousness that opened the doors of the mind onto the supreme reality. But it was the invisible side of nature and the psychic and spiritual powers latent within man that were of the utmost importance to Iamblichus and were also the source of his traditions most profound and powerful experiences. In reflecting on the visionary experience of spiritual ecstasy, Iamblichus details two different types of ecstasies that can be imparted on the intellect:

> It is necessary from the beginning to make the distinction of the two species of ecstasies, of which one causes degeneration to an inferior condition, and fills with imbecility and insanity; but the other imparts benefits that are more precious than intelligence. The former species wanders to a discordant and worldly activity; but the latter gives itself to the supreme cause, which directs the orderly arrangement of things in the world.

In continuing Iamblichus says:

> The mediumistic trance, leads to a deterioration of both mind and body. But the divine ecstasy imparts health to the body, virtue to the soul, purity to the mind. It removes the cold and destructive quality of the mind and brings the whole man into accord with the soul. The higher part of our nature is awakened, and begins to long vehemently for its universal source.

Proclus

Probably the last great Neo Platonic philosopher to have speculated on pagan mystic ecstasy and the experience of union with the divine was Proclus the apostle of Iamblichus. Proclus lived from 410-485 A.D. Proclus, like many of his predecessors, attributed to the human soul, to a faculty above thought, by which it was said a man can attain the experience of the one. This is the unitary faculty, which attains the ultimate principal of spiritual ecstasy. Proclus also said that the soul ascends through the different grades of virtue in its ecstatic union with the primary source of life more commonly known in Neo Platonic teachings as the one. Proclus distinguished three general stages in the soul's ascent as Eros, truth, and faith, truth he said leads the soul beyond the love of the beautiful and fills it with knowledge of true reality, while faith consists in the mystical silence before the incomprehensible and inevitable experience of the divine. Proclus like many of his predecessors spoke of these teachings in many cryptic ways, never fully disclosing to the unpurified and the uninitiated the secret source or method of how these divine experiences were created. Like many of his Neo Platonic predecessors, Proclus was also known to have participated in many mystical religious rites and rituals of the classical pagan world. In his discussion on the mystery traditions, Proclus, following Iamblichus, gives us this important and interesting statement and mystical visionary description:

> In all the Perfective rites and mysteries, the Gods project many shapes of themselves, and display many changing figures; there will be a formless luminance radiating from them; then again it will be represented in a human form, and again it will go into some different shape... Some of the figures were *empousae* and not Gods, and excited alarm; others were attractive, and other encouraged. [29]

In elaborating on the mystery traditions, Proclus goes on to say that the beholders, (epopoe) or seers, were the individuals engaged in being initiated and (perfected)." In Greek, an epopt, seer, or beholder, was a person admitted to a higher degree of initiation. Proclus goes on to say that "the perfective rite leads the way as the *muesis* or Mystic initiation, and after that the individual reaches Epopteia and becomes a beholder." Theon described this mystic initiation as containing three degrees, "the purification, the initiation, and the beholding of the divine vision." [30]

Both Proclus and Iamblichus were known to have stated that both the Gods and spirits were known to have appeared in the sacred rights. It was the power of this visionary element that gave these mystery cults their most profound importance in the ancient world. By looking at the NeoPlatonic tradition and the visionary experiences that were the base of their philosophical thought, we can see that the most potent and powerful of the ancient world's visonary experiences were those that were also some of the most primal, the most ancient, and the most closely connected to the mysteries of nature. In attempting to uncover the mysteries of pagan philosophy, we are drawn to the study of ancient religion itself and the experiences that are known to have been at the very foundation of its most important and ancient religious practices. In studying the Neo Platonic tradition we are left to understand their world through the few surviving writings these ancient people are known to have left us as well as the experiences they are known to have described.

Ch 4
The Mysteries of Egypt

The mind, O Tat, is of God's very essence.
Hermes, the Corpus Hermeticum

The Greeks are known to have had many difference Gods, cults, and religious rites, but of them all the most visionary and most powerful were the Eleusinian Mysteries, but the Greeks were not the only ancient culture known to have created visionary experiences for mystical and religious purposes. In fact from the most remote periods of antiquity the mystical religious experience was of the utmost importance to the religions of ancient Egypt. In the later years of Egyptian history, particularly during the Hellenistic age, formal Egyptian Mystery traditions had begun to emerge from the old Egyptian ways and started to be documented and recorded by outsiders, particularly by immigrating Hellenistic Greek peoples. Before the Greeks came to rule the lands of ancient Egypt, Egyptian mysticism and religion was very secretive, and closely guarded by the Egyptian priesthood, particularly from outsiders. Like the Greeks, the Egyptians had Mystery traditions of their own and like the Greeks, the Egyptians kept the secrets of their temples and religious initiations very closely guarded. One of the oldest and most popular mystery traditions of the ancient Egyptian civilization was the religious tradition of the ancient Egyptian God of vegetation and resurrection, the god man Osiris. Osiris had a unique relationship to vegetation, life, death, and the experience of rebirth. From the very earliest times in Egyptian history, Osiris and Isis, known as the Egyptian mother goddess and the wife of Osiris, were known to have held a unique position in the religious thought of ancient Egyptian peoples. The Historian Herodotus noted in his day that "no other gods were worshiped in the same way by the whole of Egypt save only Isis and Osiris." The worship of other deities varied from place to place in different sections of the country. By comparison with these the related cults of Isis and Osiris were undiversified, and their hold on the religious loyalties of the Egyptian people remained more or less constant not only in different localities as the cult spread, but in various ages of time as well. It is surely an impressive fact that in later Graeco-Roman times the reformed and Hellenized cult of Isis and Osiris functioned just as vigorously as the same older antique Osirian religion had functioned in the times of the great Pharaohs hundreds of years before. [1]

This brief summary of the Osirian tradition suggests that, in the religious thought of Egypt, Osiris was a dying and reviving god, much like Attis and the Greek Dionysus were, and as such a personification of the yearly rebirth of vegetable life in the ever recurrent struggle of life and death in the natural world. In later years when the Greeks came to rule the lands of Egypt, the Greeks came to identify Osiris with their own Dionysus and Isis with Demeter. Both Gods and Goddesses functioned in the very similar manner and symbolized very similar things. So similar were the two mystery traditions that when the Greeks took control of Egypt during the rule of Alexander the Great, they instituted a union between the two gods, creating a one unifying principal.

In examining the religious cult of Osiris as it was seen in later Hellenistic times, we look to the information that was handed down to us from antiquity. What little literature is known to have survived regarding this ancient religious tradition comes down to us from the historical records of the Historian Herodotus. While his historical accounts of the Osiris cult and its rituals are scanty at best, they are yet still sufficient to detail the general character of these religious celebrations. When we examine his writings on the rituals festivals of Osiris we find that they were in the nature of a passion drama and they featured lamentations in which the spectators participated. The suggestion is an obvious one, the death and resurrection of the great hero Lord Osiris constituted the subject matter of this drama and that the lamentations were the traditional lamentations of Isis for her dead husband. [2]

According to ancient Egyptian legend, Osiris was once both king and God of the Egyptians long, long ago. Typhon the brother of Osiris was very jealous of Osiris, and plotted to kill him. Later, at a feast provided for Osiris' pleasure, his brother Typhon brought a large chest, beautiful in workmanship and valuable in the extreme. Typhon offered the chest as a gift to whoever possessed a body which would best fit into the chest. When Osiris entered the box, Typhon caused the lid to shut and fastened it, sealing Osiris inside. Then his jealous brother Typhon took the chest and through the whole chest into the Nile. Currents carried it to the lands of Byblos known today as

Phoenicia, and cast the chest ashore at the foot of a large Acacia tree. The tree grew rapidly and soon encased the chest holding the body of Osiris. When Isis, faithful queen, learned of the fate of her husband she set out in search of the body. Meanwhile the King of the Land where the Acacia was growing found the Acacia holding the body of Lord Osiris, admiring the tree's beauty; he cut it down and made of its trunk, a column. Learning this, Isis became nurse to the King's children and received the column as her pay. In the tree trunk, was preserved for all time the body and soul of Lord Osiris, and from that day forward the Acacia tree came to be symbolized by the Egyptians as containing the spirit of Osiris himself. But Osiris never really died he was instead reborn, reborn as ruler over the realm of the dead, the realm of dreams and reborn in his son the living Horus. Because of this myth and its importance in ancient Egyptian culture, Osiris had became known as the God of vegetation, regeneration, and the ruler of the dead. In remembrance of Osiris and the regenerative forces of life, death, and nature that he represented, miniature mummy cases representing Osiris were sown with grain and left out in the rain until they sprouted, an emblematic statement of the life rising from death and the life giving regenerative forces of nature that Osiris clearly represented. [3]

In ancient Egyptian times the Osirian cult included both public rites and secret ceremonies. Certain things were done and certain explanations were made which were regarded as matters of great secrecy. During the early part of the afternoon, Isiac shrines were left open, and the images of the goddess were exposed to the silent adoration of the worshipers. Prayer, meditation, and contemplative devotion were thus encouraged. The daily liturgy was brought to a solemn but joyful close with the chanting of hymns, the dismissal of the people, and the closing of the shrine. By services such as these, regular and somewhat elaborate, the faith of the people in the Alexandrian and Egyptian divinities was renewed from day to day. In addition to these public ceremonies, there were special religious rites which were private in character and fostered a very individualistic type of religious experience. The Osiris cult had come to be unified in Hellenistic times with the Egyptian goddess Isis the mother goddess and wife of Osiris. Isis served as a feminine side within the ancient Osiris Egyptian tradition. Membership in the Osiris/ Isiac community, as in the other mystery cults, was contingent upon participation in certain prescribed initiatory rites and rituals, the details of which were kept closely protected and strictly guarded secrets among members. The private ceremonies of the Hellenistic Osiris/Isis cults in Egypt were a direct development from the much older esoteric rites and rituals of ancient Egypt, where the priests of Osiris reserved certain interpretations and ceremonies, and imparted them only on the promise of secrecy. The most valuable and almost the only source of information concerning these important mystic rites came from Lucius Apuleius' in an account of his own initiation at Cenchraea. By following his narrative, it is possible to trace, step by step, the procedure taking place in an Isiac/Osiris initiation. One is impressed at the outset by the genuine eagerness of Lucius for the grace of admission to the order of Isis, an eagerness tempered by a distrust of his own ability to attain initiation. While awaiting the desired privilege, Lucius lived the life of a recluse in the cloisters of the temple, attending reverently on the regular services of worship. Such a novitiate as this was apparently expected of those who desired initiation, and rooms were provided for them in connection with the temple where they lived with the priests in a sort of monastic temple community. [4]

The ritual of Osiris and Isis had its daily liturgy as well as public festivals at different seasons of the year, festivals that were conducted with an elaboration of a pageantry or play. Most solemn, most stirring, and quite the most popular of these was the November festival celebrating the passion and resurrection of Osiris. It was a festival of great antiquity, directly elaborated from the dramatic performances at Abydos and elsewhere, in which, from the Twelfth Dynasty onward, the sufferings of Osiris had been reproduced. While a great deal of evidence exists outlining the outer elements of the cult and the vireos ritual process, very little is known about the inner ritual experiences of the Osiris initiation. What evidence does exist, demonstrates that it was based upon a very real and powerful mystical religious experience. But little has come down to us to explain how these experiences were created or exactly what took place in the inner ritual sanctum and during the peak of initiation. What little has survived regarding the most inner and intimate of these ritual events have come down to us not only from ancient Egyptian tomb and wall depictions describing them, but also from within the later writings of Lucius Apuleius. In his writings we find that on the afternoon on the day of baptism, the High Chief priest imparted to Lucius certain secret instructions and commanded him to observe various abstinences for a period of ten days just before his initiation. The ascetic prescriptions included an abstinence from meat, wine-drinking, and other pleasures of the flesh. Strict chastity was a particular point of insistence. It was this moral requirement particularly that made Lucius hesitate to apply for admission into the Egyptian Osiris Isiac order. It was this requirement of purity that also made later erotic Latin poets rail so loudly against the Egyptian goddess in later Roman times. [5]

After a ten-day period of ascetic isolation of this kind, Lucius was ready for the initiatory rites. On the tenth day at sunset the initiation was held. After the priest had presented gifts to Lucius according to ancient custom, the uninitiated were commanded to depart. The high priest would then take the candidates by the hand and lead them to "the most secret and most sacred place of the inner temple" where the initiation ceremony itself is said to have taken place. Here the curtain falls and it is here that Lucius refrains from telling us exactly what happened. He conscientiously kept his vow of secrecy. Stating "You would perhaps demand, studious reader, what was said and done there: truly I would tell you if it were lawful for me to tell; you would know if it were convenient for you to hear; but both your ears and my tongue should incur the like pain of rash curiosity." The curtain of secrecy, however, is but a thinly drawn veil intended to protect the God and others from the charge of sacrilege; for he immediately proceeds to give a general impression of the ceremonies without describing a single rite or repeating a single formula. From this general characterization it is almost impossible to get a clear or concrete conception of exactly what took place in the holy of holies of the Isiac sanctuary. But from what few detailed writings Lucius has left us about his experiences with ancient Egyptian Osiris initiation. We are left with only one small, cryptic but interesting statement regarding the inner nature of his profound ritual experience, in this Lucius states the following:

> Understand that I approached the bounds of death, I trod the threshold of Proserpine, and after that I was ravished through all the elements, I returned to my proper place; about midnight I saw the sun brightly shine; I saw likewise the gods celestial and the gods infernal, before whom I presented myself and worshiped them. [6]

Egyptian priests are known to have characterized Isiac initiations as "a voluntary death and a difficult recovery of health." This suggests that a ritual death and resurrection were the central features of the initiation ceremony. Since this was an Isiac initiation, the ritual could have been none other than an adaptation of the ancient Osirian rites that in Egypt from antiquity had been practiced on the living Pharaoh. In the periods of remotest antiquity these rites, so the devotees believed, had been efficient in causing the regeneration of Osiris after his passion; and now they were practiced on the initiates, they themselves also might realize regeneration and gain access to the secret worlds of the Gods and there by experience the world of spirits, the dead, and spiritual immortality. At the beginning of the ritual it seems that the initiate approached the bounds of death. This could be taken literally. Osiris was known as the lord over the dead and it was also over the Lord Osiris whom the vivifying funeral rites were originally performed. So while many elements of the Osirian rituals may never be fully understood, it is clear that what ever took place in the inner sanctum of this ancient Egyptian initiation, was an experience that gave those that experienced it a very real and powerful experience of rebirth, regeneration, and the visionary contact with the worlds beyond. [7]

As you have seen, mysticism and religious experience seem to have been deeply rooted in the ancient Egyptian consciousness, but as Jeremy Naydler goes on to state in, <u>Shamanic Wisdom in the Pyramid Text</u>, "it is a curious fact that the subject of mysticism in ancient Egypt has come to be a controversial topic among many Egyptologists today. From the beginning of the twentieth century, there has been a broad consensus within Egyptology against the existence of any form of mysticism in ancient Egypt, something that largely still remains the situation today. While there have been occasional challenges to the non mystical basis of ancient Egyptian religion among Egyptologist over the years, their current efforst have not yet succeeded in fully dislodging it. The main reason for this is that many Egyptologist tend to view mysticism as a dangerous subject best to be avoided. So, instead of mysticism, attention is focused on the funerary beliefs of the ancient Egyptians. Indeed, the counterpoise to the denial of mysticism in ancient Egypt is the undue weight given to the funerary interpretation of ancient Egyptian religious texts and rituals. This emphasis on the funerary interpretation has served only to de-potentize Egyptian religion and to distort our current understanding of ancient Egyptian religious sensibility. It does this by treating, as mere belief or external ritual of what were, for at least some of the Egyptians, real intense inner experiences ritually undergone while still alive." [8] "If we are to understand the character and significance of the experiences described and detailed on ancient Egyptian tombs and religious artifacts, we need to approach these experiences not simply from an Egyptological standpoint, as products of the ancient Egyptian culture. We need to approach them from the stand point of the Phenomenology of religion, as a specifically religious phenomenon that reveals extraordinary possibilities of human consciousness. One of the primary aims of approaching ancient Egyptian text from the stand point of the phenomenology of religion is to position ourselves as far within the religious consciousness from which these texts originated." In studying ancient Egyptian religion, there is something potentially problematic in taking a purely Egyptology approach to the study of Egyptian religion: namely, that unless the Egyptologist adopts a frame of mind that takes the whole sphere of human religion and religious experience seriously, then the attempt to penetrate ancient Egyptian religion with real understanding is unlikely to be successful. The fact is that the spiritual universe of the ancient Egyptians does in fact have a great deal in common with that revealed in the literature of shamanism. In the shamanic literature, we read account after account given by people for whom the spirit world is a reality, just as it was for the ancient Egyptians. In shamanism, as in the ancient Egyptian religion, we are only marginally concerned with belief systems, for central to shamanism are actual human experiences. It is simply not possible to approach and understand these experiences unless one accepts that they relate to a dimension of existence of a different order from the sense-perception world that normally captures our awareness." [9]

In fact, "it was because of the perceived mystical basis of ancient Egyptian religion that across the ancient Greek and Hellenistic world, ancient Egypt had a reputation for being the fountainhead of esoteric knowledge and wisdom. Many Greek and Roman accounts of ancient Egyptian religion are not only respectful and sensitive towards its deep spiritual import, but they also affirm that the mystical experience was the wellspring of this deep esoteric wisdom. Egyptian priests are portrayed by classical writer as spiritual practitioners who had direct knowledge of spiritual realities beyond the physical world. According to our Greek and Roman sources, this knowledge was less the result of philosophical reasoning or speculation and more the result of direct experiences." [10]

"In the Greek world at large, as well as in the Roman world, people were firmly persuaded that the Egyptians had been some of the first people to organize formal state religious cults. Men of these less ancient nations were prepared to admire quite uncritically the temples and rituals of the ancient Egyptians; even the land of Egypt itself was intrinsically holy. The priesthood, which retained little of the vast social and political power it had once wielded under the Pharaohs, enjoyed a strong reputation among men of Greek and Latin culture. Even the wisest representatives of other traditions such as Moses among the Jews, Salon, Pythagoras and Plato among the Greeks, were all acknowledged to have sat at the feet of the Egyptian priest. In the Imperial Roman period men continued to believe sufficiently in the ancient mystical wisdom of the Egyptians. Many even traveled there to seek out its far famed temple dwellers, leaving behind clouds of awe struck graffiti which may still be read on the monuments along the way. By the fourth century A.D. the Neo Platonic Philosopher Iamblichus thought it no Anachronism to impersonate a learned Egyptian priest as he him self is known to have done." [11]

The Spirit World in Ancient Egypt

In ancient Egypt, the spirit world was conceived as a realm, which they called the Dwat. Naydler says, "that the Dwat was believed by the ancient Egyptians to exist alongside the physical realm that we inhabit during our life time. The Dwat is an invisible region that borders on, and interpenetrates, the world of the living. In this region, the region of the Dwat, are found the gods, demons and spirits of the dead. It is only through having entered this region that one can experience inner spiritual illumination and becoming what the ancient Egyptians called an *akh.* The connotation of the word *akh* is that of inner illumination as well as primordial creative power. Used in its initiatory sense, an *akh* might best be translated as "an enlightened being" or one whose consciousness has become open to the reality of the spirit world." [12]

As New Kingdom esoteric texts that are found to appear in the tomb of Ramesses VI, and elsewhere make clear, the Dwat was an interior realm into which people go when they die, and was an object of intense interest for the Egyptian priesthood. The title of this text is the book of what is in the underworld (Dwat), and in its introductory sentences we read that the text is concerned with (the knowledge of the power of those in the Dwat) including (knowledge of their secret rituals to Ra, knowledge of the mysterious powers, knowledge of what is in the hours as well as their gods). Now, it might be argued that the whole of this text along with the contents of all the rest of the massive body of literature dealing with the Egyptian (otherworld) is not knowledge at all, but mere priestly speculation about something essentially unknowable. But it could equally be maintained that this knowledge was the outcome of a type of mystical experience that involved crossing the threshold of death while still alive, an experience that is so characteristic of shamanism. There is ample evidence that rituals existed in ancient Egypt that served the purpose of projecting the soul across the threshold of death even when still alive. The title of various ancient Egyptian high officials from all periods, indicate that many of those officials may also have had direct knowledge of spiritual realities. One such title was master of secrets, or in its longer form master of secrets of heaven, earth, and the Dwat, which we find, for example, in the titulary of the New Kingdom vizier Rekhmire, of whom it was claimed, there is nothing on earth, in heaven or in any part of the Dwat in which he does not have knowledge. It certainly seems more likely that the type of knowledge referred to here had an experiential basis than that it was merely a memorizing of the context of sacred text." [13]

As you have seen, the role of the shaman as mediator between the non-ordinary reality of the spirit world and the ordinary reality of the sense-perceptible world is a characteristic attribute of shamanism. As Naydler relates, "this is in many respects paralleled in ancient Egypt by the king, whose role is similarly to act as a mediator between worlds. Such important shamanic themes as the initiatory death and dismemberment followed by rebirth and renewal, the transformation of the shaman into a power animal, the ecstatic ascent to the sky, and the crossing of the threshold of death in order to commune with ancestors and gods are all to be found in the ancient Egyptian pyramid text, text that have direct relevance to actual experiences undergone while still alive, experiences of a secret and initiatic nature. If within shamanism these motifs correspond to actual experiences undergone by the shaman, then one clearly fails to do full justice to the same motifs when they arise in the Egyptian Pyramid text. This is not to say that life of the old kingdom Egypt should be similarly reclassified as a type of shamanism. There are several elements in classical shamanism that are absent from ancient Egyptian religion. Most obviously we do not find the single figure of the shaman in Egypt, entering into trance states in order to retrieve souls, heal the sick, or journey into the spirit world, in the same way in which this is described in classical shamanism. We do, though, find a variety of figures in ancient Egypt, be they priests, magicians, healers, or the king himself, who, taken together, fulfilled practically all the roles of the traditional shaman, using more or less the same means." [14] "Of all the different religious frameworks, shamanism could be regarded as the most primal. So while Egyptian society, including its highly structured religious organization, may not correspond to traditional tribal cultures in which classical shamanism is practiced, the mystical experiences that we meet in the Pyramid Text have a distinctive quality that is best described as being Shamanic in nature and containing many striking elements that can be classified as shamanic in origin. The interpretation of religious texts requires that we recognize that not only do they arise out of actual religious experiences, but that they also refer to spiritual realities that need to be understood precisely as such." [15]

"The early sacred literature that survives from ancient Egypt includes tomb inscriptions, offering list, and brief prayers, but there are no long consecutive religious texts until the Pyramid texts appear in the pyramid of Unas at the end of the Fifth Dynasty, roughly 4,350 years ago. The Pyramid texts are not only the earliest example of ancient Egyptian sacred literature-they are also the earliest example of any piece of extended writing worldwide. They are of immense value to us today because they open up a window into the religious consciousness of human beings who lived under very different spiritual, psychological, and sociological conditions from ourselves today. This religious conciseness plumbed depths of spiritual experience that we fail to understand or appreciate if we regard the pyramid text merely as representing the funerary beliefs of the ancient Egyptians. Only by setting this assumption aside does it become possible for the text to reveal themselves as the proto type of a mystical tradition that has it roots not only in later ancient Egyptian religious life but also in the subsequent later Western mystical and esoteric traditions." [16]

"The Pyramid texts are of the oldest versions of a literary genre of religious texts produced during the course of Egyptian history. This includes the Middle kingdom coffin text and the New Kingdom Book of the Dead papyri, both of which derive from, and are developments of, the earlier Pyramid text. As mystical texts, the Pyramid texts describe the human encounter with spiritual realities. The spiritual world that the Pyramid text discloses is one that is revealed only once a certain existential threshold has been reached and consciously crossed. Rather than speculations or beliefs, the contents of the Pyramid text should be regarded as direct experiences and knowledge received. A system of experiences and knowledge that is quite "other" than what we are normally aware of today. A system of experiences that is most closely related to the many mystical and visionary experiences found in many shamanic traditions today." [17] The possibility that the ancient Egyptian religion demonstrates shamanic roots should come as no surprise when the wide variety of ancient Egyptian mystical religious beliefs falls into the realm of direct initiatory experiences. Evidence that ancient Egyptian mystical religious beliefs are based on real initatic experiences can be found throughout the ancient Egyptian religion, but they are seen most clearly in the later writings of the Egyptian Hermetic tradition.

The Egyptian Hermetic Tradition

While the true depth of the ancient Egyptian religion is only beginning to be understood by modern scholars there is another element of the Egyptian religion that is known to have developed in the later parts of Egyptian history that came to have had a particularly profound impact on the religious development of the ancient world, particularly on the religious practices we know today as Gnosticism. In considering the visionary and initiatory traditions of the ancient Egyptians, we are lead to examine a divinity in the ancient Egyptian religion that is known to have taken a much more important and open place in the Egyptian religion in the much later parts of Egyptian history. This was the religious and philosophical tradition of the Egyptian God Thoth, a tradition which came to be known in later Hellenistic times as the Hermetic tradition. The Egyptian Hermetic tradition was a religious philosophical tradition that had its roots in the much more ancient Egyptian priesthood and was known as the religious traditions of the ancient Egyptian scribes. Thoth was one of the most ancient of Egyptian Gods; he was originally known as, "the Lord of Divine words," and the God of wisdom, writing, and records. The God, who the native scribes and priests of ancient Egypt ascribed the inspiration and authorship of all their sacred holy books. Thoth was also known as the keeper over all of the Egyptian houses of life. The Egyptian house of life is where the Egyptians kept all their sacred medical knowledge, literature, and writings. Thoth was among the most diverse and popular of all the Egyptian Gods. Like many of his colleagues, he was also a powerful national God who had certain specialties and local associations. In particular, Thoth was regarded even in the most primitive period as the moon god; from this lunar association arose many of his most distinctive functions. Just as the moon is illuminated by the sun, so Thoth derived much of his authority from being secretary and consular to the solar divinity Ra. The moon, 'ruler of the stars' distinguishes seasons, months, and years. Because of this, Thoth became the lord and multiplier of time, and the regulator of individual destinies. Indeed, so important were the moon's faces in determining the rhythms of Egyptian national life that Thoth came to be regarded as the origins of both the cosmic order and of the religious and civil institutions. [18]

Thoth presided over almost every aspect of the temple cults, laws, the civil year, and in particular, over all the sacred rituals, text, and magical formulae. Thoth was also known to pervade over the magic and healing arts as well. Because much of the Egyptian magical arts were also related to healing and the innate properties of plants, stones, and other natural substances, Thoth became known as the keeper of all Egyptian botanical, medical, and early scientific knowledge. In Egyptian mythology Thoth was most fundamentally known as the divine scribe of the Gods, inventor of writing, and the lord of wisdom. Because of this, the priesthood attributed much of its sacred literature to him, including, for example, parts of the <u>Book of the Dead</u>. Thoth was acknowledged as the source of the Egyptian's knowledge of the secret occult powers latent in the material and supernatural world that were handed down in the ancient Egyptian cults and mystery traditions. His magical powers made of him a healer and a doctor, and when the body of a person had finally succumbed to mortality, it was Thoth who conducted the dead to the kingdom of the gods, and participated in the weighing and judgment of the soul.

The Egyptian Hermetic literary tradition is a very ancient one, yet the Corpus of text that we know today was not attested to until comparatively late in Christian times. The Hermetic tradition is known to have first originated from the ancient knowledge and writings of the Egyptian God Thoth, but came to be later known as Hermetic when the Greeks came to later dominate the lands of Egypt labeling the Egyptian books of Thoth as "Hermetic" in order to bring together and fuse the two similar theological ideas and traditions under one unifying principal. In Alexandria Egypt this was particularly common to find inscriptions to duel gods in many areas, all expressing this underlying unity, (items such as, Osiris –Dionysus or Thoth and Hermes.) The Greeks did this because they saw the Egyptian gods as very similar to their own and thus tried to unify the two gods into one spiritual idea. This was done so the people could all worship the same oneness via any particular god or goddess that appealed to them without being in contradiction with their neighbors who happened to choose a different divine face. This merging of religious system was first introduced under the ruling of the Greeks in

Egypt, and Egypt was the first places in the classical world to experience this great diverse mixing and sharing of ancient theological beliefs. In Hellenistic and Roman times, Egypt was peculiarly productive of a distinctive variety of religious systems and temperaments. These Religions were notably high in their mystical and emotional elements, as well as markedly ascetic in their tendencies, the teaching and religions developing out of Egypt at this time in history were also above all, supremely desirous for absorption into the divine and into union with the mystical and visionary experience of God. [19]

Hermetism & Gnosticism

Hermetism takes its name from the Greek God of magic and writing: Hermes. Hermes in turn was so-called Trismegistos or Thrice-Greatest Hermes because of his identification and similar association with the great Egyptian God of wisdom, writing, and magic: Thoth. Thus, Hermes Trismegistos the thrice greatest was created and became the name for Thoth. Even the name *Thôth* is a Greek attempt to phonetically render the original Egyptian world *Tehuti*, the late antique form of the very much more ancient Egyptian name *Djehuti*. This was a Greek effort to express Tehuti's full majesty while writing and copying his sacred text. While Thoth was now associated with Hermes in later Hellenistic dominated Egypt, the deep seated tradition of Thoth had still not lost his ancient supremacy or his ancient Egyptian roots or associations. This can be represented in the main philosophical Hermetic texts we have today which are contained in the *Corpus Hermeticum*. The *Corpus Hermeticum* is a collection of approximately seventeen treatises originally composed in Egypt and written in the Greek language. The exact date for the composition of the texts is unknown, but most scholars place at least the main texts of the Corpus in the second or third centuries A.D. Technical Hermetica range more broadly, and are tentatively dated to a period spanning the first century B.C. to the fourth century A.D. It is quite possible however, that at least some of the texts were based on many significantly earlier models. Egyptian Inscriptions alone prove that Hermes Trismegistos was already a name for Thoth at the location of Saqqara as early as the second century B.C. [20]

In 302 A.D., an Egyptian priest made a compilation of eighteen sacred documents, the Corpus Hermeticum, intended to prove to the rulers of the Roman Empire that there was nothing in his religion deserving of official suspicion, and that its teachings were calculated to foster loyalty to the Empire and its rulers. Something that was quite common for religions at the time to do, for the Roman Empire had a long history of problems with and the persecution of many religious systems of the time, Christianity was in no way the only one. [21] We know that in the first century A.D. there were people who thought, felt, and desired in their writings ways that are also found and represented in the Hermetic writings, of this we may be assured. Whatever the date of the original writings, the Hermetic religion itself was far older. A religion is always experienced and lived long before it is ever recorded. Its mythology, its literary structure, its magic, and its reverence for things Egyptian point in this direction and the combination of these with Greek and Oriental elements is such a product as would come from that religious mixing house of the Hellenistic world. [22]

In a comparative study of religious phenomena that existed during the earliest first centuries of the Christian era, comes the question for the dating of these ancient hermetic documents, and is one of considerable importance. If for example, the Hermetic Corpus was a third-century product and recorded only post-Christian developments, one would hardly be justified to give it consideration in connection with the genesis of early Christianity. Unfortunately, critical opinion concerning the original and exact dating of these documents is still in a very chaotic and controversial state. But a great deal of evidence does seem to indicate that many elements of the Egyptian Hermetic tradition very well predate early Christian history. So by understanding the Hermetic tradition and the profound experiences it was known to have created in its ancient rituals, we can gain a greater insight into the earliest roots of Christian history and in the development and experiences found within the larger and much more mysterious Gnostic movement. [23]

The Egyptian Hermetic tradition has been defined as a form of Gnosticism. It represents a non-Christian lineage of Hellenistic Egyptian Gnosticism. The central texts of the Egyptian Hermetic tradition are known as the Corpus Hermeticum. The Corpus Hermeticum was lost to the west in the classical times. Their rediscovery and translation during the late fifteenth century by the Renaissance court of *Cosimo de Medici*, provided a seminal force in the development of Renaissance thought and culture. The fifteen tracts of the Corpus Hermeticum, along with the perfect sermon of Asclepius, are the foundation documents of the Hermetic tradition today. The texts of the Corpus Hermeticum represent only a portion of the once great flood of literary works that were once attributed to the Egyptian god Thoth that later came to be known as Hermetic when the lands of Egypt came under Hellenistic political domination. [24]

While there are many elements that can be seen to have influenced the late classical Egyptian tradition of Thoth, Flinders Petrie, a well noted archeologist and founding father of Egyptology, dated the Hermetica to the era of 500-200 B.C. Petrie concluded that the texts are essentially later Greek translations of much earlier Egyptian philosophical compositions. To summarize the entire story of his research on this matter, it is likely that the Hermetica is only a tiny surviving portion of a flood of Egyptian knowledge that was created by the Greeks as they vigorously copied all writings and things Egyptian into the Greek language. Because of this fact it can be reasonably assured that the Hermetic text demonstrate an older Egyptian tradition, one that most possibly even pre dates the arrival of the Greeks in 320 B.C. Evidence to further support this can be found within the writings of the classical writer and philosopher Iamblichus who has informed us that an Egyptian priest named Bitys was supposed to have translated some of the hieroglyphics text of Thoth into Greek, and made use of the Greeks philosophical vocabulary in doing so. Iamblichus also stated that many of the Egyptian priests learned to express themselves in Greek philosophical words, giving rise to a whole collection of wisdom texts that circulated under the name of Hermes, but drew their essentials from the Egyptian tradition, particularly from the ancient wisdom of Thoth. [25]

In Late Antiquity, Hermetism emerged in parallel with other forms of Gnosticism, as well as Neoplatonism and early Christianity. Today Gnosticism is described as a general term describing various mystical oriented groups and their teachings, which were most prominent in the first few centuries of the Common Era. The term Gnosticism comes from the Greek word for knowledge, *Gnosis* which refers to type of knowledge which is gained through experience. It can also be understood as a type of knowledge gained from mystical or intuitive insight for which some one knows or gains knowledge of something through an experience of it. The origins of Gnosticism are not clearly known, but there is general agreement that the threads of their teachings arose in the Middle East and Asia Minor, areas in which several ancient cultures converged and synthesized their ideas. Many scholars find the roots of Neo-Platonism in Gnosticism, which similarly devalues matter and regards the spirit as the true reality. Because of this, most scholars today believe the origins of Gnosticism to have come from the mixing of theological ideas that emerged out of the Egyptian and Mesopotamian civilizations during late antiquity. The study of Gnosticism is important today because it provides us profound insight into what was once at totally unknown theological tradition from the ancient world and the visionary and mystical experiences found within Gnostic writings are virtually unparalleled any ware in ancient literature.

Part II:

Identifying Gnostic Visions

Ch 5
Gnostic Rituals

For where the mind is there is great treasure.

I said to him, Lord, now does he who sees the vision see it through the soul or through the spirit? The savor answered and said. He does not see through the soul nor through the spirit, but the mind which is between the two. That is what sees the vision.

(Jesus in the Gnostic Gospel of Mary)

The Gnostics

In 1945, near the banks of the River Nile, a jar was unearthed which contained one of the greatest manuscript finds of modern history - the Nag Hammadi codices. Like the Dead Sea Scrolls, discovered two years later, this library of ancient documents, dated to 350 A.D. contained religious and philosophical texts, many relating to early Christianity, lost and buried ancient Christian documents that the contemporary world had never before seen. The Dead Sea texts discovered a few years after belonged to an earlier, Jewish group, but the works from Nag Hammadi in Egypt belonged to a later branch of Early Christians and other theological movements we now call Gnosticism. Gnosticism bears many similarities to the Egyptian Hermetic tradition which is itself defined as a form of Gnosticism, particularly an Egyptian form. [1]

The Gnostic documents from Nag Hammadi first showed up in Cairo in 1946 when Togo Mina, Director of the Coptic Museum, purchased one of the manuscripts for 250 Egyptian pounds. Mina and Jean Doresse, French graduate students in Egyptology, thought the find was of great historical significance and worked together to reunite the rest of the collection. In 1948 the world was informed of the discovery, but the announcement caused barely a ripple. In 1950 Doresse tracked down the original site of discovery to Nag Hammadi, 280 miles south of Cairo. Some peasants in the area directed him to the site of the ancient town of Chenosboskion. The name of this city is an ancient Coptic name, which is translated as "The Acacias of Seth." Many of the ancient Gnostic Scriptures honor and claim descent from a man named Seth. Seth was said to be the righteous son of Adam and Eve, the first two humans, as in traditional Jewish and Gnostic legends, Seth was the man from whom it is said the Gnostics' race descended from, and whom many Gnostics said would also some day return to earth as an elect soul to save mankind with divine knowledge. [2]

Gnostic Texts

The jars found at Nag Hammadi containing the Gnostic codices were unearthed near an abandoned Christian cemetery at the foot of a mountain called Gebel et-Tarif. In the cliffs above the cemetery are caves, the burial places of ancient Egyptian officials. Nearby are the ruins of a monastery established by St. Pachomius, known in church history as one of the "desert fathers" who established monastic communities in the Egyptian desert. Much of what St. Pachomius used as a model for his early Christian Monasteries he established from the text of the Jewish historian Philo regarding the contemplative life of the long lost group of Jewish mystics and healers, the Therapeate. The text that Philo wrote about the Therapeate was written only a few hundred years earlier before the arrival of St. Pachomius, but by then, the Therapeate were already long gone. Some scholars have proposed the idea that perhaps it was pressure from such early Christian communities as established by St. Pachomius, communities that became widely spread out and known for their strict Christian orthodoxy, which caused the last of the Gnostics to hide their books. [3]

Evidence supporting this comes from a surviving letter from Pachomius' successor dated 367 A.D., condemning heretical writings. This also corresponds to the dating of the finds. The documents that were found are called codices. Bound in leather, they were a forerunner of the modern book. At the time of their composition, the codices had begun to replace the scroll because it was more durable and easier to read. There were 13 codices in all. Containing 52 tractates (separate texts). Forty of them were entirely new to the modern world. They were written in Coptic-the Egyptian language written in Greek characters, and probably translated from an original Greek text long before that. [4]

The lengthy time it took to translate these ancient texts was a tremendous frustration for biblical scholars because they knew that the codices would contain answers to important historical questions. Despite repeated efforts, the Gnostic scriptures would have to wait 30 years to be properly translated. The American theologian James Robinson was instrumental in finally gathering a team to translate the texts. The Nag Hammadi Library, published in 1977, is a result of this effort. For the first time in over 1500 years the wisdom and mystery of this once great library could now be shown to the world, read, and a key to understanding the many great and important mysteries it was hiding could now be understood and shared with the world. [5]

The Nag Hammadi Library is a collection of religious texts that varied widely from each other as to when, where, and by whom they were written. Even the points of view diverge to such an extent that the texts are not to be thought of as coming from one single group or movement. Since their discovery in 1945, scholars have long pondered their contents, and questioned their interconnected relationship to modern Christianity. But one of the most fascinating and interesting things about the Nag Hammadi Library is not just its mysterious lost teachings and beliefs coming to the surface in the modern age, or its relationship to early Christianity, but the mysterious wide array of visionary literature and religious experiences the texts are known to contain.

In approaching Gnostic texts, one is immediately struck by the many concepts which have a root in visionary and esoteric tradition. The texts are mysterious, elusive, and sometimes even incomprehensible. Though certain texts claim to be secret teachings, many of the texts are also secret inner teachings of Jesus to a select disciple. Two of the most famous books of this type are the Gospel of Mary Magdalene and the Gospel of Thomas, both which lay claim to deeper secret teachings of Jesus Christ. The book of Thomas is a book largely based around the direct words and teachings of Jesus, constructed much like a dialogue or sermon. When the texts in the Gnostic Nag Hammadi library regarding the words of Jesus are compared with the quoted words of Jesus from the Orthodox Christian Bible, there are almost twice as many more quoted words of Jesus Christ found in the Gnostic Gospels than there are in the entire modern day Orthodox Christian Bible. It seems quite remarkable to me that so many words of this Great Christian Prophet have come to be banned, burned, and outlawed by the Orthodox Christian church, only to be rediscovered in our modern age, in the Egyptian desert.

While many of the texts found in the Nag Hummadi library are mystical ancient Christian texts, many more of the texts found in the Nag Hammadi library are ancient literary works having little to do with Jesus at all and are instead far more complex and mystical in their character. Many are very different from what one would traditionally see in the bible or most other traditional religious texts we know or use today. Many of these esoteric texts do not even relate to Christianity at all, or even Judaism for that matter, but demonstrate a perversely undiscovered and totally unknown lost theological tradition that had immense importance and influence on the tradition and development of early Christianity. Probably the most important facts regarding these ancient books is that they show that many of the earliest Christian disciples, as well as many of the earliest followers of Christ, were not only Jews, but Gnostics as well. From examining Gnostic texts we know that many of Jesus Christ's own disciples were Gnostic Jews, people who were known to have had profound religious experiences, experiences of direct contact with divine spiritual realities, even claiming direct contact with the very mind and experience of God. But this claim of secret direct spiritual knowledge, as it is seen in classical Gnosticism and within these secret Christian books, has been a very hot topic of debate and controversy among many theologians and academic scholars of Christianity for many years. Outside of this theological controversy, the main problem with these ancient texts is that modern scholars have no idea how such experiences were created among these ancient people. Because the Gnostics were so secretive, and left us so little information in their writings on how these experiences were created, the method for how these experiences were created has become completely lost and unidentified by modern scholarship. Just because the methods for how these experiences were created has come to be lost or unidentified by modern scholarship, does not mean that the answers to how these experiences were originally created cannot be found, or that it does not exist. In fact, when we go on to examine Gnostic texts in closer detail, find direct evidence indicating that these experiences were in fact repeatedly created by very real, natural, and available means.

To understand how Gnostic visionary experiences were created, you must first understand the rituals used to create them. Like the Pagan mysteries, the Gnostics also closely guarded the secrets of their inner rituals. Clement of Alexandria stated that the Gnostics were known to have had both outer mysteries and inner mysteries, but relates that the Gnostics were only following the example of the pagans and philosophers who perpetuated similar inner and outer mysteries long before them. Clement of Alexandria goes on to relate:

> The existence of certain doctrines which are beyond those which are openly taught and do not reach the multitudes, is not a peculiarity of Christianity only, but is shared by the Philosophers, for they had some doctrines which were exoteric and some esoteric. [6]

This tells us that like the mystery traditions of the Greeks or Egyptians the religious rites of the Gnostics were also shrouded in secrecy. Clement of Alexander also tells us that in early Christianity there were likewise lesser mysteries for beginners on the spiritual path and the Greater Mysteries which were a secret higher knowledge, which lead to full "initiation." This Greater Mystery was, "The Secret tradition of true Gnosis," (Knowledge) he explains, which had been transmuted "to a small number, by a succession of masters, and not in writing." Saint Clement, Bishop of Alexandria who lived between 150 and 200 A.D. suggested that this Gnosis (secret knowledge) was given in a form of a mystery, and that certain purifications and instructions were given before the mysteries were revealed. Clement writes this regarding them.

> It is not wished that all things should be exposed indiscriminately to all on Sunday, or the benefit of wisdom communicated to those who have not even in a dream been purified in soul. Nor are the Mysteries of the Logos to be expounded to the Profane. [7]

The writings of Clement indicate that the full source of Gnostic mysteries were never fully written down and had been handed down verbally or through the experience of initation. From examining Gnostic texts, we can see that the secret of Gnostic rituals was to induce a very powerful visionary religious experience. Many mystical and visionary experiences are described in Gnostic texts, but the method of how these visionary experiences were created has been left out. So to understand how these visions were created we must not only look at Gnostic rituals but we must also look at the visionary experiences that they described and look for any similarities these visionary experiences have to similar visions that are known to take place in the world today. In beginning to unravel this long lost mystery, I am going to start by detailing some of what we already know about Gnostic rituals, by doing this you will start to understand what type of methods they used to create the powerful visions they described.

Gnostic Rituals

In Gnostic rituals, the visionary experiences they created were nothing less than a religious and mystical experience created through what is now a lost and unidentified means. Its purpose was uniformly salvation and transformation through an experience with the divine. It was also a means to restore the primordial unity of the human person or soul with that of the divine mind. Vivid manifestations of divine beings also occur in Gnostic texts. Many of the visions portrayed figures whose souls themselves had a heavenly origin such as Jesus or Seth. The Gnostics believed that salvation was achieved by the return of the soul to its original state, in union with the divine, not by a belief or a recitation of words from an impure and corrupt material realm.

Throughout Gnostic texts this ritual experience of enlightenment is seen to have been directly associated around the ritual of baptism as well as the death and resurrection of Jesus Christ. Many of the early Gnostic Christians understood the death and resurrection of Jesus Christ in a very different sense from the atonement and redemption that the Roman Catholic Church would later come to adopt. While the modern Christian rite is known to contain four steps the ancient Gnostic rite was known to contain five. These five steps were known as the ritual of the five seals. This ritual of the five seals was primarily practiced by early Sethian Gnostics, while the more Christian Valentinian Gnostic also had a five step initiation process, in Christian Gnosticism each of these five steps did not go by the name of a seal; instead they were known as a mystery. [8] To demonstrate the relationship the ritual of the five seals had with the visionary experience of gnosis within Sethian Gnosticism we can look to the following quote which relates the following:

> These are the glories that are higher than every glory, that is, [the Five] Seals complete by virtue of Intellect. He who possesses the Five Seals of these particular names has stripped off [the] garments of ignorance and put on a shining Light. And nothing will appear to him that belongs to the Powers of the Archons. Within those of this sort darkness will dissolve and [ignorance] will die. [9]

This quote indicates a direct relationship between the ritual experience of the five seals and the acquisition of knowledge and an experience of light. Like the Egyptian Hermetic tradition, the Gnostics also attributed the acquisition of divine knowledge to the ritual initatic experience. In fact, the experience of the gnosis as it is seen in classical Gnosticism is virtually identical to the experiences of Gnosis as it is also described and in Egyptian Hermetic text. The similarity between these indicates a strong link between the visionary experiences the two groups were known to have had. From examining the above quote, it is clear that the experience of knowledge and union with the divine was the primary purpose. But what exactly was this ritual, and how was it responsible for creating the visionary experiences we find in Gnostic writings? In studying Gnostic rituals we find that there were fundamental five rites in Gnostic rituals. The first was baptism, while its origins lie in the sphere of purification, it seems to be an initiatory rite generally practiced only once as the initial break with one's flawed past and a way to cleanse one for an entrance into a new state of spiritual birth and purification. The other four rites found in Gnosticism seem to be repeatable acts but are also, all closely associated with baptism. These are the acts of *Chrismation* and *Investiture*, which early Christian texts often treat as a postlude to baptism.[10] In many Gnostic rituals both *baptism* and *Chrismation* were known as "seals." The idea of seals is found most prominently within Sethian Gnostic texts and it is this name that is given to most Sethian Gnostic ritual elements. This idea of seals is usually associated with marking one as sealed, reborn, and belonging to God. [11] While these rites appear to be unrepeatable acts of initiation, the sacral meal, and the sacred *Eucharist* are often known to follow baptism and are seen as something repeatable. In some Gnostic groups such as the Valentinian Gnostics there was also a sacral marriage between God and the initiate. [12] This was the fifth step and final mysteries in the Valentianian Gnostic initiation process, a rite that was also known as the B*ridal Chamber*. While the ritual of the bridal chamber had its origins in biblical metaphor, it was primarily used to symbolize the union of the human mind or spirit with that of the mind and spirit of God. While this mental union with the mind of God is particularly intrinsic to the Gnostic tradition and its experiences, it seems that this peculiar ritual metaphor of sacred marriage was particular to this sect of Gnosticism, particularly of a more Jewish origin. Besides the major ritual elements that were shared between all Gnostic groups, there was also the ritual use of speech, especially prayer formulas, hymns, recognition formulas, as well as ecstatic utterances and chants. All of these ritual items can be included in a cross comparison of ritual similarities between the various known Gnostic Groups. [13]

Sethian Baptism

In studying the Sethian Gnostics, we come to find that the Sethian Gnostic treatises from the Nag Hammadi Library are of the oldest in historical lineage within the Nag Hammadi library. Sethian Gnosticism is believed to be where many of the Gnostics first originated from. The texts of the Sethian Gnostics show us a group of people whose traditions and beliefs extend far beyond the known Christian era, even possibly far beyond known Jewish history. The most remarkable feature of these texts is the fact that the Sethian Gnostic texts are known to contain not only numerous accounts of visions of the transcendental world and its contents, but also numerous references to baptisms, washings, anointing and sealing, as well as numerous instances of various prayers, doxologies and hymns mentioning or directed to a rather fixed set of divine visionary beings. [14]

These references generally occur in stanzaic, even hymnic, passages which can be found most especially in the Gnostics texts of the *Gospel of the Egyptians, Zostrianos Apocalypse of Adam, Apocryphon of John* and *Melchizedek.* They apparently refer to a sequence of ritual acts involving a kind of baptism, which the texts often designate by the term "the Five Seals," the Sethian texts providing the most detail about the Five Seals. *The Gospel of the Egyptians* gives us the most details regarding these rituals, but do not reveal the precise character of the Five Seals. It is believed that this was done in order to keep the rituals a secret among members. Because of this, much of these rituals were clearly never fully written down and must be reconstructed from the rather allusive illustrations to them as they are found within these writings. While this order of secrecy seems to have been heavily practiced among many initiatic mystery religions of the time, the ritual of baptism, one of the most prominent rituals of Gnosticism, is an extremely well-attested rite in the early Christian world. [15] In Sethian Gnostic texts, the various symbolic acts that originally comprised this rite are called "seals." In the past scholars studying Gnostic texts were puzzled by the meaning of the term "five." Did it originally refer to a single act performed five times, like a quintuple immersion in water contrast to the typically triple immersion of Christian baptism, or was it referring to five mysterious transcendental beings, names of beings, or symbols used in the rituals or the most likely meaning, that the term five instead referred to the five ritual acts that originally comprised the rite. By way of comparison, the normal Christian baptismal rite as you can see bellow, is known to contain at least four out of the five original Gnostic procedures:

(1) Renunciation of the evil and the devil, removal of all outer garments
(2) Anointing with oil
(3) Baptismal, immersion, and re-clothing in white garments
(4) The Chrismation or the drinking of the Eucharist. [16]

While the original theme in many Gnostic rituals is known to have centered on a five step ritual process, the Sethian Gnostic texts are unusually elusive in that, perhaps to a greater degree than most other Gnostic groups, they conceive the baptismal rite as a series of visionary experiences resulting in complete enlightenment and therefore total spiritual salvation of the ritual participant. In spite of the allusions to visionary ritual acts found throughout Gnostic literature, the rituals that we find in Gnostic texts were indeed enacted by ordinary human beings and the importance of these rites lay primarily in the visionary and spiritual plane, indicating that it was within these rites and rituals that these visionary religious experiences were taking place. This also seems to be a clear characteristic emphasis of many Gnostic Christian and non-Christian Gnostic baptizing circles throughout the first century. [17]

Sethian Gnostic literature from the Nag Hammadi library gives us the most information for the reconstruction of the ritual acts that originally comprised Sethian baptismal rituals. The *Gospel of the Egyptians* details this baptism as involving the begetting of the saints through invisible secret symbols, the "killing" and renunciation of both the world and the "god of the thirteen aeons," and the invoked presence of certain holy, ineffable beings of light, along with the light of the divine Father. While Seth, the divine son of Adam is said to have appeared in the primeval world to deliver his race from the Archons (also understood as demons) and the destructive acts of the flood, the great divine Mother now sends him into the world to save mankind for a third time. In this text, he appears along with certain divine beings or angels who are sent to guard the incorruptible race until the consummation of the new age, the "great man" also known as "the great Seth" receives a vision of various spiritual beings whose names occur repeatedly in other baptismal sections of Sethian treatises. The repeated appearance of these visionary beings throughout these texts and there association with these rituals indicates that the supernatural beings encountered in these rituals were encountered within the visionary experience, visions that were created as the result of five inner ritual acts. [18]

Evidence for visionary ritual activity abounds in these texts. In one such text it is said that through the incorruptible man one receives illumination. Those who are worthy of the invocation and the renunciations of the Five Seals will then be the baptizer who will then be the receivers as they are instructed about them. This then follows a long prayer in which the initiates are baptized. As this occurs, the baptized starts praising the Living Water "Yesseus Mazareus Yessedekeus" as the eternal Jesus who truly is, the glorious name that is now upon and within him, granting him immutability and the armor of light. The stretching out of their hands while still folded; the baptized apparently symbolically portrays the cup or containment of the inner light by all those who have received enlightenment. The Gnostic initiate then praises the man (Seth) who raises up the man (Jesus) in whose name the baptized will be purified. [19]

Following this, in one of the most important parts the text states:

> This great name of thin is upon me, O self-begotten perfect one, who art not outside me…I shall declare thy glory truly, for I have comprehended thee,…O Aeon,O God of silence, I honor thee completely. Thou art my place of rest, O son…the formless one

who exists in the formless ones, who exists, raising up the man in whome thou wilt purify me into thy life, according to theine imperishable name. Therefiore the incense of life is in me. I mixed it with water….

(Gospel of the Egyptians)

This quote is important because it is one of only a very few places in Gnostic text that indicate how the Gnostics visionary experiences are created. This quote describes a ritual experience in which a visionary and mystical experience is occurring and the initiate then states that it is taking place because they have received the incense of life and mixed it with water, resulting in the initiate being purified and then raised up into the union with the divine. This provocative statement is one of the only Sethian Gnostic references indicating a link between the use of an additive within their baptismal drink and the creation of their mystical experiences. Because the incense of life, as it is described in the gospel of the Egyptians, is described as an additive to water and seems to have been drank or consumed by the writer, and it is also identified with the visionary experience, its presence in this texts clearly demonstrates that the Gnostic visions described in this texts were being created as the result of a yet unidentified visionary additive within a ritual drink.

In examining this text further, we find that there are other ritual acts which are described that give us an idea of their general character. They describe a series of references to certain gestures and verbal performances capable of ritual enactment, these include: renunciation, invocation, naming of holy powers and doxological prayer all directed to these sacred living waters, receipt of incense, manual gestures, and baptismal immersion. Whether any of these acts comprise the Five Seals is difficult to tell, and if so, which ones; certainly renunciation, invocation, and the extension of the arms were frequently part of the baptismal rite in the wider Christian church, throughout the use of the passive voice for ritual actions and the use of plural references to the saints begotten "through instruction" suggest a community ritual in which there were initiates and officials, as well as a tradition of prescribed actions and declarations. Because of its character many scholars have pointed out that it may be that the entire *Gospel of the Egyptians* and not just its conclusion that has a ritual or liturgical function. When we examine the text further we can see that there are five completions of various stages within the text cosmology. These stages seem to have intended to invoke a fixed set of divine beings. So if the term "Five Seals" originally designated a fivefold or five-stage baptismal procedure, it may be that *The Gospel of the Egyptians* was read aloud during the administration of each phase of the ritual. After the reading of each of the five sections of the text, the baptized might have repeated this cosmology or prayer to invoke protection from these divine beings before entering into the visionary realm, as well as affirming the receipt of each of the Five Seals. [20]

A similar correlation between baptismal sealing and depictions of the structure and deployment of the transcendent world are also known to occur in the text of *Zostrianos*, although in this text, the sealing is clearly given a celestial rather than earthly setting, largely because the text is written in a first person account much like a personal experience of divine worlds. Furthermore, in both *the Gospel of the Egyptians* and the *Trimorphic Protennoia*, the final act of salvation is described as the descent of Seth in the form of the logos (logos being the great mind or thought). The Sethian Gnostics believed that the logos came into the world in the form of Christ and Christ put on the logos, in effect, the early Christian Gnostics believed that Jesus Christ was the logos, a man in possession of this divine mind. The Gnostics also believed that the five seals imparted this divine mind onto the ritual participant, but only temporarily. This union of mind is what made up and characterized Gnostic knowledge and enlightenment. Many times this divine mind was associated with the mind or spirit of Jesus Christ and other times, among other Gnostic sects, the effects of ritual union of mind was associated with Seth or some other divine consciousness such as Barbelo the divine feminine. [21]

The Gnostics were known to have associated the effects of their visionary rituals to the receiving of the logos and experiencing the divine mind. This visionary religious phenomenon is seen almost universally within classical Gnosticism, making it a defining characteristic of the Gnostic tradition. The experience of divine mind and Gnosis is also represented in the Egyptian Hermetic tradition. In the Hermetic book, *the cup or the Monad*, the Hermetic initiate receives a cup that is given to man from god and thus receives part of the mind and knowledge of God upon the cups consumption. From examining these Hermetic Gnostic texts, it becomes apparent that it was through the use and consumption of this ritual cup that the visionary experiences of divine Gnosis were created in Gnostic and Hermetic rituals.

In another important Gnostic text known as the *Apocalypse of Adam* the author goes on to describe a dream vision revealed to Adam by three glorious men who narrate a third saving mission to him that is conducted by a spiritual illuminator whose origins are said to be unknown to the evil powers. The text states that:

> He comes from a great invisible aeon to enlighten his elect. This spiritual illuminator experiences neither birth nor generation, nor does he receive nourishment, glory, or power. He comes from the beyond where he comes down to the water. [22]

The text goes on to say that, the illuminator is not baptized in the waters of the Jordan, which the author regards as polluted and chaotic. Instead, the Illuminator remains above in the light where he resides with the three imperishable illuminators Yesseus, Mazareus, Yessedekeus. His first appears in the world not at his own "birth" or baptism, but at the time he baptizes his seed, the Sethian Gnostics who receive his name on the water. At the same point, angelic beings will bring the truth to the earthly Sethians in a way independent of the written word of the evil creator, a truth that is communicated only by a holy baptism through a logos-begotten illuminator who descends "into" the living waters during the baptismal experience. [23]

The clear distinction for Gnostics between the holy baptism with Living Water and a baptism practiced by God's servants or other non-Gnostic groups who are known in Gnostic texts as "those who have polluted the water of life," this begs to ask what type of living water was used to illuminate the Gnostics and give them these profound visionary experiences of knowledge. It seems clear that the Gnostic's living water baptism was seen as a much greater and more superior liquid than the symbolic washing in a river alone. From examining these texts, is seems that the Gnostics who wrote these texts believed that the "living waters" used in their rituals were distinct from ordinary baptismal water traditionally used to wash and purify. The living waters associated with visions were used to give divine knowledge, visionary experience, and to communicate something greater that regular water just could not do. The Gnostics believed that water was a symbol of life; this same view is still held by the modern Mandaean Gnostics today. But the ancient classical Gnostics, unlike the modern Mandaeans, believed that water alone gave no visionary rebirth, only empty ritual dogma. We see evidence for this in texts like the *Apocalypse of Adam*, *Zostrianos*, and the *Paraphrase of Shem*, texts that also speak of an impure baptism in a dark water that enslaves, evidently a warning against practicing ordinary water baptism extracted of all its transcendental visionary qualities. [24]

Evidence that traditional water baptism could hold negative connotation to what the ancient visionary Gnostics considered being a lower and inferior baptism that was traditionally undergone by non-Gnostic Christians can be found when we examine later Gnostic texts and history. In examining this we find that the Gnostic group known as the Archontics, whom Epiphanius presented in his writings as an offshoot of the Sethians, were known to have completely rejected the baptism and sacraments of the Roman Christian Church, and saw them as deriving from the inferior law-giver Sabaoth; to shun baptism is to enhance the prospect of acquiring of the true gnosis, enabling their return to the Mother-Father of the All. When the statement of this ancient Gnostic group is taken into account, one thing becomes clear: baptismal water for the early Sethian Gnostics was understood to be of a celestial and visionary nature and not just a material submersion in water. For the Sethian Gnostics, baptism water was understood as a symbol of life. But there was also another form of ritual baptismal liquid that was considered to be of a much more divine and celestial nature. The term living water is used throughout Sethian Gnostic texts and is seen to be used most frequently during the ritual drinking of the living waters. Probably the most important aspect of this investigation comes from the direct symbolic correlation between this drinkable living water and the experience of visionary light, gnosis, and spiritual enlightenment that these living waters are associated with. This seems to indicate that the living waters being consumed in these rituals were the same living waters that were responsible for creating the visionary experiences of divine light, Gnosis, and enlightenment that are so characteristic of classical Gnostic literature. [25]

While in earlier Sethian treatises this rite is usually said to be "received," later treatises portray it as a self-performable technique that could be enacted either by means of ritual or independently of ritual actions. This indicates that the rite could be self performed and that the living water was in fact something received, and upon its receiving or consumption, an experience of divine light, gnosis, and visionary religious experience were induced on the participant. The Egyptian Hermetic texts as well as the Sethian Gnostic literature depict the use of this ritual and associate it with this same type of characteristic visionary experience. The Hermetic texts are probably the most outspoken in attesting to the use of a sacred ritual cup and outlining it as responsible for inducing these entheogenic experiences of visionary light, gnosis, and mental union with the divine that so heavily characterize Gnostic experiences. While the Hermetic texts refer to the use of this cup as being responsible for creating these experiences, Sethian Gnostic texts begin to witness the use of this cup being replaced in these texts with a more cryptic reference to the use of "living waters." These living waters as they are described in Sethian Gnostic texts are likewise associated with the acquisition of gnosis and the visionary experience, juts as the cup of the monad is in Hermetic documents. This relationship further supports the liquid nature of the Gnostics' visionary ritual additive. By examining Sethian Gnostic ritual literature, we can conclude that the Five Seals of Sethian Gnosticism were a five step ritual purification process where the mind and body was purified and dedicated to God. It was a ritual that ended with the consumption of "living water" or a liquid sacrament in which a visionary religious experience was subsequently created, an experience that was at the core of Gnostic beliefs and religious initiation experiences. The effects of this ritual drink, as the text indicates, brought the participants into some type of mental union with the divine mind of god and into an experience that induced visionary enlightenment as well as an experience of spiritual salvation and rebirth. [26]

Valentinian Rituals and the Sacred Marriage

While the visionary experiences found in Sethian Gnosticism may represent some of the most vivid visionary experiences recorded in Gnostic literature, the psychological effects of this mental union with the divine and the knowledge it imparted is also found to be an intrinsic property of Christian Valentinian Gnosticism as well. In Valentinian Gnosticism similar visionary metaphors and similar visionary rituals are also described, rituals just like those found in Sethian Gnostic texts. The gnosis of Valentinian Gnosticism is known as the most well defined form of classical Christian Gnosticism. The Gospel of Philip is known to be one of these Christian Gnostic books, a book originally written by the Jewish Gnostic disciple of Jesus, a man named Philip. In the Gospel of Philip, *the chrism of fire* was understood as an intense visionary light which gives both form and beauty. One is begotten again (reborn) by baptism in water and anointing with the chrism through the Holy Spirit as a sort of "baptism" in light. It seems that this is the same light that is kindled in the bridal chamber, and this same visionary experience that is experienced in the bridal chamber is the same experience Sethian Gnostic texts associate with, the cup of living waters. In examining Valentinian Gnostic rituals in greater detail, we find that Valentinian literature refers to a Valentinian rite of anointing, which was performed either before the first baptism or simultaneously with it, enabling the recipient to overcome the power of the devil, who dominates the flesh and the struggles against God. *The Gospel of Philip*, like many other Gnostic texts, lists five steps in the ritual initiation process:

> The lord did everything in a mystery, a baptism, a chrism, a Eucharist, a redemption, and a bridal chamber (*Philip, the Gospel of Philip*)

Like the Sethian Gnostics the Christian Valentinian Gnostics also had a five step ritual process. The five steps in the Valentinian initiation process are named in the Gospel of Philip as, a baptism, a chrism, a Eucharist, a redemption and a bridal chamber. In Christian Valentinian Gnosticism, the bridal chamber was considered the final step of the ritual process, a process also known as the final stage in the process of redemption. This ritual was also conceived as a heavenly marriage between the human initiate and the soul and spirit of Christ represented as the Logos or divine mind of God. For them, Christ was the Logos. He was seen in their rituals as the great pure mind, he was "The Word" who had shown the way to triumph and rule over the lower elemental powers of the lower material world and help mankind overcome his spiritual ignorance. The metaphor of marriage and the bridal chamber is a Jewish Hellenized theological idea. The idea is that the human soul is feminine to the divine force of God, and when one enters the holy of the holies in the inner temple, one is united with God. This special unification was also much like entering into the bridal chamber of a virgin bride on her wedding night. While traditionally God was seen as duel, both male and female, within the Jewish mystical theological tradition, it is only in many later parts of Jewish history that we start to find the idea of god as male and being named as Father in its singular sense. In the Christian bible today, Jesus is also known to refer to God as, God the Father, or my father. It is only in Gnostic texts that we find Jesus ever talking about God in this duel sense of both male and female or being described as containing both masculine and feminine principles. [27]

The ritual of the bridal chamber in traditional Valentinian Gnosticism can refer to both the experience of spiritual reunification with god as well as to an overtly sexual union. In either case, the underlying idea of Christ coming into the world and to the Gnostics was to reunify mankind with God. This was seen as the recreation of the primal androgyne through the union of male and female into spirit, whether that is taken as man and woman, intellect and soul, or the earthly seed and its angelic counterpart. As enlightened beings, the Gnostics generally considered themselves alone in being capable of understanding the true significance of sexual union. The Gnostics largely considered the non-Gnostic as worldly and animalistic, experiencing not love, but only lust. [28]

While in some later Gnostic practices this view of sacred union manifested as a form of sexual sacramentalism, most if not almost all Gnostic sects thought this type of sexual sacramentalism as a perverted distortion of the truth and was seen as very wrong and sinful. So I would like to put to rest the idea of anything otherwise that may be circulating, for I have seen this claim of sexual sacramentalism being perpetuated by many contemporary Christian groups as a means of denouncing early Gnostic teachings as a perverse heretical movement of impure pagan Christians, when in reality the Gnostics were anything but. The Idea of the bridal chamber to the Valentinian Gnostics was symbolized as a spiritual and mental ecstatic union between the individual person with the mind and soul of god. It was not the physical sexual ecstasy that is portrayed by some modern Christians today. For to the Gnostics the body was only corruptible material flesh.

The Valentinians made the most extensive use of the metaphor of marriage as a designation for the eschatological reunion of the savior Jesus with Sophia. Sophia was known as the divine feminine wisdom and her spiritual seed the angels or beings of light. In this Valentinian Gnostic myth, the savior Jesus and Sophia are interpreted as the bridegroom and bride, and their place of union is in the "bridal chamber," also known among Valentinians as the divine realm of the Pleroma of spiritual aeons. Thus the Pauline metaphors of the Church as bride and Christ as bridegroom are combined with the story of the fall and restoration of wisdom, the cosmic soul, and the restoration of the individual psychic beings created by the divine feminine wisdom of God. As Christians, the Valentinians maintained the Christian rites of Baptism, Eucharist, and the Chrism, but seem to have developed their own ritual enactment, enactments that seemed to have been associated with an eschatological marriage to their celestial angelic counterparts and associated with the experience of gnosis and union with the mind of God. [29]

According to *The Gospel of Philip*, becoming a son of the bridal chamber is the only means to receive the light. As in Sethian Gnostic rituals, this was a ritual that gave both mental union with the divine as well as communication with a higher spiritual force. The Gnostics believed that the experience of this light could grant absolute realization of the divine and complete forgiveness of sin throughout the rest of ones life as though one were already living in the Pleroma, this experience inspired one to be pure and holy, never forgetting this powerful experience of divine union experienced in initiation. The theme of restoration of man's primeval unity is thereby projected onto the macrocosmic plane, where it symbolizes the reintegration of the Pleroma to its pre-cosmic state, according to this form of Gnostic thought. The Valintinian bridal chamber induced an experience of union with this higher cosmic power as did the Sethian Gnostic rituals. The microcosms can be understood as the inner worlds or inner planes of reality the macrocosms are the outer worlds and outer planes of reality. The macrocosms are the world we live in, the earth, space, and the stars. The microcosms can be seen as the inner worlds and inner planes of consciousness and the inner realms of the mind. [30]

According to the *Gospel of Philip*, becoming perfect comes about by acquiring the spiritual resurrection while still on earth. This enables Christians to bypass post-mortem suffering and proceed directly to God at death. Such perfection, as in the Sethian Gnostic rituals, was enabled by no less than five sacraments. Philip goes on to say that in baptism, one strips off the old self and puts on a spiritual body; the chrism confers the Holy Spirit, creating the spiritual or pneumatic person; the eucharist does the same, except using the symbols of bread and a cup of wine mixed with water, probably on a repeated basis. The redemption seems to be an oil rite, perhaps a sort of confession or extreme unction (like the modern day Gnostic Mandaean Masiqta ritual). The bridal chamber is the final and most sacred ritual, where it seems to be an enactment of one's final entrance into the heavenly realm. These rites are arranged in an ascending order, the chrism is superior to the baptism, and baptism can include redemption the chrism and the Eucharist. Yet despite this ascension of five ritual acts the supreme rite is the bridal chamber. The bridal chamber is at the end, the last and is the final ritual where it is said that one comes in union with the divine mind, hence the name Bridal Chamber indicating this sacred divine unity. [31]

The underlying purpose of Gnostic rituals was to achieve spiritual salvation and rebirth through ritual initiatic awareness and unification with the mind of the divine. The Gnostics believed that the primordial sin or fault underlying the human existence had to be overcome. According to this Gnostic thought it was the creator's ignorant act of separating this originally androgynous creation into separate male and female persons that made this fault in the material world. This idea is also reflected in the Greek creation story of Zeus making the human race. In Jewish culture, the offspring was thought to receive his human form from the male, while its physical and emotional essence was provided by the female. The same was held for the spiritual world as well; spiritual perfection lay in a balance of both, so when a spiritual being such as Sophia undertakes to produce offspring without a male consort, according to Gnostic Valentinian thought, the result was defective, a formless abortion lacking the male element of form. This being the character of her offspring, both her son, the creator of the natural world, and his cosmic product, the universe, are likewise defective and corrupt. So as a result, we have the corruptible material world we know today. So the rectification of the faulty creation depends on introducing re-unification, and bringing back the human soul into union with the divine. Which as the Gnostics believed, could only be done by true contact and union with the mind of God, an act that could only take place through their own ritual initiation process. [32]

The Sethian Gnostic myth likewise conceives the separation of the original androgynous soul to be the fault and birth of human sin. In Sethian Gnostic mythology this is accomplished when the image of God (Adamas), the original human androgynous soul, is primordially projected as the first soul upon which the creator unwittingly bases his own human copy. Once he realizes that his androgynous copy is superior to him, he splits it into male and female. Because the Gnostics, especially the Sethian Gnostics, believed that the creator of the material realm was an inferior and an evil being, it was only in spiritual union with the divine that one could surpass this inferior material force and rise to the higher realms of light with the true supreme God of creation, who of course was the essence of both male and female principals, the source of all life, time, matter, and sprit, both visible and invisible. But according to Sethian Gnostic religious mythology it was too late. In spite of the creator's attempts to subvert the primal couple, by reuniting themselves they can now recreate their original harmony, which they do in the birth of Seth, the "other seed." Like the divine Adams, he is a true male child, as is the "immovable race" he engenders, and the Gnostic myth of Seth is born. While a few Gnostic groups sought to replicate this primeval union through non-reproductive sexual union, most, like the earlier Sethians shunned and this sacred ritual sexual union, which they considered to typify the adulterous race of Cain. One might therefore affect this divine union on the transcendent plane through ritual means. The Sethians achieved this spiritual union through the visionary baptismal ascension rituals of the five seals. The Valentinian Gnostics created a similar visionary ritual that were associated with the same type of experience of divine union in the form of an eschatological sacred marriage, a union of the human mind and soul in the ritual bridal chamber with that of the soul and mind of god. While it is clear that both Gnostic groups had deeply sacred rituals that induced an experience of creating the divine within, that was a spiritual and mental union with the divine force of life, it is also clear that that this visionary experience also always took place with the ritual use of a cup and a ritual purification of baptism. This mystical initiation was the central factor of Gnostic experiences and was responsible for creating the visionary experiences so well documented in the religious literature of these early Christian and non-Christian Gnostic groups. [33]

Valentinian Ritual and Enlightenment

The Valentinians understood the first baptism as the forgiveness of sins, but whose effect seems to be the same as the "redemption" or second baptism: it elevates the recipient out of the world into the aeon or spirit world. In both treatises, the first baptism seems to be connected with an anointing and a eucharist, although the significance of the latter seems to be attenuated. In the *Gospel of Philip*, which seems to refer to the rites of redemption and bridal chamber as a sort of second baptism, the chrism becomes the central part of the baptismal rite, overshadowing the eucharist altogether. Just as the treatise *Zostrianos* portrays the Sethian practice of visionary ascent as a series of baptisms, washings and sealings, *the Gospel of Philip* draws an explicit connection not only between the experience of vision and baptism, but also to vision and the chrism, and further associating both with rebirth and the restoration to the condition and primordial union with the divine. Because the chrism also seems to be associated with the use and drinking from a cup, and the chrism is also closely associated with the sacred ritual of the bridal chamber and the visionary experience, it seems that the visionary experience taking place in the bridal chamber is the same ritual experience taking place in other visionary Gnostic rituals, visionary experiences that were created through the use and consumption of a sacred ritual drinking cup, whose contents had unique and characteristic visionary effects. [34]

In examining the interplay between the educational symbolic mythology of the Christian Gnostics and the ascent myths found in Sethian Gnostic literature, we find that the various Gnostic myths surrounding the founding prophets of these Gnostic sects have a unique similarity between their visionary rituals and the visionary experiences they described. The relationship between these mythological narratives are best represented in the earlier Sethian texts which portray the advent of salvation of Jesus Christ as coinciding with the third and final manifestation in this world with the divine Feminine spirit named by the Sethian Gnostics as Barbelo. As the myth goes, it is she who confers the gift of salvation in the form of a baptismal rite called the Five Seals. According to the so-called *Gospel of the Egyptians*, on the third and final descent of the heavenly Seth into the material world of mankind to save his progeny seed, or children of earth, he is equipped with a Logos-begotten body prepared for him "by the virgin" this spiritual body, is in the providence of the supreme deity, in order to "establish the holy baptism" for the elect. A reference to the inaugural baptism of Jesus is also then coincidentally mentioned. By this he will "put on" Jesus, through whose crucifixion he defeats the powers of the thirteen aeons. [35] Barbelo the great feminine mother descends for the third time as the Logos or mind, who confers the ritual of the Five Seals, and finally puts on Jesus, removing him from the cross, and bears him and her seed aloft into the holy light and into union with the divine creator. Similarly, the Apocryphon of John depicts the figure of Pronoia (Barbelo), as conferring the Five Seals on her third and final descent into the material world, the first two manifestations occur in primordial times, and the primary actor behind the scenes is the divine Mother Barbelo, who appears to be a higher, unfallen double of Sophia, the divine wisdom, seen to the Christian Gnostics as the Devine feminine counter part of God. The imagery of water, and light, as well as visionary ascent and descent found in these texts seem heavily indebted in the mystical Hellenized Jewish wisdom tradition of the time. [36]

This mythological narrative not only outlines the unique relationship between Jesus Christ and the divine man Seth, but it also shows the relationship these two important figures had to the experiencing the divine Gnosis that characterized much of the Gnostics literature. The myth allows us to understand the relationship these two figures had to the ritual of the five seal found in Sethian Gnosticism, a ritual that was said to have imparted the same visionary experience of gnosis and union with the divine mind that is found in later Christian Gnosticism. The Similarities in these rituals and the effects that they created, show that the characteristic visionary experiences that were taking place in Hermetic and Sethian Gnosticism were also taking place in Valentinian Christian Gnosticism as well. This relationship indicates that all three of these Gnostic groups were experiencing similar mystical visionary experiences and were thus utilizing the same visionary substances to create them.

Identifying Gnostic Visions

The purpose of Gnostic rituals was to facilitate visionary mystical awareness of the divine. From studying Gnostic text we know that the visions of the Valentinian Gnostics, Hermetic and Sethian Gnostics shared a common theme and effect. Because of the Gnostics profound influence and importance on the development and genesis of early Christianity, identifying the source of the Gnostic's visions and how they were created has become one of the most important unsolved mysteries of the ancient world. It is a mystery that if solved adds immense value to our understanding of early Christianity and the ritual and visionary practices of the ancient world. In studying Gnostic visions we are lead to examine the research that has been conducted by one of the first scholars to have proposed a clear link between the human mind and Gnostic experiences. The Swiss Physiologist Carl Jung believed that Gnostic teachings and myths originated in the personal psycho spiritual experience of the Gnostic sages. "What originates in the psyche bears the imprint of the psyche," he said, hence the close affinity between Gnosticism and what Jung believed was an in-depth study of psychology and the human mind. Jung saw the Gnostic effort as involving deep insight into the ontological self, and thus as analogous to the best in depth study of psychology. Jung himself did not reduce Gnostic teachings to an in-depth psychology, but rather pointed to in-depth psychology as a key in helping to understand Gnosticism and its remarkable experiences. [37]

In the past, many scholars have proposed many different theories attempting to identify the original method of how Hermetic and Gnostic experiences were created. While it is clear that the Gnostics were having visions, and that these visions took place within the minds of the Gnostic initiates, there has yet to be any conclusive answer identifying how these experiences were created. Because of the important and profound nature Gnosticism presents to the modern world and to the further understanding of the ancient religious practices and experiences of early Christianity, some attempts have been made in understanding and identifying the source of these experiences, most never fully taking into account the full scope of Gnostic rituals, the psychological dynamics of Gnostic visionary experiences or the available psychoactive agents in the region of the world these experiences were created able to create such experiences in the first place. Out of the handful of theories proposed in the past that have attempted to identify the source of Gnostic experiences, all have been unable to successfully identify how Gnostic visions were created or successfully account for the wide variety of unique and characteristic cognitive elements present in Gnostic experiences. In the past, many scholars have supported theories for the creation of Gnostic visions by such claims as the possibility that Gnostic visions were created by means of autosuggestion or various visualization practices. Robinson, one of the leading proponents of this claim, goes on to say:

> Visualization practices were used to induce visions of images that had forms. The visualizations were known to be fabricated, but the visions that they triggered were thought to be unfabricated. These reflections on the visions were made during the visionary state while in the company of the envisioned souls or angels. Initiates postulated the reality of a mind that was responsible for ideas that took visionary form as images. This mind was not manifest to the initiate, but the images that manifested its ideas were. (*Disc. 8-9* 63; Robinson 1988:326)

This unfortunate statement actually stands in stark contrast to the visionary rituals and experiences described in Hermetic and Gnostic religious literature. First of all, there is no visualization practice ever described in any Gnostic or Hermetic texts. Secondly, there is no way that a visualization practice could ever have taken on the shear visual, auditory, mental and emotional complexity that the mystical visionary experiences of the Gnostics were known to have demonstrated. Furthermore, there is no way that any peoples, even ancient peoples, could have been so primitive and ignorant to have believed that a visualization practice of any type was in fact as real and as independently tangible as those described in Gnostic texts. Finally, this proposition in no way satisfactorily explains the function of the ritual drinking cup associated in these texts with the experience of visions and the acquisition of knowledge that is so characteristic of Hermetic and Gnostic rituals. It is as if, the author of this theory was either unaware of these fine details or ignored them all together. This attempt at identifying the source of Gnostic visions with visualization rituals has no basis in literary fact and in no way satisfactorily explains how the complex visionary experiences of the

Gnostics were created. To say that Gnostic visionary experiences were created through the use of visualization practices is completely miss-founded.

The use of visualization techniques is only one of a few theories that had been presented over the years that have attempted to identify how Gnostic visions were created. Another theory that has been presented in the past claimed the following:

> A curious sacrament of auto-suggestion, or having attained unity with the God whose thought was the universe, a Hermetist was presumably empowered to work magic by commanding his thoughts. [38]

Again this theory clearly fails to take into account the Hermetic texts own statements regarding the source of their experiences and is clearly more in the realm of speculation with no foundation in real literary facts. To suggest that hypnotic auto suggestion was responsible for creating the complex visions of the Gnostic Hermetist not only dilutes the intelligence that created these astounding books but also dilutes the reality and independent nature of the visionary experiences that inspired them. This proposal also goes into stark contrast too the Gnostics own experiences and written text regarding their rituals and the visonary experiences they created.

While a handful of theories have been put forward proposing the how Gnostic visionary experiences were created, none have yet been able to hold ground. Out of them all probably the most widely accepted theory that has come out over the years attempting to explain how Gnostic experiences were created has comes from the theories proposed by Jung and his associates that meditation or deep ontological reflection of self were responsible for the creation of Gnostic experiences and that this was the primary means for how Gnostic knowledge and visions were created. While these theories may have seemed probable to early Gnostic scholars and psychologists completely unfamiliar with entheogenic plants and their long history of use around the world, upon closer examination of Gnostic texts it becomes clear that the Gnostics were not using solitary practices of meditation to create the complex ritual visionary experiences they described.

In studying Gnostic text, rituals, and religious practices in greater detail, we find that there is little evidence indicating that the Gnostics ever utilized the practice of meditation and there is no evidence that meditation was ever used for creating visionary experiences in a ritual or group setting. Techniques such as meditation are also not able to create the same type of characteristic and powerful visonary experiences found in Gnostic ritual literature. The experiences induced by meditation are noticeably different from the visionary ascents we find associated with Gnosticism. The other problem with this theory is that the practice of meditation is virtually never mentioned in Gnostic texts at all or in the creation of group ritual visions. By looking at texts such as "the cup or the monad," it is also clear that the text is identifying the acquisition of Gnosis being created with the use and consumption of a ritual drink with visionary powers. At no time does this text state that the practices of personal meditative agencies were responsible for creating these visionary ritual experiences. While evidence can be found that meditative practices were known about and practiced by the ancient Egyptians, there is no evidence that these practices had ever been used in group rituals or in the creation of the visionary experiences that we find in Hermetic and Gnostic writings.

Gnostic Cup of Visions

One of the greatest mystery that has perplexed scholars since the rediscovery of these ancient Gnostic and Hermetic documents is how these visionary experiences described in these texts were created. The texts of the Corpus Hermeticum like to books of the Sethian and Valentinian Gnostics are filled with ancient firsthand accounts of visionary transcendental experiences and encounters with the divine. It is in these experiences that the texts ascribed the very foundations and source of their mystical and esoteric knowledge. In Hermetic thought this spiritual endowment of visionary experience was directly connected with the rite of baptism. The apparent connection between the practice of baptism and the visionary experience is described throughout Gnostic and Hermetic writings. Much of these texts also find themselves concerned with God, the nature of reality and the mystical knowledge obtained through the visionary experience. Until now, there has been a great deal of speculation into how Hermetic and Gnostic priest created these experiences. In studying Hermetic text we find one of the very first and probably most important peaces of evidence explaining how this visonary gnosis was created. In the Hermetic text known as, *the cup or the Monad,* Hermes states:

> Why then did God, O father, not on all bestow a share of Mind?...
> He willed, my son, to have it set up in the midst for souls, just as
> it were a prize...And where hath He set it up? He (God) filled a
> mighty Cup with mind, and sent it down, joining a Herald [to
> it], to whom He gave command to make this proclamation to
> the hearts of men: Baptize thyself with this Cup's baptism, what
> heart can do so, thou that hast faith thou canst ascend to him that
> hath sent down the Cup, thou that dost know for what thoudidst
> come into being! As many then as understood the Herald's tidings
> and doused themselves in Mind, became partakers in the Gnosis

(knowledge); and when they had received the Mind they were made perfect men. [39]

Hermes goes on to say that:

> But they who have received some portion of God's gift, these, Tat, if we judge by their deeds, have from Death's bonds won their release; for they embrace in their own Mind all things, things on the earth, things in the heaven, and things above the heaven - if there be aught. And having raised themselves so far they sight the Good; and having sighted it, they look upon their sojourn here as a mischance; and in disdain of all, both things in body and the bodiless, they speed their way unto that One and Only One. This is, O Tat, the Gnosis of the Mind, Vision of things Divine; God-knowledge is it, for the Cup is God's. [40]

In this text, Hermes tell his son Tat how God had taken a cup, filled it with mind and spirit and sent it down to men, entrusting it to a messenger, who was commanded to preach and baptize people allowing them to become partakers in this divine cup (and its contents) so they may douse themselves in mind and become partakers in the knowledge and gnosis of God. Hermes relates that such knowledge was not the result of sense-perception and reason, but it stood in stark contrast to them. Hermetic enlightenment was a special type of mental enlightenment, a gift of God, a gift which freed men from the illusions of sense and gave them insight into reality and the purpose of existence. In this way the Hermeticist interpreted the mental emotionalism of his religious experiences as a gift given to mankind through a cup endowed with mind and spirit and equipment with the gnosis of god. As a result of this sacred cup and the visionary properties it contained, the Hermetic initiate underwent spiritual visionary rebirth and an experience of divine mind and Gnosis, an experience that came to be a central and unique aspect of the Hermetic ritual tradition. After the consumption of this cups now unidentified contents, the Hermetic initiate had a profound experience of union with the mind and spirit of the divine. The individual felt himself possessed by such divine power that he could live an upright moral life, and could face the future assured of spiritual immortality.

By examining these important Hermetic quotes we find a clear indication that it was through the use of this cup that the experiences of divine gnosis and visions were taking place in Hermetic baptismal rituals. With the source of Hermetic Gnosis now being related to the use of a cup with divine powers, the question now stands, what were the contents of this important sacred cup, and what could it have contained to have created such a profound and unique experience? Earlier in this book we looked at another prominent and important mystery cult of the classical world also known to have created ritual visionary experiences by means of a ritual drinking cup, the Greek Eleusian Mysteries. In the past, some scholars have speculated into the contents of the Hermetic visionary cup but with little or no success. The main reason for this is that the Hermetic text left us no information describing the contents of this sacred cup or how it was able to create such unique and characteristic visionary experiences. Like the Valentinian and Sethian Gnostic traditions, the Egyptian Hermetic tradition was known to have induced a particular type of mystical experience, one that is characteristically marked by an experience of knowledge and mind and closely associated with the experience of visions and encounters with the divine.

The Hermetic tradition as well as many other similar Gnostic religious philosophical movements of the time has been marked by modern scholars as "Gnostic" because of the emphasis they were known to have put on a unique and particular mystical religious experience of knowledge that was known to have characterized their religious tradition. This was not just an experience of knowledge but an experience of things divine and a direct knowledge that could only come through an experience of the mind through initiation. Through the knowledge and experience of the divine that took place in these rituals one could not only know and experience god, but one could obtain spiritual salvation through knowledge and awareness of God and as the Hermetic and Gnostics claimed become aware of ones true divine origins. This particular element is what has defined the Gnostic tradition today as well as the experiences and beliefs it was known to have maintained.

For many years, the method for how the Gnostics created these experiences remained unsolved and the methods used to create them shrouded in mystery. Because of the lack of successful academic inquiry into the source of Gnostic experiences and the blatant denial on the part of Gnostic scholars to explore the use of altered states of consciousness in creating the Gnostics' experiences, it seems clear that the only way to understand Gnostic experiences and to identify the substances responsible for creating them, is to identify what type of substances are available in this region of the world that could have been used to create the same type of uniquely and characteristic experiences that we find described within their texts. If the biochemical mechanisms required for creating these Gnostic experiences can be identified and the availability for their use in the ancient world demonstrated, then a theory can be built to uncover evidence for the use of these substances in the visionary ritual experiences of the Gnostic and Hermetic traditions. If suitable psychoactive ingredients can be identified, and the effects of this substance can be examined, and evidence can be found to directly relate the effects induced by this substance to the experiences documented in classical Gnostic literature, then a relationship can be presented showing the similarity in effects between the use and effects of this visionary compound and the visionary experiences documented in Gnostic and Hermetic writings. If a successful relationship can be demonstrated between these two experiences then the identification of the Gnostic sacrament can finally be made.

Ch 6
Biochemical Foundations

In the court of Heaven...
Are many jewels so precious and beautiful
That they are inconceivable out of that realm.

Dante

In studying the visionary experiences found within Gnostic writings, it becomes apparent that their visionary experiences were created by means of some yet unidentified additive within their ritual drinking cup. Evidence to support this can be seen in many places in Gnostic literature. As you have already seen, in Sethian Gnosticism, baptismal water was understood to be a sacred symbol of life and purification, but there is also a reference to another second form of sacred Living Water, one that was of a drinkable and visionary nature as well. This second living water or drinkable living water was not only associated with the same sacred rituals and use of a sacred drinking cup, but it is also known to have given the drinker the experience of visions, light, the experience of Gnosis and divine mind that was so central to the Gnostic's visionary experiences. From examining the texts of the Nag Hammadi Library, the rite itself seems to have been conceived as a series of visionary experiences resulting in complete visionary enlightenment of the drinker. Salvation was said to have been achieved through the effects of the ritual experience and the inner spiritual transformation it was said to induce. This ritual was known in Sethian Gnosticism as the ritual of the Five Seals. The ritual of the Five Seals was interpreted as a five-stage ritual of psychic ascent: the investiture of the stripped Spirit with light, its enthronement, and its baptism in Living Water, and the final inner rapture into Gnosis into the divine mind. Similar baptismal motifs have also been found in other texts such as the Odes of Solomon, a Jewish Gnostic text in which the writer describes the drinking of Living Water, as stripping away of folly, and investing with radiance and enlightenment. The sequence of acts in the Sethian Five Seals is also nearly duplicated in the modern Mandaean Masbuta ritual as summarized by Kurt Rudolph, with only the visionary elements extracted. The ritual demonstrates investiture, entrance into the "Jordan," triple self-immersion, triple immersion by the priest, triple signation with water, triple drinking, crowning or wreathing, invocation of divine names, ritual handshake, and ascent from the "Jordan." [1]

The historical text of Hippolytus reported that one swears to be silent about the mysteries as one "drinks from the living water, which is for them a baptism (loutron), a source of living water springing up. For there is a distinction, he says, between water and living water that brings enlightenment and salvation. In Sethian theology and cosmology, a similar distinction is maintained between the transcendent luminous living water in which the divine spirit of Barbelo emerges as a faithful reflection of the Invisible Spirit's thought, indicating that it is this living water that is responsible for creating the experience of Gnostic Gnosis (knowledge).Within Sethian literature, the few passages that associate Seth with baptism usually also mention the figure or name of Jesus. Outside the Gnostic Sethian literature, Seth does not seem to be associated directly with baptism. But on one occasion with the word [sinvcircumflex]êt, meaning "Seth," which is a derivative of [sinvcircumflex] atah, "drink") Translating in the text as: the drink of the soul by the sweet stream of wisdom (sophia). Although no baptismal or other ritual reference is detectable here. This reference may point to a tradition in which Seth was identified as the bearer of a divine wisdom portrayed with liquid and aquatic metaphors. In other wisdom texts, one can point to many more aquatic metaphors for wisdom as well as aquatic metaphors for the acquisition of wisdom such as the drinking of wisdom, being washed in wisdom, and so on. [2]

The Gnostic religions had their baptism, to be sure, but the most important thing was not the physical rite but the hyperphysical immersion in the spirit and mind that the ritual was said to entail. This endowment with divine spirit brought with it, knowledge known in the Greek world as "gnosis," which according to the Gnostic scheme, was prerequisite to salvation. As I pointed out earlier, there were many different sects and branches of Gnosticism: the Sethian Gnostics, the Egyptian Hermetic Gnostics, the Christian Gnostics and the less well known Chaldaean Gnostics, each with its own particular form of religious mythology and ritual. One thing seems to unify these diverse mystical visionary groups. This is the nearly universal visionary Gnostic belief in the use of a particular initiation ritual that was practiced among their groups for attaining mystical esoteric knowledge and union with the knowledge, mind, and essence of the divine. While the experience of Gnosis is what defines Gnosticism today, it is the visionary experiences the Gnostics described, that so closely relates to the entheogenic experiences created by Ayahuasca. In Hermetic Gnosticism, as in other Gnostic sects it was the experience of visionary knowledge that was responsible for the individual's salvation and a necessary requirement for the individual to become spiritually born again. While many Gnostic sects asserted this fact, Hermes goes on to say that, "the knowledge (gnosis) of God is man's salvation, by this alone can a soul become good." We see this even in the very first event mentioned in Tat's regeneration which is the driving out of ignorance by the gnosis or knowledge of the divine. This was a real and direct experience of the mind and knowledge of God that came from drinking the contents of the sacred Hermetic ritual cup. In examining the apparent relationship the contents of this cup had to the botanical world as it is seen in the Hermetic tradition, we are lead to examine many mysterious references to the practice of alchemy and the mixing of various plants, herbs, and other natural substances to achieve spiritual or supernatural ends. The Egyptian Hermetic texts also detail the clearest and least encrypted statement that the experience of Gnosis not only came through the use of a cup with divine powers of mind, but that "the keys to experiencing spiritual rebirth…" were as Hermes Relates: "Found in herbs and spices containing occult divine power," a statement that directly supports the botanical identity of this cups visionary contents.

To identify the pharmacological contents of this ritual cup, we must first understand what type of experiences the Hermetic and Sethian Gnostic created. Now that we know this we must then understand what types of substances are available that are capable of created these same types of experiences. In search for answers we are lead to examine potential candidates that are known to create the same type of experiences the Gnostics described, experiences that are still taking place today. When we compare the visionary experiences of the Gnostics to similar experiences that are known to take place today, we find that Gnostic experiences share the most resemblance to experiences that are described in the mystical visionary literature of near death states. In both near death experiences and Gnostic visionary experiences, we find similar manifestations of visionary spiritual events taking place. In both experiences we find remarkably similar reports of encounters with supernatural beings of light, spiritual mental rapture into living intelligent light, absorption and union with divine mind and many other characteristic visionary and spiritual cognitive phenomena.

The relationship between Gnostic experiences and Near Death experiences has been a relationship that has been pointed out many times in the past, and by many Gnostic scholars, but with little knowledge regarding the biochemical mechanisms of how these experiences were created or how such experiences could have been replicated by ancient Gnostics on demand. This has left many scholars at a stand still, mystified into exactly how such experiences could have been created or their apparent similarity to visionary near death experiences. Then in the 1990s a remarkable discovery was made that finally opened up the doors to this biochemical mystery. Shortly after a biochemical relationship between near death experiences and a naturally occurring visionary substance was identified in the human body, an independent discovery in ethnobotany was made from plants in the Middle East, a discovery that showed a direct link between these plants and the visionary experiences seen in both near death states and Gnostic visions.

Biochemical Foundations

Every religious institution on earth holds the belief that mankind has an innate visionary capacity and an inner desire to understand and connect with the divine. What many people in the world today do not know is that this innate visionary capacity has recently been uncovered and found to be closely related to a powerful naturally occurring visionary neural transmitter in the human brain, a substance known today as di-methyl-tryptamine or DMT. DMT has recently been found to exist naturally in all our bodies, but for many years DMT was only known as a synthetic chemical to western science. It was first synthesized by the Canadian chemist R. Mancke in 1931, but only its basic chemical properties were investigated. Then in 1946, Goncalves de Lima isolated an Alkaloid from the root bark of the Mimosa Hostilis plant. He named his discovery nigerine, not recognizing it as the same chemical earlier synthesized by Mancke. The first clinical studies of DMT didn't initially take place until the early 1960's. This research included injections of the pure molecular substance, eventually ending because the researchers thought the drug too over powering and unpredictable claiming at the time that it had no redeeming qualities. [3]

It would only be in later years of research that the chemical "di-methyl-tryptamine" was found to be a naturally occurring and extremely potent psychoactive substance found within in the human body. The substance DMT is now known to be a naturally occurring neural triptamine with an apparent but not yet fully understood function in the human and mammalian brain. More recent studies have also found DMT to be one of the most common naturally occurring visionary substances on earth. It can be found in mammals, plants, marine animals, grasses, peas, toads, frogs, mushrooms and molds, barks, flowers, roots, trees, bushes, and a wide variety of life forms on earth. DMT is a very simple chemical, structurally very similar to the well known brain chemical serotonin. It has been found to be a very widespread substance throughout the natural world. As Alexander Shulgin titled his book <u>Tihkal</u>, "DMT is everywhere," stating findings of trace amounts of the substance being found throughout the plant and animal kingdoms, especially among mammals. [4]

The brain is where DMT exerts its most interesting effects. The sites rich in these DMT-sensitive serotonin receptors are involved in mood, perception, and thought. All of which are expressed at the very core of human cognition and thought. The brain is a highly sensitive organ, especially susceptible to toxins and metabolic imbalances. The brain has a nearly inpenetrateable shield of defense against such undesired or toxic substances; it's called the blood brain barrier. This blood brain barrier prevents any unwelcome agents from leaving the blood and crossing the capillary walls into the brain tissue. This defense system extends even to keeping out the complex carbohydrates and fats that other tissues use for energy. The brain instead only burns the purest form of fuel: Glucose or what is otherwise known as simple sugar. Although the brain denies access to most drugs and chemicals, for some reason the brain has a particular fancy for DMT. When DMT is exposed to the brain, the brain readily takes it in and utilizes it. [5]

Probably one of the most important discoveries relating to DMT and its relationship to the human brain came when Japanese scientists discovered that the brain actively transports DMT across the blood brain barrier and into its tissues. Once the body produces or takes in DMT, there are certain enzymes, called Monoamine Oxidases (MAO) which occur in high concentration in the blood, liver, stomach, brain and intestine. These naturally occurring MAO's start too quickly break down the DMT and because of these MAO's widespread presence in the human body, the effect of DMT is very short lived. Whenever or where ever it appears, the body makes sure that it is used up fast. In a way it could be said that the brain handles DMT like glucose its precious source of food. The brain actively recognizes it transporting it quickly across its defense system and just as rapidly breaks it down as it is used. This has lead some to believe that DMT on one level or another is necessary for maintaining some form of normal brain function in the human brain. It is only when the levels of DMT get too high that we start to encounter strange and unusual phenomena. [6]

The fact is that the brain is still largely a mystery to science and research into the brains mysteries is ongoing and ever constant. Despite all of the controversy surrounding DMT and its unknown but apparent function in the human and mammalian brain, one thing can be said about the location and creation of DMT in the human body. It is now largely believed by scientist that the Pineal Gland is responsible for creating DMT in the human and mammalian brain and from this place it is created and transported throughout the body. Originally the Pineal Gland was most widely known to be the source for the production of Melatonin, the necessary agent in sleep rhythms and our internal clock. But the pineal gland also contains the necessary building blocks to make DMT. Likewise, Serotonin is used throughout the brain, and the pineal gland posses the highest levels of serotonin anywhere in the body. Serotonin is also a critical precursor for pineal Melatonin creation. The unique enzymes that convert Serotonin, Melatonin, and Tryptamine into psychedelic compounds are also present in extraordinarily high concentration in the Pineal Gland. Researchers believe that DMT is created in the brain from enzymes being transformed in the pineal gland, a process that is now known as "Methyltransferases." This process is believed to work by attaching a Methyl group that is one carbon atom and three hydrogen atoms, into these other molecules, thus Methylating them. Simply put, creating the substances know as Methylate Tryptamine, another compound also known to exist in the brain. When this is done twice, the substances fuse and the body creates the substance DMT, but science has no idea what the substance is used for, or why the brain would have mechanisms for its transportation and creation. [7]

Probably the most extraordinary phenomena that has recently been uncovered in the role and function of DMT in the human body, is its newly discovered relationship to the Near Death Experience. Much of the literature, on Near Death Experiences commonly describes the experience as a mystical, psychedelic, spiritual, and overwhelming psychological experience. A near-death experience or (NDE) is the perception reported by a person who has nearly died or who was clinically dead and then revived. They are now somewhat common, especially since the development of cardiac resuscitation techniques and our modern advancements in medical technology. NDE's are now reported in approximately one-fifth of persons who have been revived from clinical death. In the west, the experience often includes an out-of-body experience, and many times the experience of contacting the supreme source of life in the universe represented in the form of a multi-dimensional intelligent mind, and existing as a supreme and infinite light. This type of divine encounter is also seen throughout Gnostic visions and is one of the defining elements that links Gnostic visions to the experiences reported in near death states. [8]

The Near Death Experience and DMT

In 1990 Dr. Rick Strassman practicing Psychiatrist and a tenured professor at the University of New Mexico was approved by the FDA to conduct live research on the chemical compound DMT. In his research Dr. Strassman used "experienced" volunteers, to whom DMT was administered intravenously. In his research with the substance, he came away with a wealth of information about the substance's effects as well as reports of its remarkable similarity to experiences described in many near death reports. In this study, volunteers described many shocking and vivid real life encounters with supernatural visionary entities and other powerful visionary religious phenomena that are directly described and encountered in Near Death Experiences. In these experiences, volunteers reported real life encounters with real other worldly entities, being of light and experiences of contacting the supreme source of life represented in the form of a multi dimensional supreme and infinite light. These reports and the remarkable experiences described in his research have shaken open the doors of neural science and have opened up the study of the Near Death experiences to new levels of complexity and scientific discourse that not only demonstrate the biochemical doorways of the NDE, but also its shear and unexplainable connection to biological life processes, for which DMT has now been found to play a vital role. [9]

The phenomenology of NDE usually includes many physiological, psychological and transcendental factors such as subjective impressions of being outside their physical body, visions of deceased relatives and religious figures such as Jesus, angels, beings of light, among many others. After the experience occurs many people also report the feeling of a new found belief in the transcendence of ego and life of the mind or soul after the death of the physical material body. Typically in western countries the NDE follows a distinct progression, starting with the sensation of floating above one's body and seeing the surrounding area followed by the sensation of passing through a tunnel or light, meeting deceased relatives, and concluding with encounters of the divine or semi-divine beings of light. Usually at the 'core' of a near-death experience is an increased feeling of peace, joy, and harmony, followed by insight and mystical or religious experiences. [10]

While out of body experiences seem to be void in most Gnostic visions, Gnostic visions do share many of the same visionary elements found in near death states and associated with DMT. In one near death experience reported by J. Timothy Green, Ph.D. we find some of the following:

> I was driving to an appointment, and I remember seeing a sign for Coco's restaurant. Suddenly, I was flying down this really big, dark, black tunnel, but I could see white light at the end. I was thinking that the light of the tunnel was really scary, but for some reason because the light was there-I felt everything was going to be ok. I remember I could not wait until I got to the light. Something

about it seemed like it was really wonderful. Anyway, I got to it and I went right into it. After I was in it, I started noticing other lights around me. And they all looked the same, but they were people. I could feel that they loved me. Then, all of a sudden, I looked at one of the lights and it was frank... He said, "it is not your time and you need to go back." I just said, "Ok." The next thing I knew I was back in the tunnel ... The next thing I felt was the left side of my head, and it was hurt really bad. I was leaning over in my car. My body was halfway between the seats, and the pain in my head was so terrible-it hurt so much - that I felt like I left my body again, only this time I went right into the light. When I went into the light, there were all of these lights again. And there was a big light or major light – I don't know if I would call it God or Jesus, but it was definitely a higher being that has something to do with why we are all here. Anyway, I went back into the light, and there were all of these people, and they were all letting me know they loved me. I knew one of these lights was [my deceased friend] frank...I felt like we were walking around or moving around, there were more lights that were beings, all letting me know that they loved me. And I could hear the most beautiful music. It was absolutely beautiful. I have never heard music like that on this earth. And then Frank said, "Well, you really do need to go back."... I really did not want to go back I told him... I started to come back but I really didn't want to... He kind of laughed and told me not to worry, that life was only the blink of an eye.... [11]

Many of the common properties associated with the Near Death Experience Phenomena have been defined as (1) a sense of being dead, (2) peace and painlessness, (3) an out-of-body experience, (4) a tunnel experience, (5) meeting people of light, (6) meeting a being of light, (7) a life review, (8) a reluctance to return, and (9) a personality transformation. While the list of exact properties may vary slightly from researcher to researcher depending upon each scientist's personal emphasis, it can certainly be agreed that the most common properties are the review of life events, encountering living intelligent light, and meeting with deceased loved ones and/or a religious figure. [12]

Recognizing these characteristics in the NDE does not mean that everyone experiences each and all of them during any given NDE. Different people experience different combinations of these characteristics. Although it seems that the events usually end with a sense of being pulled back to the experience's material body or sometimes sent back with the warning that the experience's time to die had not yet come. These various characteristics give the impression that they are dead as well as the feeling that they are out of their living body. Many experiences also report floating above their bodies and witnessing events outside of their normal range of perception while in the state of death or a near death state. Normal time and space seem irrelevant within this experience of reality. Experiences sometimes witness normal events in our normal reality during the NDE. Unfortunately, reports of normal real events witnessed during the out-of-body portion of the NDE and the accuracy of such out of body reports have been very controversial and sometimes plagued by discrepancies, so this particular form of evidence has not been fully accepted by the scientific community at large despite strong and compelling evidence that many cases of this type have in fact proven themselves to be true. [13]

At some point in the experience the person near death is brought back to life by the efforts of a medical team or by chance. The re-animation of life occurs in spite of the momentary brain death of the person. When a patient is revived, he or she is materially yanked back into the normal world by a medical team or by some active stimulus of the body. Sometimes, this stimulus comes from within the visionary near death state, many ND experiences have been 'told' during the experience that his or her time has not yet come and they are suddenly forced back into normal reality by the consciousness itself. The consciousness may realizes life was not completely disrupted and is able to reorganize or reconstitute itself, with the fundamental chemical reactions of the body then jump starting the living process once more. After the NDE, a person generally undergoes clear and specific changes in personality, literally a transformation of the self. These changes usually include a loss of fear of death, increased compassion, and an increased spiritual and ecological awareness. Personality transformations by the 'light' gives a person having experienced it an acute awareness of a far greater and more comprehensive physical universe than is currently suspected by modern science. [14]

In 1990 when Dr. Rick Strassman was approved by the FDA to conduct research on the chemical compound DMT, and its relationship to the human brain and to the NDE it was the only clinical study on the effects of DMT since the 1960s. At the time this was the first new research on a psychedelic compound in the United States in over twenty years. One thing that made Dr. Strassman's research unique is that it would be the first human trials of a naturally occurring human and mammalian psychedelic brain transmitter. The project lasted about 5years and concluded with a wealth on knowledge and a list of numerous phenomena of experiences being reported by the many research subjects who claimed that the experiences undergone in the research forever inspired and changed their lives. But some of the most extraordinary experiences were those in which the subject reported vivid other dimensional like contact with very real other worldly entities as well as experiences in which the participants believed they contacted the source of all life in the universe, many times being depicted in a strikingly similar fashion to the experiences documented in Near Death Experiences as well as the experiences found in ancient Gnostic literature. [15]

In his book <u>DMT and the Spirit Molecule,</u> Rick Strassman goes on to explain the scope of his research and examines the various mechanisms responsible for the production and creation of DMT in the human body as well as the substances relationship to the Near Death Experience. In his research, Strassman goes on to relate that, "during a Near Death Experience there is a massive surge in stress hormones during this near death state. We also know that levels of naturally occurring DMT in the body rise in the patient's blood stream during such high stress and near death states. This surge in stress hormones on the brain may be what allows the protective mechanisms of the pineal gland to be inactivated, allowing for naturally occurring DMT to flood the brain to induce these experiences, in effect, opening up some sort of biochemical doorway. We also know that DMT levels rise in animals exposed to high levels of stress." [16]

But why is this, why would the brain have such unusual mechanisms and what is DMT's role in all of this? Well, some of the most current researchers on this topic including Dr. Strassman believe that it is because of these Methyltransferase enzymes that help form DMT in the brain. If this theory is correct then it is the conversion of these Methyltransferase Enzymes in the Pineal Gland that creates DMT in the human body, but exactly what it is used for is still not yet fully understood by the scientific community. As Dr. Strassman goes on to relate, "Other than having an apparent role in creating or facilitating the profound experiences encountered in near death states, DMT is also suspected in having a role in another naturally occurring altered state of consciousness, the realm of dreams. The most likely time for a dream is also the time when melatonin levels are the highest, since melatonin itself has such mild psychological effects, it suggests a role for another pineal compound whose levels also parallel those of Melatonin. Many doctors have suggested that Pineal-derived Beta-Carbolines (MAO Inhibitors) may mediate dreams. But researchers are still uncertain as to the full psychological effects of MAO inhibitors. By virtue of the pineal Beta Carbolines or increased levels of MAO inhibitors within the sleeping state, it could certainly boost the effects of DMT. If this process was taking place then it could indirectly stimulate aspects of the dream process. While many mysteries still surround the brain and the functioning of DMT in the brain, one thing is clear. DMT is found naturally in the human brain and body and the chemical tools are there for its manufacturing, use, and controls." [17]

In considering the manufacturing and function of DMT in the human Pineal Gland, Strassman has suggested that this is a very strategic location for its roles in our lives. "The Pineal Gland is located near the middle of the brain, and from this location it is surrounded by the emotional centers of the limbic system, and nearly touches the visual and auditory sensory relay stations of the brain. Its position allows for instant delivery of its products directly into the cerebrospinal fluid. Now the effects of melatonin do not justify immediate access to the colliculi and limbic system, these deep brain structures regulate perception and emotion. The pineal does not need to be in the middle of the brain if this location were just to support melatonin's role in our lives. However, DMT production certainly warrants this strategic location. DMT released directly onto the visual, auditory, and emotional centers of the brain that the pineal gland nearly touches, would profoundly affect the individual and ones inner experience greatly. Experiences encountered under the effects of DMT are many times varied. But despite the wide range of experiences they are always profoundly powerful."[18] Probably the most extraordinary phenomena associated with this substance is the fact that many times the person experiencing it encounters what they believe to be contact with sentient independent intelligences, or beings through which contact or communication takes place. One of the most remarkable discoveries Strassman encountered in his research was not only related to many NDEs like reports of heavenly realms and contact with divine beings and intelligent universal light, but also an even more unusual collection of phenomena of very real and sometimes frightening encounters with independent sentient intelligences, beings of a seemingly extra dimensional independent existence.

While reports of entity contact are just some of the many visionary phenomena associated with the DMT, they are also some of the most characteristic phenomena found in Gnostic visionary literature outside the experience of Gnosis and encounters with the divine. Many people who have experienced this phenomenon while taking DMT have reported that the experience is more like being blown into a parallel dimension than it is like taking a traditional psychedelic drug. Many people who have reported these experiences are fully convinced that the beings or creatures they encounter are in fact real and are somehow derived from their own independent sentient existence. Many informants have also stated that the experience is nothing short of some of the most remarkable and extraordinary experiences they have ever encountered in their lives. In the past, some scholars have pointed out similarities between near death experiences for which naturally accruing DMT is known to play a role, and the visionary experiences described in Gnostic text, but with no background knowledge about how such experiences could have been safely created or duplicated by the Gnostics short of inducing a near death state, all of their theories quickly came to a halt. It has only been in more recent years, that enough research has been collected about DMT and is widespread availability around the world that science is truly beginning to understand the chemical transport systems of DMT in the human body, as well as its apparent common place throughout the botanical world. [19]

DMT in Plants

The identification of the visionary neural transmitter DMT allows us to understand and identify Gnostic visions because of the similarity Gnostic visions have to the DMT experience. While DMT is still something of a mystery to the psychological and scientific community, investigation, and exploration of its profound visionary effects is remarkably nothing new. One of the most remarkable facts about DMT is that it is found in many places throughout the natural world, but one of the places DMT is found most abundantly is throughout the botanical kingdom and the world of plants. There is literally hundreds of types of plants throughout the world that are known to contain DMT naturally in their tissues, but only some of these plants contain DMT in high enough levels to be used by people. One of the places with one of the highest concentrations of plant species anywhere in the world is known as the Amazon rainforest, located in South America. The Amazon Rainforest holds more biodiversity in plant and animal life than anywhere else on earth. The Amazonian Indians, as well as forest dwellers everywhere have a tremendous depth of understanding of the chemical properties of plants indigenous to their habitat. Extracts of plants are prepared and used by the natives as medicines that are used both in the western pharmacological sense, and a little less known to the western world, in the supernatural sense. The Amazon basin has more psychedelic plant species containing naturally occurring DMT than almost anywhere else on earth; it also has more plant species containing natural MAO inhibitors than any other place on earth.[20]

The fact that these plants are known to contain these compounds and that early indigenous peoples in this region came to discover and mix them together is quite remarkable considering that one of the most interesting compounds the Pineal gland is known to make are compounds known as Beta- Carbolines. These compounds inhibit or stop the breakdown of DMT by the body's Monoamine Oxidases (MAO). As a result, these Beta Carbolines, also known as MAO inhibitors, allow DMT to be orally activated. One of the more striking examples of how these Beta-Carbolines or MAO inhibitors work in the body comes from the study of plants and the long history of the indigenous use of plants known to contain these MAO inhibitor compounds in the Amazon area for their mixing and use. When the plants that contain these MAO inhibitors are mixed with other plants that contain DMT, these plant mixtures create a powerful, psychoactive, entheogenic brew that is unparallel to almost any other naturally occurring psychoactive substance on earth. When the two plants are mixed and consumed the MAO inhibitors in these plants allow the DMT to become orally activated, inducing its profoundly visionary effects on the human body. If it were not for these Beta-Carbolines, the MAO in the gut would rapidly break down this swallowed DMT plant based material and it would have no effect on the human mind. The Beta Carbolines or MAO inhibitors in these other companion plants are what allow the plant based DMT to be utilized, enhancing and prolonging its effects. [21]

Ayahuasca "Vine of the Soul"

Deep in the heart of the Amazonian rainforest there grows a sacred vine known by the native people of the region for its healing and mystical powers. This vine is known by many names, but the most well known of them, is Ayahuasca (aye-yah-wah-skah). In the Quechua language, aya means spirit or soul, and huasca means vine or rope. So Ayahuasca is translated as meaning "The Vine of the Soul" and it is said that those who consume this vine of the soul are bestowed with the ability to commune with spirits of the forest, diagnose illness, treat disease, and even talk with god. While the existence of this vine is certainly no big secret, it is only recently that western science has decided to study the magical properties of this sacred and ancient indigenous medicine. The Ayahuasca vine contains these Beta Carbolines or the MAO inhibitors naturally in its plant tissues. When the vine of the plant is mixed with other plants that contain DMT, a powerful botanical biochemical synergy is created that allows for the psychoactive effects of the DMT to work in the human body. The MAO Inhibitors in the vine have a small psychoactive ability on their own, but when they are mixed with DMT a totally new and much more powerful visionary experience is created, one that is profoundly spiritual, visionary and directly imbedded in nature. [22]

Ayahuasca the Entheogen

The mixture of the MAO inhibitor containing vine plant Banisteriopsis caapi with various DMT containing plants of the Amazon such as Psychotra Viridis is what is required in the traditional making of the visionary Ayahusca libation. When consumed, the botanical visionary brew Ayahuasca is known to induce a powerful visionary alteration in the drinker's wakeful state of consciousness. Other non-perceptual cognitive effects are also manifested.

These include personal insight, intellectual ideations, and profound spiritual and mystical experiences. Moreover, Ayahuasca introduces those who partake of it to what are believed to be other very real spiritual realities. Those who consume the brew may feel that they have gained access to new sources of knowledge and that the mysteries and ultimate truths of the universe are being revealed to them. All of this may also be accompanied with encounters of divine realities and even the divine itself. The effects of Ayahuasca can be extremely varied depending on many different factors. For a very long time western science had no accurate description for the experiences and states of mind that many of these Shamanistic societies were encountering under the use of this or other similar plants in their indigenous rituals. So in 1979, a group of ethnobotanical scholars created the term entheogen to more accurately and appropriately describe the experiences many of these various indigenous peoples were encountering from the use of Ayahuasca and other similar visionary substances used in their traditional healing religious rituals.

As you have seen earlier in this book, the word entheogen means "creating the divine within." The word Entheogen is a modern term derived from two Ancient Greek words, *entheos* and *genesthai*. *Entheos* means literally "in God," more freely translated "inspired." The Greeks used it as a term of praise for poets and other artists. *Genesthai* means "to cause to be." So an entheogen is that which causes (a person) to be in God or more accurately translated as "creating the divine within." In its strictest sense, the term refers to a psychoactive substance (most often some plant matter) that occasions enlightening spiritual or mystical experience within the parameters of a ritual or cult. In a broader sense, the word "entheogen" refers to a natural substance, usually a plant or fungi, which induces alterations of consciousness similar to those documented for ritual ingestion of traditional shamanic inebriants, the term creating the divine within or "Entheogen" replaces the judgment-laden misnomer "hallucinogen" and the culturally freighting term "psychedelic." However, many people object to using the word "entheogen" to describe taking psychedelic drugs for recreational and not spiritual/religious purposes.[23]

The fact is, that the Ayahuasca brew is the ultimate entheogen, but in addition to its spiritual or visionary effects, it is overly known as a purgative used in healing rituals among various ethnic groups of the upper Amazon area and in Colombia, Ecuador, Peru, and Brazil. It is used among these traditional indigenous groups as a natural visionary entheogenic sacrament used for healing and manifesting the divine from within. A number of anthropological studies of this psychoactive plant mixture are known, including symbolic studies for the Tukano Indians of Colombia. The complexity of the Ayahuasca-related rituals and their corresponding symbolism varies greatly among these ethnic groups depending on the degree to which the particular group may have been influenced by western industrial culture. [24]

The benefits of Ayahuasca can be divided into three main categories. The first is physical healing, second, emotional healing and moral growth, third, mystical or visionary insights. First and foremost, Ayahuasca is a very strong purgative that makes you throw up and will cleanse your entire system. The brew has a mysterious ability to clean out not only your intestinal track, but your whole physical being, including built up emotional stresses and difficulties. One of the traditional uses of the purge was to get rid of intestinal microbes and parasites. Without denying the importance of modern hygiene, antibiotics, and vaccines, there is evidence that when a jungle community abandons its use of Ayahuasca, its overall health deteriorates. Even non-natives like whites and mestizos, who discount Ayahuascas spiritual nature don't hesitate to acknowledge its efficacy in treating jungle illnesses. Historically, non-Indians first became interested in Ayahuasca because of its healing power, not for the mystical visions it inspires. It can be noted that one can find a number of conventional doctors in Colombia and Brazil who encourage their patients to attend Ayahuasca rituals because they have found that it is particularly effective in curing illness caused by toxins and emotional stress. In modern urban life we are exposed to countless toxins and impurities, such as alcohol, cigarette smoke, food preservatives, air pollution, pesticides, and other environmental toxins. Even conventional medicine recognizes that such things can cause heart problems, cancers, or even compromise our natural immunity to viral diseases. [25]

Purging serves to eliminate toxins in our bodies before they can cause problems. It is interesting to note that until a few centuries ago, purging was an integral part of Western medicine, but fell out of favor when natural healing methods were displaced in the western world by synthetic chemical drugs, invasive surgery, and other harsh assaults on the body. Fundamentally drinking ayahuasca is a holistic and therapeutic experience. The Shamanic initiation rites themselves are known to entail a lengthy period of preparation, which included social isolation, sexual abstinence, as well as strict dietary restrictions before novices get to ingest ayahuasca with the curandero (Healer), a connoisseur of the chemically induced healing visionary state, the curandero provides guidance to those who wish to embark upon the ayahuasca vision quest. The curandero is unquestionably the master of ceremonies, the key figure in the ayahuasca drama. After nightfall, the bitter sweat brew is passed around a circle from mouth to mouth, and the shaman starts to sing about the spirits, the visions, and the experience of healing. Listening to his chant, the novices feel some numbness on their lips and warmth in their guts. A vertiginous surge of energy envelops them with wrenching, vomiting, and diarrhea, sweeping through the intestinal coils like liquid draino for the soul, cleansing the body of parasites, emotional blockages, and long-held resentments. [26]

It is for good reason that Amazonian natives refer to *la purga* when speaking of ayahuasca, the Vine of the Soul. One cannot help be impressed by the remarkable health-enhancing effects attributed to the purging action of the vine. There have even been anecdotal reports of the complete remission of some cancers after one or two ayahuasca sessions. The rejuvenating impact of *la purga* would help to explain the exceptional health of the *ayahuasqueros*, even those of advanced ages. In addition to purifying the body, ayahuasca encourages self awareness and self knowledge, its teaches a universal ethical code, and ultimately, it offers direct personal contact with higher facets of human consciousness and what one would describe as real and direct contact with the divine. [27]

Pharmacological Western Uncovering

While ayahuasca has been known about and used in traditional South American jungle societies for thousands of years, the knowledge and awareness of ayahuasca and the plants required to make it have only emerged and been present in the industrialized western world for little over a century. The western knowledge of ayahuasca ceremonies was only first recorded in the 17th century by Jesuit missionaries who condemned the use of the brew as "diabolical potions" prepared from jungle vines. The ruthless attempt to eradicate such practices among the colonized inhabitants of the Americas was part of an imperialist effort to impose a new social order that stigmatized the ayahuasca experience as a form of devil worship or possession by evil spirits. But the ingestion of ayahuasca for religious and medicinal purposes continued among the native peoples, despite the genocidal campaigns of the conquistadores. Archaeological evidence dates ayahuasca use in Ecuador back five millennia; however, knowledge about the vine of the soul and the botanical use of DMT containing plants with it, only first came to the light of western science in 1851 when the English botanist Richard Spruce departed to explore and study the botanical diversity of the Amazon Rainforest in hopes of finding new plants species to bring back with him to study in England. Upon his encountering the native peoples of the area, Spruce was greatly intrigued by their deep knowledge and understanding of the plants and animals native to the forest around them. A group of Tukanoan Indians invited the British botanist and explorer Richard Spruce to participate in one of their ceremonies which included a visionary drink they called Caapi. Spruce only drank a small amount of the "nauseous beverage," but felt little to no effects. The Tukanoans showed Spruce the plant from which the Caapi drink was made, and he was able to collect good specimens of the plant in full flower. Spruce named the primary plant in the brew Banisteriopsis caapi. Further research led Spruce to conclude that Caapi, Yage, and Ayahuasca were all Indian names for the same tea made using the vine as the primary ingredient, a vine that he now called by the western scientific name Banisteriopsis Caapi. [28]

Richard Spruce would be the first scientist and botanist to study the plant and the first to bring back samples to Europe for study. In a hope to identify the active principal responsible for the profound effects of the brew, a chemical compound was later isolated in 1927 from the Banisteriopsis Caapi vine, which at the time was named Telepathine. At the time it was this chemical that was believed to be the chemical compound responsible for the acclaimed telepathic phenomena associated with its effects. Only later was the compound Telepathine not found to be responsible for this acclaimed telepathic experience. While still very controversial, the central reason for this phenomenon is still, to this day, unknown. It would not be until the discovery and chemical investigation of another plant containing similar chemical properties, found growing on the other side of the world that the chemical properties of the Ayahuasca vine would finally be understood and its complex biochemical synergy come to be understood. [29]

Soon after Richard Spruce brought back samples of the Ayahuasca vine for further study to England, the western academic interest in the plant mixture continued to grow and become explored. But it was not until the first half of the 20th century that the brew witnessed the initial scientific study of these plants and the mechanisms for how the brew is made and how it works in the human body. This scientific investigation started to shed light on the botanical sources as well as the active chemical constituents that facilitate the effects of this powerful visionary jungle mixture. In 1957 the alkaloids Harmine and Harmaline that were first earlier identified from the Middle Eastern plant Peganum Harmala/ Syrian Rue, were identified to be the same chemical compounds found in the Ayahuasca vine. The active psychedelic principles of Harmaline were first isolated in 1841, from the plant Peganum Harmala also known in the United States as Syrian rue. Its chemical structure was established in 1919, and it was first synthesized in 1927 by Richard Manske. Later in 1923, Fischer isolated an alkaloid from the Ayahuasca vine that he named telepathine. The same year, Barriga-Villalba and Albarracin isolated two alkaloids from this same Ayahuasca drink; they called these Yajeine and Yajeinine. Five years later in 1928, Lewin isolated Banisterine from the vine. Shortly afterward, Wolfes, as well as Rumpfand Elger, asserted that all these alkaloids were the same identical substances: they were the chemical called Harmaline, an indole derivative found years earlier from the seeds and roots of the Middle Eastern plant Peganum Harmala. This chemical conclusion was in doubt for some time, until a researcher working with the plants clearly identified botanicals, and further demonstrated that all these substances inside these plants were in fact all the same Harmaline alkaloids. [30]

Later in 1969 Naranjo identifying 18 different species of Banisteriopsis vine in Peru, out of a total of 100 in the Amazon area. In 1972, Rivier and Lindgren 1972 published the first interdisciplinary papers on this plant mixture reporting on the alkaloid profiles of the Ayahuasca brews and source plants collected among the Shuar people of the upper Rio Purús in Peru. At the time, their paper was one of the most thorough chemical investigations of the composition of the tea and the source plants from which it was made. The report also went on to discuss numerous admixture plants other than the vine that were added to the brew to help potentate its visionary and entheogenic effects, plants such as Psychotria Viridis or Diplopteris cabrerana known to contain DMT. This in depth scholarly outline for the first time provided evidence indicating that ayahuasca admixture technology was complex, and that many species of plants could be used to create it, species of plants that even lived outside of the Amazon rainforest, plants that are known to contain the same pharmacological properties as the brew Ayahuasca. It was not until the isolation of Harmaline and the discoveries of the MAOI's and their psychedelic transport system that gave science an understanding of how the plants worked in the human body. With the discovery of Harmaline from the Middle Eastern plant Peganum harmala/ Syrian Rue, researchers were finally able to uncover the chemical properties of the vine which contains similar MAO inhibitors. Once the properties of Ayahusca had been discovered and the long history and sacred mythologies surrounding the plant had been categorized and written down from the seemingly countless groups of Indigenes Rainforest peoples, this small bushy arid Middle Eastern weed from which the MAO inhibitors were first discovered had almost received no more further attention. [31]

Peganum Harmala, Keys to an Ancient Mystery

With the discovery of MAO inhibitor's in Peganum Harmala, Middle Eastern researchers wondered if Peganum Harmala had ever once been used by people of the Middle East for similar visionary healing purposes as the Ayahuasca vine had been used for in the Amazon. But because no groups in the modern Middle Eastern region were currently known to have utilized the Peganum Harmala plant for its visionary properties or in the same way native peoples of the South American Amazon were known to do with Ayahuasca researchers were quickly led to believe that the pharmacological potential of the plant was largely unknown. But upon a much more thorough examination into the history and use of the Peganum harmala plant in Middle Eastern history, scholars came to conclude that the plant was in fact used in ancient times for a wide variety of medical and magical purposes and that its modern uses as a sacred incense to ward away the evil eye were only modern vestiges from a much more ancient use of the plant. While the presence of Peganum Harmala in the area was now known it was not to long until plants were discovered in the region that were found to contain DMT. It has recently been discovered that certain types of acacia trees growing in the same regions of the Middle East and Egypt, have been found to contain relatively large amounts of DMT naturally in their tissues. In reference to this statement, I have included a list of various different Acacia species known to contain DMT alkaloids; this report comes from TiHKAL (by Alexander Shulgin):

A. baileyana	0.02% tryptamine and β-carbolines, in the leaf
A. maidenii	0.2% to 0.39% DMT and NMT, in the stem bark
A. albida	DMT, in the leaf
A. confuse	DMT and NMT, in the leaf, stem and bark
A. cultriformis	tryptamine, in the leaf and stem
A. laeta	DMT, in the leaf
A. mellifera	DMT, in the leaf
A. nilotica	DMT, in the leaf
A. phlebophylla	DMT, in the leaf
A. podalyriaefolia	tryptamine, in the leaf
A. Senegal	DMT, in the leaf
A. seyal	DMT, in the leaf
A. sieberiana	DMT, in the leaf)
A. simplicifolia	DMT and NMT, in the leaf, stem and trunk bark

| *A. vestita* | tryptamine, in the leaf and stem [32] |

With the discovery of the two plants required to make this visonary Ayahusca analog brew now present in the Middle Eastern region, the possibility that at some point in history these two plants were mixed with one another and consumed for their visionary properties is an event that must now be considered. To identify if the Gnostics had ever used these plants to create their visions evidence must be found that can demonstrate that the two plants required to make this visionary brew were known about and used in ancient times. As you can see, the two plants required to make this powerful visionary entheogen were available to ancient people in the region of the world that the Gnostics lived. The question now stands: is their any evidence that these two plants were ever used for their medicinal or visionary properties? With the availability and discovery of Peganum Harmala, the required MAO inhibitor, and the more recent discovery of psychoactive DMT compounds in various Acacia species, the possibility that the knowledge of these two plants' pharmacological potentials could have been uncovered and used by ancient peoples in this region of the world for visionary ritual purposes is apparent and demands further examination. Because of the similarity between the Gnostic's visionary experiences and the experiences reported regarding the effects of DMT and Ayahuasca, it seems likely that the pharmacological properties of the two plants were known about and mixed with one another at some point in antiquity. To identify if this was in fact the case and the mixture and consumption of these two plants was taking place and was responsible for the visionary experiences of the Gnostics, it must be demonstrated that the two plants required too make this visionary libation were known about and utilized in antiquity. If evidence can be demonstrated that the two plants required to make this Ayahuasca analog were known about and consumed in antiquity, then a theory for their mixing and use can finally be presented. If the potential for the ancient mixture and consumption of these two plants can be found, then a full examination of this brew's visionary effects can be cross-examined with the visionary experiences reported in Gnostic and Hermetic writings. If a similarity can be found between these two experiences, then the long lost identify of the Gnostic sacrament can finally be made.

Ch 7
Zoroaster and Peganum Harmala

> Ohrmazad the sacred spirit, creator of the righteous and corporeal existence, took the hand of Zoroaster and put liquid omniscient wisdom into it, and said "drink it." and Zoroaster drank it and omniscient wisdom was mixed into Zoroaster.
>
> (Zand I Wahman Yasht III, 6-22)

Peganum Harmala

About Ten grams of Peganum Harmala/ Syrian Rue seeds provide about 400mg of total Beta-Carbolines, about the same amount in a typical dose of Ayahuasca. The seeds, as well as the roots, of Peganum Harmala contain a mixture of the Harmala alkaloids, Harmine and Harmaline. These unusual alkaloids are psychoactive derivatives of B-carboline, when administered to humans, they are extremely potent, short term MAO inhibitors. Peganum Harmala, or Syrian Rue, is the plant from which the psychedelic chemical Harmine, Harmaline, and Tetrahydro Harmine were first isolated from. Total contents run almost 4% by weight in the seeds of the plant. The Peganum Harmala plant is a perennial, shrubby, hardy, arid succulent with a wide botanical distribution. It grows naturally throughout the Middle East, eastern Mediterranean, and Africa. Aspand or Isfand is the common Persian / Dari / Farsi name for the plant. The name is also translated as Espand, Esfand, and Esphand, and the plant itself is given the regional common name Harmal or Harmala in Pakistan and India. Syrian Rue as it is also commonly called in English, grows in semi-arid conditions. It originated in Central Asia, and is held in high esteem today throughout Asia Minor as a medicinal, aphrodisiac, and dye plant. It is sometimes known as "ruin weed" since it often grows on the tells covering the ruins of ancient cities in the Near East. It now grows wild in Eurasia and has recently been spread from the Middle East to the American southwest where the dry conditions have allowed it to thrive. [1]

Peganum Harmala /Syrian rue is characterized by a strong particular odor, which issues from the leaves when disturbed. The plant is made especially noticeable to herdsman such as the Indio Iranians and nomadic Bedouins by the fact that grazing animals such as camels, goats, donkeys, and sheep will not eat of its fresh stems and leaves even in the face of near starvation. Its foliage is not actually toxic but the composition of the plant is believed to give a bad taste or nauseousness to grazing livestock. This avoidance of the living herb by livestock may make it seem strangely protected. It appears that the properties of being shunned by animals may have been regarded as drawing attention to the plant by ancient herdsmen. [2]

This avoidance by grazing animals is also clear in that the plant stands and is left isolated as the surrounding vegetation is consumed. Thereby, Peganum harmala becomes one of the most available plant materials remaining after the large herds have made their way through the land after grazing. But come fall, it is one of the most common materials available for fires. In Iran and throughout other parts of the Middle East, the scent from its smoke has traditionally been regarded as incense. The smoke contains appreciable amounts of Harmine and Harmaline the psychoactive potential of which must be considered in evaluating the historical origins of the traditional burning of Peganum Harmala seeds. [3]

It has apparently been present longer in areas where it is also known as a weed especially characterized by its association with human occupation growing out from trash heaps and the sites of ancient ruins. The smoke of Peganum Harmala builds rapidly in the human body and the pharmacological potential of the smoke is quite notable even when smoked. Largely, psychedelic plants are seen as having spiritual and mystical qualities especially among indigenous and native peoples living in the regions the plants are known to grow. One way to validate the plant's psychedelic potential as being understood by early nomadic peoples and ancient tribe's men of the region comes from evidence directly linking the plant with the sacred and supernatural world. Since the experience of such realities has been traditionally linked to the use of psychoactive substances and altered states of consciousness by anthropologists around the world, the probability that Peganum Harmala was once used for creating such experiences considering its pharmacological properties and widespread availability and use in the region, demands further consideration. In considering the ancient importance and spiritual psychoactive use of Peganum Harmala in antiquity, it is important to point out that the Peganum Harmala is well known throughout the modern Middle Eastern world as holding sacred, spiritual, healing, and protective supernatural qualities for which its visionary pharmacological properties must also have once been used for.

Peganum Harmala in Modern Iran

Throughout the history of Islamic Iran to the present day, Peganum Harmala has been chiefly esteemed for its apotropiac power or power to avert evil, and is the chief plant regarded as having such power today. Allusions to its use in the very earliest of what is known as New Person literature shows that this practice was a very clear continuation of Pre-Islamic beliefs and traditions regarding the plant's supernatural qualities. In particular, the burning of the Peganum Harmala seeds is mentioned quite frequently in classical Persian literature, and is still practiced to this day throughout Iran. Many modern day cases for the present day burning of the Peganum harmala/Esfand seeds are accompanied by the recitation of formulated verses whose content reveals the essential attitude shown towered the plant. This verse asserts that the use of Peganum Harmala, also known in Iran as Isfand or Esfand is sanctioned by the most revered sources of religious authority in Islamic Iran. [4]

> Esfand and Sepand:
> Our prophet collected it,
> 'Ali planted it, Fatima collected it for
> Husayn and Hasan.
>
> Isfand and Esfand seeds, Isfand of thirty-three seeds, for relatives and friends and strangers, all who go out by the door, all whom come in by the door. May the eye of the envious and of the envy be blind, Saturday born Sunday, born Monday, born Tuesday, born Wednesday, born Thursday, and born Friday. Who planted it? The prophet. Who gathered it? Fatima. For whom do they make it smoke? For the Iman Husan and Imam Husayn. By the grace of the king of men, turn away misfortune and pain.[5]

Throughout the Islamic world, the burning of the seeds is believed to cast away evil spirits and bad energies. Wherever there is suspicion of the evil eye, Isfand is said to cleanse the evil spirits, protect the household, and ward off evil. Throughout much of the Middle East today, the seeds of Peganum Harmala or Isfand can be found as a critical element in numerous amulets and the capsules that contain the seeds which are frequently strung together to make what is called a Panja, that are displayed in conservative Iranian households even today. These Panja are also hung outside the entrances to many Bedouin tents throughout the Middle East and are used for the very same purposes, to keep away evil, and ward off the evil eye. The widespread importance of Peganum Harmala is also reflected in North African Islamic data, where women will throw Peganum Harmala seeds on their door steps and over their shoulders saying, "The Harmel is sacred, O prophet of god, protect us from bad male Jinn and bad female Jinn. (Jinn are known as Spirits). This assertion that Peganum Harmala/Syrian Rue is sacred is expressed among the Bedouin Nomads as well as in Iranian folklore, folklore with pre-Islamic roots and traditions of a much more ancient Iranian origin. [6]

Incense and Intoxicant

> While burning of the seeds is the primary use reported for Peganum Harmala in modern Iran, there is evidence in the much older folk religion that an extract of the plant was also drank at one time. Evidence demonstrating this can be found within the ancient writings and scrolls of the Mandaeans. The Mandaeans are known to have many written materials on the sacred use of the plant, and are known to have recommended the drinking of a preparation of the Peganum Harmala plant for healing and procreation. However, the Mandaean texts also recommend ingesting the plant for totally apotropic spiritual ends as well. In the following Mandaean passage where the plant is called by its modern Persian name ispand, we find the following:

> Solomon then asks, "O demon, what is the charm that exorcises thee?" ... The demon replies giving a recipes and various, for instance: black ispand in milk of a red cow: boil it over the fire and eat it" [7]

The text from the Mandaean library is not the only piece of surviving literature from the ancient world known to have given descriptions of the plants ingestion and use. In a much later Islamic quote, a preparation of the plant's smoke is also recommended with completely spiritual and protective motivations in mind. In Islam, according to the Shi'a hadith, Muhammad was commanded by God to have his people ingest Isfand for bravery. This Hadith is interesting in the present connection because it is followed by the recommendation not that Isfand be ingested, but that it be burned instead. The hadith goes on to conclude:

> He ordained that it (Isfand) be the incense chosen by the prophet. No smoke rises to heaven more quickly than its smoke, which expels devils and averts misfortunes. [8]

Another Islamic Hadith is quoted in stating that:

> An angel is appointed over every leaf and seed of Isfand.

In comparing the use and consumption of Peganum Harmala in these two texts, there seems to be a distinctive change in the methods used for the ingestion of the plant within the Middle Eastern world. The much older Mandaean texts seem to indicate that the plant was once consumed in liquid preparations that later came to be replaced in Islamic time as a plant used only as a sacred incense with spiritual supernatural smoke. While there is evidence connecting the burning of Peganum Harmala with its ingestion, it is insufficient to explain the fact that burning its seeds has been the chief mode of using Peganum Harmala throughout the Islamic period of Iran. When we go on to look to the much older Pre-Islamic Iranian practices regarding the plant, we find that the placing of incense on fires was a dominant motif in ancient Iranian iconography and was of great importance in ancient Iranian rites. The focus of these rites was of fire, for which fragrant fuel was required. Since Sauma/Haoma of ancient Iran was also considered the most sacred of plants it should have also been the most preferred offering within ancient Zoroastrian fire rituals, the religion of pre-Islamic Iran. Today Frankincense and sandal wood are the incenses favored by Zoroastrians but the seeds of Peganum Harmala still have not lost their sacred associations and are also still regularly burned in offerings to open fires by Zoroastrians today. The seeds of Peganum Harmala are also used and found to be present in many other important Zoroastrian rituals such as weddings, funerals, and other important rituals of the Zoroastrian religious calendar year. In the nineteenth century, the seeds of Peganum Harmala were known to have been exported by the Zoroastrians of Iran to those in India for their use in incense as well. So while clear literary evidence exists demonstrating that the plant was once consumed, later literary evidence seems to indicate that the consumption of the plant fell out of favor and was instead replaced with only its sacred association with fire and incense, a mystical religious association and tradition that still largely remains dominant in the region today. [9]

Medical Properties

In attempting to identify evidence for the visionary consumption and pharmacological use of Peganum Harmala in antiquity, we are lead to some of the greatest collections of literary evidence demonstrating its ancient use, and consumption among ancient peoples. From what we can gather from direct literary historical references to the plants use, we find that Peganum Harmala was widely acclaimed throughout the ancient world for its herbal medicinal properties. Evidence for its strong medical values are still well represented even today in modern folk memory and traditional healing practices. Modern

Egyptian studies that have investigated the plant have found that extracts of the plant are markedly fungicidal and antibacterial due mostly to the harmine. This could have made the plant very useful when needed in herbal remedies for fungal or bacterial infections in ancient times. Modern uses of the plant have also reported it as being used as an incense spice, abortificant, narcotic, aphrodisiac, sedative, emetic, soporific, and medical purgative. It is also reported to have been used in India for syphilis and fever. In North Africa, it is known to be used for hysteria, malaria, neuralgia, parkinsonism, prolepses of the womb, rheumatism, colic problems, and even asthma. [10]

In Iranian folk medicine today, Peganum Harmala is recognized as having both healing and psychotropic properties. If one swallows an infusion of the seeds. It is known to bring on a purging and cleansing effect on the body to help rid the body of parasites and illness. An extract made by boiling Peganum Harmala seeds in vinegar is still used for toothaches in many parts of central Iran. In one account, an Iranian doctor reported that his great aunt had related to him this medical folk knowledge of her youth. She told the doctor that once in her childhood she was administered this medication and accidentally swallowed it despite the warnings that doing so would lead to madness. The medication was made of Harmel or Peganum Harmala extract. She recalled that after she swallowed it "she saw everything moving in front of her, and she beheld wells in the earth," though she could understand, she was unable to speak during the entire day, most of which she spent asleep. [11]

Probably the most interesting facts regarding the medical properties of this plant does not come from modern descriptions of modern folk remedies or herbal medical discussions on the plant, but rather from much more ancient medical text that have come down to us from the most ancient of sources. One example of this comes from the written record of the plant found in Greek medical texts which were later translated from the Greek into Arabic many years later. In 78A.D. the Greek Dioscurides wrote about the plant's medical quality, and later in 180 A.D. by the Greek author Galen. This clearly demonstrates that the Peganum Harmala plant's medical properties were well known and widespread throughout the ancient world. Since the plant is not known to traditionally grow in Greece, finding evidence of its ancient use there demonstrates the widespread use of its importance among ancient peoples, particularly in association with healing and the use of its pharmacological properties, outside of its traditional Iranian and Persian homeland. The following ancient Greek text is quoted in saying:

> The seeds expel tapeworms from the intestines; it is used as a colic,
> sciatica and coxalia in a pubic compress. It purifies the chest and
> lungs of viscid mucus and dissipates visceral flatulence. We at the

Marw hospital use the seeds to expel black bile and vareus kinds of mucus by means of diarrhea. It is also of the greatest use in treating epilepsy. [12]

This quote clearly indicates that the purgative properties of Peganum Harmala were well known and used in the ancient world. It also directly demonstrates the knowledge and use of the plant by the ancient Greeks, who it is believed received their knowledge of the plant from the Egyptians some time during or after Greek domination over Egypt. Egypt is the chief location for Peganum harmala to have been first introduced to the Greeks as the Egyptians are known to have had the most extensive history of contact with the plant's eastern origins. Because it is necessary for the seeds of the plant, containing the purgative pharmacological properties, to be consumed in order to obtain their effect, the text is also indicating that the pharmacological properties of the plant were well known and used in ancient times. This indicates that the pharmacological properties of the plant were not only being used medically in the Persian world, but by the time of Greek supremacy the Peganum Harmala plant was also being used and consumed for its medical properties by the Greeks who clearly also had knowledge of its mind altering properties, as they were also consuming it for the chemical properties it contained. This demonstrates that the pharmacological properties of the Peganum Harmala plant were once well known and widespread in the ancient world.

It is believed that many years after the fall of the classical world, later Islamic authors writing about the medical properties of plants may have first derived much of their original information from much earlier Greek medical texts. Much of the later Islamic writings regarding Peganum Harmala are believed to have originated from these earlyer Greek sources, sources that were derived even earlier from Persian and Egyptian physicians. In examining some of the historical accounts relating to the medicinal uses of the Peganum Harmala plant, we find the following quotes which have been noted from Islamic sorces regarding the medical properties of Peganum Harmala:

Galen(180 AD): It is warm and dry in the 3rd degree. It loosens thick Viscid Humors and removes them from the urine.
Masih al Dimashqi(850 AD) The seeds expel tapeworms from the intestines. It is used against colic, Sciatica and Coxalgia in a puplic compress. It purifies the chest and lungs of Viscid mucus and dissipates Visceral Flatulence."
Isa ibn Massa (9th AD) We at the Marew hospital use the seeds to expel black bile and various kinds of Mucus by means of Diarrhea. It is of the greatest use in treating Epilepsy."

> Al Razi(925 AD) Harmal obstructs and breaks up pain. It induces the flow of menstruation and urine. Some Physitiions say an infusion undoes the black bile, purifies the blood and softens the womb. [13]

With evidence now demonstrating the medical use and consumption of Peganum Harmala in antiquity, we are able to see that the uses of the plant's medical properties were once widespread in the ancient world. Evidence now exists that the uses for the plant stretched all the way from Persia throughout Mesopotamia, the Middle East and Egypt all the way into the lands of the Greeks where it is also known to have been prescribed for use and consumption by Greek physicians for its acclaimed medicinal properties. From examining these texts you can see that the pharmacological properties of Peganum Harmala were not only well known in the ancient world, but that the plant was being used and consumed by many ancient peoples over a very large geographic region. This demonstrates that the medical properties of the plant were not only known about and used by ancient Iranian peoples where the plants originated, but that its use eventually extended, spreading the knowledge and medical uses of the plant all the way into the lands of Egypt, Greece, and the eastern Mediterranean. But incense, good luck charms, and herbal medicines were not the only important uses for the plant in ancient times. One of the most surprising pieces of research that has been uncovered in regarding the ancient importance and use of Peganum Harmala, came when a group of scholars studying the pre-Islamic history of Iran and the importance of Peganum Harmala on Middle Eastern history and culture, presented strong and convincing evidence that identified Peganum Harmala/ Syrian Rue with the ancient visionary religious sacrament of pre-Islamic Zoroastrianism, a religion that has had a profound influence on western history, religion, philosophy, and culture.

Zoroastrianism

Zoroastrianism is one of the oldest religions on the earth, and has been immensely influential in the theological and cultural history of the western world through today. Zoroastrianism is known to have originated from a people called the Indo-Iranians. The Indo-Iranians were an ancient people who had their homeland somewhere in Central Asia. About 4,000 years ago they split into two distinct groups. One group, the Indo-Aryans, moved south to the Indus Valley through the fabled Khyber Pass, around 1,500 B.C. while the other became the ancient Iranian peoples. Both preserved a vast body of religious oral literature which only later came to be written down. [14]

The sacred scriptures of these two ancient peoples are known today as the Rig Veda which is the holy book of Hinduism, and the Avesta, the holy book of the Zoroastrians. There are two distinct groups within Zoroastrianism, one that follows mostly (or exclusively) the teachings of the original Gathas, and those who believe that the later traditions are also important. These sacred texts include the original words of their founder Zarathushtra, preserved in a series of five hymns, called the Gathas. The Gathas represent the core text of the religion. The Gathas are abstract sacred poetry, directed towards the worship of the One God, understanding of righteousness and cosmic order, promotion of social justice and individual choice between good and evil. The Gathas have a general and even universal vision. At some later date (most scholars say many centuries later), the remaining parts of the Avesta were written. These deal with laws of ritual practice and the traditions of the faith. The Zoroastrian community is sharply divided between those who would follow exclusively the teachings of the original Gathas, and those who believe that the later traditions are also important and equally divinely inspired. [15]

The religion of Zoroastrianism was founded by a man named Zarathushtra (Zoroaster in Greek). Conservative Zoroastrians assign a date of 6000 B.C. for the founding of the religion, but other followers estimate 600 B.C. Historians and religious scholars generally date his life sometime between 1500 and 1000 B.C. on the basis of the earliest style of writing known in Zoroastrian texts. Although this date cannot be completely verified, due to the lack of knowledge on how far back in antiquity the religion remained an oral tradition, either way, Zoroaster lived in the land of Persia or what is today modern Iran. The oral tradition of the Zoroastrians included stories about God, the creation, the ethical and cosmic conflict between good and evil, the divine judgment, and the end of the world. The tradition would also include the well-known Zoroastrian symbolism of fire, light, and darkness, as well as stories and prayers about the Yazatas, or intermediate spiritual beings, and the Prophet Zarathushtra. These are all elements of what might be called "classic" Zoroastrianism. [16]

The Zoroastrian beliefs included a single God, named by the Zoroastrians as Ahura Mazda. Ahura Mazda's communication between himself and humans is by a number of attributes called Amesha Spentas or Bounteous Immortals. Within the Gathas, the original Zoroastrian sacred text, these Immortals are sometimes described as concepts, and are sometimes personified. One school of thought promotes a cosmic dualism between an all powerful God, Ahura Mazda who is the only deity worthy of being worshipped, and an evil spirit of violence and death, Angra Mainyu, who opposes Ahura Mazda. The resulting cosmic conflict involves the entire universe, including humanity who is required to choose which to follow. Evil, and the Spirit of Evil, will be completely destroyed at the end of time. Dualism will come to an end and Goodness will rule all and be all. Another school of thought perceives the battle between Good and Evil as an ethical dualism, set within the human consciousness. Zoroastrianism's importance to humanity is much greater than its current numbers might suggest. Zoroastrian theology has had a great impact on Judaism, Christianity, and many other later monotheistic religions. Its beliefs can be found in the ideas surrounding God and Satan, heaven and hell, and the dualistic idea of good and evil, a spiritual savior, the future resurrection of the body, and even the final judgment. Zoroaster was one of the first to teach many of these doctrines, doctrines that become familiar articles of faith to much of mankind, through borrowings by Judaism, Christianity, and Islam. [17]

The early history of Iran goes back well beyond the Neolithic period, it only begins to get more interesting some time around 6,000 B.C. when people began to domesticate animals, and plant wheat and barley. The number of settled communities increased, particularly in the eastern Zagros Mountains where early handmade painted pottery appears. Throughout the prehistoric period, from the middle of the sixth millennium B.C. to about 3,000 B.C., painted pottery is a characteristic feature of many sites in Iran. The Persian Empire is the name used to refer to a number of historic dynasties that have ruled the country of Persia (Iran). Persia's earliest known kingdom was the proto-Elamite Empire, followed by the Medes, but it is the Achaemenid Empire that emerged under Cyrus the Great that is usually the earliest period to be called "Persian." It wasn't until the Achaemenid period that the religion of Zoroastrianism spread into Southwestern Iran, where it came to be accepted by the rulers and through them becoming a defining element of Persian culture. The religion was not only accompanied by a formalization of the concepts and divinities of the traditional (Indo-) Iranian pantheon, but also introduced several novel ideas, including that of free will, which is arguably Zoroaster's greatest contribution to religious philosophy. By the 5th century B.C. and under the patronage of the Achaemenid kings, Zoroastrianism came to be the central religion of the Persian state spreading Zoroastrianism into all corners of the Persian Empire. [18]

Zoroastrian Sacrament

The one thing that makes Zoroastrianism so influential to understanding the mystical and visionary practices of the ancient world, particularly in association with Gnosticism and the research of this book, comes from the fact that in both the scriptures of the Zoroastrians, the Avesta, and in the scriptures of the Indians, the holy book of the Rig Veda, there are works in which rituals are preformed and a plant with psychoactive properties is consumed. The plant is called Soma by the Indians and Haoma by the ancient Zoroastrian Iranians. Although some of the descendants of these ancient peoples still perform their rituals, the ancient identity of the sacred plant has been lost and non-psychoactive substitutes are now used in their place. Because of this, much controversy has surrounded the identity of these various psychedelic ritual plants. Many people have suggested over the years that the identity of Soma in the Indian Rig Veda, was the Amanita Mascara Mushroom, but most researchers have now concluded that Soma was actually a changing term for a variety of available psychoactive plants and fungi used for their visionary powers for which the red and white Amanita was just one. While the exact identity of the Soma may still remain somewhat controversial, it is the recent identification of the ancient Zoroastrian ritual entheogen that holds the most profound implications for the further understanding and research of this book. [19]

For a long time, the true identity of the Zoroastrian's ancient visionary ritual plant sacrament was a very hot topic of controversy among many academic circles. The main reason for this was the fact that the modern Zoroastrians no longer use a psychoactive plant in their Haoma rituals and a non-psychoactive substitute has taken its place, in this case, it is the Ephedria plant. While the modern Zoroastrians use the Ephedria plant in the place of Haoma, the ancient books of the Zoroastrians clearly state that a plant with visionary properties was once used, and the Ephedria plant is a stimulant with no psychoactive properties. Because of this, it was believed by early scholars that the original visionary plant used in the original Haoma rituals was replaced at some point in its later history with a non-psychoactive plant with similar physical characteristics. Because of the similar physical characteristics of the Ephedria plant has to Peganum Harmala, the Ephedria plant would have been an ideal candidate to replace the more controversial and psychoactive plant Peganum Harmala in its later years of history and persecution. The most likely time for this change to have occurred is largely believed by scholars today to have been some time during or before the early Islamic era almost 1,400 years ago. The Peganum harmala plant is the most likely candidate for the role of the ancient Zoroastrian psychoactive sacrament Haoma largely due to the fact that it was the only plant known to grow in the region that contains psychoactive properties. In researching evidence for the use and availability of Peganum Harmala in ancient Iranian religious rites, researchers discovered a startling correlation between the use and effects of Peganum Harmala and reports of the older Zoroastrian sacrament as its was described in older Zoroastrian religious literature. Upon further examination they uncovered a relationship between these ancient Zoroastrian writings regarding this plant and similar texts of other outside groups that were known to have described and documented their own use of the Peganum Harmala plant. It is believed by some scholars that these groups known to have used Peganum Harmala may have come to adopt their uses of the plant from the Zoroastrians. It is believed by some that this may have taken place some time in antiquity when the two groups were in contact with one another and when the Zoroastrians were still utilizing Peganum Harmala as a religious sacrament.

Identification of Zoroastrian Haoma

Throughout the Middle East today, Peganum Harmala is belived to hold sacred and mystical spiritual powers. Many researchers believe that this belief in the plant's mystical qualities is actually quite ancient and goes back to before known written history. The plant Peganum Harmala is believed to have originated in and around the mountainous regions of what is known today as the lands of Iran. The ancient Iranians who lived in these lands were known to have believed in a spirit world, a world that was hidden and unseen but just as real if not more so than our own. They also held the belief and the need to obtain information and knowledge from this spiritual world. The fact that Harmaline offers a means to see and experience such a mystical world, suggests that if they had been aware of the pharmacological properties and potential of Peganum Harmala, then it would seem clear that they would have made use of it for these very purposes. In Iranian folk medicine today, Peganum Harmala, or Harmel, is recognized as having psychotropic properties as well as being employed and consumed for many medical purposes. [20]

In Zoroastrian literature, Haoma is presented as if it existed in Iranian culture long before the arrival of Zoroastrianism, for which it then came to be used as a religious sacrament. Some of the greatest evidence demonstrating the ancient use of Peganum Harmala as Haoma the original visionary plant mixture of the ancient Zoroastrian religion comes to us from many surviving literary sources. Since the original identity of Zoroastrian ritual Haoma is unknown and lost by modern Zoroastrians today, and the visionary plants that were once included in these ancient rituals have been replaced by non-psychoactive substitutes. It has only been through modern efforts of contemporary research and scholarship that the identity of this ancient sacrament has finally been able to be rediscovered and emerge back into the modern consciousness. A great deal of evidence that has helped to identify this long lost visionary Zoroastrian sacrament has come from an in-depth investigation of known literary sources that are known to identify the plant being used in these ancient writings and its relationship with Peganum Harmala. By comparing these ancient accounts to ancient Iranian accounts of the plant preparation and its known original effects, modern researchers have for the first time in recent history finally been able to identify and uncover the long lost source of the ancient Iranian and Zoroastrian's most important ritual visionary sacrament, the plant Peganum Harmala.

As it is well documented among researchers today, there are significant differences in the patterns and effects of psychoactive drugs of different chemical compositions. The central noticeable features of the ancient Iranian religion-metaphysical outlook may be regarded as conditioned by the particular effects of the Haoma upon a tradition developed over many generations of Iranian priest in the greater Iranian area. The Pahlavi accounts of Zoroastrian literature show that the original Haoma brought about a condition outwardly resembling sleep in which visions of what is believed to be a spirit existence were seen. They also show that the experience of Haoma was the primary source of revelation in the ancient Iranian religion. Today the visionary experience is no longer sought among Zoroastrian priests or in contemporary Zoroastrian rituals indicating that the substance once used to create these visionary experiences was some how removed or stopped being utilized for the acquisition of knowledge and the visionary experience as was seen in much early traditional Zoroastrian religious rites. Today the Ephedra plant, has replaced this visionary additive. But the Ephedra plant is a characteristic stimulant with no visionary qualities. Because of this fact, scholars are able to demonstrate against the use of the ephedra plant within ancient Zoroastrian rituals, particularly for the creation of visions and the facilitating of an experience of a spirit world as it is seen and documented in ancient Iranian religious literature. In contrast, accounts such as those found in the "Pahlavi" and other pieces of older Zoroastrian literature clearly indicate defining attributes directly associated with the unique pharmacological effects of Peganum Harmala. As we continue to examine these ancient pieces of Zoroastrian and Iranian literature, we continue to find strong and compelling evidence that Peganum Harmala/Syrian Rue was being used by Zoroastrians in pre-Islamic times for obtaining knowledge and inducing visionary experiences of a spiritual existence.

Some of the most extensive research ever conducted on the identification of the original Zoroastrian visionary sacraments was done by David Flattery and Martine Schwartz. Their original research on this topic examined direct evidence for the use of Peganum Harmala in ancient Iranian culture and Middle Eastern history. In their research, they presented evidence identifying the ancient Zoroastrian visionary plant Haoma with the plant Peganum Harmala. The following is just one of many direct literary comparisons taken from their research that have been used in identifying this long lost visionary sacrament. The following is an Islamic quote regarding the Peganum Harmala plant that has been compared to its original source as it is found within Zoroastrian texts regarding Haoma:

Peganum Harmala from text of Islamic Iran

1. Use is instituted by four persons of the lineage of the founders of the religion:
The institution of Isfand including planting collecting and burning is attributed to Mohammad and or Ali and Fatima Mohamed's daughter, for the sake of her sons Husayn and Hasan.

2. Isfand is directed and endorsed by God:
Allah commands Muhammad to use isfand.

3. Brings apotropaic benefits to the house where it is kept:
The devil is made seventy houses
Distant from a house where there is Isfand.

4. Isfand instills courage:
Muhammad's people are made courageous by Isfand. [21]

Haoma in the Zoroastrian Avesta

1. Four persons, Yima, Athwya, Thrita
And Zorathushtras father pourushaspa.
Are listed as Zaraathushtra's
Predecessors in instituting the use of Haoma

2. Azura Mazada created Haoma

3. Haoma should be present in an ahurian house
so the demons flee from it.

Let contamicartion, as soon as it is manifested,
Vanish from the house as soon as one bring fourth... Haoma

4. Haoma gives courage.
Haoma I invoke thee for courage and the victory
for my body and for strength that brings salvation to many. [22]

In comparing the two texts it is clear that the two texts share many striking similarities. The Islamic text describes the association and use of the Peganum harmala with the founding individuals of Islam. The Zoroastrian text likewise lists the use and institution of Haoma with the founding members of the Zoroastrian religion. The Islamic text states that Peganum Harmala was directed and endorsed by God. The Zoroastrian text also marks the plant as sacred stating that God, known in Zoroastrianism as Azura Mazada, created Haoma. The Zoroastrian text also states that demons flee from the house where Haoma is kept. This same important statement is found stated in the Islamic text regarding Isfand/ Peganum Harmala, where the Islamic text states, "Isfand brings apotropaic benefits to the house were it is kept, and the devil is made seventy houses distant from a house where there is Isfand. In the final literary comparison between these two text we find that the Islamic text states that "Isfand instills courage, and Muhammad's people are made courageous by Isfand." This is again also related in the ancient Zoroastrian statement regarding Haoma. "Haoma gives courage, Haoma I invoke thee for courage and the victory for my body and for strength that brings salvation to many." By comparing these two texts it becomes clear that the ancient visionary ritual sacrament of Zoroastrianism, Hoama, is the same botanical substance later used and incorporated into Islam, the plant Peganum Harmala.

In examining Zoroastrian text further regarding Haoma, we find that they go on to elaborate on the experience to which Hoama intoxication is like. When these statements are related to the known effects of Peganum harmala, a distinct similarity between the effects is seen. The following are limited Zoroastrian passage from *Yasna the Hom Yasht*:

Zoroastrian *Avestan Hom Yasht:*

I ask thee, O golden one
Intoxication, power, victory, health
healing ,success, increase strength,
of the whole body.

Thou Haoma makest rich in men, more
Spenta- and more insightful whomever
apportions thee combine with Gav

Thee I invoke for courage and for victory for
courage and for victory for my body and for
 strength that brings salvation to many

O haoma , Give me healing by which thou art a healer,
 O Haoma give me thy victoriusness,
by which though art a victory.

From other Zoreastrin text

I carry on me the victoreus Haoma.
I carry on me the protector as the good thing.
I carry on me the protector of the body.

Haoma is the chief of medical Herbs [23]

The Avesta Haoma further relates:

O, yellowish one, I call down thy intoxication.
 Ideade all other intoxications are accompanied
by Violence of the bloody club, But the intoxication
of the Haoma is accompanied by Bliss- brighting Rightness.
 The intoxication of haoma geos lightly.

May thy intoxications, besetting me at their own
 impulse, not move me about as a cow's trembling.
May thy intoxication come forth clearly.
May thy arrive bringing straightness of mind.
To thee,Haoma, righteous, promoting rightness,
do I give this body, which seems to me well formed.

May thee thyself, and may these thy
Intoxications come forth to me clearly.
 May thy intoxication come forth brightly.
May thy intoxications move lightly.

To thee, Haoma righteous, driving forth truth,
Do I give this body which seems to me well-formed.
for the Active intoxication of Haoma, for the well
 being, for rightness May thou give me, righteous,
full of light, and having every comfort.

(Translation by M. Schwartz [24]

In the above Zoroastrian texts Haoma is distinguished with many characteristics that are only attributed to Paganum Harmala. An example of this is found when the text states, "May thy intoxications, besetting me at there own impulse, not move me about as a cow's trembling." This is a particular characteristic of the Peganum Harmala plants effects on cattle. This effect is not created when cattle eat leafs of the ephedra plant, which is the other leading candidate for Haoma identification. This indicates against the use of ephedra within this text. Because of Peganum Harmala effects on cattle, the plant is also widely considered a noxious weed. This noxious effect on livestock makes the plant largely avoided by grazing animals. The Peganum Harmala plant is also known to take on a yellowish color during much of the year, after it spring growth has stopped. This further shows a relationship with the plant being described in the text (a yellowish moutian plant). The intoxication of Peganum harmala's roots and seeds which contain the MAO inhibitors also brings on an effect of visual distortion and brightness of color, an atribut the text also clearly describes. Another more unique element that can be found associated with the effects of Peganum harmala is the manifestation of inner thoughts emerging into the mind of the individual consuming it. Many times these inner thoughts take on the form of good teachings or wisdom coming into the drinker's mind. This unique characteristic of mild visionary Gnosis is also characteristic of the Ayahuasca vine, a plant also known to contain the same pharmacological properties. In examining these texts in detail it seems clear that the author of the text is clearly describing a yellowish golden colored mountain plant with visual intoxication abilities that he/she is taking for receiving knowledge and for a clear alteration in consciousness.

In another Zoroastrian text we evidence of the plants healing attributes. The following is the *Hom Yasht* from the Zoroastrian Avestan:

143

Avestan " Hom Yasht"

O golden haoma, loose thy weapons
 for protection for the body of the
righteous against the yellow loathsome poison
 emitting serpent, against the evil doing,
 bloody, injurious murderous ones,
against the lying mortal sastars..
 against the truth mocker. against the sorcerus witch.

I ask this , that I may overcome all the
enmity of the enemies , demons and men
of bad spirits, pairika spirits, of sathras,
of Kavis and karapans of two legged scoundrels ,
 of two leged truth mockers, of four leged wolves,
 and of host having a broad frunt, roaring, scampering.

O haoma throw aside the plot of that
one who curses me, throw aside the
 various plats of him who stands as my curser.

Even the smallest Haoma preparation,
the smallest Haoma laudation,
the smallest Haoma potation,
 serves to smite a thousand demons.
 Let the contamination vasnish from
this house as soon as it is created,
as soon as it indeade one brings forth and
praises the exelent healing of him who confers healing,
Haoma (yasna 10.6-7)[25]

The texts indicate that the plant is a sacred healer and removes, purges, and protects against evil spirits and demons. This not only indicates the therapeutic healing property of the plants, but also its relationship to more spiritual supernatural applications, for which its psychoactive properties could also have once been used. All of these have provided scholars with evidence supporting the identity of Haoma with Peganum Harmala and its relationship to the ancient Zoroastrian religion.

Examining Zoroastrian texts about Haoma have allowed scholars to gain insight into its identity. When these texts are examined with other surviving texts regarding the plant, such as those we find in Mandaean writings, there are many other links that further support Haoma's connection to Peganum Harmala and its ancient use as a phychoactive purgative. In studying the historical importance of Peganum Harmala, scholars have uncovered many pieces of evidence identifying the sacred use and importance of the plant from many different historical and literary sources, all indicating a long history of use and veneration of the plant and its effects that span many thousands of years, possibly even long before known written history. Some of the main summarizing arguments for the identity and use of Peganum Harmala in ancient Iranian culture and religion are as follows:

1. Geographical correspondence: Haoma must have been widely available to many Indo-Iranian groups over large parts of the Iranian area, and was not a localized or rare species. No known psychotropic plant is as abundant and conspicuous as a source of psychoactive drugs over the whole Iranian area as Peganum Harmala, and Peganum Harmala has been long known in Iran to have psychoactive properties. [26]

2. Pharmacological Correspondence: The pharmacological suitability of the drug Harmel for use as Haoma is demonstrated by the parallel roles played in ancient Iranian rites by Haoma and those seen in certain South American cultures who use the vine Banisteriopsis cappi, or Ayahusca, a plant also known for containing the same psychoactive MAO inhibitory compounds. In both cases: (1) the intoxicating use of the plant is chiefly used in ceremony's supervised by trained specialists, (2) Both groups use the plant and revere it for its strong medical properties, (3) In both groups, the effects of the drug are valued for revealing a simultaneous, intangible spirit world interpreted as being a higher reality, (4) and in both groups the experience of visions was central to the beliefs of their religious institution, (5) in both groups the plant extract is the basis of mixtures of other plants, substances, or psychoactive narcotic materials. [27]

3. Literary Correspondence: Within the ancient Iranian religion, the name "Haoma" was apparently restricted to ritual context and was not the common name for the plant. In pre-Islamic Avestan and Pahlavi texts regarding Haoma, the plant is invoked in verses which: Attribute the origins of the use of Haoma to the founding figure of Zoroastrianism. The text goes on to assert that:

> Haoma brings healing, victory, salvation and protection
> Haoma originated in the mountains
> Haoma promotes child birth and is a aphrodisiac
> Haoma is the chief of all drugs

In post-Islamic Persian, Mandaean, and Turkish texts, Peganum Harmala is invoked in verses which also:

> Attribute the origins of Peganum Harmala to the founding figure of Shi'a Islam.
> Assert that Peganum Harmala brings healing, victory, salvation and protection
> Peganum Harmala originated in the mountains
> Peganum Harmala promotes child birth and is an aphrodisiac
> Peganum Harmala is the chief of all drugs ect... [28]

These all indicate the same corresponding relationships as those associated with Peganum Harmala. All of these relationships indicate that the pharmacological properties of the Peganum Harmala plant were well known and utilized throughout the ancient Iranian culture and religion long before the arrival of Islamic authors who clearly borrowed references to the plant from their original usage in older Iranian and Zoroastrian literature. In the ancient times of pre-Islamic Iran, the chief non priestly use for Haoma was as an apotropaic, that is, it was the primary substance utilized to keep away evil and to purge away illness. Haoma, as it was known in traditional Zoroastrian texts was seen as being used apotropically and burned as incense for these protective spiritual purposes. Haoma was therefore the chief incense plant during the Avestian times. Consequently, with Peganum Harmala in modern Iran, the plant is also the chief apotropaic plant of Iran today and this role has been clearly demonstrated to be pre-Islamic. Furthermore, Peganum Harmala is the most widely used native incense plant in Iran and is the only one containing known psychoactive drugs. [29]

Fundamentally the purpose of Haoma intoxication in ancient Iran was to gain knowledge from visions which could be obtained from the plant. Belief in the validity of such visions disappeared from Iran. Visions are no longer sought from rituals representing the use of Haoma and the original plant is therefore no longer consumed in them. In examining recent evidence for the psychoactive spiritual consumption of the plant today, there is almost none known. One of the most recent accounts for the use and consumption of the plant in ritual comes from a sixteenth century account written about the festival of Isfandagan. It is said that the festival occurs on the fifth day of the month of Isfadarmud or the 12th month of the year. This would be the 5th of December to you and I, also 30 days before the new year. It was written that:

> If any plant was to be consumed on Isfandagan it would be isfand
>
> Anjavi Shirazi (1973:1,53)

Another example demonstrating the plant sacred spiritual utilization today comes from an anthropologist in Morocco, Africa where the plant is also known to grow abundantly and where researchers have found that during an exorcism in Morocco, the priest would burn the seeds of Peganum Harmala in a tent. The smoke of burning Peganum Harmala seeds would fill the tent with harmel vapor during the exorcism until the demons are heard to cry out and depart from the individual. This remarkable account was first recorded in 1937 by anthropologist Vonderheyden (1937: 459). [30]

As you can see, vestiges of the distinction of Harmel as a sacred plant exist among all Iranian peoples. This unique distinction could have only come about in response to some unique properties of this plant and only if such properties were exploited and valued. Peganum Harmala/Syrian Rue is a common place weed without significant economic value as compared with other Iranian plants. Peganum harmala is the only Iranian plant to contain the visionary drugs Harmaline and Harmine. It is clear that the effects of this drug in ancient Iran could only have been interpreted in religious terms if the plant was in fact used in ancient times for its visionary and intoxicating effects. Because of this, it is to be expected that some traces of its original sacred association and use should still exist in the modern day, evidence that is clearly represented in data of ancient Iranian and surrounding Semitic cultures, evidence which as I have demonstrated is in fact the case.

Zoroastrian Extraction of Peganum Harmala

So how did the use of Peganum Harmala come to disappear from original Zoroastrian rituals and what evidence is there to demonstrate how this would have occurred? Well, one of the major factors in considering the disappearance of Peganum Harmala use within Zoroastrianism comes from the fact that because psychoactive plants are usually credited with supernatural powers, they also in many cultures closely associated with magic and occults powers or manipulation. The following Zoroastrian text indicates that the original ceremonies taking place within ancient Iranian rituals utilizing Peganum Harmala must have once been an ordeal for the priest who performed the drinking of the plant with water and called it "Zaoaras." In particular, Yasna 11 consists of an elaborate warning that woeful consequences will befall anyone who attempts to resist the effects of the drug. Also a clear underlying fear or warning against the magical manipulation of the plant and its effects for use in sorcery. The text is understood as a promise to not use Haoma for sorcery and instead use it only for the good. It also shows how the person drinking the plant is following Zoroaster, the great prophet and is surrendering his body to the Haoma and thus showing himself to be a follower of the truth and of goodness:

> O Amesa spentas, Vision of Mazda worship,
> good male, Good Females.Zaoras!
> Whoever among these Mazda-Worshipers here,
> calling himself a Mazda worshipper, an adherent
> of the truth, ruins the world with witchcraft,
> O waters,plants and Zaooras, make him known!
> Whoever of these Mazda worshipers of full age,
> invoke diligently, is not ready to recite these words
> will get the punishment for sorcery [31]

In the Avesta, the term ZaoOra means "that which is poured" hence, liquid offering. We have just seen from this part of the text that the liquid offering held powerful spiritual powers in the eyes of the drinkers and any use of this power other than for good could get one in punishment for sorcery. This indicates a clear understanding of the plant's psychoactive potential and its ability to contain magical properties. This remarkable fact is also reflected in the use of the Ayahuasca vine by shamans in the Amazon. For the same chemical properties that are found in the Ayahuasca vine are also found in the seeds and roots of the Peganum Harmala plant. It is also interesting to point out that the native shamans who drink it, do not just drink it for its healing and spiritual properties, but rather the vine is consumed for its visionary and magical properties it contains. For it is well known throughout the Amazon area that the vine is not only a strong healing herb but that it also has a strong connection with use in Amazonian magic and sorcery primarily due to its innate visionary properties. [32]

In examining the Zoroastrian tradition further, we find that the priest must drink the Haoma mixture under the scrutiny of the other priest as a test, and with all the spirits summoned as witnesses. This would validate not only its visionary properties but also the purity and authority of the priesthood. This use of Haoma as a test must have been effective in maintaining fidelity among ancient Iranian priests, all of whom must periodically assume the role of Zaotar, while at other times they must prepare the extract to be consumed by their followers. The willing participants to take the role of zaotor would be one who would demonstrate his preparedness to expose his soul to judgment, by the spirits and show his confidence to other priests. The text of "Arda Wiraz Namag" shows that the drug was not taken casually to induce visions, but was reserved for accessions when there was genuine need to obtain information and knowledge from the spirit world. In the usual conduct of ceremony there may have been little or no need to induce visions. Thus, virtually from the inception of the ceremony, the visionary drink was an institution; the extract administered in it would frequently not have needed to be the visionary additive Peganum Harmala used in the original Haoma rites, or even at its full potency. In later years during the Muslim era when the Zoroastrians were most greatly persecuted, the fact that the drinking of a plant mixture that could have been so closely associated with magical manipulation of the supernatural could have given very good reason for the consumption of the Peganum Harmala plant to have been used more and more infrequent even possibly being completely removed altogether. Only to be replaced in the rituals by more suitable plants that did not bring on such fear of magical manipulation and persecution. [33]

The Haoma ceremonies have continued throughout the history of the Zoroastrians and have remained to be the chief activity by which priests obtain their livelihood and maintain their exclusive claim to their livelihood, and not as a means of obtaining visions. This being said, I can now give another large reason for the disappearance of Peganum Harmala in ancient Zoroastrian rituals. During the later part of their history another big change took place. It was the new social structure of the priesthood. Since the ranks of the priesthood by both Iranian and Indian Zoroastrians came only in later centuries to be decided by the social process (chiefly kingship) rather than by the traditional ritual test, the need for Peganum Harmala as a magical test would have vanished. Because its consumption in rituals became associated with the occult, all need to obtain visions would have vanished.

Once this political change from traditional visionary test to assigned kingship took place, a new order of exclusive kingship had occurred. With this new exclusive kingship, it would have been essential that the new Zoroastrian priests be careful and avoid putting their fellow colleagues to the test; to hand a colleague an extract that so much tasted of Peganum Harmala /Syrian Rue could imply doubts concerning his fitness as leader and would risk insulting him. Increased political pressure coupled with this strange new courtesy has thus disallowed even a vestigial presence of Peganum Harmala to be drunk as an extract drink in any of these once prevalent visionary rituals. With the plant no longer being used by the priesthood, it would have soon enough made its way down to the common people. Because the rituals needed to go on for the livelihood of the priest, similar non visionary alternatives would have been essential for the survival of the Haoma ceremonies. Thus the ceremonies that were originally structured in controlling the intoxication of Haoma would have developed into independent rituals excluding their once visionary element, so that no amount of the original visionary plant was consumed. [34]

Sacred Persistence of Peganum Harmala use today

As you have seen, the Peganum Harmala plant has demonstrated a long history of use and veneration throughout Iranian and Middle Eastern history. The plant has been used both medicinally and as a ritual sacrament throughout antiquity. While the sacred ritual consumption of the plant may have ended in the region, the sacred veneration and importance of the plants sacred spiritual qualities has persisted and is still being well maintained and represented to this very day. While the plant may no longer be drank to create visionary experiences in modern Islam or Zoroastrianism, its connection with ancient sacred, mystical, and spiritual practices is still very strong throughout the modern Islamic world. Throughout the area once covered by the Persian Empire, the Peganum Harmala plant and its seeds are burned on charcoal to rid children of the "Evil Eye." This is a modern ritual that has survived from the most ancient times, and as I have already demonstrated, is a practice that has originated from within the earliest history of the Iranian culture. In the rites using the burning of the seeds of the Peganum Harmala plant a short verse is recited as the smoke is circled around the child's head. Isfand, as it called, is also used to bring blessings after one has performed a sorrowful rite, such as the attending of a funeral, again further indicating the seeds close relationship to spiritual protection, and the spirit world. [35]

Isfand/Peganum Harmala seeds are dropped on the red-hot charcoal. As this is done they make a popping sound and give off a great deal of fragrant smoke. A five-line rhyming spell or verse is chanted and the smoke is swirled around the heads of children in a circular pattern to protect them from evil. "To Isfand" seems to be the usual verb describing the rite. The rite consists of an invocatory prayer to a deceased but historical king of Persia known as Naqshband, this is made while burning Isfand seeds. The word Isfand or Aspand is also known to refer to a class of Zoroastrian Archangels. In considering the Zoroastrian origins of this rite both sets of my informants, from two nations, explained to me that Naqshband was not a Muslim rite but a Zoroastrian one and that despite the Muslim conquest of Persia and outlying areas, the spirit of Naqshband is still called upon to destroy the Evil Eye also known as "Bla Band." Here is the spell-prayer, as written out in phonetic Dari by a man from Afghanistan: [36]

Aspand bla band
Barakati Shah Naqshband
Jashmi heach jashmi khaish
Jashmi dost wa dooshmani bad andish
Be sosa der hamin atashi taze.

This is its English translation:

This is Isfand, it banishes the <u>Evil Eye</u>
The blessing of King Naqshband
Eye of nothing, Eye of relatives
Eye of friends, Eye of enemies
Whoever is bad should burn in this glowing fire. [37]

In the rite they ask for a blessing. As an Old Iranian woman said: "The blessing we ask for is that of King Naqshband because he was the one who taught the use of Isfand/Aspand. He obtained this knowledge from the angels of heaven. He was a holy man. The use of fire is Zoroastrian, not Muslim. It is a very old rite. It is used to remove the Evil Eye from the children, and it is good for anyone. You can Isfand/Aspand yourself or have someone do it for you. This prayer is the blessing of Shah Naqshband, an ancient King who was a follower of Zarathustra. Shah Naqshband got this blessing from the Archangels and taught it to our people. It is very effective when you must deal with bad people or sorrowful things. It removes the Evil Eye and it is a blessing to the spirit. It lightens your burdens and it is very good to Aspand." The word Aspand relates to the Tajik / Dari / Farsi / Persian word for Archangel, also known as Amesha Spenta or Amahraspand. The Archangels or Amahraspandan are listed as the following: [38]

Vohu Mano (Vohuman, Good Mind)
   Presides over cattle.
   Asha Vahishta (Ardwahisht, Highest Asha)
the Amahraspand presiding over Asha and fire.
   Khshathra Vairya (Shahrewar, 'Desirable Dominion')
the Amahraspand presiding over metals.
   Spenta Armaiti (Spandarmad, 'Holy Devotion')
the Amahraspand presiding over the earth.
   Haurvatat (Hordad, 'Perfection or Health')
Presides over water. [39]

There are further notes describing these guardian angels (Fravashis or Frohars) who "manifest the energy of God," (Yazads, called Yezidi by some), these guardian angels also including the well known Mithra and Ahriman. The archangels of Zoroastrian belief are generally said by scholars to have been created during Zoroaster's incorporation of regional Iranian gods and goddesses. These gods and goddesses were incorparated into the Zoreastrian tradition and have roots all the way back to the prehistoric period. Thus the name Spenta Armaiti or Spandermat (also spelled Spandermad or Spendarmaz) was an earth-mother goddess whose sacred herb was Peganum Harmala also known as Espand/ Isfand. In the ancient Zoroastrian calendar, the month of Esfand (beginning around February 19) marked the feast of "Spendarmat," which was dedicated to the female archangel of earthly and motherly protection, "Spenta Armaiti," whose name signifies "Holy Devotion," or "Holy Love." Among modern Iranians, this festival, known as the Esfandgan Feast, is still held on Spandarmaz day in the month Esfand, the last month of the Iranian calendar. It is a celebration of womankind, and particularly commemorates the care, kindness, and self-sacrifices of motherhood. The connections between the protective pre-Zoroastrian goddess "Spandermat," the Zoroastrian female archangel "Spenta Armaiti," and the month of "Esfand," the contemporary festival of "Esfandgan", and the protective visionary herb Peganum Harmala/ Isfand/Espand which is used by mothers in Iran to safeguard and purify their children, are clear, even to Muslims living in formal Zoroastrian territories. It is clear to them that a sacred and important connection exists between these elements and traditions, elements that all relate these ancient figures, festivals, and rites to one another today. All the Afghani, Iranian, and Tajik people who use Peganum harmala/Aspand/Isfand today, and all assert to the sacred character and very ancient nature of this rite. [40]

The sacred use of Peganum Harmala outside Zoroastrian tradition today demonstrates in favor of the sacred mystical importance of the plant in ancient Zoroastrian ritual and religion. It also demonstrates the widespread importance of the plant and its sacred associations in the world today. Due to the clear references made by modern Muslims, who have associated Peganum Harmala with pre-Islamic Zoroastrian mystical religious traditions, it is now safe to say that the modern uses and importance of Peganum harmala clearly demonstrate pre-Islamic traditions rooted in much older Persian and Zoroastrian practices. With the modern spiritual veneration and importance of the plant emerging from the much older practices that once surrounded it, it has become clear that the use of this plant spans many thousands of years of history, back to a time were it was once consumed and revered for its ability to bring someone into contact with spiritual realities, the obtaining of secret inner knowledge, and visionary experiences of a divine world.

Ch 8

Ayahuasca Analogs in Antiquity

I was baptized in the name of the divine Autogenes by those powers which are upon living waters… I became a holy angel… the name in which they wash is a word of the water…. I was baptized again by each of these powers. The four exist because they are expressions of truth and knowledge. They exist, although they do not belong to Protophanes but to the mother, for she is a thought of the perfect mind of the light, so that immortal souls might receive knowledge for themselves.

(Zostrianos)

As I have already related, in the Amazon the Ayahuasca brew is made with a mixture of two plants, the Banisteriopsis Caapi vine containing the MAO inhibitors and various other leafy plants such as Psychotria Viridis known to contain DMT. The Pharmacological agents that have been identified in the Ayahuasca brew can be imitated in other plants with similar active chemical ingredients (Harmaline/harmine, DMT/5MeO-DMT). Traditional combinations of these plants with the same chemical ingredients are typically known today as Ayahuasca Analogs. Throughout Egypt, Israel, the Sinai Peninsula, and the greater Middle East area grow two plants containing the same two psychoactive molecules found in the plants from which the powerful entheogenic visionary Amazonian brew Ayahuasca is made. The two plants that contain these entheogenic compounds are the bushy plant Peganum Harmala and various species of Acacia trees containing DMT. [1]

In modern Freemasonry, the Acacia tree is seen as one of the most important symbols of the ancient world, used to symbolize and represent the purity of the eternal soul. It is a tradition that the group says it has perpetuated from the most ancient of times, a tradition that they say was handed down to them from the last of the ancient Egyptian mystery schools and philosophers of the classical age. For it was from the last of these Egyptian mystery traditions that many of the Freemasonry ideas were first born. The Acacia tree was considered especially sacred to the ancient Egyptians particularly in late classical times, and of all the trees represented in ancient Egyptian history and culture, none were more important and sacred than the Acacia tree, Acacia Nilotica. The Acacia tree, Acacia Nilotica is known to have a very sweet smell when in full bloom. The leaves are soft green and it bears beautiful yellow flowers. The Acacia Nilotica was also a very familiar sight in Upper Egypt during antiquity as they still are today. The Acacia has a long history of medical and spiritual importance throughout ancient Egyptian culture, and was one of the Egyptian's most important mythological plants. In Egyptian mythology, the first gods were said to have been born under the Acacia tree of the goddess Saosis, also identified with Hathor in later Hellenistic times. Horus, the son of Osiris, was said to have been born and emerged from the Acacia tree. The ancient Egyptians also viewed the Acacia tree as the most sacred plant to their god of vegetation, spiritual rebirth, and the underworld: the god man Osiris. As stated earlier, the ancient Egyptians believed that the spirit of Osiris lived within the Acacia tree and it was the symbolic relationship between the Acacia tree and the Egyptian God Osiris that made the Acacia tree one of the most revered plants in all of ancient Egypt. [2]

But the sacred importance of the Acacia goes far beyond its mythical importance in ancient Egypt. In fact, the spiritual importance of the Acacia tree, particularly the species known for containing DMT such as the Acacia Nilotica, are found to be very widespread throughout Egypt and the Middle East. One of the most prominent places we find the sacred veneration of these acacias outside the culture of ancient Egypt is in the religious tradition of Judaism. In the books of Moses, the Acacia tree went by the name *Shittah* or *Sunt*. Acacia Albida, Acacia Tortilis, Acacia Iraqensis and Acacia Niloticia can all be found in the Sinai desert and the Jordan valley. The Acacia tree was very important to the early Hebrew, when we look in Exodus chapter 25, verse 10 we find that the Hebrews construction of the holy temple and the sacred Ark of the Covenant, were made out of Gold and Acacia wood. In the Torah the sacred book of the Jews, *Shittah* or acacia wood was considered sacred by God and was the only wood to be used in the building of the sacred temple, the temple artifacts, and the sacred Ark of the Covenant where God and the Ten Commandments were said to rest. Acacia Nilotica and Acacia Seyal, from which the Ark of the Covenant was made, are plants for which DMT is now known exist in the leaves, a remarkable coincidence considering the sacred nature of these same types of Acacia trees in ancient Jewish mysticism. [3]

The sacred veneration of the Acacia is not limited to Egyptian mythology or Jewish history. In fact, the Acacia tree is known to be venerated throughout many regions of the Middle East. Despite the geographical distance and cultural separation from Egypt or the lands of Israel, the Acacia tree was widely venerated as a sacred plant throughout many regions of the Middle Eastern world. In Mecca during the pre-Islamic times there was a female goddess known as Al Uzza. She was seen as a mother goddess in pre-Islamic times and seen in a very similar way to how the Egyptian mother goddess Isis or the European Gaia were seen in these other parts of the world. Most surprising is that the sacred tree of this ancient pre-Islamic mother goddess was none other than, Acacia Nilotica, the same type of acacia that was also venerated by the Egyptians and the Jews. In ancient times it was believed that the spirit of the goddess actually resided inside of the tree, an idea very similar to the Egyptian belief regarding the spirit of Osiris who was also believed to have resided inside the same sacred tree, the Acacia Nilotica. The wood of the tree was widely believed at the time, as it still is in many places today, to be a sacred wood and long before the arrival of Islam, it was the wood of this sacred tree that all idols of the Goddess Al Uzza were made from. [4]

In the ancient world the Acacia tree was most widely used not for its mythical importance but for its medical properties. Among the Egyptians, Acacia products in particular were most useful to ancient Egyptian physicians for healing where its resins were collected and used to heal wounds, and its strong wood was used for the setting of broken bones. Acacia leaves were applied in treatments of the eyes, wounds, and skin diseases. The seeds were employed for treating ailments of the fingers and toes. The sap and bark of the tree is also known to yield tannin acid, which the Egyptians used to heal burns. Acacia Nilotica also has large pods with seeds that are very bean-like and are also very nutritious. The livestock of the ancient Egyptians were said to have been fattened on these large seeds and the many pods that the tree produced. [5]

The tree's sap was also used quite predominantly throughout ancient times. The sap of the Acacia is described as either milky or reddish, and was used as the source of Gum Acacia, or Gum Arabic which is still used even today. This edible gum has a long history of use in food, medicine, incense, paints, and even glues, uses that go back many thousands of years. Plantations of these Acacia Nilotica trees could be found throughout Egypt in antiquity. The Acacia was one of the most widely known and widely used plants in the ancient Egyptian world. Different types of Acacia's were also used for different purposes. The Masai of Africa are intoxicated by the bark and root decoction of another type of acacia which they say not only imparts courage but is also used as an aphrodisiac, and with the root said to cure impotence. Certain

Acacias are also used as a nerve stimulant in other parts of Africa. In ancient Egyptian medicine, Acacia parts were used to help elevate stomach pains. The ancient Egyptians used an extract of its sap which could be added to water to help take away stomach cramps and alleviate abdominal pain. The Egyptians were also known to have taken Acacia tree parts and made them into a paste and put them on wounds or open sores to aid in the healing process. In examining this claim, it has recently been discovered that these same types of Acacia species that were popularly used among the ancient Egyptians for healing burns, wounds, and open sores are now known to have antibacterial qualities, and if parts of the plant were put on a cut or open wound, it would have helped to prevent infection and further aid in the healing process just as the ancient Egyptians claimed. [6]

Because of the importance of the Acacia trees' medical properties, the Acacia tree would have been an ideal candidate for mixing with other important medical plants that the Egyptians would have come into contact with in later parts of their history, such as Peganum Harmala. In the dry semi-arid landscape of the Middle East and Egypt, Acacia trees thrive in regions that many other plants do not, making them a relatively common sight throughout Egypt and the Middle East. It also makes them some of the most readily available medical plants available to people in these arid regions for use in herbal medicines, mixtures, and preparations. While the Acacia tree was known to be very abundant in ancient Egypt, as they still are today, Acacia trees are found in more limited numbers throughout the harsh deserts of the Sinai and Arabia. Various species of Acacias can be found throughout the world and are famous for their strong toleration to drought and are known to thrive where many other trees do not. They can live in rainforests as well as some of the driest areas on earth with some of the largest distributions of Acacia species throughout Africa, Egypt, the Sinai Peninsula, and in more limited numbers throughout the greater Middle East. In examining the many medical and material uses of the Acacia tree, we are lead to examine some of it most well known uses in ancient times. The following is a list of some of the many potential uses of the Acacia tree as it is known today:

Forage / Fodder: Leaves, tender pods, and shoots used as forage for goats, sheep, and camels. Seeds are also a valuable cattle food. Pods contain 12-15% crude protein also very rich in minerals.

Land Rehabilitation: Used on degraded saline/alkaline soils as well as in flooded areas.

Agro-forestry: Makes an ideal windbreak, shade cover for hot dry climates, and a good fixed source of nitrogen.

Tannins: Bark has high levels of tannin (12-20% for subspecies *indica*) used for tanning and dyeing leathers. Pods of subspecies *nilotica* used for tanning.

Gum Arabic: Tapped for gum Arabic by removing bark. Used in making candles, inks, matches, glues, and paints.

Medicinal Use: Extract of the fruit, rich in tannin (18-23%) has medicinal use as a powerful astringent, molluscicide, and algicide. The gum is also used in many herbal remedies and medicines.

Timber / Wood: Hard, tough wood, resistant to termites and water. Popular for railroad, tool handles, carts, oars, posts, and buildings. It is also a very attractive wood good for carving, turnery, and boatbuilding.

Firewood / Charcoal: Excellent firewood and charcoal also used today as a source of fuel for river steamers and boilers in some small industries.

Potential Psychoactive Additive: More recently it has been found by ethnobotanists that certain types of Acacia species contain relatively large amounts of the powerful psychoactive neural transmitter DMT in their leaf tissues. While the DMT is not able to be orally activated on its own, its visionary properties could be utilized if mixed and consumed with a MAO inhibitor source such as can be found in the Banisteriopsis caapi vine of South America or the Peganum Harmala plant of Egypt, Africa, and the Middle East. If an herbal libation with a botanical MAO inhibitor additive was mixed and consumed with these DMT Acacia tree parts, then a powerful psychoactive entheogen would be produced.

Visionary and Narcotic Plants of Ancient Egypt

The use of plants was very important in ancient medicine and the Egyptians are regarded as having maintained some of the most successful advances in ancient medicine and herbal healing. The knowledge of plants and the many medical properties they contain was most likely first discovered by early humans over time and through trial and error. Through this process, a small base of knowledge was acquired and was expanded over generations. While we know that the earliest human populations used plants for their medical properties from the earliest periods of human history, the earliest recorded physician in the world is credited within the civilization of ancient Egypt. The ancient Egyptian word for doctor is *swnw*. Egyptian swnw were known to have made extensive use of herbs and plants for their many healing purposes, matter of fact, herbs played a major role in ancient Egyptian medicine of the time. In addition to the flora found in the lush native Egypt, ancient Egyptians also imported certain species from abroad. Our knowledge of the treatment regimes of ancient Egypt comes to us from information contained in seven papyrus scrolls, all of which were written around 1700 B.C.; but are believed to be copies of even much older texts. The plant medicines mentioned in the Ebers papyrus for instance, include opium, mandrake, myrrh, frankincense, fennel, cassia, sienna, thyme, henna, juniper, aloe, garlic, linseed and caster oil among many others. [7]

From studying Egyptian healing and magical practices, we know that the Egyptians made uses of many types of plants for their medical, healing, and sacred properties. The surviving medical scrolls of the Egyptians are known to contain the names of hundreds of herbal preparations, medicines, and pathological conditions. In particular, the Ebers Papyrus contains the most information on drug remedies and names over 900 specific drugs. Many of these drugs have been identified based on non-medical papyrus, drawings, analogy with function, and in a few cases, based on identification of ruminants found in labeled jars; however, the bulk of drugs of vegetable origin in particular, remain to be identified. Matter of fact, out of the 160 plant products described in the medical papyruses of the Egyptians, we have unfortunately only identified about 20% of the Egyptians' plant-based drugs. This shocking and unfortunate fact only sets to clearly demonstrate the current scholarly inadequacy at understanding the full scope of ancient Egyptian botanical knowledge, understanding, and use. [8]

In the past, many Egyptologists have claimed that there was no supporting evidence for the ritual or narcotic use of visionary plants in ancient Egyptian culture or religion, but over the years, Egyptologists and historians have gained a much greater insight into the ancient Egyptian world. What many modern Egyptologists are now starting to understand is that the ancient Egyptians had a much greater understanding of the various properties of the plants around them than what has been previously understood or what we have previously given them credit for in the past. The fact is that the sacred imagery of plants is very well represented in ancient Egypt. The most common Narcotic plant represented throughout ancient Egyptian art is the plant Nymphaea Caerulea also known today as the Egyptian blue water lily. This plant is found with a very high frequency in Egyptian art and seems to clearly be expressing the sacredness of this Narcotic water flower. The flower has been represented in sacred art throughout all of Egypt and remains of this narcotic water flower have even been found buried in the tombs of the great Pharaohs. The best representation of this comes from the tomb of the famous pharaoh Tutankomon. When this tomb was uncovered, remains of this blue narcotic lily were found covering the entire top of his sarcophagus. As far back as early dynastic Egypt, the water flower of Nymphaea was regularly found in the headdresses of figures in many tomb murals throughout ancient Egypt. Figures in tomb paintings and vessels of early Egyptian dynasties are decorated with the sacred blue water lily, and pictures of this flower become quite common by the eighteenth dynasty and came to be found almost everywhere in ancient Egyptian sacred art. [9]

Consumption of the flower is known to bring on an effect of arousal, pleasure, and excitement, a light intoxication most closely related to the euphoria effects of an opiate without many of the more narcotic or pain killing properties. The Egyptians were known to have mixed the flowers with wine for royal parties and wedding celebrations. The flower itself was seen as a symbol of fertility and life and was well represented throughout ancient Egyptian art and history. But the narcotic blue water lily was not the only plant utilized for its intoxicating effects. A limestone relief from the Amarna period circa 1350 B.C. shows the healing of King, Semenkhara by his consort Meritaton using the hallucinogenic plant mandrake and the narcotic Egyptian blue water lily. These same plant motifs appear again in the eighteenth dynasty portrait of Tutankhamen on his throne with his young queen, representing the importance of these two plants and their uses within ancient Egyptian culture. [10]

In 1956 in an even more remarkable and important discovery, the Egyptian researcher Gabra discovered that the word *shepen* referred to poppy and *shepenen* to the opium poppy. These words were also known to appear in most medical papyri and in some papyri devoted to Egyptian magic, notably the Ebers Papyrus for the Egyptians. By contrast, Gabra later identified opiates in a residue from an "unguent vessel" from the eighteenth dynasty. In this find, both the narcotic opium poppy and the psychedelic plant mandrake were found in the same vessel, demonstrating the clear use of the two mind altering plants within ancient Egypt. While the opium poppy is believed to have been introduced from Babylonia, the psychoactive mandrake plant is believed to have been introduced from Canaan and grown locally since the new kingdom. The mandrake plant is thought to have been used as an aphrodisiac and mixed with alcohol to induce visions and in a much stronger dose even unconsciousness. [11]

The ancient Egyptians are known to have recorded their knowledge of psychoactive plants such as mandrake, henbane, and the even more psychoactive plant datura in the Ebers papyrus, written at about 1500 B.C. Other species of hyoscyamus/ henbane are also known to have similar properties and were occasionally also used in antiquity for their intoxicating effects. Hyoscyamus/ henbane has been known and feared from earliest classical periods, when it was recognized that there were different kinds and that the black variety was the most potent even capable of causing temporary insanity if taken in too strong of a dose. The plant is known to grow in many regions of the world from Europe and the deserts of Egypt, all the way east into Afghanistan and India, where it is also known to be employed as an intoxicant, with the dried leaves many times being smoked. The Nomadic Bedouins particularly have been known to employ it, as to become drunk, in some parts of Asia and Africa the plant is smoked with cannabis as a visionary inebriant. Since antiquity, the mandrake plant *Mandragora officinarum* was grown in Egypt both for its flowers as for its medicinal properties. The leaves were applied to tumors, the roots were said to have analgesic and aphrodisiac properties as well as being psychoactive. In the tomb of Senedjem of the 19th Dynasty there is a depiction of Osiris whose crown seems to be topped by a mandrake. [12]

A plant with very similar properties as the mandrake, but much more powerful in its visionary and intoxicating effects is the datura plant. Datura has been used from the most ancient time and has been used in both rites of passage, and in diverse forms of shamanism around the globe. Its psychoactive properties are extraordinary, and one of the usual modalities in the Datura experience is that of mystical flight, out-of-the-body sensation, and powerful visual hallucination many times bordering on madness. Since datura is pan temperate and pan tropical, the plant genus is not considered scarce in any region. As a matter of fact, the Datura plant is one of the most widespread and most commonly used visionary plants in the world. The visionary use of Datura can be represented in almost every part of the globe and by almost every population of people known to have co-existed with its powerful visionary effects. [13]

While the plant is very toxic, this has still not stopped ancient peoples around the world from using it for its visionary, mind altering effects. For many years people wondered if the powerful Datura plant was ever used for its visionary properties in ancient Egyptian culture or history. While no direct claims regarding the sacred magical use of datura have been found in ancient Egyptian writings, there is one piece of strong visual evidence from Egyptian sacred art indicating that the datura plant may have once played a much greater role in ancient Egyptian priestly rites and ritual initiations than has been previously suspected. This artifact was identified from a tomb painting that still puzzles many Egyptologists today. It is an artifact that demonstrates some of the strongest visual evidence for visionary psychoactive plant use in ancient Egyptian religious rites and rituals. It is the depiction of "Lady

TuthShena" on the stela, in which she is before the god Horus. Emanating from the sun disc on top of Horus's head are five "rays" of tubular flowers. As the flowers are flowing into the body of the lady, we see that she is painted as if in ecstasy with eyes glowing or emanating light. Interestingly enough the flower emanating out from the disk at the top of the head of Horus strongly resembles and suggests the powerfully visionary Datura flower, well known to grow throughout Egypt and documented in the ancient Egyptian Ebers papyrus. [14]

This explanation, like so many others relating to the famous depiction of Tuth-Shena and Horus, might seem almost specious if it were not for the other, associated narcotic plants that have also been identified in the same picture, plants also known for containing narcotic or psychoactive properties. The other plants represented in the picture are: the central flower and leaf of the Egyptian blue water lily, at the foot of Horus is an unguent jar that is wrapped with the narcotic water lily bud, a strand of grapes, and their leaves hanging from the opposite side of the supporting pedestal upon which these plant offerings rest; the four repeated representations of a cleft water lily leaf in the series of glyphs at the right-hand margin of the painting; and the fact that the painting is also taking place in the realm of the dead, which is evident by the resin cone on the head of Tuth-Shena. The light is the light of Horus, realized in the psychoactive flowers of Datura which "illuminates" Tuth-Shena initiation. It is the power of Horus before her which she throws up her hands in awe, a scene of clear shamanic manifestation of a most ancient Egyptian origin. The narcotic and hallucinogenic plants represented in this picture are wine grapes, Nymphaea the intoxicating blue water lily, and flowers of the powerfully psychoactive datura being the main visionary inducing element depicted in this ancient Egyptian initiation experience. The full exegesis of psychoactive plants in the context of dynastic Egypt, have also been discussed by Emboden (1979, 1981)who made the argument that these plants and their psychoactive constituents were adjuncts to the state of ecstasies among the priestly castes of ancient Egypt. These types of ancient Egyptian ethnobotanical inquiries have lead researchers to a very new way of viewing ancient Egyptian art and artifacts, as well as those of many other civilizations of the ancient world. [15]

Peganum Harmala in Ancient Egypt

In examining evidence for the availability of the two plants required to make this visionary Ayahuasca analog brew (Acacia tree parts and Peganum Harmala) in the lands of ancient Egypt, it has recently been discovered by Terence Duquesne of the Psychopharmacology Research Committee of

London that the ancient Egyptian word *ndw* identifies the plant Peganum Harmala from an ancient Egyptian medical papyrus. This discovery was independently made by Terence Duquesne who went on to link the words *nbw* with *nbyt* to which the Egyptian Ebers Papyrus 852 is also known to assign an Eastern origin. Further research conducted by Duquesne also found that the later Coptic word *Noub* identifies the plant as the "golden rue," a term that further furnishes the identity of the Peganum Harmala plant with the mysterious ancient Egyptian plant *nbw* also found occurring in the late Berlin Museum Egyptian Papyrus. The plant's reputation as a medical and magical plant in the later Hellenistic world may very well have first come from its medical and magical uses in the lands of ancient Egypt as the Egyptians would have been the first major Mediterranean civilization to have had lengthy contact with the plant's eastern origins. [16]

Considering the importance of Peganum Harmala in ancient Iranian and Mesopotamian medicine and magic, it would seem only logical to assume that as the knowledge of Peganum Harmala spread into Egypt, Egyptian priests and healers would have come to use the plant, mixing it with other plants in an attempt to uncover more of its medical and magical potential. Because Peganum Harmala seeds and roots are known to contain these mildly psychoactive MAO inhibitors, and it is well documented that Egyptian priests were interested in the medical and visionary properties of plants. Peganum Harmala would have been an ideal candidate for use in Egyptian medicine and magic, making it of great interest to early Egyptian healers and priest. The medical properties of Peganum Harmala would also have also made it an ideal candidate for mixing with other well known medical plants of the time, particularly those already commonly used in Egyptian healing, such as the very popular Acacia Nilotica, a plant whose leaves are now known to contain DMT.

Comparative Analysis and Botanical Mixing

As you can see, both plants necessary for making an entheogenic visonary libation (Peganum Harmala and Acacia Nilotica) have been utilized in ancient medicine. This evidence is documented in the surviving writings of ancient Egyptian and Near Eastern medical literature. In addition to this, both plants required to make this psychoactive brew have been revered since the most ancient of times for their medical uses, mythological importance, and pharmacological effects. Both plants are ideal candidates for mixing and consumption with one another in ancient medicine, making the probability for their visionary potential being discovered in antiquity extremely high. Considering the strong botanical basis of ancient medicine, it is very likely that the mixing of these two plants took place. The following is a comparison of these two plants shared potential for mixing and consumption as a visionary brew:

(1) **Shared Geographical Range:** Both plants required for making this visionary beverage, (Peganum Harmala and DMT containing Acacias) are known to grow in the same geographical regions of the world and demonstrate a wide geographical distribution. Because of this, both plants were available to ancient peoples and have been used by many cultures of the ancient world. This shared geographical distribution made both plants well known medical plants of antiquity with uses that spanned over many divergent populations of the ancient world.

(2) **Shared Material Importance**: Both plants demonstrate a long history of many beneficial material uses: Peganum Harmala is used today as an incense and dye plant used in making clothes and Persian carpets. The Acacia tree is used for its strong wood, tannins, making Gum Arabic, and as important nutritional for livestock. The material uses of these two plants were also well known in antiquity and were well utilized among many people of the ancient world.

(3) **Shared Medical Importance:** Both of the plants required to make this visionary brew were important medical plants in the ancient near east. Both were well known and highly regarded for use in a variety of ailments providing remedies of relief throughout the lands in which they grew. One of the strongest cases supporting the mixture and consumption of these two plants as a visionary brew in antiquity is their long standing history of shared medical uses. The fact that both plants required to make this visionary brew have such a long history of use as important herbal remedies is significant to their success and potential for mixing and consumption as visionary agents. The Acacia tree was used by the ancient Egyptians for stomach pains, healing wounds, burns, and a wide variety of other medical complaints. Peganum Harmala was likewise regarded as the chief medical plant among ancient Persian doctors and was widely utilized and consumed for its beneficial purgative properties. The medical use of Peganum Harmala has been documented to have taken place all the way from Greece the lands of Egypt into Iran, Mesopotamia and India. Because DMT containing acacia's are most prevalent around the lands of Egypt, it is thus not surprising that we find visionary texts in that region with reports of visionary experiences very similar to the effects created by the mixture and consumption of these two plants.

(4) **Shared Spiritual Significance of Visionary Materials.** Both plants required to make this visionary brew demonstrate shared spiritual significance and mythological importance by many cultures of the ancient near east from throughout ancient times through today. This important fact added to the continued veneration of these two plants today, further supports their sacred use as entheogenic sacraments at some time in antiquity. Because of the unique visionary experiences documented in classical Gnosticism and the facts that these visions are no longer taking place in this region of the world, it must be considered that the sources of these visions has been both removed and forgotten. This would seem to account for the fact that the two plants capable of creating these visionary experiences are also no longer being used in this region of the world and the groups that once had created these visionary experiences have also disappeared.

Egypt, Healing, Plants, and Magic

The word occult means something that is secret or hidden, and the ancient Egyptians were very familiar with the hidden or occult properties of plants, stones, and a wide variety of natural substances they used. This was the basis of Egyptian magic, alchemy, science, and healing. Today we know these secret occult substances as drugs or chemicals that are present in plants, animals, and a wide variety of natural substances around the world, which are used by our own modern healers and scientists. While we have identified and named countless chemical substances found throughout the natural world today, the ancient Egyptians had not yet identified the exact chemical items found in these plants; nonetheless, they knew about and studied their effects and manifestations in the natural world. This early occult science was the very basis from which modern chemistry would later emerge. This early inquiry into the hidden occult forces of plants and nature made by the ancient Egyptians was only later expanded in the continued advancements of medieval alchemy during the renaissance, which was originally born from these earlier Egyptian practices.

In ancient Egypt, temple priests were known to have attributed the knowledge and authorship of all their sacred writings to Thoth. It was also in this way that Thoth himself would have instructed a pupil into the secrets of divine Egyptian wisdom. When we study the later technical Egyptian Hermetica we find various treaties that describe and catalog the occult properties of different plants, stones, organisms, and their uses, which were mostly related to the magic and medical spheres. This tells us that Egyptian magic was fundamentally focused on understanding the innate principles that lay behind certain substances in nature. The Technical Hermetic of

Egypt for example, does not yield theoretical accounts of the workings of the cosmic sympathy as some magical texts of other cultures were known to have done; rather, they possessed characters intrinsically in the frontier between observational science, chemistry, and the popular magical lore of the time. In Egypt, these items were primarily concerned with chemistry, botany, and the innate properties and effects of various natural substances particularly when mixed and consumed.

In examining the ancient Egyptian relationship between the consumption of magical substances and the practice of healing, we find many ancient Egyptian artifacts that represent the age old relationship. At the temple of Unas, we find that the acquisition of magical power through ingestion was of the utmost concern. It is interesting to notice that nowhere does the king actually eat the Gods power himself. Rather, he ravenously consumes various attributes or qualities of the Gods and their "magic" (*heka*) or their spirits (*akhu*). The following statement from the temple of Unas further elaborates this important point:

Unas eats their magic
and gulps down their spirits.
Their big ones are for his morning meal,
Their middle-sized ones are for his evening meal,
their little ones are for his nightly meal. [17]

It is not, then, the gods that Unas eats. It is rather that he feeds on, and absorbs into himself their spiritual power. The practice of eating or consuming spiritual qualities in order to obtain magical power (as well as for healing purposes) is well attested to in ancient Egyptian texts and is by no means unique to the "Cannibal Hymn of Unas." By ingesting something, its traits become integrated within the being of the person who ingests them. To ingest spiritual quality is to know it so thoroughly that it has become part of oneself. Even today, the vocabulary of this understanding includes such "metabolic" phrases as "absorbing the meaning of something," or simply, "taking something in." Here again we find a thoroughly shamanic motif in classical Egyptian culture, for it is shamanism that we also find a strong correlation to the idea of ingesting spiritual power. In Ayahusca shamanism for instance, this idea of ingesting the spiritual powers or qualities of a substance is seen as a particularly prominent characteristic. In Ayahuasca shamanism as well as among many, if not most, tribal and shamanic groups of the Amazon, plants are considered to contain spirits, and the consumption of these plants gives the person consuming them the spiritual power residing within the plants they are going to consume in the diet or ritual. Because of the Egyptian's close relationship between magic, healing, and the occults properties of various natural substances such as plants, animals, and stones, it becomes clear that the Egyptians had a profound understanding and respect for the life giving forces of plants in the natural world as well as the magical and healing properties they are known to contain. [18]

In the <u>Ebers Papyrus</u> which is dated to about 1,550 B.C. is among the most important medical papyri of ancient Egypt. Because of the identification of the Peganum Harmala in this text, we now know that the knowledge of the plant goes back in Egyptian history to at least 1,550 B.C. and were first introduced from eastern sources, most probably from Mesopotamia. Because of the Acacia trees importance in ancient Egypt and the Persian and Babylonian world's importance for Peganum Harmala, we must consider that the medical and psychoactive properties of Peganum Harmala were known in Egypt as far back as the New Kingdom and the probability that it came to be mixed and consumed with DMT containing acacia trees in the Egyptian area took place at some point in history.

In ancient Egypt as well as in many civilizations of the ancient world, the art of healing was originally known as one of the secret sciences of the priest craft and the mysteries of its source is obscured by the same veil which hides the genesis of religious belief. In Egypt as well as in many other early civilizations of the ancient world, all higher forms of knowledge were originally in the possession of select inner castes. Because of this, much of the early science, mathematics, and chemistry of the modern western world are known to have emerged from these much more ancient roots and traditions, knowledge originally found in these ancient forms of Egyptian science: alchemy and priestly craft. The knowledge contained in these temples is the form from which modern civilization as we know it today was originally born. In Egyptian healing, most medicines were made from plants and mixtures of plants and other natural substances. These were combined together into mixtures to make various plant-based healing formulas, often these herbal mixtures were accompanied with magical prayers and verses that the Egyptians believed further aided in the healing process of the patient. When we examine the relationship between ancient Egyptian healing and magic, we come to find that the Egyptians were not too overly concerned with the exact verses or incantations said or used in these healings. Instead, we find that ancient Egyptian healers were concerned with the mysterious occult properties of the substances being used in their magical or healing workings.

By identifying Peganum Harmala in ancient Egyptian medical Papyrus, we now know that the ancient Egyptians knew about the effects and medical properties of Peganum Harmala and made use of them. We also know that they come to make use of the plant in other herbal, medical, and magical mixtures. The plants most likely to have been initially mixed with Peganum Harmala would have also contained important medical properties that the Egyptians made use of. This would have made important medical plants like the Acacia prime candidates for early mixing and use with Peganum Harmala by ancient Egyptian priest and healers. The mixing of plants for healing and magical purposes was a common practice in the ancient world. So the mixing of acacia tree parts with the seeds or roots of Peganum Harmala, another well known medical herbal of the time, would have by no means been an unusual activity for Egyptian healers or priests looking for new medical formulas to have done. When Peganum Harmala first entered Egypt, Egyptian healers would have began mixing the plant with other medical and magical preparations to try to uncover new medical or herbal formulas. This would have made ideal conditions for the mixing of Peganum Harmala with DMT containing Acacia tree parts and the discovery of the two plants visionary properties.

In examining ancient historical texts relating to the possible discovery of such a visonary brew by ancient Egyptian priests, we are lead to examine one small and largely overlooked statement known to have emerged from the ancient Egyptian temple practices and priesthood that demonstrate the possibility that ancient Egyptian priests may have uncovered plant mixtures with the pharmacological effects of an Ayahuasca analog. This is the statement that at one point in ancient Egyptian history, Egyptian priests discovered herb extracts by means of which a type of temporary telepathy or clairvoyance could be induced. While most scholars have chosen to ignore this statement as improvable claims of ancient Egyptian magic and priest craft there is a very interesting and important correlation that must be pointed out in considering this unusual ancient claim. The important point that needs to be considered in this statement is that when the Banisteriopsis Caapi / Ayahuasca vine was first discovered and studied by western researchers, the researchers who were studying it for its innate chemical properties were originally looking for the chemical compounds that they thought were responsible for its acclaimed telepathic and clairvoyant effects. When researchers first isolated the main chemical compound found in the Banisteriopsis vine they subsequently named it Telepathine because they thought, at the time, that they had discovered and isolated the main chemical compound responsible for its acclaimed telepathic properties. It wasn't until years later in 1957 that the chemical compound Telepathine was actually found to be the same compound first earlier isolated from the seeds and roots of the Peganum Harmala plant growing on the other side of the world in the lands of Egypt, Syria, and the Middle East. The compound earlier identified in the plant Peganum Harmala was already named and identified as the chemical compounds harmine, harmaline. These

Harmaline alkaloids were the same chemical MAO inhibitor compound later found in the Banisteriopsis Caapi/ Ayahuasca vine found on the other side of the world in the Amazon rain forest. Because of this, Telepathine had to be re-named in accordance with the harmaline alkaloids earlier discovered in the plant Peganum Harmala. This extraordinary discovery gives real credit to the possibility that ancient Egyptian priests discovered herb extracts that when mixed and consumed created to same type of experiences we find associated with ayahuasca, indicating a direct link between ayahuasca and the visionary experiences created by the Egyptian Gnostic and Hermetic traditions.

Gnosticism, Peganum Harmala and the Mandaeans

With evidence now presented that both plants required to make this visonary brew were known about and used by the ancient Egyptians as early as the New Kingdom, there is also evidence that the two plants required to make this visonary brew were also known about and used among the Gnostics. Evidence for this can be seen from the remarkable relationship these two plants are known to have had with the Sethain Gnostic Mandaeans. The Mandaeans are also known to go by the name "Nasoraeans," and are the last surviving group of ancient Gnostics alive today. The Mandaeans as indicated by themselves and in the written historical works of Epiphanius are descended from Sethian Gnostic origins. The Mandaeans claim that their religion was handed down since the beginning of human history from the first man, Adam also known as the Adamas or the primal man. Adam, according to Mandonic history, translated his divine wisdom to his son Seth and from Seth down an ancient line of people until it found its way into the lands of ancient Mesopotamia and Israel manifesting into two distinct sects, one known as the Hebrews, the other known as the Nasoraeans. In the Quran, the holy book of the Muslims, we see them labeled as the Sabians. Mandaeans are called Subi by their Muslim neighbors. The word Sabaean comes from the Aramaic-Mandic word saba, or "immersed in water," according to the group's website, (www.mandaeans.org), Mandaean comes from the word menda, or "knowledge." That same word when translated from the Greek is known today as Gnostic, thus making the Mandaeans the last true group of surviving ancient Gnostics. Because of the Mandaeans relationship to ancient Gnosticism and early Christianity, the Mandaeans are profoundly important in helping us to understand many important details of the ancient world that have come to be lost or unknown today. By studying the Mandaeans researchers are able to gain a profound insight into the ancient world they emerged from.

The language Mandaeans use is called Mandonic, a language that is also very closely related to Aramaic which was the same original language that was spoken by both Jesus and John the Baptist. The Mandaeans are also some of the only people left on the planet known to still speak this ancient and nearly extinct language. The Catholic Church has labeled the group *the church of Saint John* based on a comment made by Portuguese monks in the 16th century who first discovered them. Since the 1st century A.D. after fleeing Israel from the Romans, the Mandaeans have lived mainly in the borderland areas of Iraq and Iran since that time. In more recent years, many have fled the region since the 1990s due to the unstable political climate in Iraq and have immigrated worldwide. There is no official census of the Mandaeans; conservative guesses at current population size have been made in the range of only 50,000 to 80,000. Because of the more recent unstable political climate and war in Iraq, many of the Mandaeans have been marked by Islamic extremists, being heavily persecuted and even systematically slaughtered. Because of their dwindling population the Mandaeans are on the verge of cultural extinction and have been marked by the United Nations as critically endangered. While a few small groups have immigrated around the world, they have received little to no help from their Christian or Jewish companions and remain today as one of the most important and endangered religious traditions on earth. [19]

The core of the Mandaean religion, through all vicissitudes and changes, is the ancient worship of the principal of life and fertility. The great life is a personification of the creative and sustaining forces of the universe. The symbol for the Great Life is "living Water," that is, flowing water, or yardna. This is entirely natural in a land where all life, human, animal, and vegetable, clings to the banks of the two great rivers, Tigris and Euphrates. It follows that, we find that one of the central rites in the Sethian Gnostic and Mandaean tradition is immersion if flowing water. The second great vivifying power is light, which is represented by personifications (great light, light spirits, divine light) who bestow such light- gifts as health, strength, virtue, and justice. This dual application was also characteristic of the ancient Mesopotamian cults of Anu and Ea in Sumerian times and Bel and Ea in Babylonian time. Mandaean white magic or healing magic is also directly rooted in ancient Mesopotamian practices. It is an age old Mandaean custom in times of plague and sickness to bury by the threshold or by the grave of a person carried off by disease two bowls, one inverted above the other, within which are inscribed exorcisms of disease spirits, spirits of darkness, and invocation of spirits of light and life. The magic rolls have been copied and re-copied for centuries, often without comprehension, since many magic names and spirits mentioned have disappeared from the orthodox religion and are not found in the holy books.

They are often pagan in tone and represent names found in older Babylonia and Sumerian traditions. While this may seem important, it is the use and incorporation of Paganum Harmala within these Mandaean healing texts that demonstrate the most direct evidence for the ancient magical, healing and visionary use of the plant among ancient Gnostic groups.

Evidence that the oldest Gnostic groups were known to have consumed Peganum Harmala for its healing and visionary effects is found within Mandaean writings. In Mandaean manuscript 47 collected by E.S Drower in 1946, named: A phylactery for rue, an invocation of the Personified herb. The text starts off by glorifying Peganum Harmala as a great "spring of life, great healing herb, and driver out of evil spirits and illness." The text goes on to name a list of ancient Babylonian deities including the spirits of Bel, Sin, and Nanai. The texts states that this herb medicine drives away and makes impotent all evil spirits of illness, maladies and dire disease from the body. This is direct evidence that the use of Peganum Harmala for healing goes way back in Mesopotamian times. In Akkadian the term for "rue" (Peganum harmala) is sibburratu. Its Sumerian equivalent is, "Syrian washing plant". According to Akkadian text Sibburratu is described as an aromatic plant used in medicine and in magic. According to which the plant has magical power over great sickness and could expel demons and witchcraft. This provides a good parallel with the use of sibburratu in Babylonian magic, where it was also used to dispel witchcraft from a person. While the text never seem to directly report on its visionary properties, the plant is always associated in these text with magical and spiritual powers, in which the text states that, " the male gods and female astartes give favorable testimony concerning you," indicating a communication between these spirit beings and the use of the plant.

Because of the Mandaeans relationship to the antique traditions of Mesopotamia and other Sethian Gnostic groups of the ancient world such as those we find surrounding Egypt in the texts of the Nag Hummadi library, the Mandaeans are important in allowing scholars deeper insight into many of the unknown aspects of history that have been previously lost or forgotten from the time period they are known to have emerged from. Because of this, many steps have been made by outside agencies around the world to try to preserve the Mandaean's culture, religion, and ancient texts from disappearing. One of these ancient texts that is particularly important to the research of this book, it is known as the scroll of the "Safta d Sambra" translated as, "the scroll of "the wild Rue." The scroll of the *Safta D Sambra* was written by ancient peoples in and around the Babylonian area, where it was used and collected into the Mandaean library. The *Safta D Sambra* is a very ancient text written about the plant Peganum Harmala. One of the most important elements of this important and ancient text is that it directly indicates the ancient spiritual and magical importance of this plant among this ancient Gnostic group. [20]

The following is a translated portion of the Gnostic Mandaean text *The Safta d Sambra:*

> O good plant son of the god of the mountains,
> son of the lord of the mountains,
> son of the lord of the high mountains
> son of the deep ravines and son of the peaceful
> Valleys.
>
> Further I abjure thee, glorious medicine,
> by the male gods and female astartes by
> Shamish the sun that shineth on thee:
> By sin the moon that travels over thee;
> By wind, fire and water: by the mountains
> Which bore thee; by the gorges and craggy hights
> That reared thee: and by the water ways in them.
>
> I abjure thee by the mountains that bore thee,
> by the uplands that reared thee
> By the north wind that blew over thee.
> O sambra, go below like water whick gusheth
> from the peak of a high mountain.
>
> The lady of Gods and men took thee
> And carried thee off to the male gods
> And the female astartes and she gave
> favorable testimony concerning thee.
> And they sent it to everyone that was ill,
> working a cure and healing was found in it.
>
> Thou didst spring fourth of thine own strength
> and didst come forth and camest into being. [21]

The text states that the plant grow in the mountains, as has been pointed out by previous scholars, the region where the Mandaeans currently live in Iraq is in flatlands and waterways. This is so they can be close to water for purification and baptisms which is central to their religious practices. This seems to indicate that the text may have been written at a time when the Mandaeans lived in other areas. It also indicates the possibility that they may have received their knowledge of the plant at a much more ancient time or from anther outside source. If in fact they borrowed these ideas, then some evidence should exist within these texts that would show that they could have copied or borrowed them from the writings of other people also known to have used Peganum harmala in ancient times.

In speculating on the origins of Peganum Harmala use among the Mandaeans we can see that there is a close relationship between what Zoroastrian text say about Haoma and what the Gnostic Mandaean text say regarding Peganum Harmala/ *Sambra*. The similarity between these two texts has indicated to some scholars in the past the possibility that the Mandaeans may have received their knowledge and use of Peganum Harmala from these older Persian or Zoroastrian influences at a time when the Zoreastrian religion was still using the plant for its purgative and mild visionary properties. Because the Persians are believed to have been some of the first people suspected to have uses of the plant, it is probable to assume that their early knowledge and use of the plant may have entered Mandaean writings when they came into contact with the mandaeans at some point in antiquity.

The following is from the Zoroastrian *Avestan Hom Yasht*:

Avestan Hom Yasht, relates

Good is Haoma, created by Mazadah.
 I priese all the Haomas, be they thoughs
of the hights or those of the mountains,
 be they thoughs in the depths of the valles,
cut for the bundles bound by women. (Yasna 10.17)

Thou Haoma has been upon the moutians
hights through all the ages. (Yasna 9.26)

I priese the cloud and rain which make
 thy body grow on the heights of the moutians.
I priese the high moutians were Haoma thou growest.
I priese the wide broad energetic blessingd earth, they berer
I priese the field of thin earth by which thou growest. Fragrant
and swift, and the good growth of Mazda. Haoma
 mayst thou prosper;
Truly thou art the fountain of rightness (Yasna 10.3-5)

The beneficent god has placed thee upon
  high haraiti. From there you leared spenta(!)
  birds carried thee in all directions, to the peak
above the eagles, to the hundo kish,
to the star topped peaks... to the white colered moutians.
  There on thoughs moutians though growest,
  Haoma, who art of many sorts, rich in sap,
Verdant. Thy healings are connected with
  the joys of good thinking. (Yasna 10.10-12)

Haoama, who are through thin own power
  art thin own master. (Yasna 9.25) [22]

Like the Mandaean text regarding Peganum harmala, the Zoroastrian text clearly relates that Haoma is a mountain plant. While the Mandaean text outlines its strong relationship to the ancient gods and spirits, the Zoroastrian text does not; instead, it relates its importance to god, joy, goodness and to the high peaks and mountains. Both texts do seem to share a general theme. In the Zoroastrian text the writer gives a long poetic description of Haoma's relationship to the highest peaks and mountains. The Mandaean text also gives a similar poetic description of Peganum Harmala by demonstrating its relationship to the craggy heights, upland peaks, and high mountains, both texts also clearly indicate the plant's relationship to health, healing, and the ability of the plant to spring forth from the earth from its own strength and power, an attribute that is a unique characteristic of the Peganum harmala plant in spring, as it is a time when new fresh shoots are just starting to emerge from its root in the earth. [23]

Throughout the Middle East, Peganum Harmala is generally regarded as a mountain plant. Although Peganum Harmala is abundant in the mountains of Iran it is less abundant in the lowlands north of the person gulf where the modern day Mandaeans are known to live. The location of the plant growing in the mountains as the Mandaean text describes correlates with the Avesta statement of Haoma as being a common mountain plant. In addition to the plant being known to grow in the mountains the plant is probably best known for its medical and healing properties. The healing properties of the plant as well as a clear reference to the plant being drank as a sacred healer are all items that are all well represented in both Zoroastrian and Mandaean literature. The respected virtues of the plant are further demonstrated in the following part of the Mandonic, *Safta d sambra*:

Mandaean, Safta d sambra

And there will be healing, Victory,
Sealing, armed readiness, gladness, and
medicine, and joy to him that drinketh it.

...That drinketh thee, ether in wine
or in Sakir, or in water, or in the urine
of a red bull.

And the medicine bringith joy and healing
to the drinker and riches to him
Who administers it. Thou O sprig,
Givest salvation and not perdition,
for thou make them strong and art a healer,
thou workest healing and yieldest not.

Cure, my cure. Victorious medicine
my victorious healer.

Protection, son of protection art thou
lofty in thy throun. Protection son of
protection they call me.

I am sambra, the good neibour, king of all drugs. [24]

It is important to point out the place Peganum harmala holds in these texts for having powerful medical and healing properties. The reason that this is important is because there is another plant with the same pharmacological properties on the other side of the world that we looked at earlier also acclaimed for its sacred healing properties, the vine of the soul, Ayahuasca. From examining the text we find many important statements associating the plant with the Gods and having a strong spiritual even religious association. It seems clear that the plant Sambra/ Peganum Harmala was not just an important medical plant but was also revered as sacred at one point in Mandaean history. [25]

While the text *"Hom Yasht"* is represented by the Zoroastrian priest who is about to drink Haoma, the *Safta d Sambra* is recited by the Mandaean priest who administers the extract. Although mandaic is a language used only by those adhering to the Mandaean religion, and almost all literature written on it consists of religious literature. The *Safta d Sambra* is not a part of Mandaean canonical literature. The text is of a decidedly magical character, although the purpose of the drink in the text is for purging someone of sickness or demon possession, wisdom or knowledge is not among the benefits sought, nor is its intoxication mentioned in the Mandaean text, even though this effect may well have been experienced as an outcome of drinking preparations of the plant. [26]

An unusual feature, shared by both Zoroastrian and Mandaean texts regarding Peganum harmala comes from its strong association with divine and semi-divine beings. The personification of Sambra as a semi-divine deity is unknown elsewhere in Mandaean writing. These beliefs were most likely orally transmitted only later to be written down. Considering the great antiquity of most Mandaean texts the *Softa d Sambra* could easily date long before the Islamic period in the millennium when the inhabitants and Mandaeans were under Iranian or Babylonian political domination. Some scholars have pointed out that the Mandaeans during this time could have adopted many religious and magical practices from their Iranian or Babylonian neighbors. It also seems natural for them to have given attention to the most important single element of Iranian spiritual contact and ritual, the use of Peganum Harmala. [27] In continuing, the *Safta d sambra"* states:

"Safta d sambra" Scroll of the Wild Rue.

Thou hold back those evel spirits
like the lightning that is sent and
loosed against that evel Serpint,
driving it out and turning it aside
by it's force from that house.

Turn away evil serpent that makes
from him: scair it off, thou medicine
frightens it away by the potency.
And receive from me these spells
and conjureations.. harass, drive
away and makeimpotent thoughs
who hate him and all his enemies,
and Sids, demons incudi,hobgoblins,
malign spirits, amulet spirits, evil apparition,
specters and fearsome shades of darkness,
evil enchantments, wicked machinations.

Healing medicine that cureth spirit and soul,
before whom sides tremble and evil
spirits quaking are driven.

In the name of him who is a healer that healeth..
thou shatters , drivest away and renders important.
gods and male idols and all evil beings male and female
that slay embryos in the womb of there mothers
and vows curses and provocations imprecations
of gods and men. [28]

By examining the above Mandaean text we find that Peganum Harmala is associated with protection ageist evil spirits, witchcraft, enchantments, and sorcery. It is a healing medicine that cures the body as well as the spirit and soul. It drives out evil spirits and protect the body. The texts indicate that the plant is a sacred healer and purges and protects against evil spirits and demons. This not only indicates the therapeutic property of the plants, but also its relationship to more spiritual applications, for which its psychoactive properties were also once used for. These descriptions also provide further evidence to support Peganum Harmala's use and important in ancient Gnosticism.

The texts also indicate that the Mandaeans or other peoples in the Mesopotamian area may have had knowledge of the plant long before the arrival of Persian or Iranian culture. This possibility would indicate that instead of the Zoroastrians influencing the knowledge and use of Peganum Harmala onto the Mandaeans, the Mandaeans already had knowledge of the plants pharmacological potential long before Persian or Iranian influences. Evidence to support this possibility comes from other more magical texts found within the Mandaean library that seem to indicate that the magical and medical properties of Peganum Harmala may go back many more hundreds of years in Mesopotamian and Mandaean history and are not limited to Persian or Iranian influences.

Many scholars have question when these texts were first written and originally collected into the Mandaean library? While many scholars who have advocated the original identity of Hoama with Peganum Harmala have done so by comparing Mandaean and Zoreastrian texts about Haoma to try and support their claims of Haoma's relationship to Peganum Harmala. They have speculated that because various elements of Mandaean texts are not currently practiced by the Mandaeans, they must have received their knowledge of the plant from earlier Iranian sources. But upon examination of Mandaean texts about Peganum Harmala in greater detail, it seems that while the Mandaeans who originally wrote or collected these books may have incorporated some ancient Iranian elements, there is even more substantial evidence that their knowledge and use of Peganum Harmala as it is seen in Mandaean writings, may have first originated independently of Iranian influences and had descended from much older Sumerian, or Babylonian influences and traditions long before. The possibility that people of these regions could have gained knowledge of the plant's healing and pharmacological potential on their own, completely independent of later Persian or Iranian influences is a very strong possibility. Considering the proximity ancient Babylonia has to the mountain regions of Iran where Peganum harmala is known to grow and is suspected to have first been used among early human populations, it seems very likely that early peoples in these regions of Mesopotamia could have gained access to the plant and learned of its healing and therapeutic properties long before the political domination of ancient Iranian culture. If this was the case, as it appears to be from examining these Mandaean texts, then the knowledge and use of Peganum Harmala for visionary and healing purposes may have once been very widespread in ancient Mesopotamia. This would indicate that the use of Peganum harmala had a very ancient and prominent place in ancient Mesopotamian medicine and magic that could very well span many thousands of years of use.

While we do not know the exact origins or dates the text of the *Softa D Sombra* was written and put into the Mandaean library, from examining Mandaean literature regarding Peganum Harmala, it seems clear that Mandaean texts demonstrate distinctive Babylonian and Semitic elements that are clearly not of Persian or Iranian origins. This indicates that the knowledge and use of Peganum Harmala in ancient Mesopotamia may have been a completely independent tradition, with roots of use that came many hundreds and possibly thousands of years before Persian or Iranian political dominance of the region.

The main evidence to consider in this possibility is found within the scrolls of the Mandaeans regarding the ancient use of Peganum Harmala, elements that demonstrate a clear reference to Babylonian Gods and Spiritual figures, items of direct Mesopotamian origin. The "Scroll of the Wild Rue" associates the sacredness of the plant with Samash the Babylonian sun God and Sin the Babylonia moon god, both very ancient Babylonian and Samarian deities. The text is clearly of a magical and Pagan character indicating that it may not have been originally written by Mandaeans at all, but instead came down into their sacred library from earlier Babylonian or Sumerian influences. While some similarities can be seen between Mandaean texts and later Persian and Zoroastrian writings regarding Haoma, when the text of the Mandaeans are more closely inspected, a significant portion of the Mandaean text regarding Peganum Harmala indicates elements that are of much earlier Semitic and Babylonian origins with very few direct connections to ancient Iranian practices outside of a few general statements and known ritual acts. This indicates that the knowledge and use of Peganum Harmala in ancient Mesopotamia and among early Gnostic groups may have been utilized at a much earlier date among these ancient people and among other earlier Samarian or Babylonia peoples. Evidence that some Mandaean sects are also known to have descended from older Babylonian religious traditions and not to have been purely Mandaean in origin is well known and well represented in modern Mandaean scholarship. So the possibility then that the "Scroll of the Wild Rue" could have come from earlier Mesopotamian traditions is a very strong and likely possibility.

It is already well represented by historians that by the 4th millennium B.C. the most important city in Mesopotamia was the city of Uruk and by the late periods of the same millennium influences from Uruk and southern Mesopotamia were known to have reached as far as the Mediterranean and the Iranian plateau. Pottery and other objects of southern Mesopotamia styles have been found in these regions, far away from their place of origin. This has promoted much speculation about how they originally came there. Some Settlements in southwestern Iran and in Northern Mesopotamia along the Euphrates and the Tigris rivers shared so many cultural traits that they probably had direct contact with lowland Mesopotamia and might even have been early colonies. Even the exploits of the semi legendary kings of the first dynasty of Uruk which were recorded by the later Sumerian and Babylonian scribes are known to describe early trade and contact between the Mesopotamian lowlands and the high mountain regions of the Iranian plateau. In one of these ancient legends Enmerkar the early king of the Samarians, was engaged in a struggle with the city state of Aratta, which was separated from Sumerian by several mountains to the east, and thus somewhere on the Iranian plateau. It is stated by early scribes that Enmerkar needed gold, silver, lapis laxuli and carnelian to decorate the early temples and palaces of Samaria. So to obtain these precious substances Enmerkar negotiating with envoys and written tablets (in this Enmerkar is credited with the invention of writing) and by the use of armed conflict, Enmerkar succeed in securing precious metals and stones from the Iranian highlands.

This demonstrates a very ancient relationship between Mesopotamia and the highland mountain regions of Iran were the Peganum harmla plant is believed to have originated. This indicates that the Persians did not first introduce Peganum Harmala into Mesopotamia. Instead the knowledge, use, and sacred veneration of the Peganum Harmala plant must have existed in the Mesopotamian area prior to Persian dominance of the region, at a time the text was originally written and put into the mandeaen library, and at a time when traditional Babylonian and Sumerian deities were still venerated among them. The texts of the Mandaeans seem to represent a very ancient magical healing utilization of the plant among various early Gnostic and Mesopotamian peoples.

It is important to point out the relationship the plant has in these texts for being a medicine, one that not only helps to cure the body but is also used in "curing the spirit and soul before whom evil spirits are driven out." This is an important point because it demonstrates the spiritual and magical character associated with the consumption of the plant's pharmacological properties within ancient Mandaean writings. Also a great deal of medicine in the ancient world, as well as Babylonia medicine in particular, was characterized by illnesses associated with the position of evil spirits. It was believed in many regions of the ancient world, particularly in Mesopotamia, that sickness had a spiritual cause and that evil demons were in part, responsible for causing illness in humans. This spiritual purgative quality of the plant would have made Peganum Harmala a very important and attractive medical magical plant in ancient times particularly in early Mesopotamia. So much so that as the knowledge of the plant spread throughout the ancient world, so would knowledge of its use, importance, and innate pharmacological properties.

While the Mandaeans no longer utilize Peganum Harmala for anything, the presence of this plant in Mandaean literature and history gives us a clear insight into its importance and use among ancient Gnostic and Mesopotamian peoples in antiquity. While the exact age of this text cannot be substantiated, it is clear that the text presents literary and cultural elements that are both independent of traditional Mandaean practices and are of a much more ancient Mesopotamian origin. While it is unclear exactly how far back in history the knowledge and use of Peganum Harmala may have gone in Mesopotamia, it seems clear that its first introductions into Mesopotamia very well may have come from a much earlier and much more ancient time when early Samarian populations were in direct contact with peoples of the Iranian highlands in what are known today as some of the earliest historical periods of Mesopotamian history.

By identifying the use of Peganum Harmala within the Gnostic Mandaean library, I have demonstrated direct evidence that a plant with one of the two required pharmacological properties necessary for making a visionary ayahuasca analog brew were once utilized and venerated among ancient Gnostic peoples, evidence that is still well represented within the writings of a surviving Gnostic group today. While Peganum Harmala could have been used to create visions, its visionary effects are not powerful enough to create the much more powerful visionary experiences we see in the Gnostic writings of the Nag Hammadi Library or the Egyptian Hermetic tradition. This indicates that a much more powerful visonary compound must have been used. While there is no direct record from ancient writing stating that the two plants were mixed, there are references to visonary plants based mixtures that were consumed and whose effects are shown to be very similar to the effects of this ayahuasca analog mixture. While the modern mandaeans do not currently practice any visonary rituals or even currently use Peganum Harmala, it does not mean that at some point in their history other members of their gnostic sect did not mix these two plants and use them to create the visonary experiences described in their writings. Evidence to support this can be seen in Mandaean writings in which we see that they are full of mystical visonary imagery but lack the more descriptive stories of visonary experiences and visonary rituals we find in the Nag Hammadi writings of Egypt.

Because we know that Peganum Harmala was known about and used among ancient Gnostics and the mixture of this plant with DMT containing acacia tree parts would have created a powerful visonary drink with the same effects as those described in Gnostic visonary texts, it must be considered that the Gnostics not only had knowledge of Peganum Harmala but that they also had knowledge of its effects when mixed and consumed with DMT containing plants. Evidence that the Gnostics knew about and visonary potential of acacia trees can be seen in the importance they are known to have put on it. Evidence that the acacia tree was considered sacred among the Gnostics can be seen in the very place the Nag Hammadi Library was discovered, the ancient town of Chenosboskion. The name of this city is an ancient Coptic name which is translated as, The Acacias of Seth. The association of the acacia with Seth shows a direct relationship between the acacia tree and this important visonary Gnostic prophet. The importance of the acacia tree is also represented in Gnostic Mandaean mythology, were it is said to be one of the five trees growing in paradise and is associated with the Mandaean "tree of light." By demonstrating the awarness and importance both Peganum Harmala and DMT containing acacia tree's had within the Sethian Gnostic and Egyptian Hermetic tradition, I have demonstrated direct evidence that the two plants required to make this visonary brew were known about within ancient Gnosticism and used as visonary additives to create the visonary experiences the Gnostics described.

Ch 9

Identifying the Gnostic Sacrament

Man's soul shall become, when it leaveth the body, a great flood
of Light, so as to traverse all the regions until it cometh into the
Kingdom of Mystery.

(Allogenes)

As you have seen, the visionary experience was an integral part of
the Hermetic and Gnostic religious tradition. Upon examination of
Gnostic and Hermetic text, it is has been found that their visionary
experiences took place after the ritual drinking of a cup, the Gnostic/Hermetic
sacrament. Because of this, we know that it was not only within Gnostic's
rituals that these visionary experiences took place, but that these experiences
were in fact repeatedly facilitated by means of ritual consumption of what is
now an unknown entheogenic ingredient within their ritual drinking cup.
Upon further examination of Gnostic visions, we find that they are found to
maintain a set of uniquely defined characteristics and attributes, attributes
that most closely compare to the effects associated with the use and visions
of an Ayahuasca analog. Because of the prevalence of DMT containing
Acacia trees throughout the lands of Egypt and the long history of use of
Paganum Harmala in Gnosticism and within the Middle East, there is now
compelling evidence to suggest that these two plant were once mixed and
consumed for there pharmacological properties at one time in antiquity.
To truly identify if the mixture and consumption of these two plants was
responsible for creating Gnostic and Hermetic visions as I have proposed, a
direct comparison must be found between the effects of this brew and the
visionary experiences documented in Gnostic texts. If the Gnostic's did utilize
such a specific botanical mixture of psychoactive ingredients to create their
visionary experiences, then there should be a clear correlation between the

effects of this Ayahuasca analog brew and the visionary experiences induced by the Gnostic sages. If a relationship can be found between the experiences of the Gnostics and the effects induced by this plant mixture, then the pharmacological contents of this ritual cup can finally be made.

Dieting and Purification

The most basic cultural platforms that first need to be identified in outlining the relationship between Gnosticism and the Ayahuasca analog experience comes from the most basic and fundamental practice associated with Ayahuasca shamanism, dieting, and purification. As I have stated before, the Ayahuasca brew is fundamentally used in traditional jungle societies as a medical purgative bestowing on its user spiritual and supernatural effects. Because the brew is a purgative, initial purification is of the utmost importance and is strongly recommended throughout both the indigenous and non-indigenous cultures that employ the use of the brew. This purification can take on the form of bathing or washing as well as the central and primary practice of preliminary dietary restrictions aiding in both physical and mental purification and cleansing. Because the brew contains powerful MAO inhibitors, the consumption of meat is strictly prohibited prior to the consumption of Ayahuasca. If meat is eaten prior to the consumption of Ayahuasca, it will make the drinker very uncomfortable and sick during the experience. Because of this, both vegetarianism and purification are important aspects of traditional Ayahuasca shamanism as well as a vital and important prerequisite for the use of Ayahuasca.

Because of its unique properties, and the requirements they entail, it is both important and interesting to note that the Gnostics were also very well known for their practices of initial ritual purification, mostly in the forms of initial water baptism. In addition to the Gnostics holding a strong importance to water baptism as their primary means of ritual purification, they were also predominantly well known vegetarians. As a matter of fact, they were so well known for their practices of vegetarianism that many early Christian documents recorded the Gnostic's practice of refraining from eating meat. While the initial cause for Gnostic vegetarianism has been unknown in the past, many classical Christian authors have documented the Gnostic's widespread practice of vegetarianism. In a 4th Century Christian document it attest that "Heretical Gnostic Christians were still so common, and there were so many Gnostic Heretics among the clergy and monks in Egypt that in the region of Theodosius Egypt, the Patriarch Timothy made eating meat compulsory on Sundays, as a way to flush out the vegetarian Gnostics." [1]

Upon examining Egyptian Hermetic texts for this important but largely over looked detail, we come to find that the Hermetic followers also were well known for there practice of vegetarianism in addition to the practice of water baptism as their primary means of initial ritual purification. One such example of hermetic vegetarianism is found in the Hermetic book of Asclepius. In this Hermetic book the author starts his discourse in a temple, only ending it with a prayer which is then followed by an embrace and as the author relates is then completed by a "pure meal without any animal flesh in it." Ritual purification and the practice of vegetarianism are both important initial cultural distinctions required to point out in the relationship between Gnosticism and the ayahuasca practice because both vegetarianism and ritual purification are strong cultural elements in both traditional Ayahuasca shamanism as well as classical Gnosticism. If such cultural and ritual prerequisites such as vegetarianism and initial purification were unknown to manifest in Gnosticism, then it would be a possible source of evidence demonstrating against the use of an Ayahuasca analog in Gnostic rituals. But as both of these cultural elements are found in Gnosticism and both directly relate to the consumption of this specific type of psychoactive beverage, it is then possible that such a substance could have in fact been utilized for creating the unique visionary experiences we find documented in Gnostic and Hermetic literature. So it is within this unique set of cultural requirements that we find initial support for the Gnostic and Hermetic use of a purgative psychoactive vegetative brew with unique pharmacological properties that are most closely associated with the use of an Ayahuasca analog.

Music

When even the most casual reader of the Sethian Gnostic literature from the Nag Hammadi Library comes across these texts, they cannot fail to notice their numerous references to visions of the transcendental world and its contents, numerous references to baptisms, washings, anointing and sealings, as well as the presence of various prayers, songs, and hymns mentioning or directed to a rather fixed set of divine beings. Ritual hymns, prayers in the form of song and ecstatic chants, are little mentioned but are defined characteristic of many Sethian Gnostic rituals. Comparatively in the Modern Santo Daime, Ayahuasca rituals, the core of these Daime rituals, as with all other Ayahuasca rituals sessions, is the utilization and importance of Hymns as the central part of the practice. These hymns are also said to be received under the effects of the Ayahuasca by the shaman or as in the case of the Santo Diame by the prominent members of the community. In the Santo Daime, these songs are usually descriptions of visionary scenes or many times directed to a set of divine beings. In the indigenous healing tradition of Ayahuasca shamanism, Hymns and songs are most closely connected to the practice of healing and primarily used for that purpose.

It is important to point out the correlation between the use of songs in Ayahuasca shamanism to the similar use of ritual song found in Gnosticism. In Gnosticism, hymns and songs were attributed to divine luminaries or a fixed set of divine beings. These songs were used for the purpose of conjuring up ritual contact with angels and divine heavenly spirits during the Gnostic's visionary experiences and rituals. This is a very similar practice that is, surprisingly enough, also found within traditional Ayahuasca shamanism today. When we examine the effects Ayahuasca and its relationship to sound and music in the ritual space, we find that there is an enhanced conferral of meaningfulness in both the vision and in the auditory modalities. There is also an enhanced conferral of meaningfulness to the song that is listened to by the drinker. Overall, one's audition becomes subtler and more acute, and auditory stimuli sound fuller and stronger. With this, one may sense that one detects sounds that are well below the normal auditory threshold. One of the most specific auditory effects that drinkers of Ayahuasca commonly report is the hearing of a buzzing sound or vibration coming from some unknown source, many times drinkers feel that this buzzing comes from inside the head or ears but is not of a traditional auditory modality. Many times this inner sound is associated with the initial oncoming psychological effects of the brew and usually does not continue past the peak experience.

Inner sound

Within the Gnostic tradition, the experience of light and sound are described in many particular patterns, with the phenomena of inner sound being another important relationship found between the ritual experiences of the Gnostics and the effects of an Ayahuasca analog. According to the Gnostics, as in the experiences of Ayahuasca, this inner sound current is not a sound one hears with the physical ears, but only with the inner self. Accordingly, this "Heavenly Music" is, in essence, according to Gnostic thought, part of God manifested. In Gnostic text, when describing the philosophical nature of the cosmos, Gnostic writers emphasized this sound current, variously referring to it as the sound of the Logos, or the sound of silence. Many times these references are also accompanied by manifestation of a mystical light, known as The Treasury of Light, Immeasurable Light, among others. In the Gnostic book, The Trimorphic Protennoia it is described in the following way:

> I am [the Word] who dwells [in the] ineffable [Silence]. I dwell
> in undefiled [Light] and a Thought [revealed itself] perceptibly

through [the great] Sound ... And it [the Sound] exists from the beginning in the foundations of the All. But there is a Light [that] swells hidden in Silence and it was the first to [come] forth...I alone am the Word, ineffable, incorruptible, immeasurable, and inconceivable. It (the Word?) is a hidden Light ... being unreproducible, an the Aeons that belong to the mighty glory. It is the founding of every foundation. It is the breath of the powers. It is the eye of the three permanences, which exist as a Voice by virtue of a Thought. And it is a Word by virtue of the Sound ... I (the Word) became a foundation for the All. [2]

By looking at this quote you can see that there was a clear relationship between the experience of inner sound and the mystical experiences of the Gnostics. This same type of relationship is also seen within the Ayahuasca experience. In looking at this Gnostic quote it is interesting to point out the part were the writer says, "I dwell in undefiled Light and a Thought revealed itself perceptibly through the great sound." This is describing an experience that is known to also take place under the effects of Ayahuasca. Many times in the initial stages of the Ayausca experience there is an initial sound that is heard, like a buzz or hum. This sound then leads into the deeper experience of visions of mental unity with another superior thought; this thought then leads into the experience of Gnosis or the experience of knowledge which is received from this thought. It is also interesting to point out the first part of the quote were the writer says, "I am the Word who dwells in the ineffable Silence." This indicates some form of communication that is taking place between the Gnostic initiate and the visionary light that the Gnostic is experiencing, but this communication does not take place with the use of sound or hearing but instead takes place in silence, directly within the mind of the Gnostic initate. Such a phenomenon is also directly associated with the effects of ayahuasca.

Light

When one examines Gnostic literature, one of the most prominent experiences you will find is the visionary experience of light. The visionary experience of light is the most characteristic mystical visionary phenomena attributed to Gnostic religious literature. Experiences of this type have been given many names and descriptions by the many Gnostic groups and authors known to have encountered it, many different Gnostic sects are known to have described this visionary experience of light, in fact it is a very characteristic feature of their religious literature and the visionary experiences that characterize them. Many times the experience of visionary light was directly linked to the practice of ritual and the initiatic visionary experience.

Many Gnostic groups also used many different names to describe this unique visionary encounter of divine light. Some of these include: "the experience of radiance," "receiving illumination," "contact with intelligent light," "being raptured into the light," or "contacting beings or creatures made of light," among many others. The large volume of these types of experiences and the descriptions of them are found throughout Gnostic texts as well as throughout Egyptian Hermetic literature. Yet probably the most important topic related to these various characteristic visionary manifestations of light is that these same types of unique light patterns and complex manifested visionary phenomena are also encountered and described in the same uniquely characteristic patterns in the Ayahuasca experience. As a matter of fact, light experiences of this type are found to be an intrinsic phenomenon to the DMT experience as well as being a fundamental attribute of the Ayahuasca experience.

The fact is that the Ayahusca experience is truly permeated with light, and this light is very characteristic of the experience. This association of sacred light, creatures of light, and contact with intelligent or divine light is something that is also found in many near death experiences of which naturally occurring DMT in the body has also been found to play a vital role. Because light patterns of this type are found to be closely associated with the effects of DMT, and the botanical Ayahuasca analogs are known to contain these sources of DMT, finding the presence of this unique visionary light phenomenon in Gnostic text is a very strong indication of the Gnostics relationship to the use of an ayahuasca anolog for the creation of their visionary experiences. In the Ayausca experience with eyes open, colors gain unusual saturation and intensity in the Ayahusca experience, people often feel that the things around them are saturated with energy, and things radiate and shine. As in the case with eyes open, with respect to objects in the real world, so too is the case for the experience with the eyes closed and the experience of entities or beings seen in visions. During these experiences objects seen in visions are also known to shine, radiate, and glitter. When the intoxication is strong, the colors in the vision are remarkably luminous, and take on stronger visionary complexity. Complexities of light may be introduced by the number and extent of the light and color elements. This configuration of light and colors may also enter into movement. This in turn may generate patterns that people describe as lightning, fractals, or fireworks; these configurations of light may also pulsate and be invested with movement or rhythm. Geometric patterns of light and colors may yield compositions that span the entire field of ones internal visual space. Typically the colors are very luminous and exceedingly beautiful. Many times this initial flow of Geometric patterns of light and color marks the initial state of the Ayahuasca experience. During this stage when these Geometric patterns may be all embracing, and the drinker is engulfed by them, the Ayahuasca drinker may feel that he or she is being carried off or into a transcendental realm. This experience is usually very enchanting and defies any traditional, verbal, or conceptual description or analysis. [3]

Fundamentally, the Ayahuasca experience may be regarded as a grand composition of light, something that also caries over to its various visionary manifestations as well as its unique mind fold transformations. With Ayahuasca, people have visions, but they also feel that they are washed by light, that their minds are clear, that their mentalities are enlightened, that they are in what is best described as receiving a gift of Illumination. Another particular kind of light pattern that is associated with Ayahuasca is one that is always seen and known to appear when people are seen. Manifestations of this kind include halos around the head, Auras, and rays of light that radiate from the body, as well as cones or clouds of light that hover above people. All these may be seen both with eyes open in conjunction with real people or with eyes closed in relationship to people or entities appearing in the visions. In addition to the light being seen, many times it is also felt emotionally, intellectually, and spiritually, just as one can see other people shine and emanate light, one can feel oneself as enveloped by light as well as radiating energy. Typically this type of experience, when one is enveloped in light, is also coupled with profound feelings of bliss, wonder, or happiness. [4]

One of the most special light patterns induced by Ayahusca is the observation of a pattern of almost transparent fine lines of light that connect things in the real world. Many times this experience is seen near the end of the visions. Many times these lines are interpreted as manifestations of cosmic energy, the energy that is the source and fountain of all existence, much like a network system of interconnectedness going throughout the entire universe. The visual representation of interconnectedness can also be demonstrated as an experience of visionary rapture into light or rapture into the divine source of creation. In this type of experience many drinkers may have a feeling of interconnectedness with all things and mental union with a supreme source of life manifesting as intelligent universal light. This is one of the most powerful and profound spiritual experiences noted by drinkers. [5]

Divine Light

In Gnostic literature there are many references to visionary light rapture and experiences of contact with divine intelligent light. Experiences of this type are also described throughout Anthropological literature regarding the effects of Ayahuasca. Out of the many visionary light phenomena associated with the the Ayahuasca experience; the experience of rapture into visionary light is very special. Visionary light rapture is fundamentally an experience in which the drinker becomes saturated, transformed, transported, or consumed by all encompassing visionary light. The experience takes on a deep visionary as well as an emotional complexity that defies any conceptual analysis or description. Visionary light rapture is a very special emotional experience that is most easily described as being transformed or being raptured into the divine presence of creation or life source and into union with an all encompassing living light of a sentient and intelligent nature.In addition to light being seen in the Ayahuasca experience, light can also be interacted with, even experienced as a transformation of light. There are also cases in which drinkers themselves are transformed into light, many times this is noted as a very profound mystical experience. But of all the experiences of light associated with the Ayahuasca experience, the experience of contacting or encountering the supreme living intelligent light of the divine is the most profound and spiritually powerful of all these types of Ayhuasca light experiences. [6]

Indeed these types of visionary experiences are what characterize the Ayahuasca brew as an entheogenic sacrament. Encountering the divine is clearly one of the most common and universally marked visionary characteristics attributed between Ayahuasca experiences and the Gnostic visionary religeus expereinces. The Gnostic's description of these visionary experiences of light are described in there writing and known to have also taken on the same level of deep personal, spiritual, and psychological complexity that is attributed with Ayahusca and other DMT based visionary states. Such experiences were written in Gnostic texts as clearly not only being an important and central force of their religion, but were also known to have effected them on an emotional, spiritual, and psychological leval. The experience of contacting the divine can take on many mental, visual, and emotional forms. Some have described this experience as encountering the supreme life source of nature and existence, others as a living energy saturating them in light and mind. But whatever form this experience takes on, it is undoubtedly a profoundly personal and transforming experience interpreted by drinkers as a very real encounter with the divine, with a real experience of God, and the source of the all. An experience that is not only directly described in Gnostic writings, but takes on an important and special place within their catalog of mystical religious experiences.[7]

Gnosis of Light

A few years into my writing and research of this book, I began to study and experiment with the effects of ayahuasca and vareus ayahuasca analog compounds. One of the more notable experiences I encountered in this research I found directly related to the Gnostics own descriptions of the divine as they are found within their writings. In the Gnostics experiences, we commonly find the divine described as an infinite consciousness of pure light. The Gnostics described their experiences of this in many of the same unique ways that we find are also described in Ayahuasca literature regarding the brews most astounding entheogenic effect, the experience of union with the pure consciousness of the godhead. I have taken the brew many times in the past, but there is one experience that particularly stands out. This experience took place after I consumed a particularly strong dose of the brew, one that I would not recommend anyone else try to do as I am very thankful that I did not get hurt. After drinking the brew, I began to enter deeply into the experience and much faster than I had before, as this took place I began to hear the vibratory noise arise from within my mind as it had in other times past, but this time it was much more audible than anytime before, flowing into my mind at a much faster frequency. I soon began to feel as if I was becoming surrounded by this sound with thoughts of knowledge now beginning to flow quickly into my mind. Unlike the other times these thoughts started to come into my mind at an ever faster rate. Faster and faster the thoughts came, so fast that I could no longer grasp onto them or even understand their meaning. It was as if these thoughts were flowing in my mind at an almost lightning pace, as if I was a computer being downloaded with information that was coming in too fast for me to grasp. As the experience continued I began to role around on the bed and became increasingly absorbed into the experience. As I looked around the room I started to feel that all the material objects around me or in my field of vision had became saturated with a feeling of underlying intelligence or energy, and the darkness of the room around me was gaining an energetic, jeweled, and fractal appearance.

As the experience intensified, I looked at the room around me to see all the objects and matter in my field of vision, such as the wall or my bed, and all other things in my visual surroundings, as if they were made up of an almost living network of vibrating energy. It was as if somehow within or underneath the matter in my field of vision, everything around me that I perceived was made up or imbedded with some form of life or consciousness. My mind and emotions felt this both instinctually and emotionally. I felt that these material objects in my surroundings were animated or imbedded with some form of conscious energy or logos within them. It felt as if I was perceiving some deeper order of operation within the material objects around me.

As the experience continued, I started to roll around on my bed feeling overcome by the extreme mental overload of the experience. As this took place, I closed my eyes only to find images and pictures entering my minds eye. The pictures were made of light and would flash before my inner eyes. As these luminous pictures appeared before me in the darkness, I saw what looked like chromosome shapes and images of DNA molecules. But what these images meant and why they were appearing before me I could not understand. In one instance, I remember watching parts of this luminous chromosome start to move around and rearrange themselves in front of me. It was as if some thing was showing me these pictures, attempting to communicate with me, reorganizing and changing the items in the picture before me. I felt as if something within the visions was trying to show me things and communicate information.

Then as I closed my eyes, I started to see everything as if it were flashing, warping, and being transported into a tunnel of hyper speed pure white light. I began to feel myself becoming totally submerged in the growing white light of the tunnels growing diameter, I began to find myself surrounded by this light and watching it as it flowed past me and around me in the darkness. As I layed on my bed and looked into the light flowing around me, it felt as if it was not just some inner visionary light but as if it was something more, something infused and imbedded with information. I could feel this information as it passed through me and around me in my mind. As the light continued to enclose me I felt that I was traveling faster and faster within it. As this took place I continued to roll around on my bed eventually falling off onto the floor were I only continued my actions. When I did this I felt that I was being overcome by the mental information that was flowing through my mind and the growing tunnel of pure white light that was beginning to consume my awareness. Despite my feeling of mental overextension I was fully self-aware, and at no time did I feel that I was loosing my personal identity or my core person. The mental thoughts and experiences may have come into my mind at a faster rate then my brain was normally used to receiving, but despite this, my soul, mind, or mental identity was always clear and fully intact.

As my rapture into the light progressed, I started to feel as if a form of consciousness or mind existed within the light, it was itself part conscious and aware. As the light continued to flow around me and as I traveled deeper and deeper into its embrace, I began to understand that all matter in the universe was made of energy and that all energy in the universe is imbedded on its deepest levels with this conscious force of information. As this occurred, I was becoming increasingly aware of the intelligent mind and presence within the light around me. Traveling faster and faster into the light I watched it as it continued to surround me. I felt as if I was beginning to flow into and unite with the presence of the light, and I started to feel it around me and within me. Then, while traveling at tremendous speed in this tunnel of light, I found myself sourouded in pure light and in what seemed like almost an instant, my entire awareness and state of consciousness was shattered and all awareness of my surroundings completely vanished, disappeared and the center core of my person/ mind/soul became completely saturated, absorbed and unified into the presence of infinite light and into the presence of pure divine consciousness. At that very brief but seemingly infinite instance, I not only entered and united with the pure consciousness of the light, but I had felt that I had come to be united with all energy in the universe and that all things in the universe were some how all infinitely interconnected and united with me. As this occurred my mind was totally and completely consumed by the presence of this divine mind and its infinite light of pure consciousness. At that moment I became completely aware that I was only a small part of a much deeper and much greater whole, and that at that very moment I was no longer me, I was something more, I was united with this supreme intellect that had taken me through into union with its knowledge and presence, and I had for but an instance, become one mind with the intellectual light that pervaded all things. At that brief moment I was no longer aware of time or space, only aware of the divine infinities self existence and its consciousness within me and interconnection within all things.

Experiences of this type are very private and the nature of such an experience is many times beyond the realm of words. Many times when people have attempted to put these experiences into words, (the experience of Divine light) we come to find that there are many universal attributes that have been given to this Divine encounter. Weather it comes from two thousand year old texts from the sands of the Egyptian Desert, or contemporary anthropological reports of indigenous Ayahuasca use, or near death experiences, when we compare these experiences and the descriptions of them, we find that they directly compare and are found to relate to one another despite time, location, or cultural predicament. The sheer psychological and emotional complexity of the entheogenic experience not only defines the ayahuasca experience, but also sets it apart as a primary visionary characteristic of the Gnostic religeus tradition. The appearance and prominence of this experience in Gnostic litrature defines the entheogenic experience of creating the devine within as one of the most important visionary phenomena shared between the Gnostics visionary religeus experiences and the experiences induced through the use of an ayahuasca anolog. In both Gnostic and ayahuasca experiences of divine contact, both traditions describe the experience in similar ways and with many of the same unique sets of descriptive attributes. Because the Ayahusca brew is known as an entheogen, meaning "creating the divine within," and the Gnostics primary goal was divine contact, the entheogenic potential of ayahuasca alone clearly demonstrates that if such a brew was discovered in antiquity it would have been quickly utilized by various Gnostic sects for this explicit purpose. [8]

Transformations and Rebirth

In Gnostic literature, the Gnostics spoke of encountering the divine both in the form of a great mind that gives knowledge and as a supreme source of living intelligent light. The experience of light rapture and contacting divine light is intrinsic to the DMT and Ayahuasca experience. From near death experiences and botanical plant based brews, to pure DMT, in all encounters of this type, the experience is seen as an utterly transforming experience, touching the deepest most personal aspects of the individual who experiences it. When such an experience is encountered, it leaves an impression on the individual that makes them feel forever changed, as they have experienced something so profound that the individual is changed forever and born a new individual. This profound inner transformation was what was at the very core of the Gnostic world view and it was these transformations that made the Gnostic religious experiences so unique and so personally profound.

There is no question in my mind that when people say that they have had an encounter with the divine under Ayahusca that they are referring to a genuine experience that they have had. I myself have also had such experiences. As I noted earlier, a key facet of the Ayahuasca brew is its effects and spiritual and transcendental qualities. Because of Ayahuascas potential to facilitate an experience of creating the divine within, the Ayahuasca brew has been defined by ethnobotanists as an entheogenic sacrament. Because of this innate tendency it is only natural that such a powerful and unusual experience would generate thoughts and reflections of a spiritual and transcendental type. Many natural visionary or entheogenic substances can induce experiences of the divine when taken in the right conditions, set, or setting to help facilitate a religious experience, but it is the substances who's psychoactive chemical structure most closely resemble ordinary brain chemistry that are most able to induce the most profound mystical and religious experiences on the user. For many people, perhaps most, the main reason to partake of Ayahuasca is spiritual. In all traditional and institutionalized contexts of Ayahuasca use, the consumption of the brew is seen as a sacrament and utilized as a sacred ritual.

The Transformation of light is a very profound and special experience, but the Ayahuasca experience is also known to induce mental transformations of many other types. Under the effects of Ayahuasca, people not only see, hear, and think in a special manner, they also may experience transformations in which they feel that they are subject to temporary mental transformation or metamorphosis and that their identity is altered during the experience. I myself have had experiences of this type: I have had experiences of going back into the womb, being born again, transforming mentally into the mind of a primate and learning about the deep complexities of the universe and the process of evolution. In Amazonian shamanism such transformations are of the most paramount significance. There are many types of mental transformations. Some of these include: temporary mental transformation into an animal or into the personality of another person, but some of the most profound and most closely related types of mental transformations found under the effects of ayahuasca are those having to do with experiencing either birth or death.

Birth and death are two of the most momentous events in human life, and both are also encountered within ayahuasca. In the indigenous context, Ayahuasca is intimately related with death. Evidence of this comes in the brews name: Ayahuasca, which means vine of the soul, or vine of the dead. Both the experience of self death and death of others can be experienced under Ayahusca, as well as the experience of birth or of being born again which are also very common experances throughout the ayahuasca tradition. These unique characteristics of mental transformation, rebirth or even dying and transcending into the realms of the divine are not exclusive to the effects of the Ayahuasca brew, but are experienced with remarkable similarity in both Gnostic and Hermetic religious literature. In Egyptian Hermetic literature in particular the experience of rebirth was held as one of the most prominent and important visionary transforming experiences one could go through outside of mystical union with the totality of the divine. In Gnostic literature, the experience of rebirth are described as being born into a higher state of knowledge or purity as well as dying or the passing away of the past life and the sins of ignorance of God. The experience of being born again is also found and described in the Hermetic Corpus. The experience of rebirth was thus not originally just a symbolic term used to describe the Christians new life with Christ as it is today, but was originally a term used to describe an actual mystical experience of rebirth and personal transformation, an experience that is most closely associated with the effects of an Ayahuasca analog.

The later traditions of Christianity have come to incorporate the term " born again" as a cornerstone term used to describe a new Christian's life with Jesus in the Church. But the use of this term actually stems from much more ancient mystical Gnostic roots. Originally, this term was used by the early Gnostics to signify a transcendental mystical visionary religious experience of personal transformation and rebirth. It was originally a term used to describe an actual life changing experience that was meant to be so profound that it left the individual who experienced it forever changed and mentally born into a new understanding and outlook on life, God, and reality. The prevalence of the term "to be born again" in modern Christianity today further attests to the once widespread popularity of Gnostic practices in the ancient past, long before it was incorporated into the prevailing Christian Orthodoxy. The term to be born again may have once represented a mystical religious experience of personal, spiritual, and mental transformation, but is now only used as a symbolic modern theological term used to signify a new life with Jesus Christ, a term with all of its original inner mystical significance gone and extracted from its original meaning.

Visionary Ascension

While much of the previous discussion has dealt with some of the more prominent attributes of Gnostic visionary religious experiences and a comparative analysis of their similarities to the effects of an Ayahuasca analog. Many of the most peculiar and unique properties of the Gnostic visionary experiences have yet to by fully examined, but remain as some of the greatest proponents demonstrating in favor of the Gnostic's sacraments association with an Ayahuasca analog. The previous topics discussed were elements of Gnostic visions that only manifested as small portions of many unique and equally puzzling visionary religious phenomena noted by Gnostic scholars. Upon a deeper examination of Gnostic experiences, a much more complex array of psychological visionary phenomena are found and represented as unique characteristics of the Gnostic's visionary religious tradition. In studying Gnostic visionary religious experiences, one quickly finds that one of the most unique and puzzling characteristic phenomena associated with Gnosticism is what has been defined by scholars as the visionary experience of ascension.

The visionary experience of ascension is the experience in which the individual experiencing it feels that he/she is ascending into different defined stages of the visionary experience and that these defined stages manifest in a way that makes the individual think that they are ascending into higher regions within the visionary realm. The effect that the individual is ascending into higher stages or realms of reality within the given visionary experience is also closely related to the phenomena of stages, order, and visionary progression. All of which are experiences known to manifest within the Gnostic visionary tradition. Because of the unique characteristics of visionary ascension and its importance to Gnostic visionary experience, it is both important and necessary to point out that these unique characteristics are also found to be fundamentally intrinsic to the effects induced by an Ayahuasca analog. The Ayahuasca experience is known to induce an overall enhancement of sensitivity. As a result, drinkers' perceptions become extremely refined and they come to sense and feel things they would not be able to in their ordinary state of being. The effect is pervasive, it is manifested in the acuity of perception in all sensor modalities, in sensation one has of ones own body and ones tuning in to it, in ones introspection and ability to appreciate the workings of ones own mind in general intuitive capacities.

Under the effects of Ayahuasca, as with other psychoactive agents, people feel that something very basic changes. It seems that the world is no longer the same. Even when drinkers do not have any visions, in the strict sense of the word, they usually discover that the world has altered in a very fundamental fashion during the experience. This feeling is an overall sensation of otherworldliness. The feeling is a perception that things are not as they used to be and one has entered into another hereafter or unknown reality. Let me emphasize that this may be ones subjective feeling even when the world looks as it always does, and even without one experiencing any visionary or phychoactive effects.

In addition to the effect of otherworldliness marking the general atmosphere of the Ayahuasca experience, the effect of beautification is also very typical. Colors may shine and are perceived as brighter and more saturated with color than usual. Colors seem to be richer and the overall clarity of focus in the visual field seems to be increased. In addition to visual beautification, music is also experienced as more beautiful and sounds more expressive than normal. The second feature that the brew brings out is increased meaningfulness. Symbols gain more meaning and emotion, insights are gained, and new personal understandings are reached. From this atmosphere of experiences also comes the emotional effect of enchantment and an increased state of energetic and emotional awareness and initiative insight. Such emotional effects bring about mystical and spiritual feelings on the drinker who experiences them. Such an atmosphere of effects also aids in facilitating the wide variety of mystical experiences that are also associated with the brew. It is this general atmosphere that makes the brew so profoundly spiritual as well as aiding to its many other unique and complex cognitive dynamics. [9]

Just as Ayahuasca makes the drinker extremely sensitive to various cognitive aspects that people in the ordinary state of consciousness tend to ignore, Ayahuasca also makes its drinkers very prone to shift rapidly from one cognitive experience to another. This overall state of mental fluidity brings about a very rapid influx of constantly changing cognitive material. One facet of Ayhuasca visions that regularly receive explicit treatment within Anthropological literature is the effect of stages. Many people have observed that as a session proceeds, the visions change character, and in the course of an Ayahuasca session drinkers may pass through several stages of visioning; furthermore, this progression of stages manifests within an orderly system of development. Such a system of development within the visionary experience is directly related to the visionary experience of ascension as these stages seem to develop in a defined order and as if the person having the vision is ascending into higher realms or stages within the visionary space. This gives the drinker the feeling of an orderly progression of the vision they are experancing. This visionary phenomenon of stages of visions and an organized progression of visions is also closely related to the visionary experience of assention because within this many people feel that they are assending into higher realms or deeper secret knowledge. Probably one of the most important cognitive factors to be taken into account in this examination is the fact that this unique set of cognitive effects are not only intrinsic to the Ayahuasca experience but are also noted by scholars as a common characteristic of the Gnostic's own visionary experiences. [10]

The experience of ascension as it occurs under the effects of Ayahuasca usually make the drinker feel that they have arrived to, or past through a point from one visionary realm into another higher defined reality that is distinctly different within a given visionary experience. This experience is described as ascension because the drinker has an almost instinctive feeling that they are passing through and ascending into a higher order or plain within the visionary realm. The classification of Ayhuasca visualizations in terms of stages, level, or a degree along the lines of a certain order of ascension are not just a classification of western minded scholars. The differentiation of stages and a system of structured order within the visions is a uniquely intrinsic quality to the Ayahuasca brew, and is one of the more remarkable features of the Ayahuasca experience. It is a realization reached by particularly all people whom have partaken of the Ayahuasca brew. This is the idea that one has entered a school and that this school has different classes. Such is the characteristic of one's long term involvement with the brew. The experience of ascension, progression, and stages, during the course of the Ayhuasca session is also common throughout indigenous Amazonian cultures that use the brew, in addition to other outside drinkers that are non-indigenous to the use of the brew. Because of this seemingly universal cognitive phenomenon, it is clear that the experience of visionary ascension is a marked and unique characteristic aspect of the experience regardless of race, creed, cultural background, or time period. [11]

For the Alexandrian fathers, as with the Gnostics, visionary ascension was one among several literary triumphs that could signify a mystical experience of highly varied manifested contents. In the Hermetic tradition a person who was having a vision had transcended his bodily senses and had ascended beyond the physical realm of the seven planetary heavens. The Hermetic mind found itself in a condition of existence that was entirely real, even though it was mental rather than bodily. The eighth celestial regions of Hermetic ascension was not just viewed as eight heavenly realms in space, but were understood as ascending through eight inner dimensions of reality. In Gnostic thought, these inner realms were known as Aeons. Throughout Gnostic literature, names of specific Aeons are described. As the Gnostic initiate ascended into these higher or lower realms of visionary reality, the Gnostic writer would many times describe the contents of what he would encounter within these various Aeons.

The Gnostics even had their own "maps" for these inner cosmos, believing that the soul has to pass through several different inner heavens on its way back to the one divine source, represented as living intelligent light. The Gnostics are famous for their writings and experiences of visionary ascension into higher or lower realms of reality as well as ascending into different stages and orders within a given visionary experience. Many such descriptions are represented in what scholars call the various heavenly journey apocalypse texts, such as the books of Zostrianos and Marsanes among many others. The Gnostics believed there were seven hierarchies or planes of existence. The four lower planes were responsible for purely physical creation, the world of forms visible to the eye. The three higher groups, according to Gnostic thought, could not work on the physical plane. They only helped animate subtle matter. As the Gnostic was initiated into successively higher realms, they would subsequently get closer and closer to the divine world where purer regions of light are reached, realms where life and pure virginal purity were said to reign. The cognitive phenomena of visionary ascension and visionary progression are fundamental characteristics of the Ayahuasca experience. They are also directly associated with the visionary experiences of Gnostic and Hermetic writers. Because of the unique characteristics of visionary ascension and its clear presence and abundance within Gnostic literature, the experience of visionary ascension can now be classified as another prominent attributes relating between the unique visionary and cognative effects of an Ayahuasca anolog and the visionary ritual experances of the Gnostics.

Visionary Progression

As with the visionary experience of ascension, the visionary experience of progression is also a characteristic of the Ayahuasca analog experience. With Ayahuasca in particular, one often feels that the longer one takes the brew, the greater he or she progresses with it, as if one was in a school or receiving some sort of education. Especially interesting are the long term changes in the context and themes of the visions and in the importance they have for the Ayahuasca drinker. As one gains more experience with the brew, one discovers that what happens to oneself under the experience is not haphazard, but rather seems to have an internal logic and order. It is as if there is, within the brew itself, a wise teacher who decides what each individual should experience and learn in each session. This intrinsic phenomenon is noted throughout the indigenous culture, as well as within the modern Psychological community that have studied it and who are educated regarding the experiences induced by the brew. [12]

This experience of visionary progression and its association with the acquisition of knowledge is also clearly attested to in Gnostic and Hermetic literature. Many times this is found in the more visionary ascension text such as Zostrianos where the writer goes through more and more ritual baptisms where higher realms are experienced and subsequently a progression of knowledge is described and experienced. Visionary progression of this type is explicitly represented in many Gnostic visionary experiences. It is also interesting to note that Hierarchies of the heavens are also encountered in various other non-western mythologies, notably in that of the Aztecs, a culture in which psychoactive plants are also known to have played a pivotal role. This visionary order and progression is not a mere theoretical consideration, but is a fully intrinsic cognitive phenomenon to the Ayahuasca experience. In my mind, a remarkable feature associated with this phenomenon is the realization that Ayahuasca is like entering a school, and the Ayahuasca is a doorway to the teacher. Within the Ayhuasca experience, enhanced meaningfulness and deeper senses are naturally linked to what may be regarded as the essence of things. People often feel that they are gaining access to the domain or essence of knowledge and perceiving the ultimate meanings of things, an attribute also closely characterized by the Gnostics regarding their own initatic rituals.[13]

Gnostic Knowledge & the Experience of Gnosis

With so many unique visionary and cognative phenomena found to so closely relate between Gnostic and Ayahuasca experiences, it is important to now go on to examine the most important and fundamental element Gnosticism shares with the Ayahuasca experience: the experience of knowledge. The word *Gnosis* is derived from the Greek and connotes "knowledge" or the "act of knowing." The Greek language differentiates between rational, propositional knowledge, and a distinct form of knowing obtained by experience or perception. It is this latter knowledge, gained from interior comprehension and personal experience that constitutes the Gnostic's gnosis as it is defined from the Greek. The Gnostics were a group of people who knew, not believed, that they received and experienced secret inner visionary knowledge with direct access to and experience of the divine. This belief is represented throughout their writings and it is the defining characteristic of their religion. The experience of the divine and the personal knowledge it imparted on the individual was at the very foundation of the

Gnostic tradition. As with the Ayahuasca traditions, the Gnostics view the use and ritual consumption of their sacred libation as the primary means for obtaining this knowledge. For the Gnostic, their religion was based on actual firsthand experiences, mental knowledge, and information that were received from within their experiences. The Gnostics were knowers; they were a people who knew not believed in the reality of the divine spirit. They were a people who had rituals in which profound spiritual experiences took place, of which the visionary experience of knowledge was a central factor. Thus, it is this experience of knowledge that not only categorizes the Gnostic tradition, but defines it.

To the Gnostics, the attainment of such knowledge always constituted the supreme achievement of human life. When we compare this to Ayahuasca Shamanism, we find that Ayahuasca is also seen as a vehicle, in fact, the prime one for the attainment of knowledge, and such beliefs are found to be very prevalent throughout the indigenous cultures of the Amazon that are known to employ the use of the brew. In these cultures, ultimate realty as well as all major cultural achievements are attributed to the brew. People that take Ayahuasca feel that it puts them in touch with the ultimate realty of being, and thereby reveals to them the deeper meaning of things. This experience is also commonly noted by modern syncretic religious groups who employ the brew as their religious sacrament. In both the Church of Santo Daime and in the UDV it is maintained that what the brew reveals is the ultimate true nature of reality. Within the indigenous cultures, the syncretic religious systems, as well as the non-indigenous cultures known to use the brew, the brew is universally seen to impart direct knowledge and information to the drinker. In addition to the experience of knowledge, the brew gives the user direct knowledge and experience of divine mind, known within Gnostic literature as the experience of Gnosis. In fact, the main motivating reason many people are known to take the Ayahuasca brew today out side of the healing setting, is for its association with deep personal insight, attainment of intellectual and spiritual information, and the wide variety of knowledge the brew imparts on the user. [14]

The most basic themes of many peoples Ayahuasca visions are those concerned with people's understanding of their own personality and life. The visual experience often plays a crucial role in the process of gaining psychological understanding. An example of this would be when a drinker sees people or things in visions that are especially meaningful to them, they gain a new perspective on these things as well as ones own personal relationship with these things within there own life. Such an experience facilitates both mental and emotional healing and growth of the individual drinker. However some of the most profound implications of this type do not come from what is seen or visually experienced in visions; instead it comes about by another means. In most cases, the knowledge that is received in Ayahuasca experiences comes through direct knowledge received through the drinkers mind or thoughts.

In the indigenous context, the ingestion of sacred plants in general and of Ayahuasca in particular, is considered to be the only path to knowledge. Typically, the person under the effects of the brew feels that a voice or a mind is addressing him/her and passing information or instruction. This voice is never heard but is received in the form of inner thoughts teaching the drinker important imformation about the drinkers personal life or interest; this is the very essence of the visionary experience of Gnosis and is the very essence of the Ayahuasca experience. The experience of Gnosis, as it is experienced by Ayhuasca, comes upon the drinker much like a system of thoughts or ideas flowing into or arising from some unknown source within the conscious mind of the individual during the experience. These thoughts are directing and teaching the drinker about matters regarding a wide variety of deeply personal subjects to the drinker's own personal life and physiological needs. Such experiences of Gnosis may also involve instructions and guidelines as to how the drinker should conduct his or her life. Other such experiences may be concerned with the lives of individuals and offers the drinker a better psychological understanding regarding them and other persons. The drinker's relationship to life, the world, and a review of past problems or difficulties in the drinker's life enabling the drinker to reflect, examine, and overcome such experiences through the developing help of the experience of Gnosis. This receiving of knowledge is exactly the same type of Gnosis that the Gnostics described receiving, and it is something that is by far the most fundamental and important attribute found to relate between Gnostic experiences and the experiences induced through the use of Ayahuasca. [15]

In attempting to identify the ingredients in the Gnostic's ritual drinking cup, it is the experience of knowledge that is so fundamental and uniquely intrinsic to both Gnostic and Ayahuasca experiences that identifies the use of an Ayahuasca anolog as the pharmacological agent responsible for creating there many complex and powerful visionary experiences of the Gnostics, including the most prominent, the experience of Gnosis. Becouse Ayahuasca induces such effects of Gnosis on the drinker it is the use of this brew that makes an Ayahuasca analog brew as the primary agent able to induce the Gnostics unique claim of experiencing divine Gnosis. In looking at Hermetic Gnostic texts regarding this relationship, we find the following quote in the <u>Corpus Hermeticum, The Cup of the Monad</u>:

> This is, O Tat, the Gnosis of the Mind, Visions of things divine;
> God Knowledge is it, for the cup is God's. [16]

The experience of Gnosis was the most important aspect of the Gnostic religious tradition and it was the primary source of their transcendental knowledge, wisdom, and personal relationship with the divine. In concluding this examination of visionary gnosis and its relationship to Gnosticism, I am particularly inspired to include this prayer of thanksgiving from the Nag Hammadi Library, a text that is believed by scholars to be a Hermetic Gnostic prayer intended for a group of companions after concluding a mystical ritual experience:

> We give thanks to you! Every soul and every heart is lifted up to you, undisturbed name honored with the name God and Praised with the name father, for to everyone and everything come the fatherly kindness affection and love, and any teaching there may be that is sweet and plain, giving us mind, speech, so that we may expound you, knowledge so that we may know you. We rejoice having been illuminated by your knowledge. We rejoice because you have shown us yourself. We rejoice because while we were still in the body, you have made us divine through your knowledge. The thanksgiving of man who attains to you is one thing: That we know you. We have known you, intellectual light, Life of life, we have known you. [17]

As you can see from this quote, the Gnostics are known to have spoke of mankind having the very potential to have direct spiritual union with the mind and spirit of God, and therefore know God itself. This was truly the essence of the Gnostic's world view. For the ancient Gnostics did not have faith in an unseen god, the Gnostic's knew and directly experienced this great unseen God, the Gnostics were not believers, the Gnostics had Gnosis, they had direct knowledge and experience of the divine world. Many of these experiences came in the form of direct inflow of thoughts and teachings while others came in the form of personal experiences and visions. These experiences were at the very foundation of Gnostics world view. They were also the Gnostics greatest treasure and greatest secret, a secret that was hidden in nature and only revealed to those who had been prepared for what they had to reveal.

Beings of light & Gnostic Entities: Aeons, Archons, and Emanations

As you have already seen, one of the most striking characteristic Phenomena associated with the neural transmitter DMT, as with the plant based Ayahuasca brew, is its ability to place the user in an experience that he or she is having contact with another dimension of reality, and that this space is apparently inhabited by discarnate entities of an independent and intelligent nature. The investigation of such a phenomena is also one of the most mysterious and controversial subjects in the modern cognitive study of Ayahuasca today. Such a possibility clearly takes us to and perhaps beyond the fringes of what is considered scientifically acceptable. Nonetheless, the phenomenon of apparent contact through the other side with other life forms is one of the most radical and fundamental aspects induced by DMT and the ayahusca experience. So while the experience of Gnosis may define the Gnostic tradition, it is the phenomena of entity contact that may be one of its most unique characteristics.

As you have already seen, the Gnostics claimed that the whole spiritual and material universe was peopled with countless numbers of entities and spirits that were known to make up the many varied levels of existence. These are all the successive creation of an original primordial high divine God, a God that was known to them as the great light, the great life, even the great mind. They gave the name Aeon to the higher classes of inhabitants, those which beckon humanity upwards. The inhabitants of the lower classes, those below the level of the human kingdom, they call the Archons. These entities are depicted as jealous of the higher state that mankind has reached. They constantly try to pull him back into a lower, more material realm. When reading Gnostic descriptions of the cosmos, one encounters a bewildering array of these entities, with strange and unusual names.

Today we understand these Aeons and Archons as angels and demons. But to the Gnostics, these beings were not theoretic theological ideas, they were very real creatures that were encountered and described as truly being real. The Gnostics described these experiences as real manifestations of actual experiences with living spirits and encounters of beings that they believed were from other realms of existence. The Gnostics put their understanding of these beings into many complex systems of thought. When we examine Gnostic texts regarding such beings and their encounters with them, we find that the Gnostics described performing rituals in which the initiate experiencing the ritual had a visionary experience in which he or she was entering into another reality or heavenly realm where they encounter the spirits, beings, and other luminous entities.

The past, one of the greatest hurtles in understanding the Gnostic experiences came from the fact that within Gnostic text there were descriptions of experiences in which a ritual was preformed and subsequently various beings or creatures were experienced or encountered. For many years, the possibility of such an encounter within contemporary western academia was unbelievable, unknown, and unsolved. Many scholars believed that the creatures or beings described in these texts were just mythical symbolic representations, ideas, or teachings. Yet scholars could not deny, no matter how hard they tried, the fact that within Gnostic text these beings were said to be real and described and claimed by the Gnostics to have been encountered and to have been actually experienced first hand. The Gnostics described the spirit world as a very real place, a spiritual dimension of reality that could really be experienced and encountered, a place full of mystery and spirit, a place experienced within their secret initiation rituals. Probably the most remarkable attribute found regarding the Gnostic's experience of these beings is the fact that the Gnostics described these beings in many of the same ways and with many of the same characteristics we also find attributed to the experience of luminous beings as they are encountered under the effects of Ayahuasca.

Beings of light as they are experienced under Ayahuasca are usually transparent, translucent ethereal beings which are made of light. Usually these types of beings are seen as divine or semidivine beings. Many times these winged beings of light are regarded as angels, but the winged beings seen in the Ayahuasca experiences are not wings in the standard ornithological sense, but rather, vibrating emanations of light. From just this singular cognative phenomenon alone, it seems foolish to disregard a botanical source of DMT as not being a key ingredient in the Gnostic's visionary ritual cup. The fact that the complex and unique phenomena of entity contact is present as a dominant factor within Gnosticism and Gnostic experiences strongly indicates a relationship between the effects of the Gnostic's ritual visionary drink and the effects of a DMT based Ayahuasca analog brew.

Dualism

In further examining the effects of the Gnostic's visionary drink and its relationship to the phenomena of entity contact, we find that the brew is not always good and generous; it can also have a touch of malice. The brew may be holy and sanctified, but at the same time enchanted and full of secretive and malicious forces. Overall, it seems that Ayahuasca, just like the brew of the Gnostics, leads people to conclude that the world contains both good and evil. As it is said within the Ayahuasca shamanic tradition, "it is very important to encounter the evil and get acquainted with it, for this enables one, when the situation presents itself to confront evil and overcome it." This spiritual and visionary representation of dualism found in the Ayahuasca tradition is also clearly represented in the visionary experiences and beliefs of the Gnostics. Gnostic literature clearly demonstrates the idea that both good and evil forces are acting within the material world as well as within the spiritual visionary world, this concept of visionary spiritual dualism is not just a concept manifesting within the visionary tradition of Ayahuasca, but it is a belief system created from personal experiences that are documented throughout the literature of classical Gnosticism. As in the Ayahuasca tradition, the Gnostics believed that forces both good and bad, dark and light are populating the many different layers of reality, some secretive and malicious while others are divine, enlightening, and healing.

By examining known botanical and pharmacological agents able to create the unique experiences we find documented in classical Gnostic visionary literature, I have been able to compare and directly relate the known effects of these entheogenic substances to the experiences we find documented in Gnostic writings. As you have seen, when the experiences of the Gnostics are directly compared and related to those induced by Ayahuasca and its analogs, it becomes clear that there is a direct relationship between the visionary experiences of the Gnostics and unique effects induced by the Ayahuasca analog experience. It is in fact quite remarkable that so many unique and characteristic cognitive modalities are found to relate so closely between Gnostic and Ayahuasca analog experiences. The fact that so many unique cognative elements are shared between Ayahuasca and Gnostic visions clearly demonstrates in favor for the identification of the Gnostic and Hermetic ritual sacrament. Because of this relationship, we now not only know the identity and ethnobotanical properties of this long lost Gnostic ritual libation, but we have a means to further study and examine it as well as gain a deeper insight into the experiences and profound states of mind that they were known to have induced. Experiences that became the most fundamental attributes of the Gnostic's religious rituals, experiences that were aimed at total mental and spiritual salvation through total mental and emotional absorption into the knowledge and awareness of the divine.

CH 10

EARLY CHRISTIAN HISTORY &
THE FALL OF GNOSTICISM

<hr>

Nothing is to be accepted except on the authority of scripture, since greater is that authority than all powers of the human mind.

St. Augustine

W ith research into the original identification of the Gnostic sacrament now complete, I would like to move on and explore the early history of Christianity. In this examination I will outline Christian Gnosticism and its relationship with the early changing Christian faith that would later become adopted and transformed by the Roman Empire, an event that not only ended with the suppression and extinction of the Gnostics, but the very fall and destruction of the classical world itself. When we study early Christian history, we are lead to examine not only some of the earliest moments in Christian history, but also some of its most mysterious and controversial. In studying early Christian history, it becomes clear that the facts regarding the early history of Christianity as well as the formation of the Orthodox Christian Bible have been shrouded in mystery and controversy since their earliest beginnings. As you have already seen, the four hundred years surrounding the birth of Jesus Christ could be called a renaissance of spiritual seeking and understanding. It was an era in many ways very similar to our own. By about the year 30 B.C. the Roman Empire had consolidated most of the lands surrounding the Mediterranean Sea. Its great highways and shipping routes enabled populations to freely intermingle and exchange cultural and religious ideas. Its system of law unified the vastly divergent populations that it ruled. The first 200 years after the birth of the Christian era were generally peaceful ones, allowing a high achievement in spiritual and philosophical ideals. Though Rome was unbending in its demand of obedience to the state, it tolerated a remarkably free expression of religious thought. Within its borders could be found groups adhering to ideas of Eastern Buddhism, Persian Zoroastrianism, the Egyptian Hermetic tradition, Jewish monotheism, the sun worship of Mithras, Greek Platonic thought, Gnosticism, Literalist Christianity as well as the wide array of gods, cults, and mystery traditions. [1]

Early Christianity was a very diverse religion born out of mystery and conflict. Understanding the early history of Christianity should be vitally important to all Christians. The fact is that the early history of Christianity is far deeper, more mysterious, and more complex than what has been traditionally portrayed in church or biblical scriptures regarding the early history, roots, and development of the Christianity we know today. Because most Christians today receive their knowledge and education of Christianity and its early history from the church and biblical scriptures alone, many if not most orthodox Christians know very little about the truth of Christianity's early history, development, and diverse background. It is because of this fact that so little is known or understood about Christianity's early development and ancient roots. It is also because of this unfortunate tendency that so much of early Christian history is so fundamentally misunderstood by a large portion of Christians today

Birth of Christianity

The religion of Christianity itself is believed to have started out as a largely Jewish sect from the lands of Israel, but due to the ongoing research into early Christian history, historians also now believe that many of Jesus' first followers were not just Jews, but were various pre-Christian Gnostics, both Jewish and none Jewish alike. One of the greatest facts that demonstrate this point comes in evidence found from the surviving Gnostic Mandaeans, also known today as the church of Saint John the Baptist. According to Mandaean history, Jesus, as well as the Mandaeans great prophet, John the Baptist, were both Jewish Gnostics known as Nazarenes. While Jewish Gnostic Nazarenes may have lived in the lands of Israel surrounding the Jordan River, many if not most other Gnostic groups are accredited with living in and around the lands of Egypt. In considering this point, it is important to point out that many of the first locations considered being early Christian strong holds and gathering places were also the areas surrounding ancient Gnostic habitation, particularly in the lands surrounding ancient Egypt. At the time, Egypt was one of the largest gathering places of Gnostic sects known anywhere in the ancient world. From what we can gather from ancient Gnostic texts, many Gnostic sects were waiting for the return of the Seth, the righteous son of Adam, to come back into the world to teach mankind righteousness and save mankind through divine knowledge. Many of these early Gnostic groups believed that God was going to send this divine soul into the world to save mankind, so when Jesus came, many, if not most of these Gnostic groups, came to believe that Jesus was this divine man and came to be many of his earliest followers, considering Jesus as their great divine prophet and appointed savior. This added to the already large Jewish following of Jesus which resulted in a great swell in the cult's popularity following his death and crucifixion. [2]

Diversity of Early Christianity

There were two defining ideas within early Christianity which, until recently, have been largely unknown or misunderstood within Christianity today. This is that at one time Christianity had both inner and outer teachings. The inner teachings were the deeper more esoteric mysteries of Christianity while the outer were related to its dogma, traditions, books, and rituals, rituals that have been extracted of their once mystical contents and experiences. Because many of Jesus Christs' early followers were Jews and Gnostics, many, if not most, of the early secret inner teachings of Christianity contained these more mystical and esoteric Jewish and Gnostic elements, while the outer parts of Christianity came to be concerned with faith, rituals, and the literal interpretation of approved biblical scripture. The difference between the inner and outer mysteries of Christianity began to divide the early followers of Christ between those who knew and practiced the more ancient and mystical side of Christianity, and the more literal outer parts of the religion. These two forms of early Christianity are known today as the Gnostic movements and the literalist movement. The Gnostics claimed the inner secrets and mysteries of Christianity, while the literalist came to take the teachings and books of Jesus as historical literal truth and as the direct literal words of God. The Roman empire came to adopt this literal viewpoint and as such the Roman Orthodoxy wanted to eradicate all of the inner mysterys of Christianity as well as any and all teachings or beliefs that did not exactly line up to their approved written scriptures. Because of this, the Gnostics came under heavy persecution once the Roman Empire claimed this literal viewpoint as Orthodoxy, and all other sects of early Christianity from that time on were deemed as heretical and the followers of these sects became labeled as heretics, being persecuted and even systematically slaughtered. [3]

Roman Christianity came to adopt biblical scripture as the literal written word of God and thus all things in the bible needed to be viewed and taken literally. The Gnostics on the other hand had a very different view of Jesus and the religion of Christianity. Primarily, the Gnostics offered initiates Gnosis, the doctrine of salvation by the experience of the divine. The Gnostics had a baptism that gave the initiate true contact and knowledge of the divine; this was the secret of their Gnosis and their inner rituals. For many of the Gnostics, the reason Jesus came into the world was to give mankind salvation through holy divine knowledge, and the teachings of righteousness to show him how to live good and upright. For many of the Gnostics it was in the initiation experience that this divine knowledge could also be received, not from a book or a priest, but instead through the experience and initiation which came directly from God itself, directly from the mind and thoughts of the divine. Many of the early Gnostic Christians also viewed the spirit of Jesus as being directly associated with their secret initiation experience, a ritual that gave an experience of knowledge and access to an experience of the very mind and knowledge of Christ. The same man who the Gnostics came to believe was the mouthpiece for the logos and was possessed by its divine mind.

While the Gnostics offered divine knowledge through mystical experience, the Roman Orthodoxy on the other hand offered the hope of a heavenly afterlife through believing in the historical and the exact literary authenticity of Jesus and the written gospels. They looked at biblical texts as literal, and thus defining their claim to truth and the Christian theology. While Gnostic Christians knew about and very well may have read many of the biblical scriptures, the Gnostics never looked at these books in a completely literal way. The Gnostics looked at their sacred books with a more open, symbolic, and mystical eye, taking them as a guide to living a holy and righteous life as well as giving them insight into the sacred inner mysteries of God and the divine inner worlds that they were so intimately aware of through initiation rituals that were taking place long before the birth of Jesus Christ or the rise of Christianity. [4]

There were many dividing factors between the different early Christian sects and their teachings. It was in many of these basic dividing concepts that the early Christian communities became divided right from the start. When the teachings of Jesus spread from the Jews to "the gentiles," Christianity had started drifting away from traditional Judaism as more and more of its followers were non-Jews. By the middle of the 2nd century, most Christians were gentiles and not Jews, they had rejected all the rules of the Jewish Law the laws of circumcision, and all the other laws proscribed by Moses, but the controversy still raged. The Christians wanted the Jewish scripture, but not Judaism. They therefore proclaimed that since the Jews had rejected the savior who god had sent them, they had forfeited there spiritual heritage, which we must say now legitimately belonged to the Christians. The Gnostic Christians on the other hand had rejected the Jehovah concept of God found in the Old

Testament of the Jews all together in favor of a more mystical conception of God as a supreme oneness, identical to how God was seen by the Philosophers and initiates of the Pagan Mysteries. [5]

Early Christian Conflict

From the beginning of its history up to the present time, Christianity has been a religion of schism and conflict. There is not a single document in the New Testament that does not worn of false teachings or talk about division even despite having the creed of Nicaea the Christian church remained in conflict. This conflict and division in Christianity can be found throughout Christianity's long history, many still remaining to this day. This inherent intolerance and division is not something new to Christianity, as Celsus writes at the end of the 2nd century before the birth of Roman Orthodoxy, it seems to have been a problem that has continued for a very long time:

> Christians, it is needless to say, utterly detest each other. They slander each other constantly with the vilest forms of abuse, and cannot come to any sort of agreement on their teachings. [6]

Celsus continues in saying:

> At the start of their movement, they were few in number, and unified in purpose. Since that time, they have spread all around and now number in the thousands. It is not surprising, therefore, that there are divisions among them - factions of all sorts, each wanting to have their own territory. Nor is it surprising that as these divisions have become so numerous, the various parties have taken to condemning each other, so that today they have only one thing in common- the name " Christian." But despite them clinging proudly to their name, in most respects they are at odds. [7]

From the 2nd century onward the Christians wrote numbers of long and abusive documents against the Jews. They even started to denounce their own other sects, sects like the Gnostics, who the literalist Roman church would later claim as a corrupted and impure form of Christianity that had been manipulated by pagan influences. To finally grapple Christianity away from the Gnostics and build a centralized religion based on common dogmas, the Roman bishops needed to counteract the influence of the large numbers of Gnostic gospels circulating at the time. They therefore set out to create a canon of acceptable scripture as a definitive statement of Christianity and dismiss all other texts as heretical and spurious. [8]

Christian Persecution

The conflict between the inner and outer mysteries of Christianity came to a peek under the pressure of the Roman persecution of the Christians. The Gnostic Christians and literalist Christians both took this persecution in very different ways. For the literalist Christians at the time, Jesus had been a martyr for the sins of the world and for their salvation, therefore to meet one's death was a sign of following gloriously in his footsteps. Cyprian who died in 258 C.E. vividly described the delight of the lord with the "sublime, the great the acceptable spectacle" of "flowing blood which quenches the flames and the fires of hell by its glorious gore." Because of statements like this, many literalists Christians actively sought to be martyrs for Jesus Christ and actively sought their deaths. They believed that through suffering they could purchase for themselves eternal life in heaven. [9]

The Gnostics, by contrast, view the idea of being a martyr as ensuring salvation as a complete misunderstanding of Christ and Christianity. They believed that one should accept ones god given fate, including meeting a martyr's death, but they regarded it as ridiculous and diluted to actively seek out martyrdom, as a quick way into heaven. For the Gnostic's spiritual enlightenment was to be found through the mystical realization of gnosis and not in grand gestures. The Gnostics did not believe that Jesus literally died as a martyr, but that his death symbolically represented a profound mystical truth. To die to what the Gnostics called ones own lower material self and to be resurrected as the Christ within was to imitate Jesus and it was not to be courting martyrdom, or show that by blind faith they know the truth. To the literalist Christian on the other hand, such Gnostic attitudes made the suffering of the martyrs appear to be futile. The author of a letter attributed to the Christian Ignatius writes this regarding these historical points:

> But if, as some say, Jesus suffering was only in appearance, then why am I a prisoner, and why do I long to fight with the wild beast? In that case, I am dying in vain. [10]

Another long and heated debate taking place in the early years of Christianity's development was the belief in the second coming of Christ. There was a widespread belief that humanity was about to enter a glorious era and that it would begin when Christ returned to set up his kingdom, to reward the faithful, punish the wicked, and restore physical life to those whose flesh had died in his favor, but the Gnostics held no such beliefs. We find no mention of the second coming or even a physical resurrection. Just as the crucifixion was understood in a totally different way from how it was by many of the Roman Christian groups, a physical resurrection held no attraction to the Gnostics because they knew that the true victory lay in transcending the physical body, not carrying it into the afterlife. For them, the resurrection was something that happens inwardly, not outwardly. It happened in the mind and soul of a person and it was through direct religious experience that Gnostic knowledge and salvation was received. Because of divisions like this, the literalist branch of Christianity began to see the Gnostics as traitors to Christianity; they saw them as people who were undermining their attempts to unite the church in the face of oppression by offering a theological justification for cowards. Gnostics on the other hand, saw the literalists as fanatical extremists leading the gullible to pointless suffering with untrue false promises and empty rituals. [11]

The traditional history of Christian persecution paints a picture that the Roman Empire had a particular hatred for the new religion, but in all actuality things were not so. The fact is that Rome was constantly purging itself of mystics, philosophers, and religious cults, which it saw as a threat to its stability. The Romans truly had a love-hate relationship with their mystery cults, and the Christians at the time were just another part of it. The followers of the mysteries of Dionysus, like the later followers of Jesus, were accused of conspiracy to overthrow the state. From as early as 186 B.C. the Mysteries of Dionysus had been prohibited in Rome and the shrines destroyed throughout Italy. Huge numbers of initiates were executed, sometimes many thousands at a time. Even at various times during the first few centuries it was almost a crime to philosophize in Rome. Even the great philosopher Epictetus was exiled, along with countless others. Like the Christian's martyrs after them, many philosophers were sent to their deaths for refusing to compromise with the tyrannical Roman authorities. [12]

After Jesus' death, his following started to spread like wildfire throughout the Roman Empire, but the growth and popularity of Christianity in the first three centuries was not unique, but was part of the general uprising of monotheistic mystery cults throughout the ancient world at this time in history. Christianity was just another monotheistic mystery cult, one of many. The religion and success of the Mithraic Mysteries into the Roman Empire is a great example of this. In the year 304 A.D., just 17 years before Christianity became the state religion, the Persian savior Mithras and the mysteries of Mithraism had been spreading extremely rapidly throughout the Roman Empire. It entered the Roman Empire some time around the first century and developed until about the third century A.D. At the height of its popularity, Mithraism was practiced from one end of the empire to the other. [13]

Mithraism was emphatically a soldier religion, for this is where it received its greatest adherents and popularity. Its foremost apostles were the legionaries, where it spread first from the frontier stations of the Roman army. At the same time, Eastern slaves and foreign tradesmen were maintained its propaganda in the cities. Mithraism had a Eucharist and a sacred meal. The sacred meal was celebrated with bread and Haoma juice for which wine was later substituted. The first principle or highest God was, according to Mithraism, "Infinite Time" and was symbolically represented as a human with the head of a lion and a serpent coiled about his body. He carried a scepter of lightning as sovereign high god and held in each hand a key, as the lord and master of the heavens. He had two pairs of wings to symbolize the swiftness of time. His body was covered with zodiacal signs and the emblems of the seasons. Mithraism was a monotheistic fusion of Persian and Chaldaean philosophy, Persian Dualism, and Chaldaean star science. It was a mystery cult with a belief in one God venerated as pure light and its inner mysteries were said to have come from the days of old, where the greatest source of its mystical power and lore were said to have been contained. [14]

By the end of the second century, the Roman Emperor Commodus was initiated into the mystery rites of Mithras, an event which created an immense stir in the Roman Empire and lead to a great swell in the cult's popularity. A number of emperors after Commodus also attempted to make the Persian religion of Mithraism the state religion of Rome. Over the years other Roman leaders had tried with different degrees to make different mystery religions the one universal religion of the Roman Empire. Marc Anthony had styled himself on Dionysus. Claudius had looked at Attis. Vespasian had worshiped Serapis, Domitan honored the Egyptian God of vegetation and rebirth, the lord Osiris. [15]

To endorse their claim of "One empire, one Emperor" in the face of increasing fragmentation and un-stabilization of the Roman empire, the Emperor needed a one unifying religion, something that all the people of the empire could follow and believe in. The empire needed "One Faith," a universal religion to bring together and unite the empire. The Persian religion of Mithraism was the leading competitor to early Christianity in those early years. Many cults had been proposed at different times, but all without any successes. It was not until the first half of the 4th century that the Emperor Constantine tried Christianity. It was an ideal candidate for the role. The Romans needed a popular monotheistic mystery religion because they were always so popular with the people, but mystery religions were lead by mystics and philosophers who had the audacity to question and undermine the authority of the empire, and the authority of the state. It is historically clear that the strict Roman Empire had many problems with these developing mystery cults as well as many of their teachers and philosophers, but Christianity was unique. Christianity had a sect and a set of teachings separate from its inner mystery traditions, a sect separate from its inner mystery rites. [16]

Constantine believed, as many of the emperors did, that it was only religion that could unify the Roman Empire and seat him as Rome's all powerful emperor. However, Rome also needed to be purged of its many mystery religions as well as all of its troublesome intellectuals and secret inner mysteries. There was one sect of Christianity that was already an authoritarian religion, which encouraged the faithful followers to have blind faith in those holding positions of power. This is exactly what the Roman authorities wanted, a religion without mystics, a religion with only the outer mysteries, free from its troublesome inner mysteries. [17]

In year 321 A.D. emperor Constantine became the first Christian emperor, making Christianity the state religion. Like most Roman emperors, Constantine was a vicious and ruthless man, and he clearly did not become more compassionate with his conversion to Christianity. Almost immediately after presiding over the Christian council of Nicaea, the council that created the Nicaen creed for the Roman Catholic Church, he had both his sons and their stepmother Fausta murdered. He even deliberately postponed his own baptism until just before his death on his very death bed, so that he could continue living as he wished and yet be assured of a heavenly afterlife. Constantine's reputation was such that not even the Roman Catholic Church could face making him a saint. [18]

The inspiration for Constantine's Christianity came from his mother Helena, who had become a Christian sometime before. She was forced into exile under the implication for murdering Constantine's step mother, so she went to the holy land. Here she miraculously found the cave that Jesus was born in, along with the remains of the three crosses used to crucify Jesus and the two thieves of Golgotha. This truly was an extraordinary miracle since thousands of other Jews had been executed in the 300 years that had elapsed since Jesus supposedly met his death! [19]

It is one of the great ironies of human history that the great Roman Empire eventually came to embrace Christianity, not just as a new mystery cult, but as the one and only true religion. It seems incredible that having completely laid waste to the state of Israel, the Roman Empire should end up adopting a religion with Jewish history in its sacred text, and based on a Jewish prophet that was said to have been executed by a Roman governor. [20] After Constantine, the Roman Empire became increasingly Christianized under successive and even more intolerant Orthodox Christian emperors, except for one emperor, Julian in the year 360 A.D. For a brief spell, Julian tried to reinstate the old philosophies and open religious beliefs back into the empire. He was himself a Platonic philosopher, he was noted for his humility and who wrote a beautiful hymn to the one God. Emperor Julian was also initiated into both the inner mysteries of the Person Mythras and the Greek Dionysus. He proclaimed toleration for all religions. He even attempted to rebuild the Jewish temple in Jerusalem, but much to the delight of the anti-Semitic early Christian church, he never succeeded. Julian's pagan renaissance was short lived and after it, Christianity was reinstated and enforced with even greater force and vehemence. [21]

Two churches

Once the Roman Church had claimed orthodoxy of Christianity, and clearly decided that the Gnostics were heretics, some Gnostics tried, like the great Valentenus, to maintain the original version of the Jesus mysteries by attempting to hold together the ever widening rift between the outer and inner mysteries of Christianity. Following in the original Christian tradition of Paul, sages such as Valentinus viewed the church as necessarily comprised of two parts, the "psychic," also known as the literalists, and the "pneumatic," which were the inner more mystical Gnostic Christians. Paul wanted all Christians to confess the same thing," so to avoid a destructive schism within the community. Paul advised the Pneumatic Christians to keep their deeper Gnostic understanding a secret "between yourselves and God." The Valintineans likewise did not discuss the fact that they taught inner mysteries, but still participated in all the outward ceremonies with the literalists. In a document from Irenaeus we find that he found it frustrating trying to argue theology with Valentinus, for Valentinus would complain the following:

> They keep asking us how it is that when we confess the same things and hold to the same doctrine, we are called Heretics! [22]

By the beginning of the 3rd century the Valintinean Christians came to be split between those in the east who had given up on the literalists as a lost cause and regarding them as outside the "Body of Christ," and the western Valintineans who still fought to unite the rift in Christianity. The Gnostics covered Asia and Egypt while the literalists were gaining more and more power and influence throughout the Mediterranean. [23] The Gnostics were the mystics and intellectuals of early Christianity who commanded the respect of large numbers of Christians. Valentinus was a heavy force in early Christianity for he was a highly educated Alexandrian philosopher and poet who was elected bishop of Egypt until Gnosticism was violently suppressed in the 4th and 5th centuries. Gnosticism is the path of directly experiencing the divine as the path to salvation. Mysticism, Gnosticism, and the Jewish Kabbalah are all very similar. Their path to God is to look for God within ourselves and understand God as a spirit of mind and totality. If we take the view that God is within everything, and that nature and the universe is the very embodiment of God, then our own inner self is the most accessible point for experiencing the divine and the all-pervading supreme reality of its existence. Probably one of the greatest biblical quotes that reflects this Gnostic view point is powerfully presented by Jesus in Luke 17:20-21:

> And when he was demanded of the Pharisees, when the kingdom of God should come, he answered them and said the kingdom of God cometh not with observation: Neither shall they say, Lo here!, lo there! For, behold, the kingdom of God is within you. (Luke 17:20-21,)

Extraction of Gnostic Rituals

In examining later Gnostic literature and history, it becomes clear that later Gnostic treatises begin to witness what seems to be a gradual extraction of the clearly repeatable visionary components from the original baptismal ritual setting, something that also directly coincides with the early Christian history of the time. Historical texts clearly show that it was the loss of these inner mysteries that the great Valintineus tried so hard to protect, and prevent from being lost during the early rise of Christian Orthodoxy in later centuries. Later Valentinian Baptism rites further demonstrate that the clearly repeatable ritual practices that facilitated the religious experiences of his group, were being extracted of their mystical significance due to increased Orthodox Christian persecution. Valentinian baptismal practices were known to have functioned on three basic features. The first is the presence of two separate baptisms among the Valentinians: the "psychic," which was the "normal" Christian one, while the "pneumatic" was the inner secret one that could allow people to gain closer contact with the divine by a second inner rite which Irenaeus and Hippolytus called the "redemption." [24]

In examining these later historical Gnostic texts, we find a strong division growing between the inner secret rituals of the Gnostic Christians and the outer rituals of the Orthodox Christians. The only difference between them was that the Orthodox Church had symbolic ritual acts while the inner rites of the Gnostics were not symbolic but were based on real mystical religious experiences. This fight for orthodoxy and extraction of the inner mystical traditions of early Christianity is what was taking place during the early decline of Gnosticism and the rising power of Roman Christian Orthodoxy.

It was a series of events that would eventually lead to the Gnostic's eradication at the hands of the Roman Catholic Church and the eventual decline and suppression of all other pagan non-Christian religious pursuits. The extraction of the Gnostic's inner visionary rituals can also be seen in some of the beliefs expressed at the time. Rather than devaluing the standard psychic baptism, Theodoto demonstrated great concern for the psychics. These visionary rituals were seen as salvation sacraments to the Gnostics, but soon enough the visionary elements of these rituals eventually came to be replaced by only outer symbolic acts and a baptism used only for the remission of sins, with all evidence of a second and inner secret baptism being extracted. Evidence of this is seen in the Excerpta ex Theodoto which characterizes the first water baptism as a "sealing" done in the name of the Father, the Son, and the Holy Spirit, which gives Christians power over sin, allowing them to be reborn, control the impure spirits, and gain entry to the marriage feast in the end times. Symbolic acts like this were increasingly being introduced into Christianity and were intended to override the need for the Gnostic's second inner visionary baptism with more suitable symbolic acts. [25]

According to Hippolytus, Marcus taught that a second washing or baptism, called the "redemption," was available to Christians through him. Valentinian taught that the redemption was part of the bridal chamber and thus made the second inner baptisms of the Valentinian Christians the most secret and sacred visionary ritual of ancient Gnostic Christianity. The Gnostic teachers stated that this ritual normally required special and extensive instructions beforehand, but a bishop could also administer it to those who were on their deathbed. Anyone undergoing the rite of redemption belonged to "the perfect power and inconceivable authority," and was no longer affected by sin. Redemption, on the other hand, was brought by the spirit of Christ descending on the man Jesus with the aim of perfecting him; this demonstrates another instance of the widespread Gnostic adoption of the traditions about Jesus' inaugural baptism in which he sees the heavens opened, and receives both the Holy Spirit and is adopted as the son of God. In the Sethian tradition, the descent of the spirit upon Jesus at his baptism justified the distinction of the Gnostic's own secret visionary baptism rituals, rituals that were also said to have imparted a visionary knowledge and experience of the divine. Indeed Irenaeus spoke of the Valentinian tendency to gather gospel allusions such as Luke 12:50 or Matthew 20:20 to support the necessity for another inner or more secret ritual baptism being practiced by his tradition. The remission of sins is linked to baptism, and thence to repentance, the psychics, and the ministries of John and Jesus. Redemption, on the other hand, is linked to pneumatics, perfection, and the spirit of Christ descending on the man, Jesus. This is also what was known by the Valentinian Christians as the inner and outer mysteries of original Christianity. [26]

Valentinian Christians are themselves baptized through the same redemption of the same name which descended to redeem Jesus at his own baptism. These angels are baptized "for the dead," that is, for the earthly Valentinians, who also imparting to them the name of the son by which they are enabled to pass through the vail and into the Pleroma of the divine reality.Valentinian baptism was thus equivalent to the redemption, or the second baptism just mentioned. Redemption occurs when one enters the bridal chamber, which is also equivalent to entering a state of enlightenment, and mental union with the divine. This was the effect of the inner ritual of the bridal chamber, a ritual that was also associated with this second or secret inner baptism of Christianity. It is the ritual, which, above all others, functioned as the seal of the union between the author's community and God who grants knowledge of himself in exchange for the believer's confession of his newfound faith and newfound awareness in the existence of the divine.[27]

As the divide between the inner and outer mystery of Christianity grew, the inner visionary rituals of the Gnostics continued to be replaced by symbolic acts, something that many traditional Gnostics still rejected. One later Gnostic quote relates that "the true redemption occurs only through inner, spiritual awakening of man's knowledge of the ineffable greatness." The clear distinction between the inner visionary experiences of the Gnostics and the outer beliefs and teaching of the Christians can be seen in many later Gnostic treaties. One such later Gnostic quote relates the following:

> The Pleroma or Heaven is as the bridal chamber in which the elect spiritual beings will experience ultimate restoration as the bride of the savior, while the "called" psychic humans, the "men of the Church," will serve as attendants outside the pleroma in the aeon of "images," until they receive instruction, upon which all will receive the restoration together. [28]

This Gnostic quote is explaining that heaven is like a sacred union in which the soul of a person is united with the spirit of the divine all upon death. It then goes on to say that the elect spiritual person or Gnostic, will experience ultimate restoration of this union with the divine right away after death. But the people of the church who have not been saved through the rituals of the elect will serve as attendants outside of this sacred union. While they wait, they will lay in rest in the aeon of images until they receive instruction in this realm. Once this instruction is complete they can enter into heaven and join into union with the elect and the divine.

The Destruction of Gnosticism

Even after literalist Christianity had become the state religion of the Roman Empire, Gnosticism remained a powerful force. In the 4th century Heretical Christians were still so common, the Cyril of Jerusalem had to warn the faithful to be careful not to step into a Gnostic church by mistake. In the year 381 A.D Theodosius finally made heresy a crime against the state. Gnostic writings were condemned as a "hotbed of manifold perversity," which "should not only be forbidden, but entirely destroyed and burned with fire." All philosophical debate was entirely suppressed. A proclamation from this period declares:

> There shall be no opportunity for any man to go out to the public
> and to argue about religion or to discuss it or give any counsel. [29]

Augustine, the great spokesman for Catholic Christianity, expressed the mood of the times when he explained that coercion was necessary since many people respond only to fear. Military force was "indispensable" in suppressing heretics for their own good, of course. Augustine proclaims: "filled with fear myself, I fill you with fear." The spirituality of St. Paul and Jesus was love and knowledge and now only a few hundred years later was replaced by the Roman churches religion of obedience and terror. [30]

The reason why much of the early history of Christianity has become lost and is so greatly misunderstood today is because of the fact that after the Roman Empire claimed to hold the one true source of Christianity, thus claiming orthodoxy, they named all other forms of Christianity including the Gnostics as heretics, viewing their religious beliefs as well as all other religious traditions of the ancient world as perverse forms totally misguided from the one truth that was the written word of God. Soon after, the Roman Catholic Church came to claim orthodoxy. They began to persecute and systematically eradicate all forces of division within their ranks including the Gnostics. When the early Roman Church began to do this, the Gnostic's beliefs and teachings were systematically suppressed and outlawed, slowing eradicating the very esoteric roots and traditions from which the great prophet Jesus Christ originally emerged from. Like his cousin John the Baptist, Jesus was a Jew, but not the traditional Rabbinic Orthodox Jews we know today. Instead, Jesus and his cousin John the Baptist were part of a more ancient and mystical side of Judaism, a group of Gnostic Jews known as the Nasoreans.

The mystical Jewish tradition these two men emerged from commanded some of the most radical, mystical, religious experiences documented from the ancient world. When the Gnostics began to be persecuted and their religion became outlawed, what began to disappear was not just the secret mystical side of Judaism and early Christianity, but also the very original traditions that helped shape the very life and teachings of Christ himself.

But if Gnostic rituals were so profound, why did literalist Christianity triumph over Gnostic philosophy? Well, by its nature, Gnosticism attracted people of a deeper and more mystical disposition, while literalism, on the other hand, attracted people only interested in establishing a religion. The Gnostics were concerned with personal enlightenment, not in creating a church. By their very nature, the Gnostics had an anti-establishment ideology while they knew the need for such things; it was never in their desire to do so. Literalism on the other hand was originally the outer mysteries of Christianity, designed to attract initiates to the spiritual path. They were meant to be more popular and appealing than the inner mysteries. If the initial integrity of the Jesus mysteries had survived, the popularity of the outer mysteries would have led more and more people into the deeper inner mysteries of Gnosis that characterized Gnosticism and the tradition of early Christianity, but unfortunately, the Gnostics and the literalists were two distinct traditions in conflict with each other, and inevitably it was the literalists that won. Above all however, the early literalist had one quality that eventually decided the fate of the teachings of Christ and that was intolerance. This intolerance divided the church, widened the rift, eventually suppressing and destroying all existence of its original inner mysteries and eventually leading to the complete destruction and eradication of the Gnostic tradition. [31]

The holy conquest of the Roman Christian Orthodoxy would not stop with the Gnostics. The newly constructed state religion of Rome would only get more and more intolerant of other religions and spiritual traditions, continuing its campaign of cultural eradication and religious conversion. Soon enough, all pagan traditions, writings, and temples were in the eyes of the Holy Roman Empire and the beginning of the end of the classical age had finally begun. By the late 4th century, persecution of pagans by Christians had reached new levels of intensity. Temples and statues were destroyed throughout the Roman Empire, and pagan rituals were forbidden under punishment of death. In 391 A.D. Emperor Theodosius ordered the destruction of all pagan temples, and patriarch Theophilus of Alexandria complied with this request. Socrates Scholasticus provides the following account of the destruction of the temples in the great city of Alexandria Egypt: [32]

> Demolition of the Idolatrous Temples at Alexandria, and the
> Consequent Conflict between the Pagans and Christians, at the
> solicitation of Theophilus bishop of Alexandria, the emperor issued
> an order at this time for the demolition of the heathen temples
> in that city; commanding also that it should be put in execution
> under the direction of Theophilus. Seizing this opportunity,
> Theophilus exerted himself to the utmost to expose the pagan
> mysteries to contempt. [33]

In Alexandria Egypt the Alexandrian school of Neo Platonism was once known as a center for the investigation in the department of the special sciences and for the labor of commenting on the works of Plato and Aristotle. Hypatio, the principal Neo Platonic teacher at that time, (Best known for his murder in 415 A.D by a fanatical mob of Christians) wrote on mathematics and astronomy. It is also said that he was known to have lectured on Plato and Aristotle, but with the growing power and influence of the Christian Church, the Metaphysical and religious interest began to retreat to the foreground, the once multiplication of intermediary beings so characteristic of Iamblichus and Proclus teachings began to be abandoned and little attention was paid to the doctrine of ecstasy that was once so popular years before. In the later commentaries of the school we find that they paid more and more special attention to the more logical works of Aristotle. The Neo Platonic school at Alexandria gradually lost its specifically pagan character and became rather a "neutral" philosophical institute: logic and science were obviously subjects on which Christians and Pagans could meet on more or less common ground. It was this growing association of the school with Christianity that made possible the continuation of Hellenistic thought at Constantinople. The doctrine of salvation as it was found in the philosophical schools was a doctrine of ecstatic union with the Godhead and like the Gnostics and the Egyptians, Hellenistic Philosophers held a strong reverence for these experiences, their cultivation and the knowledge they imparted. Soon after the death of Proclus, and because of the growing influence of Roman Christianity throughout the empire, classical philosophy began to see a sharp decline. [34]

By the year 529 the Roman Emperor Justinian finally forbade the teachings of Philosophy at Athens, and Damascus, together with Simplicius and five other members of the last Neo Platonic school went to Persia, where they were received by the King Chosroes. Then in 533 they returned to Athens, apparently disappointed with the cultural state of Persia. Soon after this, it is not apparent that there were any more Pagan Neo Platonists surviving shortly after the middle of that same century and the once great philosophers of the classical age were finally silenced making Neo Platonism the last great breath and intellectual flower of classical pagan philosophy. [35]

Soon after this, came the closures of the temples and the eradication of the mystery traditions, all secret and philosophical teachings regarding ecstatic union began to quickly disappear. Soon after this, all evidence that the visionary and ecstatic experiences that were once so central to late classical philosophical thought and religion, became hidden, with many of their teachings and books being burned and sent to the fires. All knowledge of these once great experiences were finally successfully suppressed and eradicated by the growing power of Roman Catholic Orthodoxy. With no one left to initiate people into these once great mysteries, and with no one left to pass on these secret rituals and teachings, all knowledge of these once great cults and religious institutions disappeared. All knowledge of these experiences and the methods used to create them became lost with all knowledge of their source completely disappearing from the European world. With the mysteries no longer being perpetuated, the Roman Christian church had become successful in suppressing the already secret Pagan practice of creating the divine within and had succeeded in eradicating the last great mysteries of the classical western world.

In Egypt, the once great mysteries of Osiris that had continued from the most ancient and early periods in Egyptian history up until almost the 6th century A.D. on the island of Philae in Upper Nile, was finally destroyed. The Theodosian decree (in about 380 A.D.) to destroy all pagan temples and force worshippers to accept Christianity was ignored there. However, Justinian dispatched general Narses to Philae, who destroyed the Osirian temples and sanctuaries, threw the priests into prison, and carted the sacred images off to Constantinople. At about this same time, it is believed that the great library of Alexandria was sent to the flames with many of its great collections of ancient scrolls being burned, stolen, and destroyed. Civil wars, decreasing investments in maintenance, acquisition of new scrolls, and generally declining interest in non-religious Christian pursuits, likely contributed to the further reduction in the body of books and written material available in what had once serviced as the largest and greatest library in the ancient world. [36]

In 325 A.D. Roman orthodoxy was sealed in two ways. Constantine declared Christianity the only state religion, and the council of Nicea declared that Jesus was identical with the one and only God of the universe. Dissenting voices were tolerated a while longer, but in 381 A.D. the emperor Theodosius I officially recognized one single branch of Orthodox Catholicism. This opened the way for even more extensive sanctions, including violence against the Gnostics as well as the many other cults and religions of the ancient world, many with roots and traditions that ran back many thousands of years. In its zeal for absolute authority, the Roman church attacked with equal fervor the pagan religions and age old mystery traditions. In a rampage it destroyed ancient temples and monuments, with its attacks eventually extending into systems of pure philosophy, knowledge, and science, with the subsequent great library of Alexandria eventually being sent to the flames. The following is a quote attesting to the burning and destruction of all non-Christian books at the hands of the Roman Catholic Church during the fall of the classical age.

> Innumerable books were piled together many heaps of volumes drawn from various houses, to be burnt under the eye of the judges as prohibited. Owners burnet their entire libraries, so great was the terror that seized everyone. [37]

In the coming years the Roman Empire would fall into increasing decline, corruption, and war. Soon after this would come the fall and destruction of the once mighty Roman Empire herself and the lands of Europe would fall into a cultural and economic collapse, and shortly after, western civilization would fall hopelessly into the dark ages.

Part III:

Other Visions and a New World

CH 11

MYSTERIES OF DARK AGE MAGIC

For this quest is the most sublime that was ever instituted, the quest for the Holy Grail, which holds in store for him who shall see it through such honors as passes man's imagining.

(King Author: The Quest for the Holy Grail)

The dark ages refer to the initial five hundred years following the fall of Rome. It is thought of as beginning around 450 A.D. and continuing till about 1000 A.D. The Dark ages lasted over 500 years and were a period in history when Christianity increased its power and control over early medieval Europe. During this time period Rome and other cities deteriorated because of the invasions of barbarians from northern and central Europe. Since there was no longer an imperial authority with the power to protect the citizens of the cities, the urban population declined sharply during this period of history. Another consequence of the lack of a strong central power was the development of the feudal system especially from 900-1150 A.D. During this feudal age, most parishes had rural populations, and towns tended to be smaller and less numerous. Wars and civil wars filled the land. This brought about the creation of castles and walled towns that were guarded by the feudal lord's armies that provided security and safety to the peasants and townspeople from the invading barbarians. One of the great strengths of the church in the dark ages is how it highlights that the Roman Empire's fall would enable the church and the papacy not only to endure, but in its interaction with the barbarian invaders, to fashion a new and vibrant Christian culture, one stronger and more widespread than ever before. With the fall of the Roman Empire, the Catholic Church was able to gain even more power, control, and continue its campaign as the ruling hand of God's authority on earth. It continued gaining power and influence over the people by continuing its campaign of converting souls and concurring lands. With its continued growing power, the Roman Catholic Church continued its religious campaign of conversion and cultural assimilation, resulting in the complete successful suppression and eradication of the last indigenous religious practices on the European subcontinent with Christianity eventually covering all the lands of ancient Europe. [1]

In the ancient world, particularly in ancient Europe, plants were used for a variety of material and healing purposes, but like many ancient cultures, ancient Europeans had a particularly close relationship to plants for their importance in magic and the supernatural. As Roman Christianity spread throughout ancient Europe, it came perpetuating the idea that all contact with the spiritual supernatural world was to be feared, and when opened, only opened doorways to demonic control and manipulation. As a result of this view point, all indigenous peoples that early Christianity would later came into contact with who were found to still be practicing these ancient techniques for contacting the spirit world, were deemed as dangerous. The church viewed the people who practiced these ancient forms of occult religion as needing to be converted and the religions that they practiced suppressed and eradicated assimilating the people into the prevailing Christian culture. Over the centuries as Christianity expanded, all non- Christian peoples came under heavy persecution eventually driving virtually all indigenous religious practices in Europe into extinction. Today, only a handful of myths, legends, and folk beliefs are known to have survived. What does still survive from these ancient traditions attests to the religious practices of ancient Europe and the indigenous pre-Christian peoples who lived there, a world that as we will come to find was heavily steeped in the practices of the ancients and in the experience of the mystical. When we take a closer look into the ancient religious and spiritual traditions of ancient pre-Christian European peoples, we find a system of religious beliefs and traditions that was not only very old, but one that was very closely intertwined with the very spirit of nature.

It was once said:

> That the sages of old were instructed in the occult knowledge of trees and herbs, as well as the sacred art of healing, divination, enchantments and prophecy. This was given to mankind in very remote times by the Gods, by other accounts it was the Nymphs, tree spirits, Fairy- folk, genii, and the rustic entities allied unto the dominions of the wilderness. In many traditions it was the trees and herbs themselves, or the land wherein they were rooted,

who taught the ancient plant doctors their art, often revealing themselves by way of a unique "language of the trees" where by vegetable powers were accesses by song or incantation. With the ascendance of power hungry Monotheistic cults, a great many of these plantluminaries were assimilated to a false lexicon of demons, and the inner magical arts, once the pursuit of sages, was made heresy. Eventually Nature herself came to be viewed as an evil spirit, and cursed. Representative of powers only to be bound, exploited, and civilized. [2]

In studying some of the ancient religious practices of pre-Christian Europe, I think it is important to touch upon one of the last indigenous religious traditions known to have converted into Christianity, the traditional priests and healers of pre-Christian Celtic society, the Druids. Today druids are known to have designated the priestly class in ancient Celtic societies, which existed throughout much of Western Europe north of the Alps and in the British Isles until they were supplanted by the Roman government, and later, Christianity. Druidic practices were part of the culture of all the tribal peoples called "Keltoi" and "Galatai" by Greeks and "Celtae" and "Galli" by Romans, which evolved into modern English "Celtic" and "Gaulish." Druids combined the duties of priest, arbitrator, healer, scholar, and magistrate. Druids were also traditionally known as "wise men" or "the ones who know." The druids claimed direct contact with the spirit world, they practiced visionary rituals, and were known as the keepers of the Celtic peoples most secret and ancient mystical knowledge. [3]

The druids were fundamentally known to have venerated nature and the elements as physical manifestations of the divine, such as the sun, the moon, and the stars, looking to them for "signs and seasons," they also venerated other natural elements, such as the oak, certain groves of trees, tops of hills, streams, lakes, and even plants. Fire was also regarded as a symbol of several divinities and was associated with the sun, cleansing, and rebirth. The druids taught of the omnipresence of a spiritual otherworld, that is sometimes accessible to us, and particularly close at certain times of the year. There was a great sense of connection and continuity between life and death. Because of this, the ancient Celts are known to have not feared death, but instead viewed it as a transition phase in the course of a long and eternal life. So strong was the druidic doctrine of the immortality of the soul, that Celtic warriors would enter battle and fight without fear of death, a phenomenon that puzzled not only Roman historians but also Roman military strategists as well. [4]

Fire-worship was also central to Celtic religion as it certainly played a pivotal role in the four annual fire festivals. Poetic inspiration is said in druid legends to be a fire in the head. Fire was also known as the main source of energy in a time without electricity, but the Celtic's veneration of fire primarily comes from a much more ancient time. The Celtic veneration of fire is believed to have originated from the prehistoric times when their descendents, the earliest European peoples, lived in caves and the first fire was captured and utilized. [5]

While the sacred veneration of fire may represent the antiquity of the druidic traditions, it was song and poetry that communicated druidic wisdom and spirituality. Druidic wisdom was always primarily communicated through poetry. Even as the later Christian scribes were recording the oral literature of the people, the magic poetry of the druids was so inseparable from the narrative that many fragments have survived in translation. The poetic tradition in druidism was also related to the oral-transmission method that the Celts used to trace their lineage and history. In an Irish myth there was a deity of poetry named "Brigid" and he had a particular style of poetry associated with him called Roscanna, which has its purpose in the construction of magical incantations. A druid was expected to see the past, present, and future for any given person, object, or situation. This is why they were the chosen advisors of kings. This is also why it is said that they would sit at the king's right hand, and why they were entrusted with the magical and spiritual well-being of the tribe. [6]

While it is relatively well known that supernatural nature beings such as elves and fairies are known to have taken an important and prominent role in ancient European, Celtic, and druidic mythology, our historical knowledge of Druid priests is very limited. We know that druidic lore consisted of a large number of verses learned by heart and it has been claimed that twenty years were required to complete the full course of study. There was a very advanced druidic teaching centre at Anglesey, which was said to have been centered on a magical lake. Druids went there from all over Europe to learn their secrets, but what was taught there or at other druid teaching centers is mostly lost and unknown today. Of the druids' oral literature, we know that there were sacred songs, formulas for prayers, and incantations, as well as rules of divination, prophesy, and magic. Unfortunately, not one verse has survived, even in translation, nor is there even a legend that can be called purely druidic without a Roman and/or Christian overlay or interpretation in them. While much of the ancient knowladge of the druids has been lost, there are many defining symbols of European magic and mythology that have their roots in these much more ancient European Druidic practices. One of these is the symbol and use of the wand. The symbol of the wand and the idea in the wand's ability to cast magical spells comes to us in folklore from a handful of surviving druid legends. There are some legends that show druids using wands, staves, and rods to direct their energy when working spiritual or magical tasks; usually this was done only on certain occasions or by certain druidic groups. Many times this rod or wand was made from hazel wood and had to touch the thing that it was directing its energy at. Today this concept is seen in modern mythology as the wizard's staff or represented as a witch's wand, elements that are all a clear continuation of these much more ancient European religious practices. [7] Another prominent symbol that is associated with indigenous European magical and spiritual practices is the use of the cauldron. Two prominent Celtic deities were particularly known to have used magical cauldrons, the Irish Dagda and the Welsh Cerridwen, both of these cauldrons were said to possess the property of granting wisdom to any who drink from it. Archaeologists have uncovered several cauldrons and buckets that may have also had ritual magical or spiritual uses associated with them. Fundamentally, it is believed that various psychoactive agents were added into these caldrons to create various psychoactive brews that were used by the druids in traditional Celtic religious rituals, particularly for creating visionary experiences and healing. Druids are well known to have used various plants and animals for spiritual, medicinal, decorative and religious purposes. One ritual which was called the Tarb Feis requires the Druid to sleep under the skin of a freshly killed bull, so that the spirit of the bull could send prophetic dreams to the sleeper. Some druids were also known to have used colorful bird feathers in their cloaks to denote their rank. [8]

One of the most popular of druidic plants that is still used today is Mistletoe. On continental Europe, druids used mistletoe for its magical and healing quality. The use of sacred plants in old European paganism was so strong that the Catholic Church forbid the presence of mistletoe and holly in its churches for almost 500 years. Today mistletoe stands as an icon of the modern winter holiday season, but its use and importance actually stems from very ancient traditions and beliefs. On the sixth night of the moon, a white-robed druid priest would cut the oak mistletoe with a golden sickle. The mistletoe was then caught in wicker baskets and never allowed to touch the ground. Two white bulls would then be sacrificed amid prayers that the recipients of the mistletoe would prosper. Later, the ritual of cutting the mistletoe from the oak came to symbolize the emasculation of the old king by his successor.

Mistletoe was long regarded as both a sexual symbol and the "soul" of the oak. It was gathered at both mid-summer and winter solstices, and the custom of using mistletoe to decorate houses at Christmas is a survival of the druid and other pre-Christian traditions. The Greeks also thought that the plant had mystical powers, and down through the centuries it became associated with many folklore customs. In the Middle Ages and later, branches of mistletoe were hung from ceilings to ward off evil spirits. In Europe they were placed over house and stable doors to prevent the entrance of witches, but the belief in the magical powers of mistletoe has long outlived the druids. In medieval times, the plant was called allheal, and used medicinally for a variety of ailments from epilepsy to cancer. Sprigs were hung in stables to protect livestock from the mischief of fairies, and over cradles to protect babes from the vexation of witches. In Scandinavia, its branches were fashioned into dowsing rods to search for treasure. An old English superstition held that as long as a sprig was retained in the home, so would love be retained. From this it became custom to insure that a fresh sprig of mistletoe was installed in the household every year, this lead to the custom of kissing under the mistletoe that was hanging in the home, a tradition that is still largely followed today. [9]

Fundamentally, the druids were masters of nature. The druids were famous for their ability to talk to nature spirits, trees, forests, and other elemental powers. In some Celtic legends there are stories of druids conversing with babbling brooks, talking trees, or springs. The most likely cause for these experiences seems to have come while under the effect of the various psychoactive substances they employed in their many religious and visionary rituals. It was also said that the druids could read the writings of destiny in the sky, and were masters of magic and the healing arts. They lived with a foot in both this world and the otherworld; they were also poets, healers, and masters of spiritual ecstasy. The mystical, religious, and magical practices of the druids were closely and intimately intertwined with nature, and it was from within nature, and the secrets it offered these ancient peoples that the greatest of the druidic mysteries came to be revealed. [10]

The use of plants and the properties they contain have long been used by people all over the world. In ancient Europe, plants are known to have played a major role in healing, medicine, magic and the religious rites and rituals of its ancient peoples. Since antiquity, several members of the nightshade family have been closely associated with magic, witchcraft, and the supernatural throughout Europe. The use of these plants were said to have enabled witches to perform feats of occult wonder and prophecy, to hex through hallucinogenic communication with the supernatural and go into visionary trances where they would transform into animals, fly, even contact nature spirits for healing or prophecy. Herbane, Hyoscyamus, Belladonna, and Mandrake all have a long history of use as visionary magical plants throughout Europe. Connected with European magic, witchcraft, and superstition, the extraordinary reputation of these plants is due primarily to the bizarre psycoactivity they induce, and their similarities in effects are the result of their similarity in chemical coposition. [11]

All of these plants contain relatively high concentrations of Tropane alkaloids, primarily Atropine, Hyoscyamine, and Scopolamine; it seems to be the scopolamine that produces the primary psychoactive effects. The effects of these plants induces an intoxication followed by a strong and bizarre state of delirious visionary trance, in some of the strongest effects it will usually lead to a transition state between consciousness and sleep, in which a visionary experience is induced accompanied by a strange state of delirium. Atropine has several chemical models for the synthesis of several other psychoactive and hallucinogenic compounds. The effects of Scopolamine differ from those of other usual psychoactive agents in that they are also extremely toxic; and the user usually remembers little of the full intoxication, loosing all sense of reality and falling into a deep sleep much like an alcoholic delirium that is accompanied with powerful visionary trance-like images. [12]

In ancient Greek literature Homer was known to have described magical drinks with which the effects described are clearly indicative of Henbane as a major ingredient. The effects are partially described as giving delusional raving visions as well as experiences of strange light. One of the first uses of the plant as recorded in ancient Greek texts states that the plants were also used in serving as a poison to mimic insanity as well as to help enable man in prophecy. Hyoscyamus or Henbane has been known and feared from earliest classical periods, when it was recognized that there were different kinds, and that the black variety was the most potent and capable of causing insanity. The ancient Egyptians also recorded their knowledge of Henbane in the Ebers papyrus, written in 1500 B.C. in which the plant is seen as an additive in numerous magical potions. [13]

The Mandrake and Others

The Mandrake plant was also famous in European magic and witchcraft because of its powerful narcotic effects, as well as the bizarre form of its root, which is strangely shaped just like a man. Hence the name Mandrake or man root. This strange root shape brought about many myths and beliefs regarding the plants power, beliefs that have been handed down from the earliest of times. Curious beliefs about the need to exercise great care in harvesting the root grew up and surrounded it. Theophrastus in the 3rd century B.C. wrote that collectors of medical plants drew circles around Mandrake, and they cut off the top part of the root while facing west. The remainder of the root was gathered after collectors had preformed certain dances and recited special formulas. This ritual harvesting of the plant clearly indicates a very ancient and sacred reverence for the plant's mystical and visionary powers. [14]

Mandrake was usually extracted in wine by the Greeks. Julius Caesar once escaped from pirates who had captured him by promising them double the ransom they were asking, and then sealing the deal with a party at which he served mandrake wine. It is also said that Hannibal won a battle in Africa by faking a retreat, and leaving behind jars of mandrake wine, then falling upon his stupefied enemies after they drank his gifts. Theophrastus, in his history of plants, ca. 230 B.C. was the first to record elaborate rituals performed by the (rhizotomists) or root cutters when gathering the plant. First, three circles were inscribed on the ground around the plants, then the first cut was made while facing west and speaking as many words related to the mysteries of love as one could think of. After the root was ritually removed from the ground, it would be used in creating various ritual magical potions. [15]

Use of the Mandrake plant is one of the oldest demonstrated old world intoxicants. Knowledge of the plant's effects and the writings about them go back to even the earliest books of the Bible where in the book of Genesis, Racheal trades Jacob to Leah for a night in exchange for some mandrake root, so that she might conceive. The Hebrew word for mandrake is duday from the word Duwd, a pot or cauldron, from the root word probably meaning "to boil," and thus by analogy, "to love," or "love object." In the Christian King James Bible Mandrake has been translated as "love apples." The Mandrake plant has undoubtedly received its name from the strange appearance of its root which is that of a human form, an appearance that has also been noted by many other ancient peoples. According to Dioscorides, the resemblance of the root to the human form was noted by the great Greek Pythagoras. Later in the Middle Ages it is said that Mandrakes had to be pulled from the earth by a dog, and when the plants were uprooted, it was said that they would shriek. The mythology of Mandrakes shrieking when pulled from the earth is a very ancient myth, one that has continued through to modern day in such famous magical stories as Harry Potter. [16]

The lore of the mandrake root's fame started to fade some time in the late 16th century, for it was at this period of time that many herbalists began to doubt many of the large tails associated with the plant. As early as 1526 the English herbalist Turner had denied that all mandrake roots had a human form and protested against their anthropomorphism, but the ancient and long standing superstitions that surrounded the plant were so strongly engrained in the culture and lore of European people that many of the superstitions surrounding the plant still persisted in European folklore well into the 19th century. In 1558 Giambattista della Porta went on to include a number of recipes in his book <u>Natural Magic</u> for both sleeping potions and madness potions using Datura, Belladonna, and Henbane. Porta described recipes and effects for potions of mandrake, Datura, and belladonna, one of which would make a man believe he had changed into a bird or beast. Porta was said to have tried this on some of his friends. He described how one of his friends he had given the potion to thought he was a fish, and tried to swim on the ground, and how another thought he was a goose and would eat grass and flap his wings. [17]

All of the Tropane containing plants were also all major ingredients in the various "Flying Ointments" of European witches along with other dangerous substances such as water hemlock (Cicuta Virosa), hamlock (Conium maculatum) and monkshood (Aconitum Napellus). Other substances that were also added in flying brews to give a number of other magical effects or characteristics, items such as opium poppy (Papaver Somniferum), soot, toad's sweat, animal fat and bats blood. People at the time were known to have kept toads for pets, toads that are well known for their secretions of psychoactive substances. It is fairly well known that many toads of this type were also known to have been used in witch's brews. The effect of these toads psychoactive secretions is also why the toad has became so closely intertwined into European magic, myths, and mythology. Today the toad is primarily regarded in association with witches and for having supernatural qualities. This is also why the toad came to be seen as a witch's animal, primarily during the times of ancient Medieval Europe, and why magical legends of these toads have persisted in folklore and fairy tails even to this day. [18]

By the fifteenth century, a number of learned and scientifically-inclined men, including Porta, had observed and written about the effects of witch's flying ointments. According to some modern scholars, the inquisition was notably uninterested in flying ointments, they were in their own way looking for actual appearances of Satan, and not the drug induced hallucinations of the peasants. But most witch craft accusations were tried in local civil courts, and possession or use of plants associated with "witches" was at the very least highly suspicious. Still by far, the majority of the thousands and thousands of deaths at the hands of witchcraft trials, the trials had little to almost nothing to do with plants, flying, herb lore or goddess religion. Fundamentally witch accusations had to do with sour milk, infertility, failed crops, and the nastiness of poverty. [19]

Mushrooms and the Faerie

Probably one of the most widespread visionary substances naturally endemic throughout the lush green regions of northern Europe and the Mediterranean are various species of wild psychoactive mushrooms. While there is very little conclusive archeological evidence that pre-Christian indigenous European peoples consumed psychoactive mushrooms for their visionary properties, there are considerable cultural, mythological, and literary references to indicate visionary mushrooms were used by ancient European peoples, particularly within various Celtic and Scandinavian traditions and myths. Most of these are based around the gods or heroes drinking magical ecstasy- inducing drinks from cauldrons. Primarily, it has been believed that various psychoactive plants were included in these cauldrons, plants such as Mandrake or others, but because visionary mushrooms are very widespread throughout Europe, it is logical to assume that if these people were already utilizing various psychoactive plants in the region, then when the case presented itself, they would have also utilized various psychoactive mushrooms as well. Today more than a half a dozen varieties of Psilocybin mushrooms are currently found throughout the British Isles, Sweden, Germany, and northern Europe. The climate conditions conducive to the growth of such mushrooms are also known to have existed during the Bronze Age and even long before. So the possibility that these mushrooms were known about and utilized for their visionary and magical properties is not only possible but must be considered in examining the use of visionary and psychoactive substances available to indigenous European peoples.

One such piece of evidence indicating ancient European people used and consumed various visionary mushrooms comes from the fact that the dark rimed Psilocybin containing Mottlegill Mushroom is widely distributed throughout Europe. It grows on dung-fertilized grassy earth, particular in horse pastures and in conjunction with horse manure. Research now suggests that this particular type of mushroom has had a long symbolic relationship with the horse and was sacred to the German God of wisdom and ecstasy, Wodan. In another example found in the forth chapter of an ancient Scandinavian text known as <u>Eiriks Saga Rautha</u>, the text gives a fairly detailed description of a woman named Lill-volvan, a "seeress" who travels from farm to farm predicting the future for the land owners. Unlike earlier Scandinavian shamanic myths, this account is filled with many mushroom motifs that are highly suggestive of psychoactive Psilocybe mushroom metaphors.

In the text, the seeress is dressed in a very special way. She wears a blue cloak, jewels, and a head piece of black lamb decorated with white cat skin and caries a staff. It would seem that her outfit is clearly a shamanic ritual costume, but also serves as an entheogenic metaphor. Lill-volvan wears a black and white fur cap. It may be merely coincidental, but the cap of the Psilosibe Semilanceata, the most common and most potent of the psilocybes found in Scandinavia, is frequently black and white, as well as having a very furry look. The seeress also wears a blue cloak, which immediately brings to mind the tendency of Psilocibe mushrooms to turn blue when they are picked or handled. Furthermore, the text says that she sits on a cushion of chicken feathers. This is also similar to the mushrooms natural growth pattern, for when the mushroom is picked one often sees white downy material loose at the base. This is part of the mycelium a network of fungi cells under the base used by the mushroom to consume material for food. As if her black and white cap, blue cloaked body and white fury cushion were not metaphors enough, it is stated that the seeres wears a belt with mushrooms hanging from it. Moreover, on her belt hangs a pouch in which the text says she keeps a "magical substance" that most likely also contained visionary mushrooms.[20]

In examining evidence for the use of visionary mushrooms among ancient indigenous European peoples, we are lead to one of the most prominent examples demonstrating evidence for their mystical and magical use in ancient Europe, which can still be found in the symbolism surrounding the European world's most popular supernatural spirit being, the fairy. Traditionally the fairy is known as a nature spirit and are many times depicted with, on, or around mushrooms. What many people do not know today is that the association of fairies with mushrooms is no accident. This relationship is actually something that goes back to the most ancient times in European myths and history. A fairy (sometimes seen as faery or faerie; collectively wee folk) is traditionally known as a spirit or supernatural being that is found in the legends, folklore, and mythology of many different cultures, but most notably in European and Celtic legends. They are generally portrayed as humanoid in their appearance and many times have supernatural abilities. Although in modern culture they are often depicted as young, sometimes winged, females of small stature, they originally were of a much different image: tall, angelic spirit beings as well as short, wizened troll like beings of light. Some of them commonly mentioned as fay. The small, gauzy-winged female fairies that are commonly depicted today did not appear until the 1700 and 1800s, and are really only a very modern manifestation of this age old mythological spiritual entity. [21]

Traditionally, the belief in fairies and the fairy tradition came from the European Faerie faith. The Faerie faith is the set of folk beliefs and folk religious practices that entered the Celtic culture when Christianity became the official religion. The Faerie Faith has no priests or ministers of any kind, nor does it have established churches or complicated theology. Its scripture is now only folk memory. Its professionals were traditionally "wise women" also known as "faerie doctors," individuals who had experienced the faeries and carried the knowledge and skills necessary to see them, identify their handiwork, and occasionally cure any ills caused by them. The Faerie Faith includes a number of superstitions and taboos designed to prevent insulting or angering the faeries. When the Faerie Faith was most widespread, it was common to seek out a wise woman or faerie doctor to cure a disease in cattle or humans when the medical doctors or priests were unable to do so. It is important to point out that throughout many shamanic traditions of the world, the use of a spirit helper or spiritual being and ally are essential elements in many Shamanic traditions around the world. In the traditional European shamanic traditions, it was these fairies who served this purpose. The same purpose that guiding spirits have done for shamans in traditional societies around the world for thousands of years. Like those spirits, fairy familiars helped watch over people and acquire practical knowledge, like where a stolen object might be or how to cure or even hex someone. [22]

In traditional European and Celtic traditions, fairies were often friends and companions as well. Witches generally first encountered a fairy familiar while being under extreme stress, family member's sickness, overworked, hungry, and fearing the worst. This is much of the same sort of deliberate preparation required to encounter a guiding spirit that many shamans in traditional societies around the world use by engaging in things such as fasting, depriving themselves of sleep, or creating other physical extremes to induce visionary experiences. While the knowledge of these methods may be known about and understood by traditional societies, they are never the most advised or desired methods for contacting spirits. In many ancient cultures, particularly in ancient pre-Christian Europe, one of the most notable tools, especially in ancient European spirituality and magic used for contacting the spiritual supernatural world, was through the use and consumption of mind altering plants and fungi. One of the most common and peculiar symbols that represents this relationship between this age old spirit being and the mushroom comes from a popular story surrounding many species of fungi that grow on old tree stumps and roots under the ground that come up from the ground in the form of a rind. This mushroom ring pattern is known today as "Fairy Rings." Fairy rings are the familiar narrow rings of bare ground, of almost any size, found in fields and lawns. The name fairy ring comes from old folk tales in ancient Europe. People once believed that mushrooms growing in a circle followed the path made by fairies dancing in a circle or ring on a midsummer's night. This indicates an ancient connection between the supernatural nature spirits known as the fairy and the secret mysteries of the mushroom.

Fairies are well represented in European myth and folklore even today. They can be found depicted in pictures, art, statues, and sculptures. Many of these types of depictions can be found in book stores, markets, and malls all over Europe and North America. Interestingly enough, one of the most popular symbols directly associated with the fairy is its association with the mushroom, particularly intoxicating or visionary mushrooms. Anyone who has ever seen fairy art can tell you that fairies are commonly depicted in paintings and art on, near, or around mushrooms. The most common representation of this type of fairy pictures are pictures of a fairy sitting or standing on top of mushrooms known for their visionary effects. One of the most popular of these is the red and white Amanita Mascara mushroom, widely used shamanically for its intoxicating effects when dried and consumed. Because fairies were traditionally known as nature spirits, they are also many times depicted in and around the forest, particularly, with images of mushrooms very close by. Forests are also a very prominent place for psychoactive mushrooms to be found, particularly in Europe.

In Celtic legends and myths, fairies are understood as nature spirits, they are many times closely associated with mushrooms and the mystical powers of the forest, the same locations where mushrooms are known to grow and are harvested by mushroom hobbyists in Europe today. Forests are also many of the same places visionary mushrooms were found and harvested by the ancients and they are also the same locations where the spiritual supernatural fairy beings were said to be seen. The Celtic peoples as well as the druids were well known for their use of magical and visionary plants and fungi, substances that have still held their symbolic representation even today.

The relationship between the early appearance of fairies in European culture and the use of visionary mushrooms first came to me not by their appearance in art or mythological tales, but through a startling first hand encounter with the phenomena myself. The experience took place during a high dose Psilocybin mushroom experience I had while alone in the mountains. The experience took place while I was hiking in the mountains after eating a large number of the vision inducing mushrooms. After the effects began to take hold, I encountered and was approached by only what I can best describe as two somewhat small winged beings of light about 3 feet in size. They flew in front of me and appeared to me as if they were made out of some form of light or energy. As the event took place, the small beings of emanating light flew in front of me in my field of vision. They then opened up what felt like or appeared to be some sort of multicolored fractal jeweled visionary portal. They asked me, in my mind and thoughts, if I wanted to go with them and to see what was in their world. They were talking directly into my mind, saying that this was where they were from and where they lived and that they wanted to take me there to show me the secrets of their world.

They were not clearly defined; their wings were made out of what looked like vibrating light emissions. As they hovered before me, my impressions of them were not distinctly visual, but more on an emotional and mental level, and it was in this way that I perceived them. I could not see distinctive details about their shape and there was no clear characteristic of their form in sharp detail such as a face, eyes, or clothing. They looked more like somewhat short, winged beings made out of vibrating light with a distinctive feminine-like energy that felt like what I can only best describe as fairy-like. As the two beings continued hovering on either side of this open portal, I told them in my thoughts that I did not want to go with them and that I was comfortable here in my world and I did not feel safe going with them. As I did this these two small winged beings of light, emanating a feminine fairy like presence, flew into the open portal before me. As they did this, the portal closed behind them and they disappeared.

To this day, my best description of these beings would be some sort of fairy-like entity. I say this based on the way I felt when I encountered their presence. They also did not feel fully divine or angelic, nor did they feel bad or evil. In interpreting the experience at face value, I would have to describe them as more like some type of semi-divine entity that I would have to say most closely fits the same descriptions found associated with the ancient European fairies. In reflecting upon this experience and the visionary fairy phenomena associated with it, I have now come to believe the fairy tradition, as it is represented in European culture, mythology, and history is a universal human cognitive phenomenon directly associated with the long standing history of psychoactive mushroom use throughout ancient Europe. A use that has manifested within the history, mythology, and culture of western civilization as the supernatural nature being we know today as the fairy.

European Age of Rebirth and Discovery

From the earliest of times shamanism has been oppressed, forbidden, and destroyed by expanding hierarchically organized peoples, peoples who have acted in a violent and imperialistic manner. In ancient Rome, the shamanic cult of Dionysus was fought to the death, and any of its followers who were discovered were brutally slain. It was exactly the same in the ancient Germanic areas. The seeresses and the priests of Wodan were killed. Later, the "witches" who had remained heathen in their nature worship were persecuted and burned at the stake during the inquisition. After the rise of Christianity, the ancient cultures, gods, myths, and mystery traditions of the classical world had been eradicated or assimilated into the prevailing Christian culture. The classical world had disappeared into the past and its ancient libraries and temples had long been burned and destroyed. The age old mystery traditions had been eradicated and what little had survived of these ancient practices on the European subcontinent remained only in a handful of myths and legends. Christianity had succeeded in gaining a strong grip on the minds and lives of the people of the European world.

With the European dark ages nearing an end and Christianity deeply infused in the minds and hearts of the European people, the European world was again going to change, but this time it was going to be reborn and enter a transformation that would forever change the course of human history. This period of European transformation is known today as the Renaissance. During the Renaissance, the rediscovery of ancient scientific texts was accelerated after the fall of Constantinople in 1453, and the invention of printing would democratize learning and allow a faster propagation of new ideas, information, and knowledge. With this came the birth of the scientific revolution. The scientific revolution built upon the foundation of ancient Greek learning, as it had been elaborated in medieval Islam and the universalities of medieval Europe. The Renaissance is understood as a historical age in Europe that followed the Middle Ages and preceded the Reformation, spanning roughly the 14th through the 16th century. The term Renaissance meaning rebirth, or Rinascimento in Italian, as used to indicate the flourishing of artistic and scientific activities beginning in Italy in the mid 13th century. With this age of scientific and intellectual rebirth also came one of the greatest discoveries in all of western history, the discovery of a new world, the discovery of the Americas. [23]

Ch 12

Shamanism and the New World

Apparently there is a great discovery or insight which our culture is deliberately designed to suppress, distort and ignore. That is that Nature is some kind of minded entity. That Nature is not simply the random flight of atoms through electromagnetic fields. Nature is not the empty; de spiritualized lumped matter that we inherit from modern physics. But it is instead a kind of intelligence, a kind of mind.

The Great Insight Terence McKenna

In 1492 the European world officially discovered the lands of the Americas, the lands of the new world, but they were not the first people to have arrived in this new world. The native peoples of the Americas first came to the new world during the last ice age in search of foods to hunt and gather. A commonly agreed-upon date for the first migrations of humans to the new world is 20,000 B.C., although there are some who want to push the migration back as far as 40,000 B.C. based on the still-controversial analysis of several ancient archeological sites in North and South America. In either case, it is generally believed, based on DNA studies, that the first human immigrants to the Americas originated in Siberia, where shamanism is known to have been practiced at least since the Neolithic period and probably even much earlier. Given the prevalence of shamanistic beliefs throughout the Americas, anthropologists have assumed that the immigrants brought their shamanic practices with them across the Bering Strait. Thus, shamanism became the starting point for the later development of all indigenous religious culture in the Americas. [1]

One thing that makes the Americas unique is its unusually high concentration of psychedelic plant species, far more than in the old world. As a result of this, the native peoples of the Americas are known to use a much larger array of psychoactive and visionary substances than peoples in the old world. When the Spaniards came to conquer Mexico in the 16th century, what they found both fascinated and repelled them, this was the Indians' widespread use and incorporation of the numerous psychoactive plants native to the land. From the Spaniards point of view, these plants served a simple purpose, to conjure up visions of demons and devils and to take individuals from their daily life to the supernatural realms believed by the Spanish and catholic priests to have come directly from the devil. [2]

Spanish writers of the sixteenth and seventeenth centuries left us relatively detailed accounts of the use of psychoactives in central Mexico. Historical documentation for the use of psychedelic plants among the Aztec civilization is probably the best documented among the various native civilizations of the Americas at the time of the European conquest. From these historical documents we also know that Aztec priests were rigorously trained from childhood in a kind of priestly boot camp where fasting, celibacy, austerity, and even bloodletting were central aspects of their religious priestly training. It is also known that Aztec officials took *ololiuhqui* or morning glory seeds *and datura* seeds for the use of divination. Certain priests who engaged in prophecy were documented using other psychotropic plants such as jimson weed, psilocybe mushrooms, and peyote cactus. The practice of shamanism and the use of visionary substances to contact the spirit world were not just restricted to the native peoples of Mexico, but was instead a very widespread practice throughout the Americas. In Central and South America the practice of shamanism seems to have also been continuous since the arrival of humans in the region about twenty thousand years ago. By the time Andean civilization began to flourish as early as 2,000 B.C., formal priesthoods had evolved in the region, taking over many of the roles of shamans as mediators between this and other realms of being. Archeological evidence indicates that psychotropic sacraments derived from indigenous plants played an important role in ancient Andean priestly rites. Just as they have in many other shamanistic traditions in the Americas as well as around the world. [3]

Celib Tree

Throughout the Americas many different types of plants and fungi are known to expand consciousness, increase awareness of self, and initiate one into the nature of spirituality. They have been used sacredly and successfully for their sacred, visionary, and healing properties for many thousands of years, many with a very ancient history of use spanning well into the realms of pre history. One of the oldest psychoactive plants known to have been used in the Americas is a tree known as the Celib. In the Atacama desert in northern Chile there is an oasis called San Pedro De Atcama. The art historian and archaeologist C. Maual Torres excavated and studied over six hundred prehistoric graves there. The result of his archaeological work in this location lead him to the astonishing finding that nearly every person buried there was accompanied for their last journey to the underworld with numerous tools dedicated to the ritual sniffing of the psychedelic Celib tree. The name Celib designates the tree (Anadenanthera Colubrina) as well as it seeds, which can induce a strong psychoactive affect when smoked, sniffed, or eaten. [4]

The Puna Region of northwest Argentina is the oldest archeological proof of ritual shamanistic use of the Celib that has ever been found. The seeds of these trees have been smoked and eaten in this location for well over 4, 5000 years. Numeras ceramic pipes have been found in certine caves in the region. Occasionally the bowls of the pipes were found to contain Celib seeds still in them. The shamans of the Wichi, known as the Mataco Indians of northwest Argentina, still use the snuff made from the Cebil tree even today. The shamans smoke the dried seeds preferably in a pipe or rolled in a cigarette. The Celib is seen to the people as a manner of speaking, a gateway to a visionary world and to another reality. The shamans say that this is just how their ancestors smoked the seed five thousand years ago. This makes the northwest of Argentina the place with one of the longest uninterrupted ritualistic or shamanistic use of a psychoactive plant known anywhere in the world. [5]

The local people of the area are called the Matacos Indians. They have lived in this area long before the arrival of European culture. So as some Matacos Indians have converted to Christianity in recent years, they have come to fuse aspects of biblical or Christian mythology with elements of their own culture. One of the more interesting elements of this evolving fusion is the fact that many of the native people have come to identify the sacred Celib tree with the biblical Tree of Knowledge, but native people do not see the Celib as a forbidden fruit. Rather, they see it as a holy tree which is used by their healers and shamans for obtaining knowledge of the spirit world and healing the sick. [6]

San Pedro Cacti

Another very interesting and important psychoactive plant found in the deserts of central and South America that has also been identified by Ethnobotanists in some of the earliest archeological discoveries in the Americas comes from stone carvings found in a Chavin temple in northern Peru, artifacts that date back to 1300 B.C. Within these stone carvings are depictions of Trichocereus Pachanoi, or the San Pedro Cactus. The San Pedro Cactus is represented as one of the most ancient of magical plants found to be used throughout the desert and mountain regions of South America, with equally old finds of textiles from the Chavin area are also found depictions of the San Pedro Cactus with jaguar and humming bird figures, as well as other Peruvian ceramics made between 1000 and 700 B.C. that also depict the plant in association with deer, and in other sites from several hundred years later are found depictions of the cactus with jaguars and stylized spirals illustrating aspects of the psychedelic experience induced by the plant. On the southern coast of Peru, large ceramic urns from the Nazca culture have also been found dating between 100 B.C. to 500A.D. with other clear depictions of the San Pedro cacti and its association with sacred rituals and spiritual shamanic uses. [7]

The modern use of the San Pedro cactus is still known to be maintained along the coastal regions of Peru and the Andes of Peru and Bolivia today. Like many other indigenous practices, the indigenous use of San Pedro has been greatly affected by Christian influence, influence that is seen even in the name that is now applied to the plant, "San Pedro." The name originates in the Christian belief that St. Peter holds the keys to heaven. So since the native people believe San Pedro also holds the keys to the doorway of heaven, the name was coined and the plant came to be known as "San Pedro" or St. Peter. [8]

The San Pedro cactus is still currently used by the indigenous peoples in this region for traditional healing and spiritual practices. The plant is employed in curing a wide variety of illnesses as well as an affective treatment against alcoholism, sickness, and insanity. The plant is also used for many other purposes by the native people such as in divination, finding lost objects, undoing love witchcraft, and to counter all kinds of sorcery. Today the San Pedro Cactus as well as the Peruvian Torch cactus are primarily used by healers in the north coastal region of Peru. A region predominantly populated by mestizos, many of whom know little of the pre-hispanic culture of their area. The native people were ravaged by the Spanish invaders in the sixteenth and seventeenth centuries, and according to some anthropologists, no indigenous language, textile, farming practice, or social organization has survived fully intact. Only a handful of native peoples in the Andes have maintained aspects of their original language, beliefs, and traditional ancient healing practices.[9]

While the use of the San Pedro cactus is undeniably indigenous, the curing ceremonies have developed into a syncretic mixture of Christianity, shamanism, and magic. The Cactus is reputedly made into the psychoactive beverage called "cimora," and in Peru it is used by curanderos or healers with the tobacco plant Nicotiana. Tobacco is commonly included within the San

Pedro ceremonies, often as a liquid extract that is ingested nasally prior to the drinking of the San Pedro tea. The plant is believed to hold the sacred power of the four winds as well as being a powerful spiritual ally given by God to help mankind heal the sick and see into the realms of spirits. [10]

The Morning Glory

One of the most popular yet commonly unsuspected psychoactive plants is the morning glory. The use of the morning glory for ritual and shamanic purposes was well documented by early European conquerors. A Spanish report written shortly after the conquest stated that the Aztecs have an herb called, "Coatl-xoxo uhqui" meaning (green snake) it bears a seed called "Ololiuqui." An early drawing depicts the plant, with congested fruits, cordate leaves, a tuberous root, and a twining vine habit. In 1651, the physician of the king of Spain, Francisco Hernandez identified "Ololiuqui" as the morning glory and professionally reported it. "Ololiuqui," which some call Coaxihuitl or snake plant, is a twining herb known as the morning glory flower. Soon after the Spanish inquired about this plant's power and its relationship to the Aztec people, they quickly went on to eradicate and persecute its use. The Catholic Church at the time came to associate the plant and its use directly with the devil. The negative propaganda and cultural prejudice of the Spanish Missionaries is clearly demonstrated when just four centuries ago a Spanish missionary in Mexico wrote this regarding the morning glory plant:

> The natives communicate in this way with the devil, for they usually talk when they became intoxicated with the Ololiuqui, and they are deceived by various hallucinations which they attribute to the Deity which they say resides in the seeds. [11]

As a result of this type of European propaganda and strong persecution by the Roman Catholic Church, the traditions and practices of using the Morning glory seeds for healing went deep into hiding with the western knowledge of the plant's psychoactive potential becoming completely lost and misunderstood. By 1916, an American botanist suspected erroneously that Ololiuqui was a species of datura. He reasoned that several species of datura were well known intoxicants, they were used by the Aztecs and its flowers resemble the morning glory, but no psychoactive principals were known from the morning glory family; the symptoms of Ololiuqui intoxication resemble those caused by datura, he proposed. As he further went on to say, "a knowledge of botany has been attributed to the Aztecs, which they were far from possessing...and the botanical knowledge of the early Spanish writers... was perhaps not much more extensive." Thus his misidentification at the time was widely accepted. It wasn't until 1939 that identifiable material of the morning glory, *Turbina Corymbosa*, was collected among the Chinantec and Zapotec Indians of Oaxaca, Mexico where it was cultivated for use and the psychoactive components finally uncovered in its seeds laying to rest the Academic European Mystery of the visionary properties of the morning glory and the source of the Aztecs Ololiuqui. [12]

Traditionally, Ololiuqui, or the seeds of the morning glory flower are taken at night, and in contrast to peyote or mushrooms, is administered to a single individual alone in a quiet, secluded place. Usually thirteen morning glory seeds are ground up in water. The intoxication usually begins rapidly and leads to visions many times portraying people or events, sometimes the visuals can be strange and almost alien, manifesting snakes or unknown creatures, spirits, or beings. The natives say the effects last only about 3 hours and seldom have unpleasant effects. Like many psychoactive medical herbals that are taken in liquid preparations, they can be accompanied by a bodily purge in the initial stage of the ritual consumption. Primarily this is an initial stage of cleansing and purification the body induces before the onset of visions. Traditionally the seeds of the morning glory are used for healing, and the patient, who must be alone with the healer if not in a solitary silent place were he/she falls into a stage of deep mental involvement with the experience, during at which time it is said by the native peoples that the little ones, male and female, known as the plant children (bador), come and talk with the sick patient. These plant spirits help in healing the sick person. It is also said by the native peoples that these plant spirits can also help in giving information on lost or stolen objects. [13]

As with many indigenous traditions in the Americas, the modern ritual use of morning glory seeds have come to incorporate some Catholic and Christian elements. Evidence for this is found in some of the names that are now known to be used for the seeds of the plants among some native peoples, names such as (Semilla de la Virgin) or seeds of the Virgin, connecting the seeds of the flower to the Virgin Mary. Names such as this attest to the infusion of Christian elements within the original indigenous tradition. Yet a more recent report also indicates that Ololiuqui, or the morning glory, has not lost its original association with the deity that is known to reside within the plant among the native peoples. To this day in almost all villages in its home of Oaxaca, Mexico one can find the seeds still serving the natives as an ever present helper in their times of sickness and trouble. As with the sacred mushrooms and the salvia plant, the use of the psychoactive morning glory was so significant in the life of pre-Hispanic Mexico that all knowledge of its use went deep into hiding during Catholic and Spanish Rule, hiding among native peoples in the mountains and hinterlands of the region only until it's re-awakening and emergence in our own most recent century. [14]

Mushrooms

Like the seeds of the morning glory flower, psychoactive Mushrooms are also known to have played a very important role in pre-conquest Mesoamerican Indian life. Certain species, mostly belonging to the Genus of Psilosibe, have been used by the native people in this region successfully and sacredly for many thousands of years. The Aztecs called them Teonanacatl, meaning God's Flesh. Psychedelic fungi were wildly employed in Mexico and Central America when the Spaniards came. In 1656 a guide for missionaries argued against Indian idolatries, including mushroom ingestion, and recommended the extermination of their use among native peoples. Not only do many or most of the historical European reports condemn Teonanacatl, the visionary mushroom, but there are also illustrations that have been found that denounce it. There is one depiction of the devil enticing an Indian to eat the fungus, another where a devil is performing a dance on the mushroom and around the native person eating it, this type of European propaganda became well institutionalized by the Catholic Church who attempted to eradicate all evidence of the original native tradition and its sacred mushroom cult. [15]

The Spanish church persecuted the mushroom cult even more vehemently than other sacred plants such as peyote or morning glories. In 1620 the Holy Office of the Inquisition in Mexico City formally decreed that the ingestion of inebriating plants was heresy. Many aspects of the war on drugs today is still a religious war, and a war of personal beliefs and ideals that are being forced onto people, with the use of traditional plants being persecuted in many of the same ways they were just 300 years ago. When the very first Europeans came over to rule the lands of the new world, they took their religious beliefs, fears, and prejudices with them, fears and prejudices that still largely continue to this very day. [16]

The persecution of the native people by the Spanish and the Catholic Church was so strong that centuries later nothing was known of the mushroom cults that once thrived in the lands of Central America. It was even doubted by some western researchers many years later that mushrooms were ever used to create visions at all in native ceremonies. The church fathers had done such a good job at driving the cult into hiding through persecution that no anthropologist or botanist had ever uncovered the religious use of these mushrooms until early in the 20th century. [17]

In 1916 an American botanist finally proposed a solution to the identification of Teonanacatl, he concluded that Teonanacatl and peyote where the same thing. Motivated by distrust in the historical accounts as well as in the knowledge of the native Indians, he argued that the dried brownish disk-like crown of dried peyote resembled a dried mushroom, so remarkable, he said it could even fool Mycologists. It would not be until 1930 that an understanding of the role of psychoactive mushrooms in Mexico would come to light and the later scientific identification of their chemical composition would come to be understood. In the later 1930's the first two of many species of sacred Mexican mushrooms were collected and came to be associated with a surviving modern mushroom ceremony among indigenous peoples in the region. Subsequently, field research has resulted in the discovery of twelve types of visionary mushrooms in Mexico and Central America. The most widely known today is the Psilocybe Cubensis. Further research has demonstrated that the mushroom cults in fact never fully disappeared, but only went into hiding, only to re-emerge most recently. These mushrooms are now known to be employed in religious rituals among the Mazctec, Chinantec, Chatino, Miixe, Zapotec, and Mixtec Indians of Oaxaca and the surrounding mountainous regions. [18]

Evidence has now been accumulated that the sacred religious use of mushrooms in Mexico and Central America have flourished since at least 100 B.C. to the present time, making the ongoing religious sacramental use of these mushroom rituals well over 2000 years old, older even than the entire history of Christianity. There is also evidence that the religious use of these mushrooms once extended all the way down into central and South America, where other archeological artifacts have been uncovered that also directly relate to the sacred psychedelic use of these mushrooms. [19]

While there is a fairly large collection of texts regarding the use of visionary mushrooms by the Aztecs as well as by some other native pre-Colombian groups, there is little mention of this intriguing aspect of native religion among the Mayas, who lived farther to the south. The silence is the most puzzling because there has been strong circumstantial evidence of a very early religious use of sacred visionary mushrooms in the Maya highlands where there have been found mushroom artifacts in Guatemala and the adjacent lowlands in the form of more than 250 mushroom statues made of carved stone, many dating to the first millennium B.C. [20]

Mushrooms clearly played an important role in pre-conquest Mesoamerican Indian life. There use in supernatural psychological curing and magic still survives to this day in the mountainous regions of central Mexico primarily in the state of Oaxaca. These mushrooms are known to contain the chemical compound psilocybin, which is the primary psychoactive agent. Psilocybin has a very similar molecular structure as that of the common neural transmitter serotonin as well as the similar visionary neural transmitter DMT to which it is also very closely related. [21]

The Mazatec Indians of Central Mexico are known to have maintained a very long tradition of using these mushrooms. The Mazatec Indians inhabit a range of mountains called the Sierra Mazateca in the northeastern corner of the Mexican state of Oaxaca. The mushrooms are collected in the forest at the time of the new moon by a virgin girl, then they are taken to the church where they remain only briefly on the alter. They are never sold in the marketplace. Usually several members of a family will eat the mushrooms together. It is not uncommon for a father, mother, children, uncles, and aunts to all participate in these healing rituals. The mushrooms themselves are eaten in pairs, a couple representing man and woman to symbolize the dual principles of procreation and creation. To the Mazatecs the mushrooms are directly connected to the practice of healing and they have been a primary source of traditional medicine for them for many thousands of years. But the mushrooms are more than just an herbal medicine, they also come with a strong spiritual quality and attribute. It is this spiritual quality that the healers use the mushrooms for gaining knowledge and understanding, knowledge they say comes directly from or through the mushrooms. [22]

The Mazatec Indians eat the mushrooms only at night and in absolute darkness. The depths of the night are recognized by them as the most conducive to visionary insights and healing. The mushroom ceremony is an all night ritual that may include a curing ritual with chants accompanying the main part of the ceremony. The intoxication is characterized by fantastically colored visions in kaleidoscope movements manifesting from the darkness. This is also accompanied by strong mental sensitivity, auditory sounds, emotional and tactual sensations as well as the recipient receiving an impart of knowledge or information. The natives sometimes call the mushrooms, "The mushrooms that speak," for it is in the darkness of the night and in the setting of the rituals that the mushrooms teach the people wisdom, knowledge, healing, and the mysteries and perplexities of existence. It is from this thought and from this voice that the mushrooms teach and heal the people and show them the right way to live. [23]

Salvia Divinorum

Another remarkable visionary medical plant also used by indigenous peoples in Mexico is the plant Salvia Divinorum. Salvia Divinorum is a species of Sage that grows naturally in a small mountainous region in southern Mexico and is a plant that was relatively unknown to the western world until its emergence from the region only recently. The ritual use of Salvia

Divinorum in modern Mexico is remarkably similar to the ritual use of psychedelic mushrooms for healing, also in the same region. The male and female shamans of the Mazatect of Oaxaca use Salvia Divinourum, which they also call "Hoja de la Pastora" or leaf of the shepherdess. The salvia ritual takes place in much the same way as the mushroom rituals do. The salvia rituals take place at night and in complete darkness. As with the mushrooms, the leaves of salvia are fundamentally used in these rituals for healing. In these rituals the healer is either alone with the patient or there are other patients or participants present. The leaves are held over Copal incense, and some prayers are said to consecrate the leaves. The shaman then takes thirteen leaves and wraps them into a cigar shape and hands them to the patient. Both the patient and the shaman then chew and suck on the leaves. After chewing and sucking on the leaves the patient lies down and remains still and as silent as possible in the quiet darkness of the room. It is important that the rituals take place at night in complete darkness and stillness for the best healing to take place as well as for allowing the clearest impressions of the visionary world to manifest. The salvia ritual usually only lasts about one or two hours at the very most, and are not as long as the all night mushroom rituals, primarily, this is due to the difference in the length of the effects between the two substances.[24]

During the salvia ritual the healer sings songs about healing, health, and wisdom, calling on the healing forces of the body, nature, and the supernatural divine world. It is believed by western scientists that the successes of these visionary healing rituals comes from the mind altering effects of the plants, which are believed to act on the mind and body of the patient much like a very powerful mentally enhanced placebo effect, acting on both the mind and body of the sick patients during the healing rituals. Some of the plants and herbs used in these shamanic healing rituals are also known to contain purgative properties such as ayahuasca or the seeds of the morning glory. Purging helps the body eliminate illness and toxins from the body further aiding in the healing process. In addition to the singing that takes place in salvia healing rituals, many times the healer also takes the leaves of the salvia to go into the altered visionary state with the patient, seeking out the spiritual cause of the illness. If the visions are strong enough, the healer may find a solution to the problem or illness that is affecting the patient who is seeking his help. After the salvia healing ritual is completed, the healer gives the patient further appropriate advice, and any other treatments if necessary. Such as: if the patient is very ill, further herbal medicines are recommended to the patient to help further clean the body of toxins or boost the immune system. After this is done, the healer ends the healing ritual and the meeting is over.

The Aztecs are also known to have used the Salvia Divinorum plant which they called Pipiltzintzintli, or "The Purest Little Prince." Salvia Divinorum also goes by the name of diviner's sage or Aztec sage and is native to the Mazatec areas of the Sierra Madre Oriental in the high tropical mountains in the Mexican state of Oaxaca. It grows naturally in the tropical rain forest in an altitude of three hundred to eighteen hundred meters. Because of Salvia Divinorum's limited geographical habitat, it belongs to the rarest of the psychoactive plants on earth, and as of now, it is not considered banned or illegal in most places of the world. Subsequently, the use of the plant in the United States and Europe has seen a surge in interest. The use of Salvia Divinorum, also known as the diviner's sage, is somewhat of a modern development within the European western world, for the plant was almost totally unknown to the European world less than 100 years ago. [25]

Gaining popularity as an alterative smoke for aiding in meditation and shamanic activity, many shamanic herbal companies have started to ship extracts of the plant as well as the pure plant material itself into the United States and around the world from cultivation fields in Mexico. Only recently has this increase in use and interest in the plant resulted in some conflict and controversy among some western states and nations. Supporters of salvia's legal status state that due to its non-toxic, non-addictive qualities, coupled with its relatively mild and short lived psychoactive effect, in its natural form, all attempts at criminalizing the plant only demonstrate the strong cultural bias and ignorant prudence regarding anything mildly psychoactive in contemporary western culture. The supporters of salvia's legality have attempted to demonstrate the safety, sacredness, and potential cultural benofits of the plant, as well as its clear unsuitability for scheduling as a controlled narcotic substance. Legal supporters of Salvia have further pointed out the plant's safe medical and health properties when related to other culturally expectable and legal forms of intoxication such as: smoking tobacco or alcohol, which are well known and well documented to kill thousands of people a year and claim millions of addicts around the world. Salvia on the other hand is non-toxic, non-addictive and not one death has been reported or substantiated from the use of salvia. Supporters of salvia have demonstrated time and again that the plant is not a threat to public health or safety and is not a danger to society.

Yet despite these facts and the growing positive academic research around the world regarding the potential beneficial and therapeutic application of Salvia Divinorum, the plant is being persecuted, banned, and criminalized, in more and more western states around America and Europe today. The main cause for this action comes only from the fact that the plant is defined as a psychoactive and thus feared and misunderstood by the greater public and the social drug prohibition systems. This criminalization and persecution comes even in the face of strong scientific research demonstrating the plant's non-toxic, non-addictive, and therapeutic properties, all strong elements demonstrating its non-suitability for scheduling. Yet despite the ongoing controversy of this relatively new visionary plant into modern western culture, Salvia is still legal in most areas of the world, with only a few exceptions. As a result of its growing popularity by non-indigenous peoples, the plant Salvia Divinorum has been brought into modern cultivation and is now cultivated by plant lovers all over the world and this is something that we can only hope will be a freedom that can continue for many years to come.

Datura and Brugmansia

While the Salvia plant may be one of the safest and tamest of psychoactive plants when taken in its natural form, the datura plant is unarguably one of the oldest and most dangerous. In the tropical rain forest of South America, the Brugmansia is known to be the must common datura-like plant available. The psychoactive use of Brugmansia very well may have come down from the knowledge and use of the closely related datura plant that was first earlier discovered and used by ancient migrating peoples in their much earlier shamanic practices. Knowledge of the datura plant itself most likely originally came down from early migrating peoples as they advanced into the new world. It is largely believed because of the antiquity of datura use around the world and in Asia that these ancient prehistoric migrants most likely brought the knowledge of the plant with them into the Americas some time in the late Paleolithic and Mesolithic times. As they migrated southward, they encountered other new spices of datura, especially in Mexico. Upon arriving in the Andes of South America they recognized the resemblance of the tropical Brugmansia to that of datura and found its psychoactive effect very similar. The use of datura as well as the Brugmansia bespeaks of its great antiquity and the ancient tradition of its use. [26]

Datura as you have already seen is one of the oldest of old world intoxicants and it is a plant with a very long history of use as a medicine and as a sacred hallucinogen. The ancient use of datura has been found in China, India, Napal, as well as ancient, Babylon, Persia, and Egypt. It has been used throughout the Middle East and throughout the Americas. The datura plant is one of the most widespread and ancient visionary plants known in human culture, but they are also some of the most dangerous. In California, the rock art of the regions inhabited by the Chumash and Yokut Indians is found a polychromic manner of painting-particularly evident during what is known as the Santa Barbara Painted Style' a type of Native American rock art that has been associated with the use of Jimsonweed (a hallucinogenic plant of the datura genus). This plant is known to have been used by a number of Californian and

251

Mexican Indian tribes. Apparently, the first examples of Chumash rock art date back to 5,000 years ago and from this art is seen a continual use of the datura plant which is believed to have taken place in the region and to have been responsible for the cave art so characteristic of the Santa Barbara region. In addition to this visionary based cave art that is known to dot the southern California Mountains, sacred Datura inspired artwork can also be seen in the Chumash art coloring the interior walls of the Santa Barbara Mission. [27]

It is interesting to note that nearly all tribes of the Southern California region were known to have used datura in their religious and shamanic rituals. Groups like the Akwa, Yuma, Mohave, Chumash and eastern Mono. The Mono were known by white explorers to take the plant to aid in gambling luck. In southwestern California the use of datura was strongly ritualized in the Chungichnich cult of the Luiseno Indians, and northern and southern Diegueno Indians as well. According to many scholars the ritual use of this plant among some of these tribes was a more recent overlay of much older uses of the plant, over a once wider area and from a much older time. [28]

A second group of tribes in the San Joaquin basin and Sierra Nevada Foothills had a datura drink that they used ceremonially every spring for both sexes shortly after the age of puberty. In the American southwest, the Pima had a jimsonweed song, which brought success in deer hunting, and was also known to cure vomiting and dizziness in small amounts. The White Mountain Apache mixed the root of Datura Meteloides with their corn beer to make it more intoxicating. The Apache credited datura with the power to make men crazy, but denied using it medicinally or ceremonially. The Havasupai Indians are known to have eaten datura leaves occasionally for purely secular pleasures, and also use the plant in their arrow poisons. At Zuni, datura was one of the medicines formerly belonging to the Gods, and only the rain priest and directors of the little fire could use it. The rain priest grinded boards with the powdered root on it and ate it in rituals to bring rain. They also administered it to clients who had been robbed, to help discover the thief, and to patients with broken bones; the pulverized root and flower were also used with corn meal for all types of wounds. The Navaho ate the root of datura Meteloides, and sometimes while under it's influence, would run around in a frenzy trying to discover lost or stolen items, which it is said many times they discover with the help of the plants intoxication. There is also a record of a Hopi doctoring with the use of datura as well. But among all native peoples of the American South West, the Navajo were some of the best known and best documented to have taken datura for its visionary properties. Valuing it for diagnosing, healing, and for intoxication ritual, the Navajo used the plant as a means to alter consciousness and to receive messages from the divine. [29]

Amanita Mascara or Fly Agaric Mushrooms

Another old world psychedelic that has demonstrated shamanic use in the new world is Amanita Mascaria mushroom. Amanita Mascara is probably one of the most famous psychedelics in the modern world. It is also a source of many modern theories on entheogenic religion: Wasson thought it was the sacred Soma of the Indian Reg Verdia holy books as well as the possible source and origin of religion itself. John Allegro thought that Christianity was really an Amanita Cult, and that Jesus was a code word for the fly Agaric mushroom. One of several Protégés of Wasson and Allegro, Clark Heinrich, thought that Moses was initiated into a secret Fly agric cult before seeing the burning bush, as well as the mushroom being the Holy Grail and the Elixir of life of the Alchemist in later centuries. According to Andrija Puharich, the sacred mushroom was so highly revered by the Egyptians and so secret that it wasn't even part of their language. Carl Ruck finds the mushroom hiding in the Golden Fleece, and in the fire of Prometheus. Blais finds Amanitas within secret orders in Christian monasteries. Yet despite its fame and the many modern inquires into the visionary uses of the Amanita mushroom whatever they may have been, one thing is for certain. That the red caped mushrooms has a long history of shamanic use throughout Siberia, Northern Europe, China, Japan, Korea, and may other areas where it is known to grow naturally. [30]

The first settlers of the Americas came in from many of these same regions in Asia, slowly crossing the baring strait, while others traveled down the coastline by boat. As a result, Anthropologists have found many Asia related or remnant culture traits that are known to persist in the Americas. One of these is demonstrated in the ancient use of the Amanita Mascara mushroom both by native peoples in Asia and Siberia as well as native peoples just over the baring strait into Canada. Recent discoveries have uncovered the religious and shamanic importance of the fly Agaric mushroom that has indeed survived in North American native cultures from these earliest of times. Indications for this have been found among the Dogrib Athabascan peoples who live on the Mackenzie Mountain range in northwestern Canada. They are known to use the mushrooms in a very similar fashion as has been documented in the traditional shamanic use of the mushrooms in Siberia. Also more recently, the religious shamanic use of Amanita Muscaria has also been discovered in an ancient annual ceremony practiced by the Ojibwa Indians or Ahnishinaubeg who are known to have lived on Lake Superior in northern Michigan. The mushroom is known in the Ojibwa language as "Oshtimisk Wajashkwedo" or the red topped mushroom. [31]

Mescal seeds

Another powerful mind altering plant that was popular among native peoples of North America particularly in the shamanic rituals of the Plains Indians was known as Sophophora secundiflora a plant also known to produce the red Mescal bean. Mescal, as it is more commonly known, was first commonly employed by many southern planes Indians as a ritual shamanic intoxicant before the arrival of the Europeans. The beans of the plant Sophophora secundiflora contains a highly toxic narcotic alkaloid sophorine, which somewhat closely resembles nicotine on a molecular level, as well as in its physiological action, the contents of the bean are said to induce nausea and if taken without proper supervision can induce convulsions and even death by asphyxiation. Yet regardless of this danger, the powerfully mind altering effects of the beans have had a long history of use among many of the tribes of the southern planes Indians in North America. [32]

The plant Sophophora secundiflora is known as an evergreen shrub bearing two or three tough shelled red seeds or been like pods, known in Mexico as "toleselo" and elsewhere as the mescal bean. The intoxication of the seeds productizes a delirious exhilaration followed by a deep sleep. The intoxicating effects of the seeds can be represented in this great old Apache story in which a Coyote trickster pounded up a number of the seeds and gave them to people to eat. While the people were out of their minds, the coyote trickster cut off their hair in patches to show them that they were all crazy. While the maddening effects of these toxic beans were well known to the Indians, the effects of the beans were most often used in ritual dances to induce states of trance and to create visions. The Pawnee and Oto used the mescal bean ritually and the Iowa were also known to have had a full fledged ceremony called the Red Bean Dance in which the participants would dance in an all night vigil under the intoxicating effects of the beans to induce both trace and an alteration in consciousness as a means to see visions and create waking dreams that gave them divine messages. [33]

There is a legend that surrounds this ancient mescal rite. It is said by the Iowa and Pawnee Indians that the society of Mescal was originally founded by a faster who dreamed in a fast that he had received his knowledge of the bean from the deer, for the red beans (mescal) are sometimes found in the deer's stomachs and are also known to intoxicate. From this faster, the Indians learned of the sacred nature of the bean and came to use it to receive knowledge and messages from the divine. While the Mescal bean is no longer consumed in Native American rituals, Anthropologists that have studied the use of the Mescal bean among native North American Plains Indians have come to affirm that the mescal cult goes back at least 10,000 years, which is back to the Paleo-Indian Hunters Period at the end of the Pleistocene period in the Americas. The impressive Pecos River paintings in Texas have also been associated with this prehistoric mescal cult. Archeological excavations carried out in the areas where these paintings were found have also revealed mescal seeds and clear evidence in which the use of the seeds is known to go back at least to 8,000 B.C., when Carbon-14 dated. Along the same regions in the lower Pecos river in Texas, there have also been found rock paintings of spirit beings, and other supernatural and entopic patterns that have all been associated with the ancient Native American Indian use of this very ancient and visionary native American plant.[34]

Formally widely used by the Indians of the southern plains to produce dream like visions at certain ceremonies, the ritual use of mescal bean has now been supplanted by the more powerful and far less toxic peyote cactus. Many of the plains Indians were already familiar with the practice of visionary rituals, so when they were introduced to peyote, the use of the mescal bean quickly became replaced and was set aside as an only ornamental ritual element within the emerging peyote cult. The ritual presence of Mescal seeds in the Plains Indian peyote rituals attests to its long history of use and importance among them. It was from this popular transference by the plains Indians that the use of Peyote spread into the larger Native American population and would later spread into what is known today as the greater Native American church. [35]

Peyote Cacti

Throughout this chapter you have seen the many visionary and psychoactive substances popularly associated with indigenous Native American visionary shamanic practices of Central and South America as well as to the native people of Mexico and North America. But out of all of the sacred and psychoactive plants native to the Americas and used by the indigenous people for sacred, spiritual, and healing purposes, the one plant that has probably had the greatest influence on the indigenous and native peoples of North America in the last 100 years is the Peyote Cactus. Ever since the arrival of the first Europeans in the new world, Peyote has provoked controversy, suppression, and persecution. Condemned by Spanish conquerors for it's satanic trickery, and attacked again by local governments and religious groups, the plant has nevertheless continued to play a major role among the Indians of both Mexico, and in the last 100 years, that of North America by what is now the greater Native American Church. The Peyote plant is currently used by members of the NAC in their religious rituals, as their most holy religious sacrament and most sacred spiritual ally.

An early Spanish Chronicler, from Fray Bernardino de Sahagun, estimated on the basis of several historical events recorded in Indian Chronology that Peyote was known to the Chichimeca and Toltec Indians of Mexico at least 1,890 years before the arrival of the Europeans. This calculation would give the cactus native to Mexico a history extending over a period of some two thousands years and possibly even longer. Many years after this, the Danish Ethnologist Carl Lumholts did his pioneering work with the Chihuahua Indians, who suggested to him that the Peyote Cult is far older than previous known dates would allow. He showed symbols employed in the Tarahumara Indian ceremonies which appeared in ancient ritualistic carvings and cave paintings preserved in Mesoamerica lava rocks, many dating well over thousands of years in age. [36]

The history of Peyote also known as Lophophora Williamsii, goes back far beyond known human history. More recently, the archeological discoveries in dry caves and rock shelters in Texas and Mexico have yielded specimens of Peyote. These specimens have also been found in a context suggesting ceremonial use. Radio Carbon 14 dating of these specimens indicates that the sacred use of the cacti in this region is more than seven thousand years old. The earliest European records concerning this sacred cactus are those of Sahagun, who lived from 1499 to 1590 and who dedicated most of his adult life to the Indians of Mexico. Most of the early records in Mexico were left by missionaries who opposed the use of Peyote in religious practices. To them Peyote had no place in Christianity because of its pagan associations. Since the Spanish rulers were intolerant of any cult but their own, fierce persecution resulted, but the natives were reluctant to give up their peyote cults that had been ongoing and well established from centuries of tradition. [37]

Several seventeenth century Spanish Jesuits testified that the Mexican Indians used peyote medicinally and in ceremonies. The name of Peyote is derived from the Aztec word *Peyotl* and was used by Indians in central and northern Mexico in Pre-Columbian years. During the last decades of the nineteenth century, the explorer Carl Lumholtz observed the use of peyote among the Indians of the Sierra Madre Occidental in Mexico, primarily by the Huichol and Tarahumara Indians. However, no anthropologist ever participated in or observed a traditional Peyote hunt until the 1960s when anthropologists and a Mexican writer were permitted by the Hoichol Indians to accompany several of their pilgrims. [38]

The Hoichol Indians

The Hoichol Indians are the only Indigenous Native peoples of Mexico to have maintained their pre-Columbian traditions. Because of this, they are of a great interest and importance to the Anthropological community today. Once a year the Hoichol Indians make a sacred trip to gather "Hikuri," as the sacred Peyote cacti is called. The trek is lead by an experienced "mara' akame" or shaman, who is in contact with "Tatewari" known as grand father fire. Tatewari is the oldest of Hoichol spirit gods. The preparation for gathering Peyote involves ritual confession of misdeeds or sins as well as bodily purification. Following the confession and the purification rituals, the group sets out to Wirikuta known as their sacred ancestral mountains. Upon arrival within sight of the sacred mountains of "Wirikuta" also known as Paradise, the pilgrims are ritually washed as they prey for rain and the fertility of the earth. [39]

Upon arrival at the place where the Peyote is to be hunted, the shaman begins ceremonial practices, telling stories from the ancient Peyote tradition and invoking protection for the events to come. After another set of rituals, the Peyote hunt begins with basket fulls of the plants eventually being collected. On the following day, more Peyote is collected, some of which is to be shared with those who remain back at home for later religious rituals in the coming year. The Hoichol Peyote hunt is seen to them as a return to Wirikuta or Paradise, and it is their yearly tradition of returning there, and gaining their most sacred and holy spiritual power, the power of the Peyote. This can only be done by returning to paradise in their yearly pilgrimage back to Wirikuta. [40]

Peyote in North America

In North America it was the Kiowa and Comonche Indians who apparently visited native groups in northern Mexico, and who first learned about this sacred plant. At this time in history the Indians in the United States of America were restricted to conservation camps or reservations for the last half of the nineteenth century. At this time much of their cultural heritage was disappearing, in fact, disinagrating. Faced with this disastrous inevitability, a number of surviving North American Indian leaders, especially from tribes in Oklahoma, began actively to spread a new kind of Native American religion, with Peyote as the central sacrament. [41]

Its use quickly spread north to the Indians of the United States and Canada around the 1890s. The Kiowa and Comanche were apparently the most active proponents of this new religions movement. The success in spreading this new peyote cult resulted in a strong opposition to its practice from Christian missionaries and local governmental groups, so in an attempt to protect their rights and religious activities from further eradication and persecution, American Indians organized the Peyote cult into a legally recognized religious group known today as the greater Native American church. In 1993 the NAC numbered 300,000 members strong in the United States alone, from among seventy different tribes. The sacrament Peyote is considered illegal by the U.S. Government due to the cacti containing the controlled psychedelic compound mescaline. It is only in the religious exemption of the Native American church that Native American Indians can partake of the cacti in the religious ritual setting. To this day, strong persecution and imprisonment are still very common throughout the United States for anyone who would use peyote for personal religious activity outside the constructs of a NAC gathering or if they are not of Native American descent. [42]

In examining Native American traditions and beliefs regarding this sacred plant is found this following important Native American legend:

It was once said that:

> Long ago the Indians lived with this land and in peace with god the Great Spirit. But then the white man came, he came to take the land, he came by force and brought much suffering to its people the Indians. So God took pity on the Indian, and gave them Peyote that he had created. God wanted to bless the Indians, and to give them some of his power. So God put some of his power into the Peyote for it to be used for all Indians, as a tool, a tool to give them back some of his power. [43]

The quote you have just read is one of the legends perpetuated regarding Peyote and it relationship to Native American peoples. Followers of the Native American Church say that they take the Sacrament Peyote to absorb gods power which they say is contained within the plant. This is done in much the same way that the white Christians take the sacrament bread and wine during communion. The term "power" is an English term used by the Indians for the supernatural force called Mana by anthropologists; it is the equivalent to the New Testament *pneuma*, translated as Holy Spirit or Holy Ghost. In the Native American tradition, the Great Spirit also known as God lives throughout all things in the universe and is said to pervade all of matter. So it is the use of Peyote that allows them to have to ability to come into contact and communion with the Great Spirit during their sacred rituals. The Native Americans who use Peyote use it as a sacrament where it is consumed to gain good knowledge and good wisdom on life, healing, and the earth, knowledge that the Indians say is obtained directly from God with the help of the spirit of peyote. Among American Indians, all psychotropic drugs (including tobacco) were invariably used only in religious or sacred context, because of the belief that the effects of using these substances were evidence of supernatural "power" in them. It in interesting to note that when problems arise from the employment of narcotics, they arise after the narcotics have passed from the ceremonial to the purely hedonic or recreational use. [44]

The Indians say that peyote works from the inside out and is a teacher who can show a man the right way to live and answer his questions by giving him an experience to live through. Spiritually, peyote is used to obtain knowledge. This knowledge is obtained by learning from Peyote. Used properly, peyote is an inexhaustible teacher. A common statement on this is that, "one can use peyote all their life, but you'll never get to the end of what there is to be known from peyote. Peyote is always teaching you something new." The experience of knowledge is a very common theme in the Native American tradition, particularly with the use of Peyote as the tool for obtaining this knowledge.

But the mere act of eating peyote does not in itself bring knowledge. The proper ritual behavior has to be observed before one is granted this knowledge through peyote. Physically one must be clean, having been bathed and put on clean clothes. Spiritually one must put away all evil thoughts. Psychologically, one must be conscious of his personal inadequacy, humble, sincere in wanting to obtain the benefits of peyote, and concentrate on it. Peyote teaches in various ways. One is through heightened powers of introspection during a Peyote session. During a Peyote session a great deal of time is spent in personal introspection. This heightened introspection leads to a heightened sensibility of oneself and with others. There is also another deeper heightened sensibility to others that manifests in what one might call a form of telepathy. This is to say that, one sometimes can either feel that he knows what others are thinking, or feels that he or she influences, or is influenced by the thoughts of others around him. This mental connection phenomenon is a relatively frequent phenomenon among native peyote rituals and has been labeled by the Indians as the speaking in tougues. [45]

The 2nd way peyote teaches is by means of revelation, called vision. The vision is obtained because one has eaten enough peyote under proper ritual conditions to obtain the power needed to commune with the spirit world. The vision provides a direct experience (visual, auditory, or a combination of both) of God. Peyote is considered sacred by the NAC and is seen as a divine messenger, enabling the individual to communicate with god without the need of a medium or priest. Many times also some intermediary spirit such as Jesus or the Peyote spirit, which is seen as a purification spirit, also known by the Indians as the famous Water Bird which may also been seen.

[46] Correlated with its use as a religious sacrament is its presumed value as a medicine some Indians claim that if Peyote is used correctly, all other medicines are superfluous. It supposed curative properties are responsible probably more than any other factor for its rather quick expansion to many other tribes throughout the United States in many of the early years of the cults rising. The Peyote religion is therefore fundamentally a medico religious cult. Making it a religion of both healing and religious experience, something that can be found among many other native indigenous religious traditions around the world, and a common factor found within Shamanism, a healing tradition that is interwoven with that of the religious or spiritual tradition. Peyote is therefore an essential religious sacrament as well as an important and vital healing medicine for the body, mind, and soul. [47]

The Peyote cactus Lophophora Williamsii grows naturally in the Chihuahuan desert from San Luis Potosi, Mexico, to the Rio Grande. North of the Rio Grand in the United States peyote was once found from big bend national park almost to the golf of Mexico. Today, peyote's range is largely restricted to a few small counties. This is largely as a result of habitat destruction and over harvesting. Large ranches in the Peyote growing areas or habitats of Texas have been root plowed for cattle grazing. This has torn up the soil killing the deep carrot like root systems of the native peyote plants. Grasses grow back for the cattle ranchers, but the peyote plants never return once the roots have been killed. The members of the various branches of the Native American church in the United States and Canada consume between five and ten million, peyote tops a year for ritual religious purposes. Native Americans as well as licensed commercial peyote harvesters are not able to cultivate or grow peyote according to current United States Law. Because the licensed commercial Peyote harvesters are not currently replanting or attempting any cultivation, the size of the buttons has been steadily decreasing, while the price has been going up. Not surprisingly, the amount of peyote consumed at meetings has also been decreasing. With the increased demand for land and the current misguided laws surrounding Peyote's cultivation, if something is not done to reverse this, then in the next hundred years we may begin to see a slow extraction of peyote use from many Native American rituals, with the plant becoming increasingly scarce in its natural habitat. [48]

Ayahuasca

Earlier in this book I presented research outlining the history and pharmacological properties of the entheogenic plant brew Ayahuasca. I also described the availability and importance of other plants in other regions of the world containing the same pharmacological properties as those traditionally found in the Ayahusca mixture. As you have already seen the basic principals for the indigenous uses of Ayahuasca in the jungles of Central and South America are like many psychoactive plants used in traditional societies around the world and in the Americas. They are used primarily for healing and visionary mystical insight. Ayahuasca, like all entheogens is not a toy, it is not a ride, you do not take it to get high, and you do not take it to see interesting or amazing pictures or images. The brew is fundamentally a medicine used for healing the body. It is also a spiritual biochemical doorway, a technology that temporarily and naturally fundamentally alters ones consciousness in a way that can be so totally profound that taking it without respect or fully understanding what you are about to get yourself into can be a very dangerous and shocking experience. It affects you on a physical, emotional, and spiritual plane that can be so complex and completely emotionally and mentally saturating that you must treat it with a great deal of care and respect. The brew is not for everyone, it is a sacred and powerful secret technology that must not be taken lightly and should always, repeat always, be taken under trained supervision. It should only be taken with someone who is trained and experienced with its use, and familiar with its consumption and effects, a person like a shaman. The brew is not recreational, taking it will make you throw up and vomit, it may be unpleasant at first, but it is all part of the natural process of purification required by the brew. It does not taste good and because of its chemical properties you can not take the brew if you are taking any other drugs or medications. Also as a requirement you should not eat any meat three days before drinking the brew as this will make the person drinking the brew very sick and uncomfortable. Refraining from the consumption of meat is another built in design required by the brew and it should be taken with the utmost regard.

Ayahuasca Churches

Because of Ayahuasca's powerfully sacred and therapeutic effects, the use of Ayahuasca in sacred healing practices can be found to be present in almost all of the traditional indigenous cultures populating most of central and South America today. As Christianity and increasing industrialization have begun to reshape the landscape of the Amazon, so too has the Ayahuasca brew began to witness an evolution and adaptation in the use and incorporation of its sacred properties. In more recent years emerging from some of these traditional shamanic rain forest roots, has developed religious institutions that have come to utilize the brew as a religious sacrament and a powerful healing device. One of these churches is known as the UDV or the Uniao do Vegetal, also known in English as the church of the *Union of the Vegetable*. The church is a synergistic religious sect, where the brew of Ayahuasca is employed as a religious ritual sacrament. Claiming roots as far back as the 10th century B.C members of the UDV claim the movement lay dormant before reappearing in the Incan civilization of Peru in the 4th and 5th centuries B.C. The UDV as it is known today was "re-created" on July 22, 1961 in Porto Velho, Rondônia, Brazil by the rubber-tapper José Gabriel da Costa In Brazil. [49]

As with the UDV there is another Church that has come out from the Rain forest that uses Ayahuasca as a religious sacrament and has started to spread around the world.

It is known as the church of the Santo Daime. The Santo Daime is also a syncretism religious union of indigenous Amazonian traditions with the catholic religion. In the Santo Daime rituals, Ayahuasca is consumed as a central religious sacrament. The term Daime, refers not only to the brew, but also the animated force believed to reside within or through the brew. The church of the Santo Daime was founded in the early 1930s by Mestre Irineu, also known as Raimundo Irineu Serra, a native rubber tapper of African Brazilian descent. Diame is a revealed religion and its doctrine is based on the hymns received from the Diame brew. So it is therefore the brew that is the source of the traditions wisdom and sacred spiritual teachings. [50]

Emerging from the rain forest of South America the Santo Daime and the União do Vegetal are considered to be animist, shamanist spiritualism mixed with Christian elements and religious imagery. Both the Santo Daime and União do Vegetal now have members and churches throughout the world. UDV has over 10,000 members, about 130 of which are in the United States, with a branch in Santa Fe, New Mexico and much more secretly in sparse areas of California and New York. UDV members participate in ritual consumption of Ayahuasca in a group ritual setting. The brew is used for healing and inducing mystical religious experiences and knowledge. [51]

Another fast growing religion that has also emerged out of the rain forest is known as *Gnostisismo Revolutionario de la Concienca de Krishna*. This religious tradition like the UDV and Santo Daime is an example of a spiritual community based around the use of the Ayahuasca brew as a central entheogenic religious sacrament, healer and teacher. Combining beliefs from various cultures, *Gnostisismo Revolutionario de la Concienca de Krishna* is a growing religious community which began over fifteen years ago in the Putamayo and Caqueta regions of the Colombian jungle from the native indigenous peoples and from their traditional shamanic practices associated with the use of Ayahuasca. The name, 'Gnostisismo' relates to the groups strong association with the Gnostic movement. 'Revolutionario' refers to a (non-violent) "revolution in consciousness as a means of changing the world and bringing in peace and enlightenment, 'De la conciencia de Krishna' comes from the affinity of the community with the spiritual traditions of India and the concept of the Krishna consciousness. The Krishna consciousness is the spiritual understanding of the mind of god within the Indian subcontinent. In addition to containing many Gnostic and esoteric shamanic elements, the group is also very ecologically and politically motivated, campaigning for the human rights and for the people who live in the jungle, as well as initiating ecological projects. Ayahuasca (also known to them as yaje) is drunk in twice weekly ceremonies. It is revered as a teacher and spirit guide and seen as a spiritual path that can be followed to gain access to the realms of healing, inner spiritual knowledge, as well as for maintaining an intimacy with the immediate environment and the planet. [52]

One of the newest Ayahusca institutions that has developed around the use and protection of the Ayahuasca brew is a Peruvian church known as, "Soga Del Alma" meaning "Vine of the Soul." The Saga Del Alma is an entity for the legal protection of the religious and shamanic use of Ayahuasca in the state of Peru, primarily for the many native and indigenous peoples of the Peruvian Amazon, for which the Peruvian Government largely ignores. The church is known to organize yearly conferences for those interested in Amazonian shamanism and healing as well as providing access to traditional Ayahuasca ceremonies that are managed by authentic Amazonian curandero(a) s or healers. The church attempts to maintain the traditional shamanic contents of the indigenous beliefs and practices, both in healing and in spiritual practice. The primary locations of the temples are located in and around the city of Iquitos Peru.

CH 13
MODERN GNOSIS & THE GREATEST SECRET OF THE ANCIENT WORLD.

The most beautiful and most profound experience is the sensation of the mystical. It is the sower of all true science. He to whom this emotion is a stranger, who can no longer wonder and stand rapt in awe, is as good as dead. To know that what is impenetrable to us really exists, manifesting itself as the highest wisdom and the most radiant beauty which our dull faculties can comprehend only in their primitive forms-this knowledge, this feeling is at the center of all true religiousness.

- Albert Einstein

Many prominent mainstream orthodox forms of religion in the world today teach that mankind is somehow separated from God. In Christianity this is due to sin, which started from a primordial curse on mankind from the first two humans rebelling against God in the Garden of Eden. The two largest religions on earth, Islam and Christianity, both teach that spiritual contact can only come as a result of "Divine Grace" and that enlightenment only comes to those that have been chosen by God, or that only through faith can mankind come into contact or have union with God's true nature. This is in fact not the case. Enlightenment is a normal characteristic of the human nervous system. God, the Great Spirit, the Divine Mind, whatever you choose to call it, is present within all things and within all matter in the universe, both seen and unseen. God is not some grey haired old man sitting in the clouds; god is a form of pure consciousness that prevays all matter in the universe. God is the great life force and intelligence that animates nature. God is not separated from mankind as some would suppose, and the direct experience of God does not need to come through divine choosing or by strong faith in an unseen creator. Contact with the divine has been built into the very fabric of nature, and it is through nature that people all over the world and throughout human history have come to know and experience God. This is not something I have faith in, believe, think, or was told by someone else. This is something I know and have directly experienced first hand.

A few years before I started the research and writing of this book, I had one of the most profound experiences of my life. It was a mystical religious experience and my first full fledged encounter with the divine. It was an event that was so profound it changed my entire outlook on life, and eventually led me to the research and writing of this book. The experience took place during the summer. I had hiked to the top of a secluded hill to pray and spend time in reflection after eating a large batch of freshly harvested visionary mushrooms. I chose a resting space surrounded with grass, deciding to lay down I looked up into the bright cloud speckled summer sky. As the effects started to come over me, I became filled with feelings of wonder and awe becoming struck by the grandeur and beauty of the sky before me. As this occurred I decided to pray and thank God for the beauty that surrounded me and the grandeur of his creation. As I looked around me, everything looked particularly luminous and beautiful. All the plants in my field of vision were surrounded by a faint hue of living self-emanating light that I could feel and see. As the effects started to increase, I began to become emotionally saturated into the beauty of the experience. Again, I looked at the sky. Starring into its depths, I began to enter a world where the air breathes and the sky has spirit. As I looked into the grandeur of heaven, I saw it become filled with a beautiful interconnected web of omnipresent rainbows that would slowly sway and breathe in the sky before me.

As I continued to look into the depths of the sky and into the rainbows that were now filling my field of vision, my heart became full with emotions of wonder and awe enticed by its increasing beauty. As I continued to stare into the presence of the sky above me, and at the beautiful network of breathing rainbow patterns, my heart became filled and my mind started to open like a flower. As this occurred I started to pray and thank God for what I was beginning to experience. Then, just as I did this, my mind began to be drawn to and focus on a singular rainbow within the sea of multi colored interconnected breathing patterns of faint rainbow light. As this occurred I began to feel a presence or life force within the light. Focusing on the depths of this singular rainbow, I watched as it began to expand, separate, and open up before my eyes from a singular space of white light at the center of the rainbow in my field of focus. As I continued to stare into the spreading white light, I watched as the white light opened up from between the colors. As this occurred, my mind and emotions began to be transported and engulfed by the beauty and transcendence of the experience.

Then, as if in an instance and of no will of my own, I became filled with an energy and mind of a divine universal presence, an emotional spirit and intellect not of my own. As its consciousness entered my mind, I quickly became mentally and emotionally raptured into union with its emotional intellectual presence. As this occurred, I became aware of its independent conscious nature and the deeply independent mental and emotional reality of its invisible spiritual essence, which was comprised of pure consciousness. As the presence of its consciousness filled my mind and emotions, I continued to lie on the grass in an emotional and mental state of spiritual and emotional ecstasy, completely saturated and taken away by the profoundness of the experience that had raptured my awareness. Feeling completely raptured into the awareness of this mind, thoughts not of my own began to enter my thoughts and from this, an intellect began to communicate with me. It communicated to me directly through thought, flowing thoughts, feelings, and emotions into my mind. It filled my heart with a spiritual and emotional elevation of divine presence, ecstasy, and spiritual emotional awareness that words alone cannot sufficiently describe. Its presence was both mentally and emotionally unified with my mind and spirit. It was an emotional consciousness comprised of both masculine and feminine principals united into one singular emotional conscious universal spirit, with my own personal soul or psyche being feminine to its divine embrace. While the inflow of knowledge and thoughts were similar to the experience of gnosis, I would have later have in my first experiments with ayahuasca, the experience I was having now was far more emotionally and mentally saturating. It was also much more ecstatically rapturous, and personally emotionally complex. While I had taken mushrooms alone many times before and in many different settings, this was the first time my mind had ever been opened up to such an experience.

As my mind, will, and emotions lay absorbed in the consciousness of this presence, I continued to communicate with it in my heart and mind. I yearned for more as I laid wrapped up in ecstatic awe and spiritual rapture by the awareness and communion of its overwhelming divine consciousness. As this took place, thoughts of wisdom and teachings flowed into my mind. It spoke in thought alone, telling me it was the great balancer and source of life. Its emotions were of love, wisdom, and compassion and its thoughts were of pure knowledge and its mind was of pure understanding. "To cultivate love is to life," it said, as it continued to encourage me with passion and fill me with love and an overwhelming yearning for its continued divine emotional presence. I perceived its essence as a complex emotional system of independent thoughts and personalies, structured of pure consciousness made of independent mind, emotions, and universal unseen spiritual presence.

Soon enough, my union with its force began to fade, and as quickly as it emerged into my awareness it began to disappear, eventually disappearing back inside from which it had come. After this experience occurred I knew without a doubt that what I had experienced was real and that I had a real encounter that was the most profound experience of my life. It was an experience that not only changed the way I viewed the world from that day forward, but it also forever changed my belief and understanding of God. The experience was so powerful that I continued to think about the experience for months after it took place, and I still even think about it to this day. Because of its strong effect on my life, I desperately wanted to record and capture the experience the best way I could. I first attempted to do this by writing poems and songs about my experience trying to express and describe it, but no matter how hard I tried, I felt that the words I had written could not fully grasp the true grandeur, complexity, or profoundness of what I had experienced. Because of this, I started to contemplate other ways that I could express or depict my experience. That is when I came to realize that the best way to describe my experience was visually in art, but the presence I encountered was not visually made, or comprised of any shape or visible form. So how could I express something that was invisible? Well, the beautiful thing about art, particularly sacred art, is its ability to communicate ideas through the use of pictures and symbols. This is known as artistic symbolic form or symbolic representation. So it was in this way that I was going to describe and express what I had experienced, creating a painting that I could always look at and remember the truth and reality of my experience.

At the time, I had no idea how I was going to do this, and all ideas I could come up with to symbolically describe the experience just seemed to be grossly inadequate. Then one day, a few weeks after the experience took place I woke up after having a dream. In the dream, I was painting my experience and I had hung the painting on the wall in my home. As I woke, I continued to reflect on how I was going to express this experience in art and how I could paint it and visually describe it. I had already purchased a canvas and all the needed supplies, but until that morning I had no idea how I was going to accurately describe my encounter. Then as I reflected I had an idea, I knew just how I was going to construct my painting.

Over the next few months I created a painting that you now see as the cover art for this book. The picture on the cover of this book is my own artistic symbolic representation of this event, the most profound entheogeic experience of my life. As I have said before, the painting does not depict something that I saw visually with my eyes, but was instead something I felt and encountered mentally, spiritually, and emotionally. The painting is intended to be a visual symbolic form of visual communication used to describe and represent aspects of the experience.

In examining the symbolism of the picture, you will see two eyes on the upper left and lower right sides of the painting representing the different emotional aspects of the divine consciousness. The eye on the bottom right is a woman symbolizing the feminine principle and the eye surrounded by blue energy on the top left is a man symbolizing the masculine principal. These represent the masculine and feminine principles of the consciousness. The rainbow faced flower like depiction in the center of the painting is there to demonstrate union of the masculine and feminine principles into one singular essence. As I said before, they were not individual separate entities, but were unified within one singular consciousness. The eye at the top of the rainbow flower is to further emphasize the singular nature of this consciousness. A consciousness comprised of both masculine and feminine principles. To emphasize the universal omnipresence of its nature I created the rippling circular motions of the red and black liquid-like energy background that is being torn in the center of the picture. In the center of the picture within the opening of the tear is the earth. The earth is represented as the blue and green patterns on either side of the central flower figure. This is to represent the universal omnipresence of its consciousness and its connection with all things.

The man and woman holding in sensual embrace and surrounded in rainbows just below the lower portion of the pink fractal flower is there to demonstrate the emotional presence and feelings I had during my union with this mind. These were the feelings of perfect love, balance, and purity that I felt within the raptured presence and its mental embrace to myself. It is also to show the two emotional principals of masculine and feminine unified in a singular nature. Just below the pair of sensually unified male and female figures, is an image of one light and one dark element fusing or balancing out. This image is surrounded by yellow paint which I used to symbolize energy. The image came from a science book that is used as a symbol for antimatter. I included the symbol at the bottom of the picture because it was smaller than the main ideas but it was also a perfect choice to put in the painting not only to depict the innate dualism of nature and the primary principals of reality that comprises the universe, but also to depict a symbol that was one of the central principals of this being that I experienced, the essence of balance. Just below this image of balance I included a water drop to show water as a source of life and as symbol of purity. This was another impression I received during the experience. I also included water because of the liquid nature of consciousness that I felt during the experience. The ripples in the overall background of the image are also to represent energy and the liquid nature of consciousness.

As I have stated before, experiences like this and others that may be experienced during visionary and entheogen encouters are many times some of the most important and profound events in a person's life who has had them, but when these experiences are found to be created by plants, chemicals, or drugs, they are many times devalued and seen as less than the real thing. There is a real prejudice against the use of such substances in many areas of the western world today. I think that some of this comes from the almost inherent dualism that has been built into modern western thought, where people value the experience only if it is endrogenously produced, such as through diet, personal ordeal, or near death experience. What many people fail to consider is that they are working on the same biochemical mechanisms that the brain produces in naturally occurring experiences. Just because these states of mind can be induced through the consumption of a plant, should not make them any less valued. The fact that such experiences can even be induced through plants at all, gives great credit to the natural world. In examining the full scope of these types of experiences, I have come to believe that the people who deal with consciousness in our society really do not realize how mutable consciousness really is. This has, in my opinion, held back the western development of understanding consciousness because quite simply, many of the experiences and states these substances induce I do not believe are accessible by any other means other than by drugs, and this is a great heresy to a great number of people.

As you have seen throughout this book, altered states of consciousness have been responsible for many of the most profound mystical religious experiences of human history. The fact that this experience can be induced through drumming, fasting, meditation, or the consumption of plants does not make them any less valuable. In fact, the use of plants and their importance to the history of human religion has been greatly persecuted and devalued in western civilization. As I have shown throughout the research in this book, it is the relationship between mankind and nature that have truly facilitated the greatest connections between the human spirit and the experience of the divine. This is truly the greatest secret of the ancient world, that the keys to the divine are not locked away or have been lost and forgotten. Connecting and experiencing the divine is a natural part of the human experience on this planet, and it is an experience that has been going on within human history since the very dawn of time. The keys and secrets to this experience have been passed down through tradition and ritual from the most ancient religions and traditions on the planet, many of which are now extinct.

The modern world of faith does not need to contradict the mysteries of spirit. As you have seen from reading this book, the use of such substances among the Gnostics and the many other religeus groups throughout antiquity that has been examined in this book, account for the most important mystical religious experiences of the ancient world. Of which comes the greatest and most powerful visionary experiences known to man, the experiences of the divine. The urge of the transcendental and the yearning for the mystical is a particular and unique appetite of the human soul. Its importance has defined our beliefs and inspired the most monumental events in our history. The spiritual, visionary, and mystical encounters that define these experiences lay at the center and heart of all world religions and are known to characterize nearly every religion on the planet. Their importance in our lives and interconnectedness with our history and culture cannot be denied. While the importance of the transcendental may define us as human, its relationship to the natural world has some how been forgotten or deliberately exercised from our greater cultural awareness. It is this relationship between mind and matter that defines the mystical experience, and it is the mystical experience that allows us to, if ever so briefly, bridge the gap, between the two worlds of mind and spirit.

References

Ch1. Keys to the Spirit world and the Birth of Religion

1. Samorini, Giorgio. <u>Animals and Psychedelics, the Natural World and the Instinct to Alter Consciousness</u>. Rochester: Park Street Press, 2002. pp. 57 and 58.

2. Samorini, Giorgio. <u>Animals and Psychedelics, the Natural World and the Instinct to Alter Consciousness</u>. Rochester: Park Street Press, 2002. pp. 57 and 58 also Wikipedia, "Mandrill" <http://en.wikipedia.org/wiki/Mandrill>

3. Grey, Alex. <u>Transfigurations</u>. Rochester: Inner Traditions International, 2001. pp. 52.

4. Grey, Alex. <u>Transfigurations</u>. Rochester: Inner Traditions International, 2001. pp. 52.

5. Hancock, Graham. <u>Supernatural, Meetings with the Ancient Teachers of Mankind.</u> New York: Disinformation Company Ltd., 2007. pp. 7.

6. Hancock, Graham. <u>Supernatural, Meetings with the Ancient Teachers of Mankind.</u> New York: Disinformation Company Ltd., 2007. pp. 7.

7. Hancock, Graham. <u>Supernatural, Meetings with the Ancient Teachers of Mankind.</u> New York: Disinformation Company Ltd., 2007. pp. 8.

8. Hancock, Graham. <u>Supernatural, Meetings with the Ancient Teachers of Mankind.</u> New York: Disinformation Company Ltd., 2007. pp. 31.

9. Hancock, Graham. <u>Supernatural, Meetings with the Ancient Teachers of Mankind.</u> New York: Disinformation Company Ltd., 2007. pp. 37.

10. Hancock, Graham. <u>Supernatural, Meetings with the Ancient Teachers of Mankind.</u> New York: Disinformation Company Ltd., 2007. pp. 37.

11. Hancock, Graham. <u>Supernatural, Meetings with the Ancient Teachers of Mankind.</u> New York: Disinformation Company Ltd., 2007. pp. 38.

12. Hancock, Graham. <u>Supernatural, Meetings with the Ancient Teachers of Mankind.</u> New York: Disinformation Company Ltd., 2007. pp. 38.

13. Hancock, Graham. <u>Supernatural, Meetings with the Ancient Teachers of Mankind.</u> New York: Disinformation Company Ltd., 2007. pp. 68.

14. Hancock, Graham. <u>Supernatural, Meetings with the Ancient Teachers of Mankind.</u> New York: Disinformation Company Ltd., 2007. pp. 69.

15. Hancock, Graham. <u>Supernatural, Meetings with the Ancient Teachers of Mankind.</u> New York: Disinformation Company Ltd., 2007. pp. 69.

16. Hancock, Graham. <u>Supernatural, Meetings with the Ancient Teachers of Mankind.</u> New York: Disinformation Company Ltd., 2007. pp. 69.

17. Hancock, Graham. <u>Supernatural, Meetings with the Ancient Teachers of Mankind.</u> New York: Disinformation Company Ltd., 2007. pp. 71.

18. Hancock, Graham. <u>Supernatural, Meetings with the Ancient Teachers of Mankind.</u> New York: Disinformation Company Ltd., 2007. pp. 72.

19. Hancock, Graham. <u>Supernatural, Meetings with the Ancient Teachers of Mankind.</u> New York: Disinformation Company Ltd., 2007. pp. 73.

20. Hancock, Graham. <u>Supernatural, Meetings with the Ancient Teachers of Mankind.</u> New York: Disinformation Company Ltd., 2007. pp. 73.

21. Giorgio Samorini, from Integration No. 2,3, 1992, 69-78. <Http://leda.lycaeum.org/Documents/Prehistoric_Psychoactive_Mushroom_Artifcacts.10483.shtml>. and (Anati, 1989).

22. Giorgio Samorini, from Integration No. 2,3, 1992, 69-78. <Http://leda.lycaeum.org/Documents/Prehistoric_Psychoactive_Mushroom_Artifcacts.10483.shtml>.(Anati (1989:187), and (Sansoni 1980)

23. Giorgio Samorini, from Integration No. 2,3, 1992, 69-78. <Http://leda.lycaeum.org/Documents/Prehistoric_Psychoactive_Mushroom_Artifcacts.10483.shtml>....(Lhote, 1968) and Sansoni (1980)

24. Giorgio Samorini, from Integration No. 2,3, 1992, 69-78. <Http://leda.lycaeum.org/Documents/Prehistoric_Psychoactive_Mushroom_Artifcacts.10483.shtml>. (Samorini, 1989

25. Giorgio Samorini, from Integration No. 2,3, 1992, 69-78. <Http:// leda.lycaeum.org/Documents/Prehistoric_Psychoactive_Mushroom_ Artifcacts.10483.shtml>. (Dobkin de Rios, 1984:194).

26. Giorgio Samorini, from Integration No. 2,3, 1992, 69-78. <Http:// leda.lycaeum.org/Documents/Prehistoric_Psychoactive_Mushroom_ Artifcacts.10483.shtml>. (Mori, 1975), and (Lhote, 1973 :210 and 251)

27. Giorgio Samorini, from Integration No. 2,3, 1992, 69-78. <Http:// leda.lycaeum.org/Documents/Prehistoric_Psychoactive_Mushroom_ Artifcacts.10483.shtml>.

28. Giorgio Samorini, from Integration No. 2,3, 1992, 69-78. <Http:// leda.lycaeum.org/Documents/Prehistoric_Psychoactive_Mushroom_ Artifcacts.10483.shtml>.

29. Giorgio Samorini, from Integration No. 2,3, 1992, 69-78. <Http://leda. lycaeum.org/Documents/Prehistoric_Psychoactive_Mushroom_Artif cacts.10483.shtml>.

30. Giorgio Samorini, from Integration No. 2,3, 1992, 69-78. <Http:// leda.lycaeum.org/Documents/Prehistoric_Psychoactive_Mushroom_ Artifcacts.10483.shtml>.

31. Narby, Jeremy. The Cosmic Serpent, DNA and the Origins of Knowledge. New York: Penguin Group inc., 1998. pg 38 referring to Farnsworth (1988,pp.95), Eisner (1990,pp.198), and Elisabetsky (1991,pp.11)

32. Arthur, James. Mushrooms and Mankind. San Diego, Book Tree, 2000

33. Dictionar.com: "Entheogen" Retrived (2006) from http://dictionary. reference.com/browse/entheogen?vm=r

34. Hancock, Graham. Supernatural, Meetings with the Ancient Teachers of Mankind. New York: Disinformation Company Ltd., 2007. pp. 91 and 96

35. Breaking open the head. Web page Shamanism: <http://www. breakingopenthehead.com/what_is_shaminism.htm>

36. Breaking open the head. Web page Shamanism: <http://www. breakingopenthehead.com/what_is_shaminism.htm>

Ch 2: Visions and the Hellenistic Mysteries

1. Hale, John R. et al., "Questioning the Delphic Oracle: When science meets religion at this ancient Greek site, the two turn out to be on better terms than scholars had originally thought" Scientific American. August 2003 <http://www.sciam.com/article.cfm?articleID=0009BD34-398C-1F0A-97AE80A84189EEDF>

2. Encyclopædia Britannica, "Delphic Oracle." Chigago, IL 2005 also at http://www.britannica.com/

3. Encyclopædia Britannica, "Pythia." Chigago, IL 2005 also athttp://www.britannica.com/

4. Encyclopædia Britannica, "Delphic Oracle." Chigago, IL 2005 also at http://www.britannica.com/. Also see Roux 1976, pp. 54-63. and Bowden 2005, pp.

5. Encyclopædia Britannica, "Delphic Oracle." Chigago, IL 2005 also at http://www.britannica.com/

6. Encyclopædia Britannica, "Delphic Oracle." Chigago, IL 2005 also at http://www.britannica.com/

7. Encyclopædia Britannica, "Pythia." Chigago, IL 2005 also at http://www.britannica.com/

8. Encyclopædia Britannica, "Pythia." Chigago, IL 2005 also at http://www.britannica.com/

9. Jeffrey P. Chanton, retrieved on 2006-10-01 & John R. Haleret, rieved on 2006-10-01

10. Encyclopædia Britannica, "Pythia." Chigago, IL 2005 also at http://www.britannica.com/

11. Broad, William J. (2007).The Oracle: Ancient Delphi and the Science behind Its Lost Secrets. New York: Penguin Press Broad (p. 37)

12. Broad, William J. (2007).The Oracle: Ancient Delphi and the Science behind Its Lost Secrets. New York: Penguin Press

13. Broad, William J. (2007).The Oracle: Ancient Delphi and the Science behind Its Lost Secrets. New York: Penguin Press

14. Broad, William J. (2007).The Oracle: Ancient Delphi and the Science behind Its Lost Secrets. New York: Penguin Press

15. Broad, William J. (2007).The Oracle: Ancient Delphi and the Science behind Its Lost Secrets. New York: Penguin Press

16. Broad, William J. (2007).The Oracle: Ancient Delphi and the Science behind Its Lost Secrets. New York: Penguin Press (2006, p. 152), Reporting on the spring

17. Willoughby, Harold R. "Pagan Regeneration: a study of mystery initiations in the Graeco- Roman world." 1929 <http://www.sacred-texts.com/cla/pr/pr04.htm>

18. Willoughby, Harold R. "Pagan Regeneration: a study of mystery initiations in the Graeco- Roman world." 1929 <http://www.sacred-texts.com/cla/pr/pr04.htm>

19. Willoughby, Harold R. "Pagan Regeneration: a study of mystery initiations in the Graeco- Roman world." 1929 <http://www.sacred-texts.com/cla/pr/pr04.htm>

20. Willoughby, Harold R. "Pagan Regeneration: a study of mystery initiations in the Graeco- Roman world." 1929 <http://www.sacred-texts.com/cla/pr/pr04.htm>

21. Willoughby, Harold R. "Pagan Regeneration: a study of mystery initiations in the Graeco- Roman world." 1929 <http://www.sacred-texts.com/cla/pr/pr04.htm>

22. Willoughby, Harold R. "Pagan Regeneration: a study of mystery initiations in the Graeco- Roman world." 1929 <http://www.sacred-texts.com/cla/pr/pr04.htm>

23. Willoughby, Harold R. "Pagan Regeneration: a study of mystery initiations in the Graeco- Roman world." 1929 <http://www.sacred-texts.com/cla/pr/pr04.htm>

24. Freke, Timothy., and Peter Gandy. The Jesus Mysteries. New York: Three Rivers Press, 1999.

25. http://www.pantheon.org/articles/e/eleusis.html, Encyclopedia Mythica Eleusis

26. Willoughby, Harold R. "Pagan Regeneration: a study of mystery initiations in the Graeco- Roman world." 1929 <http://www.sacred-texts.com/cla/pr/pr04.htm>

27. Willoughby, Harold R. "Pagan Regeneration: a study of mystery initiations in the Graeco- Roman world." 1929 <http://www.sacred-texts.com/cla/pr/pr04.htm>

28. Burkert, Walter, <u>Ancient Mystery Cults</u>, Harvard University Press, 1987.

29. Willoughby, Harold R. "Pagan Regeneration, a study of mystery initiations in the Graeco- Roman world." 1929 <http://www.sacred-texts.com/cla/pr/pr04.htm>

30. Willoughby, Harold R. "Pagan Regeneration, a study of mystery initiations in the Graeco- Roman world." 1929 <http://www.sacred-texts.com/cla/pr/pr04.htm

31. Encyclopedia Mythica, Eleusis: Retrived from: http://pantheon.org/articles/e/Eleusis.html

32 Encyclopedia Mythica, Eleusis: Retrived from: http://pantheon.org/articles/e/Eleusis.html

35. Willoughby, Harold R. "Pagan Regeneration, a study of mystery initiations in the Graeco- Roman world." 1929 <http://www.sacred-texts.com/cla/pr/pr04.htm>

36. Baigent, Michael. <u>The Jesus Papers</u>. San Francisco: Harper, 2006. Quotes from (rf #37 pg202)

37. Schultes, Richard E., Albert Hofmann, and Christian Ratsch. <u>Plants of the Gods: Their Sacred, Healing, and Hallucinogenic Powers.</u> Rochester: Healing Arts Press, 2001.

38. Valencic, Ivan. <u>Has the Mystery of the Eleusinian Mysteries been Solved.</u> Yearbook for Ethnomedicine and the Study of Consciousness, Issue 3, 1994, pp325-336. ©VWB - Verlag für Wissenschaft und Bildung, 1995. also (Rf 98 pg337) Handcock, Supernatural

39. Valencic, Ivan. <u>Has the Mystery of the Eleusinian Mysteries been Solved.</u> Yearbook for Ethnomedicine and the Study of Consciousness, Issue 3, 1994, pp325-336. ©VWB - Verlag für Wissenschaft und Bildung, 1995. (RF103 pg 338) Handcock, supernatural

40. Richard Evans Schultes, Albert Hofmann, and Christian Ratsch. <u>Plants of the Gods, Their sacred, Healing, and Hallucinogenic Powers.</u> Rochester: Healing Arts Press, 2001.

41. Richard Evans Schultes, Albert Hofmann, and Christian Ratsch. <u>Plants of the Gods, Their sacred, Healing, and Hallucinogenic Powers.</u> Rochester: Healing Arts Press, 2001.

42. Richard Evans Schultes, Albert Hofmann, and Christian Ratsch. <u>Plants of the Gods, Their sacred, Healing, and Hallucinogenic Powers.</u> Rochester: Healing Arts Press, 2001.

43. Richard Evans Schultes, Albert Hofmann, and Christian Ratsch. <u>Plants of the Gods, Their sacred, Healing, and Hallucinogenic Powers.</u> Rochester: Healing Arts Press, 2001.

44. Richard Evans Schultes, Albert Hofmann, and Christian Ratsch. <u>Plants of the Gods, Their sacred, Healing, and Hallucinogenic Powers.</u> Rochester: Healing Arts Press, 2001.

45. Lee, Martin A., and Bruce Shlain. <u>Acid Dreams.</u> New York: Grove Press Books, 1992.

46 Richard Evans Schultes, Albert Hofmann, and Christian Ratsch. <u>Plants of the Gods, Their sacred, Healing, and Hallucinogenic Powers.</u> Rochester: Healing Arts Press, 2001.

47. Martin A. Lee and Bruce Shlain. <u>Acid Dreams.</u> New York: Grove Press Books, 1992.

48. Freke, Timothy, and Peter Gandy. <u>The Jesus Mysteries</u> . New York: Three Rivers Press, 1999.

49. Martin A. Lee and Bruce Shlain. <u>Acid Dreams.</u> New York: Grove Press Books, 1992.

50. Freke, Timothy, and Peter Gandy. <u>The Jesus Mysteries</u> . New York: Three Rivers Press, 1999.

Chapter 3 Mysteries of Pagan Philosophy

1. Copleston, Frederick. <u>The History of Philosophy</u>, Volume 1, Greek and Rome. New York: Image Books, 1993.

2. Copleston, Frederick. <u>The History of Philosophy</u>, Volume 1, Greek and Rome. New York: Image Books, 1993.

3. Shanon, Benny. <u>The Antipodes of the Mind: Charting the Phenomenology of the Ayahuasca Experience.</u> New York: Oxford University Press, 2002.

4. Copleston, Frederick. <u>The History of Philosophy</u>, Volume 1, Greek and Rome. New York: Image Books, 1993.

5. Willoughby, Harold R. "Pagan Regeneration: a study of mystery initiations in the Graeco- Roman world." Chapter IX. The Mysticism of Philo 1929 <http://www.sacred-texts.com/cla/pr/pr04.htm>

6. Willoughby, Harold R. "Pagan Regeneration: a study of mystery initiations in the Graeco- Roman world." Chapter IX. The Mysticism of Philo 1929 <http://www.sacred-texts.com/cla/pr/pr04.htm>

7. Willoughby, Harold R. "Pagan Regeneration: a study of mystery initiations in the Graeco- Roman world." Chapter IX. The Mysticism of Philo 1929 <http://www.sacred-texts.com/cla/pr/pr04.htm>

8. Willoughby, Harold R. "Pagan Regeneration: a study of mystery initiations in the Graeco- Roman world." Chapter IX. The Mysticism of Philo 1929 <http://www.sacred-texts.com/cla/pr/pr04.htm>

9. Willoughby, Harold R. "Pagan Regeneration: a study of mystery initiations in the Graeco- Roman world." Chapter IX. The Mysticism of Philo 1929 <http://www.sacred-texts.com/cla/pr/pr04.htm>

10. Copleston, Frederick, <u>The history of Philosophy</u>, Volume 1, Greek and Rome. New York: Image Books, 1993.

11. <u>Iamblichus and the Egyptian Mysteries</u>. Feb. 2007 <<u>http://www.wisdomworld.org/setting/iamblichus.html</u>>.

12. <u>Iamblichus and the Egyptian Mysteries.</u> Feb. 2007 <<u>http://www.wisdomworld.org/setting/iamblichus.html</u>>.

13. Peterson, Joseph H. <u>Iamblichus: Theurgia or On the Mysteries of Egypt</u>. Trans. Alexander Wilder, M.D. F.A.S. New York: The Metaphysical Publishing Co., 1911.

14. Peterson, Joseph H. <u>Iamblichus: Theurgia or On the Mysteries of Egypt</u>. Trans. Alexander Wilder, M.D. F.A.S. New York: The Metaphysical Publishing Co., 1911.

15. Peterson, Joseph H. <u>Iamblichus: Theurgia or On the Mysteries of Egypt</u>. Trans. Alexander Wilder, M.D. F.A.S. New York: The Metaphysical Publishing Co., 1911.

16. <u>Iamblichus and the Egyptian Mysteries.</u> Feb. 2007 <<u>http://www. wisdomworld.org/setting/iamblichus.html</u>>.

17. Copleston, Frederick. <u>The History of Philosophy: Greek and Rome</u>. Vol. 1. New York: Image Books, 1993. and (*Ennead* V.1.7).

18. Copleston, Frederick. <u>The History of Philosophy: Greek and Rome</u>. Vol. 1. New York: Image Books, 1993. and (cf. *Ennead* III.8.4)

19. Copleston, Frederick. <u>The History of Philosophy: Greek and Rome</u>. Vol. 1. New York: Image Books, 1993.

20. Copleston, Frederick. <u>The History of Philosophy: Greek and Rome</u>. Vol. 1. New York: Image Books, 1993.

21. Copleston, Frederick. <u>The History of Philosophy</u>, Volume 1, Greek and Rome. New York: Image Books, 1993.

22. Copleston, Frederick. <u>The History of Philosophy</u>, Volume 1, Greek and Rome. New York: Image Books, 1993.

23. Fowden, Garth. <u>The Egyptian Hermes: A Historical Approach to the Late Pagan Mind</u>. Princeton: Princeton University Press, 1986.

24. Copleston, Frederick. <u>The History of Philosophy: Greek and Rome</u>. Vol. 1. New York: Image Books, 1993. and (cf. *Ennead* III.8.4)

25. Peterson, Joseph H. <u>Iamblichus: Theurgia or On the Mysteries of Egypt</u>. Trans. Alexander Wilder, M.D. F.A.S. New York: The Metaphysical Publishing Co., 1911.

26. <u>Iamblichus and the Egyptian Mysteries</u>. Feb. 2007 <http://www. wisdomworld.org/setting/iamblichus.html>.

27. Peterson, Joseph H. <u>Iamblichus: Theurgia or On the Mysteries of Egypt</u>. Trans. Alexander Wilder, M.D. F.A.S. New York: The Metaphysical Publishing Co., 1911.

28. Copleston, Frederick. The History of Philosophy: Greek and Rome. Vol. 1. New York: Image Books, 1993. also (Dillon 1977, p. 12) and (cf. *Enneads* VI.9.6 and V.2.1)

29. Peterson, Joseph H. Iamblichus: Theurgia or On the Mysteries of Egypt. Trans. Alexander Wilder, M.D. F.A.S. New York: The Metaphysical Publishing Co., 1911.

30. Copleston, Frederick. The History of Philosophy: Greek and Rome. Vol. 1. New York: Image Books, 1993.

Ch 4 Mysteries of Egypt

1. Willoughby, Harold R. Pagan Regeneration: a study of mystery initiations in the Graeco- Roman world. 1929 < http://www.sacred-texts.com/cla/pr/pr04.htm>.

2. Willoughby, Harold R. Pagan Regeneration: a study of mystery initiations in the Graeco- Roman world. 1929 < http://www.sacred-texts.com/cla/pr/pr04.htm>.

3. Willoughby, Harold R. Pagan Regeneration: a study of mystery initiations in the Graeco- Roman world. 1929 < http://www.sacred-texts.com/cla/pr/pr04.htm>.

4. Willoughby, Harold R. Pagan Regeneration: a study of mystery initiations in the Graeco- Roman world. 1929 < http://www.sacred-texts.com/cla/pr/pr04.htm>.

5. Willoughby, Harold R. Pagan Regeneration: a study of mystery initiations in the Graeco- Roman world. 1929 < http://www.sacred-texts.com/cla/pr/pr04.htm>.

6. Willoughby, Harold R. Pagan Regeneration: a study of mystery initiations in the Graeco- Roman world. 1929 < http://www.sacred-texts.com/cla/pr/pr04.htm>.

7. Willoughby, Harold R. Pagan Regeneration: a study of mystery initiations in the Graeco- Roman world. 1929 < http://www.sacred-texts.com/cla/pr/pr04.htm>.

8. Naydler, Jeremy. Shamanic Wisdom in the Pyramid Texts: The Mystical Tradition of Ancient Egypt. Rochester: Inner Traditions, 2005. pp.3 pag 254 rf 41

9. Naydler, Jeremy. <u>Shamanic Wisdom in the Pyramid Texts, The Mystical Tradition of Ancient Egypt</u>. Rochester: Inner Traditions, 2005. Rf #37 pg 15

10. Naydler, Jeremy. <u>Shamanic Wisdom in the Pyramid Texts, The Mystical Tradition of Ancient Egypt</u>. Rochester: Inner Traditions, 2005. RF. 10 Pg. 23

11. Naydler, Jeremy. <u>Shamanic Wisdom in the Pyramid Texts, The Mystical Tradition of Ancient Egypt</u>. Rochester: Inner Traditions, 2005. Rf. 14 pg. 23(Pg 14and15)

12. Naydler, Jeremy. <u>Shamanic Wisdom in the Pyramid Texts, The Mystical Tradition of Ancient Egypt</u>. Rochester: Inner Traditions, 2005.

13. Naydler, Jeremy. <u>Shamanic Wisdom in the Pyramid Texts, The Mystical Tradition of Ancient Egypt</u>. Rochester: Inner Traditions, 2005. rf3pg21. Rf. 6 pg. 22

14. Naydler, Jeremy. <u>Shamanic Wisdom in the Pyramid Texts, The Mystical Tradition of Ancient Egypt</u>. Rochester: Inner Traditions, 2005. Rf. #39 pg.16

15. Naydler, Jeremy. <u>Shamanic Wisdom in the Pyramid Texts, The Mystical Tradition of Ancient Egypt</u>. Rochester: Inner Traditions, 2005. RF #44 pg.17

16. Naydler, Jeremy. <u>Shamanic Wisdom in the Pyramid Texts, The Mystical Tradition of Ancient Egypt</u>. Rochester: Inner Traditions, 2005. pg148 ch6

17. Naydler, Jeremy. <u>Shamanic Wisdom in the Pyramid Texts, The Mystical Tradition of Ancient Egypt</u>. Rochester: Inner Traditions, 2005.

18. Fowden, Garth. <u>The Egyptian Hermes, A historical approach to the late pagan mind;</u> Princeton university press, Princeton, New Jersy.(1986) (rf52pg22)

19. Willoughby, Harold R. <u>Pagan Regeneration: a study of mystery initiations in the Graeco- Roman world</u>. Chapter VIII The New birth Experience in Hermeticism (1929): <http://www.sacred-texts.com/cla/pr/pr04.htm

20. Willoughby, Harold R. <u>Pagan Regeneration: a study of mystery initiations in the Graeco- Roman world</u>. Chapter VIII The New birth Experience in Hermeticism (1929): <http://www.sacred-texts.com/cla/pr/pr04.htm

21. Willoughby, Harold R. Pagan Regeneration: a study of mystery initiations in the Graeco- Roman world. Chapter VIII The New birth Experience in Hermeticism (1929): <http://www.sacred-texts.com/cla/pr/pr04.htm

22. Willoughby, Harold R. Pagan Regeneration: a study of mystery initiations in the Graeco- Roman world. Chapter VIII The New birth Experience in Hermeticism (1929): <http://www.sacred-texts.com/cla/pr/pr04.htm

23. Willoughby, Harold R. Pagan Regeneration: a study of mystery initiations in the Graeco- Roman world. Chapter VIII The New birth Experience in Hermeticism (1929): <http://www.sacred-texts.com/cla/pr/pr04.htm

24. The Gnostic Society Library. The Corpus Hermeticum and Hermetic Tradition. <http://www.gnosis.org/library/hermet.htm>.

25. Willoughby, Harold R. Pagan Regeneration: a study of mystery initiations in the Graeco- Roman world. Chapter VIII The New birth Experience in Hermeticism (1929): <http://www.sacred-texts.com/cla/pr/pr04.htm

Ch 5 Gnostic Rituals

1. Robinson, James M. The Nag Hammadi Library. San Francisco: Harper and Row Publishers, 1978. and <http://www.gnosis.org/naghamm/nhl.html>.

2. Robinson, James M. The Nag Hammadi Library. San Francisco: Harper and Row Publishers, 1978.

3. Robinson, James M. The Nag Hammadi Library. San Francisco: Harper and Row Publishers, 1978.

4. Robinson, James M. The Nag Hammadi Library. San Francisco: Harper and Row Publishers, 1978.

5. Robinson, James M. The Nag Hammadi Library. San Francisco: Harper and Row Publishers, 1978.

6. Freke, Timothy., and Peter Gandy. The Jesus Mysteries. New York: Three Rivers Press, 1999. Rf 60 pg 97

7. Freke, Timothy., and Peter Gandy. The Jesus Mysteries. New York: Three Rivers Press, 1999. Pg98

8. Baigent, Michael. The Jesus Papers. San Francisco: Harper, 2006.

9. Turner, John D. <u>Ritual in Gnosticism.</u> University Of Nebraska-Lincoln SBL 1994 Book of Seminar Papers, 136-181. <<u>http://www.unl.edu/classics/faculty/turner/ritual.htm</u>>

10 Turner, John D. <u>Ritual in Gnosticism.</u> University Of Nebraska-Lincoln SBL 1994 Book of Seminar Papers, 136-181. <<u>http://www.unl.edu/classics/faculty/turner/ritual.htm</u>>

11. Turner, John D. <u>Ritual in Gnosticism.</u> University Of Nebraska-Lincoln SBL 1994 Book of Seminar Papers, 136-181. <<u>http://www.unl.edu/classics/faculty/turner/ritual.htm</u>>

12. Turner, John D. <u>Ritual in Gnosticism.</u> University Of Nebraska-Lincoln SBL 1994 Book of Seminar Papers, 136-181. <<u>http://www.unl.edu/classics/faculty/turner/ritual.htm</u>>

13. Turner, John D. <u>Ritual in Gnosticism.</u> University Of Nebraska-Lincoln SBL 1994 Book of Seminar Papers, 136-181. <<u>http://www.unl.edu/classics/faculty/turner/ritual.htm</u>>

14. Turner, John D. <u>Ritual in Gnosticism.</u> University Of Nebraska-Lincoln SBL 1994 Book of Seminar Papers, 136-181. <<u>http://www.unl.edu/classics/faculty/turner/ritual.htm</u>>

15. Turner, John D. <u>Ritual in Gnosticism.</u> University Of Nebraska-Lincoln SBL 1994 Book of Seminar Papers, 136-181. <<u>http://www.unl.edu/classics/faculty/turner/ritual.htm</u>>

16. Turner, John D. <u>Ritual in Gnosticism.</u> University Of Nebraska-Lincoln SBL 1994 Book of Seminar Papers, 136-181. <<u>http://www.unl.edu/classics/faculty/turner/ritual.htm</u>>

17. Turner, John D. <u>Ritual in Gnosticism.</u> University Of Nebraska-Lincoln SBL 1994 Book of Seminar Papers, 136-181. <<u>http://www.unl.edu/classics/faculty/turner/ritual.htm</u>>

18. Turner, John D. <u>Ritual in Gnosticism.</u> University Of Nebraska-Lincoln SBL 1994 Book of Seminar Papers, 136-181. <<u>http://www.unl.edu/classics/faculty/turner/ritual.htm</u>>

19. Turner, John D. <u>Ritual in Gnosticism.</u> University Of Nebraska-Lincoln SBL 1994 Book of Seminar Papers, 136-181. <<u>http://www.unl.edu/classics/faculty/turner/ritual.htm</u>>

20. Turner, John D. Ritual in Gnosticism. University Of Nebraska-Lincoln SBL 1994 Book of Seminar Papers, 136-181. <http://www.unl.edu/classics/faculty/turner/ritual.htm>

21. Turner, John D. Ritual in Gnosticism. University Of Nebraska-Lincoln SBL 1994 Book of Seminar Papers, 136-181. <http://www.unl.edu/classics/faculty/turner/ritual.htm>

22. Turner, John D. Ritual in Gnosticism. University Of Nebraska-Lincoln SBL 1994 Book of Seminar Papers, 136-181.<http://www.unl.edu/classics/faculty/turner/ritual.htm>

23. Robinson, James M. The Nag Hammadi Library. San Francisco: Harper and Row Publishers, 1978.

24. Turner, John D. Ritual in Gnosticism. University Of Nebraska-Lincoln SBL 1994 Book of Seminar Papers, 136-181. <http://www.unl.edu/classics/faculty/turner/ritual.htm>

25. Turner, John D. Ritual in Gnosticism. University Of Nebraska-Lincoln SBL 1994 Book of Seminar Papers, 136-181. <http://www.unl.edu/classics/faculty/turner/ritual.htm>

27. Turner, John D. Ritual in Gnosticism. University Of Nebraska-Lincoln SBL 1994 Book of Seminar Papers, 136-181. <http://www.unl.edu/classics/faculty/turner/ritual.htm>

28. Turner, John D. Ritual in Gnosticism. University Of Nebraska-Lincoln SBL 1994 Book of Seminar Papers, 136-181. <http://www.unl.edu/classics/faculty/turner/ritual.htm>

29. Turner, John D. Ritual in Gnosticism. University Of Nebraska-Lincoln SBL 1994 Book of Seminar Papers, 136-181. <http://www.unl.edu/classics/faculty/turner/ritual.htm>

30. Turner, John D. Ritual in Gnosticism. University Of Nebraska-Lincoln SBL 1994 Book of Seminar Papers, 136-181. <http://www.unl.edu/classics/faculty/turner/ritual.htm>

31. Turner, John D. Ritual in Gnosticism. University Of Nebraska-Lincoln SBL 1994 Book of Seminar Papers, 136-181. <http://www.unl.edu/classics/faculty/turner/ritual.htm>

32. Turner, John D. <u>Ritual in Gnosticism.</u> University Of Nebraska-Lincoln SBL 1994 Book of Seminar Papers, 136-181. <<u>http://www.unl.edu/ classics/faculty/turner/ritual.htm</u>>

33 Turner, John D. <u>Ritual in Gnosticism.</u> University Of Nebraska-Lincoln SBL 1994 Book of Seminar Papers, 136-181. <<u>http://www.unl.edu/ classics/faculty/turner/ritual.htm</u>>

34 Turner, John D. <u>Ritual in Gnosticism.</u> University Of Nebraska-Lincoln SBL 1994 Book of Seminar Papers, 136-181. <<u>http://www.unl.edu/ classics/faculty/turner/ritual.htm</u>>

35. Turner, John D. <u>Ritual in Gnosticism.</u> University Of Nebraska-Lincoln SBL 1994 Book of Seminar Papers, 136-181. <<u>http://www.unl.edu/ classics/faculty/turner/ritual.htm</u>>

36. Turner, John D. <u>Ritual in Gnosticism.</u> University Of Nebraska-Lincoln SBL 1994 Book of Seminar Papers, 136-181. <<u>http://www.unl.edu/ classics/faculty/turner/ritual.htm</u>>

37. <u>The Gnostic Jung</u>. (Wheaton, Ill., 1982), p.11. <http://www.gnosis.org/ naghamm/nhlintro.html RF 2. Stephan A. Hoeller>.

38. Merkur, Dan. <u>Stages of Ascension in Hermetic Rebirth</u>. University of Toronto. <<u>http://www.esoteric.msu.edu/Merkur.html</u>>. and Nock (1933:12)

39. <u>The Corpus Hermeticum:</u> Published by: the Gnostic Society Library retrived at <http://www.gnosis.org/library/hermet.htm>.

40. <u>The Corpus Hermeticum:</u> Published by: the Gnostic Society Library retrived at <http://www.gnosis.org/library/hermet.htm>.

Ch 6 Biochemical Foundations

1. Turner, John D. <u>Ritual in Gnosticism.</u> University Of Nebraska-Lincoln SBL 1994 Book of Seminar Papers, 136-181. <u>http://www.unl.edu/ classics/faculty/turner/ritual.htm</u>> & Gnostic Society Library. The Odes of Solomon: http://www.gnosis.org/library/odes.htm?vm=r

2. *Mediators of the Divine: Horizons of Prophecy and Divination on Mediterranean Antiquity*, M. Berchman; Florida Studies in the History of Judaism 163; Atlanta, GA: Scholars Press, 1998

3. Pendell, Dale. <u>Pharmako Gnosis, Plant Teachers and the Poison Path</u>. San Francisco: Mercury House, 2005.

4. Pendell, Dale. <u>Pharmako Gnosis, Plant Teachers and the Poison Path</u>. San Francisco: Mercury House, 2005.

5. Strassman, Rick. <u>DMT the Spirit Molecule.</u> Rochester: Park Street Press, 2001. pp. 52.

6. Strassman, Rick. <u>DMT the Spirit Molecule.</u> Rochester: Park Street Press, 2001.

7. Strassman, Rick. <u>DMT the Spirit Molecule.</u> Rochester: Park Street Press, 2001

8. James E. Beichler, <u>Life Death in the Big city, the geometric structure of dying.</u> (2000) <http://members.aol.com/jebco1st/Paraphysics/nde.htm>. and (Morse, Conner & Tyler, 1985)

9. James E. Beichler, <u>Life Death in the Big city, the geometric structure of dying.</u> (2000) <http://members.aol.com/jebco1st/Paraphysics/nde.htm>.

10. James E. Beichler, <u>Life Death in the Big city, the geometric structure of dying.</u> (2000) <http://members.aol.com/jebco1st/Paraphysics/nde.htm>.

11. Greene, Timothy. "Journey into the Light: Near-Death Experience as an Ecstatic Initiation." <u>Shaman's Drum</u> 41 (1996): 41-54.

12 James E. Beichler, <u>Life Death in the Big city, the geometric structure of dying.</u> (2000) < http://members.aol.com/jebco1st/Paraphysics/nde. htm>.

13. James E. Beichler, <u>Life Death in the Big city, the geometric structure of dying.</u> (2000) < http://members.aol.com/jebco1st/Paraphysics/nde. htm>.

14. James E. Beichler, <u>Life Death in the Big city, the geometric structure of dying.</u> (2000) < http://members.aol.com/jebco1st/Paraphysics/nde. htm>.

15. Strassman, Rick. <u>DMT the Spirit Molecule.</u> Rochester: Park Street Press, 2001

16. Strassman, Rick. <u>DMT the Spirit Molecule.</u> Rochester: Park Street Press, 2001

17. Strassman, Rick. <u>DMT the Spirit Molecule.</u> Rochester: Park Street Press, 2001

18. Strassman, Rick. <u>DMT the Spirit Molecule.</u> Rochester: Park Street Press, 2001

19. Strassman, Rick. <u>DMT the Spirit Molecule.</u> Rochester: Park Street Press, 2001 Part4 Chapter14Contact through the veil:2 pg 214

20. White, Timothy. "Drinking Yaje in Colombia: An Interview with Jimmy Weiskopf." <u>Shaman's Drum.</u> 67 (2004): 19-31.

21. McKenna Dennis. <u>Ayahusca: An Ethnopharmacologic History</u>. (1998) Retrived from: http://leda.lycaeum.org/?ID=16806>.

22. McKenna Dennis. <u>Ayahusca: An Ethnopharmacologic History</u>. (1998) Retrived from: <http://leda.lycaeum.org/?ID=16806>.

23. Wikipedia Encyclopedia. "Entheogen" <http://en.wikipedia.org/wiki/Entheogen>.

24. White, Timothy. "Drinking Yaje in Colombia: An Interview with Jimmy Weiskopf." <u>Shaman's Drum.</u> 67 (2004): 19-31.

25. White, Timothy. "Drinking Yaje in Colombia: An Interview with Jimmy Weiskopf." <u>Shaman's Drum.</u> 67 (2004): 19-31.

26. White, Timothy. "Drinking Yaje in Colombia: An Interview with Jimmy Weiskopf." <u>Shaman's Drum.</u> 67 (2004): 19-31.

27. White, Timothy. "Drinking Yaje in Colombia: An Interview with Jimmy Weiskopf." <u>Shaman's Drum.</u> 67 (2004): 19-31.

28. McKenna Dennis. <u>Ayahusca: An Ethnopharmacologic History.</u> (1998) <http://leda.lycaeum.org/?ID=16806>.

29. <u>Wikipedia Encyclopedia</u>. "Entheogen" Aug. 2003 <http://en.wikipedia.org/wiki/Entheogen>.

30. McKenna, Dennis. <u>Ayahusca: An Ethnopharmacologic History</u>. (1998) <http://leda.lycaeum.org/?ID=16806>.

31. McKenna Dennis. <u>Ayahusca: An Ethnopharmacologic History.</u> (1998) <http://leda.lycaeum.org/?ID=16806>.

32. Alexander Shulgin, <u>TiHKAL</u>

Ch 7 Zoroaster and Pagenum Harmala

1. Most Albert, Peganum Harmala(1985) Venom Press. <Http://diseyes. lycaeum.org/dmt/harmpmp.txt>.

2. Flattery, David S. and Martin Schwartz. <u>Haoma and Harmaline:The Botanical Identity of the Indo- Iranian Sacred Hallucinogen "Soma" and its Legacy in Religion, Language, and Middle Eastern Folklore</u>. Near Eastern Studies Vol. 21. Berkeley: University of California Press, 1989.

3. Flattery, David S. and Martin Schwartz. <u>Haoma and Harmaline:The Botanical Identity of the Indo- Iranian Sacred Hallucinogen "Soma" and its Legacy in Religion, Language, and Middle Eastern Folklore</u>. Near Eastern Studies Vol. 21. Berkeley: University of California Press, 1989.

4. Flattery, David S. and Martin Schwartz. <u>Haoma and Harmaline:The Botanical Identity of the Indo- Iranian Sacred Hallucinogen "Soma" and its Legacy in Religion, Language, and Middle Eastern Folklore</u>. Near Eastern Studies Vol. 21. Berkeley: University of California Press, 1989. pp. 47 #65

5. Flattery, David S. and Martin Schwartz. <u>Haoma and Harmaline:The Botanical Identity of the Indo- Iranian Sacred Hallucinogen "Soma" and its Legacy in Religion, Language, and Middle Eastern Folklore</u>. Near Eastern Studies Vol. 21. Berkeley: University of California Press, 1989.

6. Flattery, David S. and Martin Schwartz. <u>Haoma and Harmaline:The Botanical Identity of the Indo- Iranian Sacred Hallucinogen "Soma" and its Legacy in Religion, Language, and Middle Eastern Folklore</u>. Near Eastern Studies Vol. 21. Berkeley: University of California Press, 1989.....pp. 47

7. Flattery, David S. and Martin Schwartz. <u>Haoma and Harmaline:The Botanical Identity of the Indo- Iranian Sacred Hallucinogen "Soma" and its Legacy in Religion, Language, and Middle Eastern Folklore</u>. Near Eastern Studies Vol. 21. Berkeley: University of California Press, 1989. (Drower 1943: 156...Haoma hermalain pg 63)

8. Flattery, David S. and Martin Schwartz. <u>Haoma and Harmaline:The Botanical Identity of the Indo- Iranian Sacred Hallucinogen "Soma" and its Legacy in Religion, Language, and Middle Eastern Folklore</u>.

Near Eastern Studies Vol. 21. Berkeley: University of California Press, 1989. (pg63)

9. Flattery, David S. and Martin Schwartz. Haoma and Harmaline:The Botanical Identity of the Indo-Iranian Sacred Hallucinogen "Soma" and its Legacy in Religion, Language, and Middle Eastern Folklore. Near Eastern Studies Vol. 21. Berkeley: University of California Press, 1989. (pg66)

10. Yronwode, Catherine :http://www.luckymojo.com/aspand.html

11. Flattery, David S. and Martin Schwartz. Haoma and Harmaline:The Botanical Identity of the Indo- Iranian Sacred Hallucinogen "Soma" and its Legacy in Religion, Language, and Middle Eastern Folklore. Near Eastern Studies Vol. 21. Berkeley: University of California Press, 1989.

12. Flattery, David S. and Martin Schwartz. Haoma and Harmaline:The Botanical Identity of the Indo- Iranian Sacred Hallucinogen "Soma" and its Legacy in Religion, Language, and Middle Eastern Folklore. Near Eastern Studies Vol. 21. Berkeley: University of California Press, 1989.

13. Flattery, David S. and Martin Schwartz. Haoma and Harmaline:The Botanical Identity of the Indo- Iranian Sacred Hallucinogen "Soma" and its Legacy in Religion, Language, and Middle Eastern Folklore. Near Eastern Studies Vol. 21. Berkeley: University of California Press, 1989.

14. Encyclopædia Britannica, "Zoroastrianism." Chigago, IL 2005

15. Boyce, Mary (1979), Zoroastrians: Their Religious Beliefs and Practices, London: Routledge

16. Boyce, Mary (1979), Zoroastrians: Their Religious Beliefs and Practices, London: Routledge

17. Boyce, Mary (1979), Zoroastrians: Their Religious Beliefs and Practices, London: Routledge

18. Schmitt, Rüdiger. "Achaemenid dynasty". Encyclopaedia Iranica. vol. 3. Routledge & Kegan Paul. Retrieved from: http://www.iranica.com/newsite/articles/unicode/v1f4/v1f4a109.html.

19. Flattery, David S. and Martin Schwartz. Haoma and Harmaline:The Botanical Identity of the Indo- Iranian Sacred Hallucinogen "Soma" and its Legacy in Religion, Language, and Middle Eastern Folklore.

Near Eastern Studies Vol. 21. Berkeley: University of California Press, 1989. pp. 58 #84 Flattery (Translated by E.S Drower, 1934

20. Flattery, David S. and Martin Schwartz. <u>Haoma and Harmaline:The Botanical Identity of the Indo- Iranian Sacred Hallucinogen "Soma" and its Legacy in Religion, Language, and Middle Eastern Folklore</u>. Near Eastern Studies Vol. 21. Berkeley: University of California Press, 1989.

21. Flattery, David S. and Martin Schwartz. <u>Haoma and Harmaline:The Botanical Identity of the Indo- Iranian Sacred Hallucinogen "Soma" and its Legacy in Religion, Language, and Middle Eastern Folklore</u>. Near Eastern Studies Vol. 21. Berkeley: University of California Press, 1989. pp. 58 #84

22. Flattery, David S. and Martin Schwartz. <u>Haoma and Harmaline:The Botanical Identity of the Indo- Iranian Sacred Hallucinogen "Soma" and its Legacy in Religion, Language, and Middle Eastern Folklore</u>. Near Eastern Studies Vol. 21. Berkeley: University of California Press, 1989.*

23. Flattery, David S. and Martin Schwartz. <u>Haoma and Harmaline:The Botanical Identity of the Indo- Iranian Sacred Hallucinogen "Soma" and its Legacy in Religion, Language, and Middle Eastern Folklore</u>. Near Eastern Studies Vol. 21. Berkeley: University of California Press, 1989.*

24. Flattery, David S. and Martin Schwartz. <u>Haoma and Harmaline:The Botanical Identity of the Indo- Iranian Sacred Hallucinogen "Soma" and its Legacy in Religion, Language, and Middle Eastern Folklore</u>. Near Eastern Studies Vol. 21. Berkeley: University of California Press, 1989.

25. Flattery, David S. and Martin Schwartz. <u>Haoma and Harmaline:The Botanical Identity of the Indo- Iranian Sacred Hallucinogen "Soma" and its Legacy in Religion, Language, and Middle Eastern Folklore</u>. Near Eastern Studies Vol. 21. Berkeley: University of California Press, 1989. (Cited 99n20 with her in 1975a;112*)

26. Flattery, David S. and Martin Schwartz. <u>Haoma and Harmaline:The Botanical Identity of the Indo- Iranian Sacred Hallucinogen "Soma" and its Legacy in Religion, Language, and Middle Eastern Folklore</u>. Near Eastern Studies Vol. 21. Berkeley: University of California Press, 1989.

27. Flattery, David S. and Martin Schwartz. <u>Haoma and Harmaline:The Botanical Identity of the Indo- Iranian Sacred Hallucinogen "Soma" and</u>

its Legacy in Religion, Language, and Middle Eastern Folklore. Near Eastern Studies Vol. 21. Berkeley: University of California Press, 1989.

28. Flattery, David S. and Martin Schwartz. Haoma and Harmaline:The Botanical Identity of the Indo- Iranian Sacred Hallucinogen "Soma" and its Legacy in Religion, Language, and Middle Eastern Folklore. Near Eastern Studies Vol. 21. Berkeley: University of California Press, 1989.

29. Flattery, David S. and Martin Schwartz. Haoma and Harmaline:The Botanical Identity of the Indo- Iranian Sacred Hallucinogen "Soma" and its Legacy in Religion, Language, and Middle Eastern Folklore. Near Eastern Studies Vol. 21. Berkeley: University of California Press, 1989.

30. Flattery, David S. and Martin Schwartz. Haoma and Harmaline:The Botanical Identity of the Indo- Iranian Sacred Hallucinogen "Soma" and its Legacy in Religion, Language, and Middle Eastern Folklore. Near Eastern Studies Vol. 21. Berkeley: University of California Press, 1989.

31. Flattery, David S. and Martin Schwartz. Haoma and Harmaline:The Botanical Identity of the Indo- Iranian Sacred Hallucinogen "Soma" and its Legacy in Religion, Language, and Middle Eastern Folklore. Near Eastern Studies Vol. 21. Berkeley: University of California Press, 1989.

32. Flattery, David S. and Martin Schwartz. Haoma and Harmaline:The Botanical Identity of the Indo- Iranian Sacred Hallucinogen "Soma" and its Legacy in Religion, Language, and Middle Eastern Folklore. Near Eastern Studies Vol. 21. Berkeley: University of California Press, 1989.

33. Flattery, David S. and Martin Schwartz. Haoma and Harmaline:The Botanical Identity of the Indo- Iranian Sacred Hallucinogen "Soma" and its Legacy in Religion, Language, and Middle Eastern Folklore. Near Eastern Studies Vol. 21. Berkeley: University of California Press, 1989.

34. Yronwode, Catherine <http://www.luckymojo.com/aspand.html>.

35. Yronwode, Catherine <http://www.luckymojo.com/aspand.html>.

36. Yronwode, Catherine <http://www.luckymojo.com/aspand.html>. and Tajik man: At <http://members.tripod.com/~khorasan/Miscellaneous/ aspand.html>.

37. Yronwode, Catherine <http://www.luckymojo.com/aspand.html>.

38. Yronwode, Catherine <http://www.luckymojo.com/aspand.html>.

39. Peganum Harmala and Modern Magic: Retrived (2005) From:<http://www.geocities.com/mandaeans/Sabians7.html>.(2005)

Ch 8 Ayahuasca Analogs in Antiquity

1. Emboden Jr., William A., "Ethnobotanical Tools in the Ancient Near East." Mar. 2005 <http://www.entheology.org/edoto/anmviewer.asp?a=152&z=1>.

2. Turner, John D. RITUAL IN GNOSTICISM.University Of Nebraska-Lincoln SBL 1994 Book of Seminar Papers, 136-181. <http://www.unl.edu/classics/faculty/turner/ritual.htm>.

3. New King James Bible, Oxford University Press, USA

4. al-Tawil, Hashim, Early Arab Icons: Literary and Archaeological Evidence for the Cult of Religious Images in Pre-Islamic Arabia", PhD dissertation, University of Iowa, 1993

5. Bruno Halioua, Bernard Ziskind, M. B. Medicine in the Days of the Pharaohs, Belknap Press of Harvard University Press Belknap Press,

6. Bruno Halioua, Bernard Ziskind, M. B Medicine in the Days of the Pharaohs,. Belknap Press of Harvard University Press

7. Bruno Halioua, Bernard Ziskind, M. B. Medicine in the Days of the Pharaohs, Belknap Press of Harvard University Press

8. Medicine in the Days of the Pharaohs, Bruno Halioua, Bernard Ziskind, M. B. Belknap Press of Harvard University Press

9. Emboden Jr., William A., "Ethnobotanical Tools in the Ancient Near East." Mar. 2005 <http://www.entheology.org/edoto/anmviewer.asp?a=152&z=1>.

10. Emboden Jr., William A., "Ethnobotanical Tools in the Ancient Near East." Mar. 2005 <http://www.entheology.org/edoto/anmviewer.asp?a=152&z=1>.

11. Emboden Jr., William A., "Ethnobotanical Tools in the Ancient Near East." Mar. 2005 <http://www.entheology.org/edoto/anmviewer.asp?a=152&z=1>.

12. <http:// nefertiti.iwebland.com/botany/index.html

13. Emboden Jr., William A., "Ethnobotanical Tools in the Ancient Near East." Mar. 2005 <http://www.entheology.org/edoto/anmviewer. asp?a=152&z=1>.

14. Emboden Jr., William A., "Ethnobotanical Tools in the Ancient Near East." Mar. 2005 <http://www.entheology.org/edoto/anmviewer. asp?a=152&z=1>.

15. Emboden Jr., William A., "Ethnobotanical Tools in the Ancient Near East." Mar. 2005 <http://www.entheology.org/edoto/anmviewer. asp?a=152&z=1>.

16. Flattery, David S. and Martin Schwartz. Haoma and Harmaline:The Botanical Identity of the Indo- Iranian Sacred Hallucinogen "Soma" and its Legacy in Religion, Language, and Middle Eastern Folklore. Near Eastern Studies Vol. 21. Berkeley: University of California Press, 1989.

17. Naydler, Jeremy. Shamanic Wisdom in the Pyramid Text: The Mystical Tradition of Ancient Egypt. Rochester: Inner Traditions, 2005.

18. Naydler, Jeremy. Shamanic Wisdom in the Pyramid Text: The Mystical Tradition of Ancient Egypt. Rochester: Inner Traditions, 2005.

19. <http://www.mandaeanworld.com/portuguese.html>. and E.S. Drower, The Secret Adam, A study of Nasoraean Gnosis.(1960) Oxford, London

20. Flattery, David S. and Martin Schwartz. Haoma and Harmaline:The Botanical Identity of the Indo- Iranian Sacred Hallucinogen "Soma" and its Legacy in Religion, Language, and Middle Eastern Folklore. Near Eastern Studies Vol. 21. Berkeley: University of California Press, 1989.

43. Flattery, David S. and Martin Schwartz. Haoma and Harmaline:The Botanical Identity of the Indo- Iranian Sacred Hallucinogen "Soma" and its Legacy in Religion, Language, and Middle Eastern Folklore. Near Eastern Studies Vol. 21. Berkeley: University of California Press, 1989.

21. Flattery, David S. and Martin Schwartz. Haoma and Harmaline:The Botanical Identity of the Indo- Iranian Sacred Hallucinogen "Soma" and its Legacy in Religion, Language, and Middle Eastern Folklore. Near Eastern Studies Vol. 21. Berkeley: University of California Press, 1989.

22. Flattery, David S. and Martin Schwartz. Haoma and Harmaline:The Botanical Identity of the Indo- Iranian Sacred Hallucinogen "Soma" and

its Legacy in Religion, Language, and Middle Eastern Folklore. Near Eastern Studies Vol. 21. Berkeley: University of California Press, 1989.

23. Flattery, David S. and Martin Schwartz. Haoma and Harmaline:The Botanical Identity of the Indo- Iranian Sacred Hallucinogen "Soma" and its Legacy in Religion, Language, and Middle Eastern Folklore. Near Eastern Studies Vol. 21. Berkeley: University of California Press, 1989.

24. Flattery, David S. and Martin Schwartz. Haoma and Harmaline:The Botanical Identity of the Indo- Iranian Sacred Hallucinogen "Soma" and its Legacy in Religion, Language, and Middle Eastern Folklore. Near Eastern Studies Vol. 21. Berkeley: University of California Press, 1989. #85 on pp. 58-59

25. Flattery, David S. and Martin Schwartz. Haoma and Harmaline:The Botanical Identity of the Indo- Iranian Sacred Hallucinogen "Soma" and its Legacy in Religion, Language, and Middle Eastern Folklore. Near Eastern Studies Vol. 21. Berkeley: University of California Press, 1989.

26. Flattery, David S. and Martin Schwartz. Haoma and Harmaline:The Botanical Identity of the Indo- Iranian Sacred Hallucinogen "Soma" and its Legacy in Religion, Language, and Middle Eastern Folklore. Near Eastern Studies Vol. 21. Berkeley: University of California Press, 1989.

27. Flattery, David S. and Martin Schwartz. Haoma and Harmaline:The Botanical Identity of the Indo- Iranian Sacred Hallucinogen "Soma" and its Legacy in Religion, Language, and Middle Eastern Folklore. Near Eastern Studies Vol. 21. Berkeley: University of California Press, 1989.

28. Flattery, David S. and Martin Schwartz. Haoma and Harmaline:The Botanical Identity of the Indo- Iranian Sacred Hallucinogen "Soma" and its Legacy in Religion, Language, and Middle Eastern Folklore. Near Eastern Studies Vol. 21. Berkeley: University of California Press, 1989.

Ch 9 Identifying the Gnostic Sacrament

1. Freke,Timothy and Peter Gandy. The Jesus Mysteries. New York: Random House Inc., 1999.

2. Shanon, Benny. The Antipodes of the Mind: Charting the Phenomenology of the Ayahuasca Experience. New York: Oxford University Press, 2002.

3. Shanon, Benny. The Antipodes of the Mind: Charting the Phenomenology of the Ayahuasca Experience. New York: Oxford University Press, 2002.

4. Shanon, Benny. The Antipodes of the Mind: Charting the Phenomenology of the Ayahuasca Experience. New York: Oxford University Press, 2002.

5. Shanon, Benny. The Antipodes of the Mind: Charting the Phenomenology of the Ayahuasca Experience. New York: Oxford University Press, 2002.

6. Shanon, Benny. The Antipodes of the Mind: Charting the Phenomenology of the Ayahuasca Experience. New York: Oxford University Press, 2002.

7. Shanon, Benny. The Antipodes of the Mind: Charting the Phenomenology of the Ayahuasca Experience. New York: Oxford University Press, 2002.

8. Shanon, Benny. The Antipodes of the Mind: Charting the Phenomenology of the Ayahuasca Experience. New York: Oxford University Press, 2002.

9. Shanon, Benny. The Antipodes of the Mind: Charting the Phenomenology of the Ayahuasca Experience. New York: Oxford University Press, 2002.

10. Shanon, Benny. The Antipodes of the Mind: Charting the Phenomenology of the Ayahuasca Experience. New York: Oxford University Press, 2002.

11. Shanon, Benny. The Antipodes of the Mind: Charting the Phenomenology of the Ayahuasca Experience. New York: Oxford University Press, 2002.

12. Shanon, Benny. The Antipodes of the Mind: Charting the Phenomenology of the Ayahuasca Experience. New York: Oxford University Press, 2002.

13. Shanon, Benny. <u>The Antipodes of the Mind: Charting the Phenomenology of the Ayahuasca Experience.</u> New York: Oxford University Press, 2002. pp. 302.

14. Shanon, Benny. <u>The Antipodes of the Mind: Charting the Phenomenology of the Ayahuasca Experience.</u> New York: Oxford University Press, 2002.

15. Shanon, Benny. <u>The Antipodes of the Mind: Charting the Phenomenology of the Ayahuasca Experience.</u> New York: Oxford University Press, 2002.

16. Robinson, James M. <u>The Nag Hammadi Library</u>. San Francisco: Harper and Row Publishers, 1978.

17. Robinson, James M. <u>The Nag Hammadi Library</u>. San Francisco: Harper and Row Publishers, 1978.

Ch 10 Early Christian History & the fall of Gnostosism

1. Freke,Timothy and Peter Gandy. <u>The Jesus Mysteries</u>. New York: Random House Inc., 1999.

2. Freke,Timothy and Peter Gandy. <u>The Jesus Mysteries</u>. New York: Random House Inc., 1999.

3. Freke,Timothy and Peter Gandy. <u>The Jesus Mysteries</u>. New York: Random House Inc., 1999.

4. Freke,Timothy and Peter Gandy. <u>The Jesus Mysteries</u>. New York: Random House Inc., 1999.

5. Freke,Timothy and Peter Gandy. <u>The Jesus Mysteries</u>. New York: Random House Inc., 1999.

6. Freke,Timothy and Peter Gandy. <u>The Jesus Mysteries</u>. New York: Random House Inc., 1999.

7. Freke,Timothy and Peter Gandy. <u>The Jesus Mysteries</u>. New York: Random House Inc., 1999.

8. Freke,Timothy and Peter Gandy. <u>The Jesus Mysteries</u>. New York: Random House Inc., 1999.

9. Freke,Timothy and Peter Gandy. <u>The Jesus Mysteries</u>. New York: Random House Inc., 1999.

10. Freke,Timothy and Peter Gandy. <u>The Jesus Mysteries</u>. New York: Random House Inc., 1999.

11. Freke,Timothy and Peter Gandy. <u>The Jesus Mysteries</u>. New York: Random House Inc., 1999.

12. Freke,Timothy and Peter Gandy. <u>The Jesus Mysteries</u>. New York: Random House Inc., 1999.

13. Clauss, Manfred. <u>The Roman Cult of Mithras.</u> New York: Routledge, 2001

14. Clauss, Manfred. <u>The Roman Cult of Mithras.</u> New York: Routledge, 2001

15. Freke,Timothy and Peter Gandy. <u>The Jesus Mysteries</u>. New York: Random House Inc., 1999.

16. Freke,Timothy and Peter Gandy. <u>The Jesus Mysteries</u>. New York: Random House Inc., 1999.

17. Freke,Timothy and Peter Gandy. <u>The Jesus Mysteries</u>. New York: Random House Inc., 1999.

18. Freke,Timothy and Peter Gandy. <u>The Jesus Mysteries</u>. New York: Random House Inc., 1999.

19. Freke,Timothy and Peter Gandy. <u>The Jesus Mysteries</u>. New York: Random House Inc., 1999.

20. Freke,Timothy and Peter Gandy. <u>The Jesus Mysteries</u>. New York: Random House Inc., 1999.

21. Freke,Timothy and Peter Gandy. <u>The Jesus Mysteries</u>. New York: Random House Inc., 1999.

22. Freke,Timothy and Peter Gandy. <u>The Jesus Mysteries</u>. New York: Random House Inc., 1999.

23. Freke,Timothy and Peter Gandy. <u>The Jesus Mysteries</u>. New York: Random House Inc., 1999.

24. Turner, John D. <u>RITUAL IN GNOSTICISM</u>.University Of Nebraska-Lincoln SBL 1994 Book of Seminar Papers, 136-181. found at: <u>http://www.unl.edu/classics/faculty/turner/ritual.htm</u>

25. Turner, John D. <u>RITUAL IN GNOSTICISM</u>.University Of Nebraska-Lincoln SBL 1994 Book of Seminar Papers, 136-181. found at: <u>http://www.unl.edu/classics/faculty/turner/ritual.htm</u>

26. Turner, John D. <u>RITUAL IN GNOSTICISM</u>.University Of Nebraska-Lincoln SBL 1994 Book of Seminar Papers, 136-181. found at: <u>http://www.unl.edu/classics/faculty/turner/ritual.htm</u>

27. Turner, John D. <u>RITUAL IN GNOSTICISM</u>.University Of Nebraska-Lincoln SBL 1994 Book of Seminar Papers, 136-181. found at: *Excerpta ex Theodoto* (76-86) <u>http://www.unl.edu/classics/faculty/turner/ritual.htm</u>

28. Turner, John D. <u>RITUAL IN GNOSTICISM</u>.University Of Nebraska-Lincoln SBL 1994 Book of Seminar Papers, 136-181. found at: <u>http://www.unl.edu/classics/faculty/turner/ritual.htm</u>

29. Freke,Timothy and Peter Gandy. <u>The Jesus Mysteries</u>. New York: Random House Inc., 1999.pg219

30. Freke,Timothy and Peter Gandy. <u>The Jesus Mysteries</u>. New York: Random House Inc., 1999.

31. Freke,Timothy and Peter Gandy. <u>The Jesus Mysteries</u>. New York: Random House Inc., 1999.

32. Freke,Timothy and Peter Gandy. <u>The Jesus Mysteries</u>. New York: Random House Inc., 1999.

33. Freke,Timothy and Peter Gandy. <u>The Jesus Mysteries</u>. New York: Random House Inc., 1999.

34. Copleston, Frederick. <u>The History of Philosophy: Greek and Rome</u>. Vol. 1. New York: Image Books, 1993

35. Copleston, Frederick. <u>The History of Philosophy: Greek and Rome</u>. Vol. 1. New York: Image Books, 1993.

36. Freke,Timothy and Peter Gandy. <u>The Jesus Mysteries</u>. New York: Random House Inc., 1999.

37 Freke,Timothy and Peter Gandy. <u>The Jesus Mysteries</u>. New York: Random House Inc., 1999

Ch 11 Mystereis of Dark age Magic

1. Wood. Michael. <u>In Search of the Dark Ages</u> Checkmark Books, 2001

2. 39. Pendell, Dale. <u>Pharmako Gnosis: Plant Teachers and the Poison Path.</u> San Francisco: Mercury House, 2005.

3. Liywelyn, Morgan. <u>Druids</u>. Del Rey publishing, 1992

4. Markale, Jean. <u>The Druids: Celtic Priest of Nature</u>. Inner traditions, Vemont, 1992

5. Markale, Jean. <u>The Druids: Celtic Priest of Nature</u>. Inner traditions, Vemont, 1992

6. Liywelyn, Morgan. <u>Druids</u>. Del Rey publishing, 1992

7. Liywelyn, Morgan. <u>Druids</u>. Del Rey publishing, 1992

8. Liywelyn, Morgan. <u>Druids</u>. Del Rey publishing, 1992

9. Liywelyn, Morgan. <u>Druids</u>. Del Rey publishing, 1992

10. Markale, Jean. <u>The Druids: Celtic Priest of Nature</u>. Inner traditions, Vemont, 1992

11. Markale, Jean. <u>The Druids: Celtic Priest of Nature</u>. Inner traditions, Vemont, 1992

12. Markale, Jean. <u>The Druids: Celtic Priest of Nature</u>. Inner traditions, Vemont, 1992

12. Richard Evans Schultes, Albert Hofmann, and Christian Ratsch. <u>Plants of the Gods, Their Sacred, Healing, and Hallucinogenic Powers.</u> Rochester: Healing Arts Press, 2001.

13. Richard Evans Schultes, Albert Hofmann, and Christian Ratsch. <u>Plants of the Gods, Their Sacred, Healing, and Hallucinogenic Powers.</u> Rochester: Healing Arts Press, 2001.

14. Richard Evans Schultes, Albert Hofmann, and Christian Ratsch. <u>Plants of the Gods, Their Sacred, Healing, and Hallucinogenic Powers.</u> Rochester: Healing Arts Press, 2001.

15. Richard Evans Schultes, Albert Hofmann, and Christian Ratsch. <u>Plants of the Gods, Their Sacred, Healing, and Hallucinogenic Powers.</u> Rochester: Healing Arts Press, 2001.

16. Richard Evans Schultes, Albert Hofmann, and Christian Ratsch. <u>Plants of the Gods, Their Sacred, Healing, and Hallucinogenic Powers.</u> Rochester: Healing Arts Press, 2001.

17. Richard Evans Schultes, Albert Hofmann, and Christian Ratsch. <u>Plants of the Gods, Their Sacred, Healing, and Hallucinogenic Powers.</u> Rochester: Healing Arts Press, 2001.

18. Richard Evans Schultes, Albert Hofmann, and Christian Ratsch. <u>Plants of the Gods, Their Sacred, Healing, and Hallucinogenic Powers.</u> Rochester: Healing Arts Press, 2001.

19. Pendell, Dale. <u>Pharmako Gnosis: Plant Teachers and the Poison Path.</u> San Francisco: Mercury House, 2005.

20. Pendell, Dale. <u>Pharmako Gnosis: Plant Teachers and the Poison Path.</u> San Francisco: Mercury House, 2005.

21. Pendell, Dale. <u>Pharmako Gnosis: Plant Teachers and the Poison Path.</u> San Francisco: Mercury House, 2005.

22. Leto, Steven. "Magical Potions: Entheogenic Themes and Scandinavian Mythology" Shaman's Drum. 54 (2000): 55-65.

23 Encyclopædia Britannica, "Renaissance." Chigago, IL 2005

Ch 12. Shamanism and the New World

1. Furst, Peter T. and Michael D. Coe. "Ritual Enemas" <u>Magic,Witchcraft,and Religion: An Anthropological Study of the Supernatural.</u> Ed. Arthur C. Lehmann and James E. Myers. 5th ed. Mountain View: Mayfield Publishing Co., 2001. 134-137.

2. Furst, Peter T. and Michael D. Coe. "Ritual Enemas" <u>Magic,Witchcraft,and Religion: An Anthropological Study of the Supernatural.</u> Ed. Arthur C. Lehmann and James E. Myers. 5th ed. Mountain View: Mayfield Publishing Co., 2001. 134-137.

3. Richard Evans Schultes, Albert Hofmann, and Christian Ratsch. <u>Plants of the Gods, Their sacred, Healing, and Hallucinogenic Powers.</u> Rochester: Healing Arts Press, 2001. pp. 120-123.

4. Richard Evans Schultes, Albert Hofmann, and Christian Ratsch. <u>Plants of the Gods, Their sacred, Healing, and Hallucinogenic Powers.</u> Rochester: Healing Arts Press, 2001.pp.120-123.

5. Richard Evans Schultes, Albert Hofmann, and Christian Ratsch. <u>Plants of the Gods, Their sacred, Healing, and Hallucinogenic Powers.</u> Rochester: Healing Arts Press, 2001. pp. 120-123.

6. Richard Evans Schultes, Albert Hofmann, and Christian Ratsch. <u>Plants of the Gods, Their sacred, Healing, and Hallucinogenic Powers.</u> Rochester: Healing Arts Press, 2001. pp. 166-169.

7. Entheology: preserving sacred ancient knowaldge: "San Pedro"Retrived 2006. Found at: http://www.entheology.org/

8. Richard Evans Schultes, Albert Hofmann, and Christian Ratsch. <u>Plants of the Gods, Their sacred, Healing, and Hallucinogenic Powers.</u> Rochester: Healing Arts Press, 2001. pp. 166-169.

9. Entheology: preserving sacred ancient knowaldge: "San Pedro"Retrived 2006. Found at: http://www.entheology.org/

10. Entheology: preserving sacred ancient knowaldge: "San Pedro"Retrived 2006. Found at:http://www.entheology.org/

11. Richard Evans Schultes, Albert Hofmann, and Christian Ratsch. <u>Plants of the Gods, Their sacred, Healing, and Hallucinogenic Powers.</u> Rochester: Healing Arts Press, 2001. pp. 170-175.

12. Richard Evans Schultes, Albert Hofmann, and Christian Ratsch. <u>Plants of the Gods, Their sacred, Healing, and Hallucinogenic Powers.</u> Rochester: Healing Arts Press, 2001. pp. 170-175

13. Richard Evans Schultes, Albert Hofmann, and Christian Ratsch. <u>Plants of the Gods, Their sacred, Healing, and Hallucinogenic Powers.</u> Rochester: Healing Arts Press, 2001. pp. 170-175

14. Richard Evans Schultes, Albert Hofmann, and Christian Ratsch. <u>Plants of the Gods, Their sacred, Healing, and Hallucinogenic Powers.</u> Rochester: Healing Arts Press, 2001. pp. 170-175.

15. Richard Evans Schultes, Albert Hofmann, and Christian Ratsch. <u>Plants of the Gods, Their sacred, Healing, and Hallucinogenic Powers.</u> Rochester: Healing Arts Press, 2001. pp. 156-163.

16. Richard Evans Schultes, Albert Hofmann, and Christian Ratsch. <u>Plants of the Gods, Their sacred, Healing, and Hallucinogenic Powers.</u> Rochester: Healing Arts Press, 2001. pp. 156-163.

17. Richard Evans Schultes, Albert Hofmann, and Christian Ratsch. <u>Plants of the Gods, Their sacred, Healing, and Hallucinogenic Powers.</u> Rochester: Healing Arts Press, 2001. pp. 156-163.

18. Richard Evans Schultes, Albert Hofmann, and Christian Ratsch. <u>Plants of the Gods, Their sacred, Healing, and Hallucinogenic Powers.</u> Rochester: Healing Arts Press, 2001. pp. 156-163.

19. Richard Evans Schultes, Albert Hofmann, and Christian Ratsch. <u>Plants of the Gods, Their sacred, , and Hallucinogenic Powers.</u> Rochester: Healing Arts Press, 2001. pp. 156-163.

20. Furst, Peter T. and Michael D. Coe. "Ritual Enemas" <u>Magic, Witchcraft, and Religion: An Anthropological Study of the Supernatural.</u> Ed. Arthur C. Lehmann and James E. Myers. 5th ed. Mountain View: Mayfield Publishing Co., 2001. 134-137.

21. Richard Evans Schultes, Albert Hofmann, and Christian Ratsch. <u>Plants of the Gods, Their sacred, Healing, and Hallucinogenic Powers.</u> Rochester: Healing Arts Press, 2001. pp. 156-163.

22. Richard Evans Schultes, Albert Hofmann, and Christian Ratsch. <u>Plants of the Gods, Their sacred, Healing, and Hallucinogenic Powers.</u> Rochester: Healing Arts Press, 2001. pp. 156-163.

23. Entheology: preserving sacred ancient knowaldge: "Mushrooms that speak": Retrived 2006. Found at: http://www.entheology.org/

24. Richard Evans Schultes, Albert Hofmann, and Christian Ratsch. <u>Plants of the Gods, Their sacred, Healing, and Hallucinogenic Powers.</u> Rochester: Healing Arts Press, 2001. pp. 156-163.

25. Richard Evans Schultes, Albert Hofmann, and Christian Ratsch. <u>Plants of the Gods, Their sacred, Healing, and Hallucinogenic Powers.</u> Rochester: Healing Arts Press, 2001. pp. 164-165.

26. Richard Evans Schultes, Albert Hofmann, and Christian Ratsch. <u>Plants of the Gods, Their sacred, Healing, and Hallucinogenic Powers.</u> Rochester: Healing Arts Press, 2001. pp. 156-163.

27. Barre, Weston La. <u>The Peyote Cult.</u> New York: Schocken Books

28. Richard Evans Schultes, Albert Hofmann, and Christian Ratsch. <u>Plants of the Gods, Their sacred, Healing, and Hallucinogenic Powers.</u> Rochester: Healing Arts Press, 2001. pp. 156-163.

29. Barre, Weston La. <u>The Peyote Cult.</u> New York: Schocken Books, 1975. pp. 38, 24 &25

30. Richard Evans Schultes, Albert Hofmann, and Christian Ratsch. <u>Plants of the Gods, Their sacred, Healing, and Hallucinogenic Powers.</u> Rochester: Healing Arts Press, 2001. pp. 156-163.

31. Richard Evans Schultes, Albert Hofmann, and Christian Ratsch. <u>Plants of the Gods, Their sacred, Healing, and Hallucinogenic Powers.</u> Rochester: Healing Arts Press, 2001. pp. 156-163.

32. Richard Evans Schultes, Albert Hofmann, and Christian Ratsch. <u>Plants of the Gods, Their sacred, Healing, and Hallucinogenic Powers.</u> Rochester: Healing Arts Press, 2001. pp. 156-163.

33. Richard Evans Schultes, Albert Hofmann, and Christian Ratsch. <u>Plants of the Gods, Their sacred, Healing, and Hallucinogenic Powers.</u> Rochester: Healing Arts Press, 2001. pp. 156-163.

34. Hancock, Graham. <u>Supernatural, Meetings with the Ancient Teachers of Mankind.</u> New York: Disinformation Company Ltd., 2007. an

35. Barre, Weston La. <u>The Peyote Cult.</u> New York: Schocken Books, 1975.

36. Barre, Weston La. <u>The Peyote Cult.</u> New York: Schocken Books, 1975.

37. Barre, Weston La. <u>The Peyote Cult.</u> New York: Schocken Books, 1975.

38. Barre, Weston La. <u>The Peyote Cult.</u> New York: Schocken Books, 1975.

39. Benitez, Fernando. <u>In the Magic Land of Peyote.</u> New York: Warner Books Inc., 1975.

40. Benitez, Fernando. <u>In the Magic Land of Peyote.</u> New York: Warner Books Inc., 1975.

41. Richard Evans Schultes, Albert Hofmann, and Christian Ratsch. <u>Plants of the Gods, Their sacred, Healing, and Hallucinogenic Powers.</u> Rochester: Healing Arts Press, 2001. pp. 144-155.

42. Richard Evans Schultes, Albert Hofmann, and Christian Ratsch. <u>Plants of the Gods, Their sacred, Healing, and Hallucinogenic Powers.</u> Rochester: Healing Arts Press, 2001. pp. 144-155.

43. Slotkin, J.S. "The Peyote Way." <u>Magic,Witchcraft,and Religion: An Anthropological Study of the Supernatural.</u> Ed. Arthur C. Lehmann and James E. Myers. 5th ed. Mountain View: Mayfield Publishing Co., 2001. 130-133.

44. Slotkin, J.S. "The Peyote Way." <u>Magic,Witchcraft,and Religion: An Anthropological Study of the Supernatural.</u> Ed. Arthur C. Lehmann and James E. Myers. 5th ed. Mountain View: Mayfield Publishing Co., 2001. 130-133.

45. Slotkin, J.S. "The Peyote Way." <u>Magic,Witchcraft,and Religion: An Anthropological Study of the Supernatural.</u> Ed. Arthur C. Lehmann and James E. Myers. 5th ed. Mountain View: Mayfield Publishing Co., 2001. 130-133.

46. Slotkin, J.S. "The Peyote Way." <u>Magic,Witchcraft,and Religion: An Anthropological Study of the Supernatural.</u> Ed. Arthur C. Lehmann and James E. Myers. 5th ed. Mountain View: Mayfield Publishing Co., 2001. 130-133.

47. Slotkin, J.S. "The Peyote Way." <u>Magic,Witchcraft,and Religion: An Anthropological Study of the Supernatural.</u> Ed. Arthur C. Lehmann and James E. Myers. 5th ed. Mountain View: Mayfield Publishing Co., 2001. 130-133.

48. Hancock, Graham. <u>Supernatural: Meetings with the Ancient Teachers of Mankind.</u> New York: The Disinformation Company, 2007.

49. Entheology: preserving sacred ancient knowaldge: Retrieved 2006. Found at: http://www.entheology.org/

50. Entheology: preserving sacred ancient knowaldge: Retrieved 2006. Found at: http://www.entheology.org/

51. Entheology: preserving sacred ancient knowaldge: Retrieved 2006. Found at: http://www.entheology.org/

52. Entheology: preserving sacred ancient knowaldge: Retrieved 2006. Found at: http://www.entheology.org/